I'm sorry
I had to kill
your brother.
  — Katniss
      →

Duc
seen
I think I left them
in the Gym.
Spicoli

Keep up your history studies
and please try not to maim
anyone next year.
        Mr. Dadier

Don't do anything
I ~~would do~~
  wouldn't do!
        — TOAD

To a swell kid with
tons of pep and terrific lungs!
woo-woo!!
        — Andy H.

Life moves pretty fast —
except in Mr. Stein's econ class!
        — Ferris

AVID

READER

PRESS

ALSO BY BRUCE HANDY

Wild Things: The Joy of Reading Children's Literature as an Adult

PICTURE BOOKS

There Was a Shadow (Illustrated by Lisk Feng)

What If One Day . . . (Illustrated by Ashleigh Corrin)

The Book from Far Away (Illustrated by Julie Benbassat)

The Happiness of a Dog with a Ball in Its Mouth
(Illustrated by Hyewon Yum)

HOLLYWOOD HIGH

A TOTALLY EPIC, WAY OPINIONATED HISTORY OF TEEN MOVIES

BRUCE HANDY

AVID READER PRESS

NEW YORK   AMSTERDAM/ANTWERP   LONDON   TORONTO   SYDNEY/MELBOURNE   NEW DELHI

AVID READER PRESS
An Imprint of Simon & Schuster, LLC
1230 Avenue of the Americas
New York, NY 10020

First Avid Reader Press hardcover edition May 2025

AVID READER PRESS and colophon are trademarks of Simon & Schuster, LLC

Interior design by Ruth Lee-Mui

Manufactured in the United States of America

1   3   5   7   9   10   8   6   4   2

Library of Congress Cataloging-in-Publication Data

Names: Handy, Bruce, author.
Title: Hollywood high : a totally epic, way opinionated history of
teen movies / Bruce Handy.
Description: First Avid Reader Press hardcover edition. |
New York : Avid Reader Press, 2025. | Includes bibliographical references and index.
Identifiers: LCCN 2024050593 (print) | LCCN 2024050594 (ebook) |
ISBN 9781501181177 (hardcover) | ISBN 9781501181191 (paperback) |
ISBN 9781501181184 (ebook)
Subjects: LCSH: Teen films—United States_History and criticism. |
Teenagers in motion pictures. | Motion pictures and youth—
United States. | LCGFT: Film criticism.
Classification: LCC PN1995.9.Y6 H363 2025 (print) | LCC PN1995.9.Y6
(ebook) | DDC 791.43/65235—dc22
LC record available at https://lccn.loc.gov/2024050593
LC ebook record available at https://lccn.loc.gov/2024050594

ISBN 978-1-5011-8117-7
ISBN 978-1-5011-8118-4 (ebook)

For Helen,

who endured it.

CONTENTS

INTRODUCTION

WHICH CAME FIRST, THE TEEN MOVIE OR THE TEENAGER?

Leap Day, 1940. The city: Los Angeles. The place: the Ambassador Hotel's Cocoanut Grove nightclub, where Hollywood's biggest names were gathered for the 12th annual Academy Awards ceremony. Among the stars smiling for the cameras ("aflutter in ermine wraps and shimmering gowns," as one correspondent put it): Vivien Leigh and Laurence Olivier, Clark Gable and Carole Lombard, Bette Davis, Spencer Tracy, Jimmy Stewart, Greer Garson, Hedy Lamar, and emcee Bob Hope.

It would prove to be a long evening. With dinner, dancing, and hobnobbing, the presentations didn't begin until eleven p.m., so everyone was likely sloshed enough not to mind all *that* much when *Gone with the Wind* took home the lion's share of awards, as widely predicted. In fact, the results had been leaked earlier in the evening in a misguided effort to make the morning papers back east, so most everyone knew what to expect. Nevertheless, Olivia de Havilland, who played Melanie in *Gone with the Wind*, reportedly fled to the kitchen and burst into tears after losing Best Supporting Actress to co-star Hattie McDaniel, the first African

American to win an Oscar. The movie's producer, David O. Selznick—or, in some tellings, his wife, Irene—had to run in after her, shake her by the shoulders, and give her a talking-to before she could pull herself together and return to her table.

But professional jealousy was not the evening's theme, not officially. So surely no one at the Cocoanut Grove resented the fact that by one important measure—*the* measure—the answer to the question *Who is the biggest star in the room?* was . . . *none of the above.* Just a month earlier, the nation's theater owners had conducted their annual poll and named not Gable, not Davis, not Stewart, but the young, callow, and diminutive Mickey Rooney as the nation's top box office attraction. Better or worse yet, it was his second straight year winning the crown. *Variety* had hailed him as Metro-Goldwyn-Mayer's "most valuable piece of talent" and "king of its star list." *The New York Times* dubbed him "the mighty mite of the screen world." His future first wife, Ava Gardner, then an MGM starlet, deemed him "the biggest wolf on the lot," adding, "He went through the ladies like a hot knife through fudge."

He was nineteen (and a quarter).

That night, Rooney was a Best Actor nominee, too, for his role opposite Judy Garland in the "Hey, kids, let's put on a show!" musical *Babes in Arms.* (He, along with fellow nominees Gable, Olivier, and Stewart, lost out to Robert Donat from *Goodbye, Mr. Chips.*) Rooney had been under contract to MGM since 1934, when he was thirteen, with big parts in prestige films like *Captains Courageous, Boys Town,* and the soon-to-be-released *Young Tom Edison.* But the main reason for his clout with moviegoers, and for the *Time* magazine cover he would grace a few weeks after the Oscars, was Andy Hardy, the car-crazy, girl-crazy, swing-crazy high school kid he played in a series of cheerful, not entirely bland family comedies that had been coming off MGM's assembly line since 1937, at a clip of two or three a year—*Love Finds Andy Hardy, Andy Hardy Gets Spring Fever,* and so on, until the series came to an end after fifteen pictures, in 1946, with *Love Laughs at Andy Hardy.* (Rooney's second marriage came to an end on that picture, too, when his new wife,

Miss Alabama of 1944, allegedly walked in on him in his dressing room while he was receiving a blow job from fourteen-year-old Elizabeth Taylor; he was then twenty-six.)

Younger child stars like Jackie Coogan or Shirley Temple, Rooney's immediate predecessor as box office champ, were a familiar part of the movie landscape, but a teenage star like Rooney (or peers like Garland, Jackie Cooper, and Deanna Durbin) represented something new—new because teenagers were themselves new in 1940, so new that almost nobody even called them teenagers.

It was only in the early decades of the twentieth century that the interregnum between thirteen and nineteen had begun to be seen as the distinct, passionate, and volatile, sometimes baffling phase of life we deem it today, that familiar but treacherous expanse between childhood and maturity littered with social, hormonal, and developmental land mines. As it happened, 1940 witnessed a tipping point in this evolution: that spring, for the first time in American history, a majority of the nation's seventeen-year-olds graduated from high school, and upwards of three-quarters had logged at least some time in secondary-school classrooms, even if they didn't exit with diplomas. This was a radical shift in American childhoods. Contrast 1940 with 1900, when only six percent of seventeen-year-olds, most of them well-off, had graduated from high school. The rest, in an era of lax to nonexistent child labor laws, had long since been tossed into the workforce to sink or swim or lose a hand in a factory mishap.

Adolescents in the nineteenth and early twentieth centuries were seen less as their own species than as not-quite adults—adults with training wheels, say (not so different from today's post-*Friends* twentysomethings). It was thanks to the hard work of educators and reformers that more and more adolescents began leaving the workforce to attend high school; it was thanks to high school—one of twentieth-century history's less well-known cases of an unintended consequence—that adolescents began developing their own discrete subcultures with their own sometimes-puzzling-to-adults tastes in music, fashion, and slang. What they were doing was forming their own tribe. Adults did not yet envy, resent, or emulate them; there would be no such thing as a cool mom or dad for decades; the notion of posing as a youthful rebel well into one's seventh, eighth, and ninth decades (cf. Mick Jagger and Madonna) would have been laughable in 1940, but the ground was shifting, and Rooney was both a beneficiary and a spark.

The press heralded his alter ego, Andy, as a national treasure arrived just in time to help parents and kids alike make sense of the new American adolescent. As one movie magazine proclaimed, conflating star and screen presence: "Mickey Rooney is as important to America as strawberry shortcake, Angelo Patri,* and the night before Christmas . . . Millions of parents send their children to see Mickey, and see him themselves, for a richer understanding of each other."

Rooney himself had never attended high school. Born to a pair of vaudevillians, he'd been acting since he could walk, and off screen, he and his libido could be a handful, to the consternation of his studio minders. Playing Andy Hardy was a responsibility, even a burden, one that he wore uneasily throughout his life, but he, too, recognized the role's import. As he would write in his 1991 autobiography, *Life Is Too Short*: "Through the years I keep meeting people who tell me, 'Andy Hardy? Hey, he taught me how to be a teenager.' From remarks like these, I conclude that many American teenagers and would-be teenagers went along with the celluloid ideal fashioned by Metro's writers."

If you've seen any of the Hardy movies, you may be troubled by the notion that anyone's real-life behavior was influenced by Andy's predictable misadventures—Signing an $8 promissory note to buy a broken-down jalopy? Not a good idea!—not to mention his pop-eyed enthusiasm for the opposite sex. But if Andy served as a role model for American teens, it was in part because he was reflecting them back to themselves; they had reached such a critical mass of shared experience that a role *could* be modeled.

Teenagers and teen movies would come of age hand in hand.

---

*A syndicated parenting columnist, now forgotten but once beloved and widely read.

•   •   •

The history of teen movies is also the history of a feedback loop: Hollywood would pick up on something in youth culture, sell it back to kids, who would in turn be inspired by what they saw on screen. For instance, middle-class kids in the postwar years unnerved their parents by adopting working-class totems like blue jeans and leather jackets and, scarier still, in the case of white teens, developing a taste for "race music"—prompting fears about juvenile delinquency to soar. Hollywood responded with teens-gone-wild movies like *Blackboard Jungle* and *Rebel Without a Cause*, released within months of each other in 1955. The former assisted in making a star of Sidney Poitier, the latter James Dean; both actors helped turn the simple white T-shirt into a sexy and durable fashion statement. The pictures were designed simultaneously to alarm parents and excite teenagers; Dean's character in particular could be seen, depending on your age, as either a case study in troubled adolescent psychology or the coolest thing ever put on screen. As one twelve-year-old fan, Martin Scorsese, would later enthuse, "To say that I identified with Dean in that movie as an actor and as a character—they were the same to us; there was no separation—is way too mild. The identification was total, even violent."

As America's teenage population grew and grew into the 1960s—along with pockets and purses now stuffed with allowances and after-school pay—Hollywood's less tony precincts began pandering directly to young baby boomers' tastes (as cynical B-movie producers divined those tastes). The result was drive-in sensations ranging from *I Was a Teenage Werewolf* (1957) to *Beach Party* (1963). One thing these movies had in common, aside from poor production values: parents and other authority figures were routinely portrayed as villainous and/or cretinous, if not simply ignored. You may not think much of these pictures as films, but as *products*, they had undeniable nerve and occasional brilliance.

Jump ahead another decade, when America was nursing a sour stomach post Dallas, Vietnam, Watts, Memphis, Chicago, Kent State, Watergate—the familiar roll call of bummers. The oldest baby boomers, now in their midtwenties, began reflecting on the "innocence" of their high school years. The result was a cycle of nostalgic teen movies that also threw implicit shade on the present, among them *American Graffiti* (1973) and *Grease* (1978), two of the most popular movies of the decade, and *Cooley High* (1975), the first all-Black teen movie and a touchstone for the next generation of African American filmmakers. These were the first teen movies made by artists who had more or less experienced what they put on screen, and they brought knowingness along with affection to the genre. (Meanwhile, the future cult film *Over the Edge*, which addressed the real-time problems of teens in the seventies—alienation, anomie, feathered hair—barely received a release in 1979.)

When the baby boom finally ebbed in the 1980s, it left teenagers as America's most dependable moviegoers and the teen movie as the decade's dominant film genre, excepting action spectacles starring human meat lockers like Sylvester Stallone and Arnold Schwarzenegger. The teen movie had grown so vital and elastic it could embrace rom-coms (*Sixteen Candles, Pretty in Pink, Say Anything . . .*), musicals (*Fame, Footloose*), R-rated raunch (*Porky's, Porky's II: The Next Day, Porky's Revenge!*), techno-thrillers (*WarGames*), social comedy (*Fast Times at Ridgemont High*), social satire (*Risky Business*), crime dramas (the Sean Penn as opposed to Will Smith *Bad Boys*), horror (*Friday the 13th, A Nightmare on Elm Street*), self-conscious artifice (*Rumble Fish*), talky confessionals (*The Breakfast Club*), dark comedies (*Heathers*), stoner comedies (*Bill & Ted's Excellent Adventure*), science fiction comedies (*Weird Science, Back to the Future*), film buff curios (Robert Altman's *O.C. and Stiggs*), and European art-house nihilism (*River's Edge*).

One reason for this florescence: by the 1980s, almost everyone with power in Hollywood had grown up in the postwar years and enjoyed, if that is the word, high school experiences not dissimilar from their audience's—another tipping point. In John Hughes (class of 1969, Glenbrook North High School, Illinois) and Amy Heckerling (class of 1970, New York City's High School of Art and Design), the decade also produced two teen movie auteurs, each with more than one milestone film to his or her credit. Hughes directed and/or wrote six in four years: *Sixteen Candles*, *The Breakfast Club*, *Weird Science*, *Pretty in Pink*, *Ferris Bueller's Day Off*, and *Some Kind of Wonderful*—a remarkable feat. He was improbably prolific, famous in Hollywood for knocking out scripts in days, if not hours, but his movies spoke to young audiences with a directness, empathy, and lack of condescension (some pandering, too), which at the time felt radical. As the novelist Allison Lynn has written: "Hughes would eventually teach me that it was okay to be myself"—which may read as overly dramatic but also authentically adolescent. One secret of Hughes's success was that he was a middle-aged adult who wanted to *be* a teenager, or at least he gave that impression through his tastes, interests, and choice of friends. Jon Cryer, co-star of *Pretty in Pink* (1986), said of Hughes at the time, "I think he's still trying to be popular at school."

Heckerling had an even simpler (if probably disingenuous) explanation for her success as the director of *Fast Times at Ridgemont High* (1982) and the writer-director of *Clueless* (1995), two of the finest, funniest, and least-dated teen movies ever made: "My tastes never matured, unfortunately."

Jump forward again, to 1991, when John Singleton, fresh out of film school and only four years removed from high school, wrote and directed *Boyz n the Hood*, a raw but accomplished cri de coeur about growing up in South Central Los Angeles. "I wrote about what I knew," Singleton said. "The streets, friends who fell off from gangbanging and from being in the wrong place at the wrong time and getting shot." The result was a challenge to the Hollywood status quo, an unexpected box office success, and another milestone, with Singleton the first Black director to be nominated for an Academy Award, and also, at twenty-two, the youngest of any race, eclipsing Orson Welles's five-decades-old record by two years.

Teen movies have continued to thrive and mutate into our current wretched century. With *Mean Girls*, the screenwriter Tina Fey took a topic steeped in adult alarm—she adapted a bestselling nonfiction book about female bullying written for parents—and created something that struck a chord with teenagers and in time achieved iconic status, much like what the filmmakers behind *Rebel Without a Cause* had done fifty years before, the pink miniskirts and pumps worn in *Mean Girls* being no less indelible than Dean's white T-shirt and red windbreaker. Meanwhile, in an era of so-called franchise filmmaking, two of the biggest were adapted from peculiar but wildly popular young adult novels: the five *Twilight* movies, based on the four books by Stephenie Meyer, and the five *Hunger Games* movies, based on the trilogy and prequel by Suzanne Collins. One is a gothic high school romance, the other a dystopian teen nightmare; both speak in sledgehammer metaphors. The heroine of the former series, launched on screen in 2008, is an asocial transfer student suffering from early-onset anhedonia who falls in love with an asocial 104-year-old vampire who compensates for age-inappropriateness by looking like a Milan menswear model. He loves her back, but won't sleep with her because his ferocious supernatural passion might leave her not just satisfied but dead. In other words, he's an old-fashioned gentleman! Which is arguably the story's most fantastic element of all — and maybe of too-obvious appeal to a generation raised on Pornhub and the hot-or-not dictates of social media.

The Hunger Games series, which debuted in 2012 (and returned in 2023 with a semidetached prequel), takes place in a bleak future where a totalitarian government forces impoverished teenagers to battle to the death in an annual competition that plays like *Mean Girls* with a crossbow instead of a burn book. Neither *Twilight* nor *The Hunger Games* are subtle entertainments, and, like teenagers themselves, both have wide morbid streaks — read into them whatever allegorical intent you'd like; many have and I will, too — but maybe novelists and filmmakers have to go big and dark, even flirt with silliness, to get the attention of a generation raised in the shadow of 9/11, a twenty-year war, a once-in-a-lifetime (fingers crossed) financial crisis, police violence, opioid deaths, Covid, an epidemic of school shootings, creeping authoritarianism, and, not least from a filmmaker's perspective, an infinity of other things to watch. It worked: globally, the *Twilight* and *Hunger Games* movies have together taken in over $6.6 billion.

• • •

Profitability is one way to measure success. Resonance is another. Chances are I've already mentioned *the* film that spoke to you when you were a teenager, that maybe comforted you by demonstrating your private agonies and ecstasies were shared—that you weren't the singular freak you feared you were.

Themes endure across decades: the intensity of friendships, the yearning to belong, the tyranny of hormones, the drudgery of school itself, the cruelty of cliques and pecking orders, the absurdity of parents, the emotional conundrum in which the fear of growing up jostles with a hunger for independence, the angry "Take that, world!" defiance epitomized by Judd Nelson's raised fist at the end of *The Breakfast Club*.

And parties. So many parties.

"Few stories, it turns out, are as comically and horrifyingly reliable as those set in high school," the critic Manohla Dargis observed in *The New York Times*, while giving a mostly positive review to the latest version of *Mean Girls*. That would be the hit 2024 movie adaptation of the hit 2018 Broadway musical based on the hit 2004 film adapted from the bestselling 2002 parenting book—a pedigree rendering Dargis's observation nearly tautological.

Certain aspects of adolescent life are suited to the dictates of commercial filmmaking. First off, there is graduation's ticking clock. Confinement works in favor of the high school movie, too, just as it does for the disaster movie. Put a cross section of passengers on a plane 35,000 feet in the air and add a mechanical failure, or stick a cross section of sixteen-year-olds in a lunchroom and add an ambitious crush plus an upcoming prom—either way, instant drama. Prison pictures are another obvious reference point.

So are savage comedies of manners. "Never again are we ranked so precisely by those around us, and on so many scales," the social critic Ralph Keyes has written—*not* about attending a fashionable ball in eighteenth-century London, but rather, of course, modern American adolescence. "Through the popularity polls of our classmates, and their inexperience at tact," Keyes continued in his book *Is There Life After High School?*, "daily feedback was conveyed about how we were coming across. Such merciless feedback is not easily forgotten, the last time of life we know just where we stand in the scrutinizing eyes around us." That was written in 1976, by the way, long before smartphones and social media made the feedback exponentially more pitiless and inescapable.

I would argue that teen movies have become an essential American genre, rivaling the western as a vehicle for national mythmaking. The two have more than a little in common. Both deal with the struggle to establish order and fairness in an indifferent world, whether the prairie or the high school hallway, where the law, if not absent altogether, is only what whoever has seized power says it is. The former *New York Times* film critic A. O. Scott once described the classic western hero as "a socially marginal figure, a loner who defends the fragile society of the frontier without ever becoming a part of it." He cited some obvious examples: Alan Ladd's Shane and the "righteous loners" played with minor variations across multiple films by John Wayne and Clint Eastwood. The stakes might be less life-and-death for the characters in most teen movies (if only from an adult's point of view), but Scott's character breakdown could apply as well to the misfits, malcontents, and alienated observers played by Dean in *Rebel Without a Cause*, Poitier in *Blackboard Jungle*, Richard Dreyfuss in *American Graffiti*, Winona Ryder in *Heathers*, Cuba Gooding Jr. in *Boyz n the Hood*, Lindsay Lohan in the original *Mean Girls*, Kristen Stewart in *Twilight*, and, paradigmatically, the entire cast of *The Outsiders*. These, too, are characters who stand apart from the fray while maintaining a certain moral authority. But I'm only piggybacking on Scott's argument here, since his essay was in fact about Katniss Everdeen, Jennifer Lawrence's heroine in *The Hunger Games*, whom Scott compared to an even older frontier archetype: James Fenimore Cooper's Natty Bumppo.

In Katniss's world, the stakes truly *are* life-and-death, even more so than in the average Wayne or Eastwood picture. The same holds true for Gooding Jr.'s Tre Styles in *Boyz n the Hood*. But in most teen movies the question isn't *whether* the heroes will live long enough to grow up but rather *how* will they manage the feat, and on whose terms? That, too, is a western theme, although applied to a young nation rather than just the young. But if westerns have always looked backward to explain America to itself, teen movies have for the most part done their work in real time. Moreover, since teenagers themselves have so often been the prime movers of American popular culture, the history of teen movies serves as a useful vantage point on the last eight or so decades' worth of the nation's sociocultural history.

Put another way: How did we get from Andy Hardy to Katniss Everdeen?

As there is no federal law or bureau of cinematic standards that defines teen movies, and because I am not attempting to write an encyclopedia, my focus is American movies that are *about* teens, not simply movies that teens like. Often those attributes are one and the same. But sometimes they aren't, and I've left out Elvis Presley movies, *A Hard Day's Night* and *Help!*, *Saturday Night Fever*, college movies like *Animal House* and *Revenge of the Nerds*, *Flashdance*, *Purple Rain*, the early films of Adam Sandler, any of the clever horror movies from Blumhouse, and Taylor Swift's and Beyoncé's 2023 concert films. These are significant movies that had huge teen audiences—another is *The Rocky Horror Picture Show*, which in its midnight movie incarnation has been a touchstone for several generations of queer kids—but I don't see these as teen movies in the same way that *Love Finds Andy Hardy* or *Rebel Without a Cause* or *Fast Times at Ridgemont High* are. Conversely, I'm also touching on a few works that I suspect appealed more to adults than teenagers, like Elia Kazan's *Splendor in the Grass* (1961) and Larry Clark's *Kids* (1995). No doubt I've ignored a favorite or two of yours. (Sorry, Freddie Prinze Jr. fans.) I'm writing about movies that I think have something useful and interesting to say about young people and their times—and movies about which I hope I have something useful and interesting to say myself.

Disagree! Write your own teen movie book! What's fun about this subject is that everyone has an informed opinion. Most of us have never been frontier lawmen, or private eyes, secret agents, Jedi knights, superheroes,

Disney princesses, or ex-cons setting off to pull one last heist. If we're older than twelve, however, we've also been (or are) teenagers. Which, I realize, lands uncomfortably close to the parental refrain *I was young once, too, believe it or not*. But it's true. We've lived these movies. We've earned the scars.

Two final data points from an America on the cusp of both World War II and a social revolution.

In 1941, Mickey Rooney, now twenty, was once again voted Hollywood's top box office attraction—his third consecutive crown. (In 1942, he would fall to the fourth spot, behind, in ascending order, Gary Cooper, Clark Gable, and new champs Abbott and Costello.)

1941 was also the year the word *teenager*—or *'teen-ager*, as it was initially styled—first turned up in a national periodical, according to the Oxford English Dictionary.* The citation comes from *Popular Science*— not a source I would have expected—in an article about high school students in Denver who were making educational films as part of their social studies curriculum. To research short subjects like "How to Find a Job" and "Food the Modern Way," the students had ventured out into the city to interview local professionals and business owners. The money quote: "I never knew 'teen-agers could be so serious," a dairy operator told the magazine's reporter, pulling the word out of the conversational ether and sending it on its way toward ubiquity. *Teener* was already in use, but this was the one that stuck.[†]

Not the most scintillating debut, true. But the fact that it had to do with movies made by actual teenagers, even if school sanctioned and almost certainly dull, is for my purposes a nice bit of serendipity.

*There are a handful of earlier usages in local newspapers, most dating to the late 1930s.

[†]*Teen* was around, too, as a noun but not yet an adjective.

1

PRETEENS

In America, there is no adolescence, strictly speaking.

—Alexis de Tocqueville, *Democracy in America*, 1840

Don't worry. That will be the last mention of de Tocqueville in these pages, I promise. But before I dive into teen movies proper, I think it's important to offer a quick account of how modern American adolescence evolved, and of what life was like for kids in an earlier era when no one much cared about their tastes in film, music, fashion, hair conditioner, or anything else—almost as if they were today's old people.

It's another bit of serendipity that two pillars of American modernity, teenagers and the US film industry, both surfaced at the turn of the last century.

In 1903, Thomas Edison's movie studio, the nation's oldest, released *The Great Train Robbery*, sometimes credited as the first American narrative film. It wasn't, but it may well have been our first homegrown blockbuster, a sensation at just over thirteen minutes. Formally, *The Great Train Robbery* is primitive, but with beatings, cold-blooded murders, an explosion, a chase on horseback, a gun fight, a precocious little kid, and an irrelevant comic dance number, it provided a template, however rudimentary, for much of what American cinema would soon become. Three months after its release, *The New York Times* estimated the film, which the paper deemed "certainly astounding," had been seen by more than five million people in nickelodeons and vaudeville houses across the country—an impressively large audience in a nation of seventy-six million, many of whom viewed moving pictures as disreputable.

Just a year later, in 1904, a pioneering psychologist named G. Stanley Hall, who had earned the country's first-ever PhD in the subject at Harvard, published a two-volume book titled *Adolescence: Its Psychology and Its Relations to Physiology, Anthropology, Sociology, Sex, Crime, Religion and Education*. This exhausting work, which comes to more than 1,200 pages, has been described by one historian of American childhood as "feverish, recondite, and at times incomprehensible." The book's first twenty or so pages are all that, I can attest, having made it only that far before giving up. Yet somehow, amid long skeins of opaque philosophy and poorly articulated grievances against long-forgotten branches of parapsychology, Hall made the then-novel argument that the years between the onset of puberty and full-blown maturity were a distinct phase of life, marked not only by rapid physical and intellectual growth but also heightened sensitivity and emotional tumult—"suggestive," in Hall's words, "of some ancient period of storm and stress when old moorings were broken and a higher level attained." In other words, Hall saw adolescence as a chaotic but crucial phase of life, one that was worthy of respect. He didn't invent modern adolescence, but his work would prove hugely influential, inspiring educators and reformers to build a nation in which adolescents would be protected, nurtured, and even indulged, and not just tossed into the adult workforce with all its associated predations.

In his 1999 book *The Rise and Fall of the American Teenager*, the historian Thomas Hine* describes adolescence in the colonial era: "The teenage years were part of a very lengthy, vaguely defined period of youth, which continued, practically speaking, until marriage sometime in one's early to midtwenties." For most children of most classes in most parts of the country, schooling was haphazard, and "youth" bore little resemblance to

---

*As I am not a scholar of American childhood, I am indebted to Hine and the other historians cited in this chapter who are.

a late twentieth-century or early twenty-first-century childhood. At the age of seven or so, kids were expected to begin pulling their weight around the home or family farm. Some children went to work as servants in other people's homes or were apprenticed, even future founding fathers like Benjamin Franklin, who was sent off at twelve years old to work for an older brother as a printer's apprentice. No less an authority than Thomas Paine wrote in 1778: "Nothing hurts the affections of parents and children so much as living too closely connected, and keeping up the distinction too long." Our nascent democracy had no room for mollycoddles. At the time, ten-, eleven-, and twelve-year-olds were serving as scouts and sometimes soldiers in the Continental Army.

Unsurprisingly, work was even more onerous for enslaved children, of whom there were many: half of the roughly four million people who were "owned" at the outbreak of the Civil War were sixteen or younger, and by that age more than a third had been forcibly separated from their parents (according to a Works Progress Administration survey of surviving freed people in the mid-1930s). Children as young as three labored as houseboys or housegirls for a couple of years before being sent off to the fields. "At five or six, enslaved children served as scarecrows . . . or toiled on trash gangs, hauling water and wood, pulling weeds, sweeping yards, driving cows to pasture, and cutting tree limbs for firewood," writes Steven Mintz in *Huck's Raft: A History of American Childhood* (2004). The labor only got harder as the children grew older, as did the existential toll. Citing slave narratives and oral histories, Mintz adds: "As they recalled their childhood in bondage, former slaves inevitably recollected a moment around puberty when they first confronted the reality of lifelong servitude. A whipping, an abusive epithet, a sudden change in how one was treated by white playmates revealed the full meaning of enslavement."

With the onset of the Industrial Revolution in the US, children and adolescents became an essential part of the urban workforce, with the compactness of young bodies and the nimbleness of young hands prized by factories, mills, and mines. "For most of our history, child labor was not a social horror but simply a fact of life," writes Hine. "The New York publisher Horace Greeley, for example, won a reputation as a child labor reformer when, in 1850, he advocated limiting the workday of children under twelve to a mere ten hours a day." In cities, kids entered the full-time workforce at fourteen, on average. At that age, Hine notes, they were "viewed as inexperienced adults—people with energy, who could work a full day, but might, if not supervised, fall into bad habits." You will not be surprised to learn that nineteenth-century supervision was not up to twenty-first-century helicopter-parent standards. In fact, children enjoyed all the vices their elders did. Working kids were often drinking kids, with most states disdaining legal drinking ages until the temperance move-ment gained momentum in the 1880s, while throughout the nineteenth century, the age of consent was between ten and twelve in most of the country.

Growing up was no more gentle on the frontier. Mintz quotes an English visitor to the Rocky Mountains in 1873: "One of the most pain-ful things in the Western States and Territories is the extinction of child-hood. I have never seen any children, only debased imitations of men and women, cankered by greed and selfishness, and asserting and gain-ing complete independence of their parents at ten years old."

Here is one example of that independence. Sam McDonald, born in 1884, was an African American whose family had moved west from Louisiana to California when he was six. At thirteen, while still living at home, he began work on the dairy farm that also employed his father, milking a couple dozen cows a day and doing kitchen work. At sixteen, unwilling to follow his family to Oregon, he struck out on his own, mak-ing his way around California, sometimes on horseback, sometimes on foot, doing odd jobs, including stints as an artist's model and a bouncer on a riverboat, and occasionally hunting to feed himself. At nineteen, he landed a steady job hauling gravel for roads at the recently founded Le-land Stanford Junior University. (He would remain there for the rest of his life, becoming the school's first Black administrator as its superintendent of athletic buildings and grounds.)

Theodore Dreiser's 1925 novel, *An American Tragedy*, offers a vivid, if fictionalized, account of a city boy's working life in the early twentieth century. The "vain and proud" hero, Clyde Griffiths, only in his early teens, already feels like he's well behind the eight ball because his evangelical parents have deprived him of almost all schooling and otherwise shielded him from anything that would give him a worldly leg up. "How was one to get a start in such circumstances?" Dreiser writes. "When, at the age of thirteen, fourteen, fifteen, he began looking in the newspapers . . . he found that mostly skilled help was wanted, or boys to learn trades in which at the moment he was not very much interested . . . What! Run a machine, lay bricks, learn to be a carpenter, or a plasterer, or plumber, when boys no better than himself were clerks and druggists' assistants and bookkeepers and assistants in banks and real estate offices and such." That is a long list of jobs available to an age group that today would be grappling with algebra and *The Scarlet Letter*. Clyde eventually finds a position as a bellboy at an expensive Kansas City hotel with a sixty-six-hour workweek. He is seventeen and finally living on his own—a late bloomer. One of his colleagues has been on his own since fourteen.

The historian Joseph P. Kett distinguishes modern teenagers from earlier iterations in a single pithy sentence: "They are essentially consumers rather than producers." The advances in adolescent psychology spearheaded by G. Stanley Hall played a role in that shift; so did a maturing economy that demanded a well-educated workforce—someone had to write, read, and file all that paperwork alphabetically!—along with a growing middle class that began emulating the attitudes and practices of the upper classes, whose youth had long been better educated and less gainfully employed. Teenagers' status began to change in more formal ways, too: the nation's first juvenile court was established in Cook County, Illinois, in 1899; a quarter century later, forty-six of the then forty-eight states had juvenile justice systems. "In effect," Kett writes, "adolescence had become a legal as well as social category."

High school enrollment increased steadily from the turn of the century forward; by 1920, roughly a quarter of all American teenagers were spending at least some of their days in classrooms; by 1930, the numbers had increased to near 50 percent. But that was the big picture. On the ground, progress was uneven, with enrollment increasing more quickly in towns and small cities than in rural areas, where crops still needed to be harvested, and bigger cities, where shoes needed to be shined and newspapers hawked. In the South, with its separate and unequal schools, Black enrollment trailed white.

The Depression—silver lining alert—proved to be a nationwide education accelerator: teenagers were as unemployed as everyone else, and adult workers with families to feed didn't want to compete with the likes of Clyde Griffiths for what precious jobs were still available; funneling kids into high schools thus proved a win-win solution. New compulsory education laws provided the muscle, along with the child labor restrictions included in the 1938 Fair Labor Standards Act. As Thomas Hine puts it, "Like the Hoover Dam, the American teenager was a New Deal project, a massive redirection of energy."

In the span of a generation, high school had gone from a privilege to a commonplace.* As mentioned earlier, by 1940, three-quarters of teenagers were logging at least some time in high school, and just over half of all seventeen-year-olds received a diploma that year. Better educations aside, "what was new," Hine writes, "was the assumption that all young people, regardless of their class, location, or ethnicity, should have essentially the same experience spent with people exactly their age." An unintended consequence of that—unintended at least in the eyes of earnest educators—was the growth of an increasingly distinct and sometimes oppositional culture generated by teenagers themselves.

Not that kids hadn't always devoted themselves to inexplicable fads; readers of *Little Women* will remember Amy March and her classmates turning pickled limes into a form of social currency. But by the 1940s,

*The revolution would be completed in the 1960s, thanks to the postwar economic boom and *Brown v. Board of Education*, with 95 percent of kids attending high school— and half going on to college.

teenagers had begun forming entire subcultures with dress, slang, tastes, and social mores unencumbered by adult preferences. In 1941, for instance, *Life* magazine reported on "subdebs"—high school girls from what were once called "good" families but who fell short of socialite status—as if cataloging a heretofore unknown species of bird or hippopotamus:

> They swoop in and out of parties in noisy, cohesive gangs. They love open houses where there are plenty of phonograph records, cigarets and 'cokes.' . . . The world at large means nothing to any of them; the microcosm of their gang is everything. They speak a curious lingo of their own, adore chocolate milkshakes and swing music, wear moccasins everywhere, collect quantities of quaint dolls and soft squishy animals, and drive like bats out of hell.*

In *Teenagers: An American History* (1996) Grace Palladino describes the dynamics that forged subdebs (and eventually sportos, motorheads, geeks, sluts, bloods, wastoids, dweebies, and dickheads, to cite the taxonomy from *Ferris Bueller's Day Off*): "When a teenage majority spent the better part of their day in high school, they learned to look to one another and not to adults for advice, information, and approval." In short, Palladino concludes, "They revolutionized the very concept of growing up."

Relations between generations had never been entirely smooth, but now kids began to see parents and teachers as a kind of enemy camp while adults came to view teenagers as an invasive species. Or maybe a better way to paint it is that teenagers and adults began to form a labor-management-style relationship. At any rate, the balance of power was shifting at home, at school, and everywhere else kids were asserting themselves. To emphasize this new dynamic, Palladino quotes the anthropologist Margaret

---

*One more tidbit: "Slam books contain a subdeb's frankest thoughts about her friends. They are circulated privately for feline amusement." In other words, the burn book has a venerable history that predates *Mean Girls* by more than half a century.

Mead, who had famously studied adolescence in Samoa, from an interview Mead gave to *Ladies' Home Journal* in 1951:

> When mothers cease to say, 'When I was a girl I was not allowed . . .' and substitute the question, 'What are the other girls doing?' something fundamental has happened to the whole culture.

Something equally fundamental would happen to American movies.

2

JUDGE HARDY'S SON

Look here, Dad, I'm not a child anymore and, well, a fella's just got
to have a car.

—Fifteen-year-old Andy Hardy, hoping to wheedle an auto
loan from his father, in *Love Finds Andy Hardy* (1938)

Mickey Rooney enjoyed the perks that came with reigning as Hollywood's
top box office attraction for three years running—the big house, the nice
cars, the girls, the great tables at nightclubs. His studio, MGM, even set up
a direct phone line from his bookie to his dressing room. He also appreciated the import, beyond mere ticket sales, of his screen role as America's
favorite teenager. But there was a downside to playing Andy Hardy. "I was
a fourteen-year-old boy for thirty years," he would complain in middle age.

He got an early hint of that fate, at nineteen, when he was invited to
the White House for Franklin Roosevelt's annual birthday celebration on
January 30, 1940, part of a Hollywood contingent that included Edward
G. Robinson, Tyrone Power, and Olivia de Havilland—three more stars
Rooney was outgrossing. But the affair proved deflating. When he was
introduced to Roosevelt at a luncheon, the president said, "Well, my boy,
someday I hope to be able to spare enough time so that you and I can
have a man-to-man talk"—a reference to the earnest, confessional scenes
between Andy and his father that had become part of the series' formula,

if not schtick. But Rooney didn't get that FDR was kidding him. "Yes, sir," he replied eagerly. "You say when. I can get time off from the studio any time for that." Roosevelt reportedly had a big laugh at Rooney's expense, though from the actor's point of view, given his celebrity and his princely status as the screen embodiment of American youth, it may have seemed perfectly natural that the president would want a private word. In Roosevelt's laugh, there was an echo of the films' own gentle joke at Andy's expense: the aspirational notion of his asking his father for a "man-to-man" talk in the first place. The whole point of Andy Hardy was that he wasn't yet a "man." Instead, he was helping America chart this new gray area between childhood and adulthood.

The films were set in the fictional middle-class, middle-America town of Carvel. Where Carvel was located was never explicitly stated, though everyone, even the screenwriters, figured it was somewhere in the Midwest; the Hardy films were *mid* all the way. MGM, Hollywood's richest, most glamorous studio, home to Clark Gable and Greta Garbo, *Grand Hotel* and *The Thin Man*, didn't realize at first what it had on its hands in either star or character. Rooney had been a hardworking juvenile actor for the studio, with a natural ease in front of the camera and a mischievous energy that could read as impish or streetwise depending on the part; he was good at tears, too. In the beginning, the *Hardy* series had centered on Andy's father, James Hardy—a judge, no less—but through some alchemic reaction among role, performer, and zeitgeist, Andy elbowed his way to prominence; he was the movies' breakout character, the precursor to latter-day sitcom breakouts like Fonzie, Alex Keaton, and Urkel.

Time's March 1940 cover story on Rooney, written with a tone of grudging if amused respect—*This punk is the biggest star in the world?*—described him as "a rope-haired, kazoo-voiced kid with a comic strip face, who . . . had never appeared in a movie without overacting or mugging it." That last dig wasn't wrong, just incomplete, and the magazine also credited Rooney with "a lot of talent, a lot of brass, a lot of luck." But at sixteen, when he was first cast as Andy, he'd been approaching a child star's traditional age of obsolescence. The idea of a teenage star playing distinct teenage roles was as novel as the idea of a teenager as a distinct class of human.

It wasn't that the notion of centering a movie on an adolescent character had never occurred to anyone. One early example is *Bab's Diary*, released in 1917 and now sadly considered lost (like 70 percent of all silent American features, according to the Library of Congress). A contemporary review described seventeen-year-old Bab as a "little flapper heroine" whose wealthy family "persist in treating her like a little girl." Home from boarding school, she gets into a mishap over a make-believe suitor and engenders further scandal with a V-necked dress. The picture was popular enough to generate two sequels, *Bab's Burglar* and *Bab's Matinee Idol*, both released in 1917 as well, the film business moving at a friskier pace in its infancy than it does today. Alas, Bab has not left much of a mark on movie history, though the film did pioneer a lasting teen movie trope by casting someone far too old for the part: thirty-four-year-old Marguerite Clark. But reviews make Bab sound more like a daffy, proto-screwball heroine than any kind of reasonably believable teenaged girl. The same was true of Pat, the swoony, lovestruck adolescent played by Marion Davies, then thirty-one, in the 1928 comedy *The Patsy*, which survives and is wonderful. It even strikes a still-relevant "beauty myth" note when Pat, despairing of attracting a boyfriend, tells her father, "I'd like to be entrancing, alluring, ravishing—like a stocking advertisement."

The heroine of *Flaming Youth* (1923), based on a widely popular and allegedly scandalous novel, was played by twenty-three-year-old Colleen Moore. The character is a teenager in the book; her age may not be specified in the movie, which only survives in fragments. The ads marketed it as a cautionary tale: "She smoked cigarettes. She drank. She went to petting parties. She led the pace of the gayest life in the gayest society . . . But there were certain conservative young men who were not seeking her as a wife. 'Why?' she wondered. Had she gone too far?" But the picture's surviving sequences play more like a lark, at least to twenty-first-century eyes, especially a pool party where everyone jumps in wearing their skivvies, another early glimpse of a future teen movie trope. But *Flaming Youth* and the ensuing cycles of flapper movies and college comedies weren't about teenagers per se but rather a broader swath of silly and/or misbehaving young people—"the wildest of all generations," as F. Scott Fitzgerald termed it (lacking a good crystal ball) in his 1931 essay "Echoes of the Jazz Age." Perhaps too close to the subject, he was not a fan of the era's youth movies, dismissing most as "timid, behind the times, and banal . . . The Hollywood hacks ran the theme into its cinematographic grave."

When Andy Hardy's time came, he stood out, paradoxically, because he was in many ways unremarkable. He has enthusiasms, but no real talents. He's not an athlete or a musician or a scholar, but he does have heaps of "pep," that once prized quality, which is enough to make him a big wheel at Carvel High; girls you'd think would be out of his league fall all over him. You might also know him as Archie Andrews, the comic book character introduced in 1941 by creators who borrowed much of the *Hardy* DNA.

No one sensed after Andy's first appearance on screen as a secondary character in a modest B movie that he would become an archetype. Even when he became the series' breakout character, the films still held him at arm's length as if he were some sort of novelty act, assuming an adult audience's amusement at his hormonal excesses and overeager fumbling toward manhood. Teenagers identified with him, but he wasn't a Ferris Bueller speaking directly to and for them. And unlike subsequent generational avatars such as James Dean's Jim Stark from *Rebel Without a Cause* or Dustin Hoffman's Benjamin Braddock in *The Graduate*, Andy would never trouble a parent's beauty sleep. He could be mildly rebellious, occasionally even surly, driven by ping-ponging impulses, but he was fundamentally good-natured and always, when it mattered most, obedient. His greatest act of filial rebellion isn't racing cars over a cliff or bedding a friend's mother but asking Judge Hardy not to accompany him when he finally sets off for college, lest his new classmates deem him a "pantywaist" still clinging to his father's shirttails. He would have been eaten alive a decade later attending the feral high schools depicted in *Blackboard Jungle* and *Rebel Without a Cause*. In a John Hughes movie, he'd be dismissed as a tool.

But in his own era, he was the iconic main attraction of films that appealed to audiences of all ages. These were family pictures—the notion of movies about and *for* teenagers was still well below the horizon—and they were among MGM's most profitable. By one estimate, taken as a whole, the *Hardy* films earned roughly ten times what they cost to produce, given their skimpy budgets, grossing a total of $80 million through 1946, or $1.3 billion in 2024 dollars.

Louis B. Mayer, the co-founder and head of production at MGM, liked that return on investment, but he took the *Hardy* films deeply seriously, too, believing that for all their easy laughs and silly plot contrivances they served a higher, patriotic purpose. "The best pictures [I] ever made—the only pictures I really ever took an active hand in—were the *Andy Hardy* series," he once said. "They were good and wholesome. They had heart. You can't imagine how much good they did for America . . . all over the world."

Being good for America meant that, among other things, the Hardys' world was almost entirely white, with allowances made for porters and butlers; queerness remained a subterranean menace, surfacing only rarely in the form of epithets like "pantywaist." With the encouragement of MGM's publicists, the Hardys were invariably referred to as a "typical American family" in the era's press, even in precincts that had every reason to know better. The *Washington Tribune*, an African American weekly, used the phrase not at all ironically in its rave review of the ninth picture in the series, *Andy Hardy Meets Debutante*, which the paper deemed "a tale of hilarious human comedy and poignant human drama." (It is neither of those things, though it has its moments.)

At the 1943 Oscars ceremony, MGM received a Special Academy Award "for its achievement in representing the American Way of Life in the production of the 'Andy Hardy' series of films." In a very real sense, when twenty-first-century conservatives conjure the bucolic small-town "real America" of the past and narrowing present, they are tapping into a myth crafted by Mayer, Rooney, and the rest of their collaborators, from the city of Carvel—population 25,000 as a sign in the first shot of the first film announces; not too big, not too small, *just right*—down to the literal white picket fence in front of the Hardy home. Andy, goofy and libidinal, but not *too* goofy and libidinal—also *just right*—helped sell the myth. Which meant Rooney did, too. As Mayer once told him, in all seriousness (during an argument over the actor's busy off-camera love life), "You're Andy Hardy. You're the United States. You're the Stars and Stripes."

Imagine being saddled with that. *The New York Times* profiled the star on a 1939 publicity tour of New York, on an afternoon when "the typical American boy wasn't feeling so typical." The paper described a weary, jaded Rooney struggling to stay awake on his hotel suite's couch where he lay prone "like a heroic warrior being borne from the battle on his shield," depleted by nonstop photo opportunities and deep drafts of Gotham nightlife:

> It must give him a tremendous feeling of responsibility to young America—that is, being Andy Hardy and all, the reporter cautiously observed. Mickey, lying flat upon his back with his hands behind his head and that tousled nob cradled wearily between his elbows, said it does.
>
> "I try," he solemnly recited, his eyes half closed with fatigue, "to live up to what they expect of Andy Hardy. I try to be as close to Andy as possible. I really do."

It was a strange, novel predicament for an eighteen-year-old.

The only child of performers, Rooney was virtually bred to be at ease in front of an audience or camera—to crave it, even. His father, Joe Yule, was a vaudeville comedian, his mother, Nell Carter, a former showgirl. Rooney was born in 1920 in Brooklyn, where, as an infant, christened Joe Yule Jr., he literally slept in a drawer in his mother's old wardrobe trunk. But shortly after his arrival, the family went back out on the vaudeville circuit as part of a packaged troupe. The infant, nicknamed Sonny, was an early walker and first tasted audience approval at the age of a year or so when he wandered out from backstage during a comic's act. As the story goes, he tottered his way to the edge of the stage by the orchestra pit, and started imitating the kettledrum player, earning the addictive reward of laughter and applause. By two, he had formally joined the lineup, singing and telling bad jokes. By three he had been outfitted with his own stage tuxedo. At one theater, when he drew the attention of the local Children's Society, a watchdog group on the lookout for child-labor-law violations, his father tried to pass him off as a midget performer, asking, "What three-year-old would be wearing a fifty-dollar tuxedo?" The toddler eventually received a special work permit from New York Governor Alfred E. Smith, a friend of the troupe's manager.

Decades later, the gossip columnist Hedda Hopper asked Rooney, "Are you conscious of never having been in show business?" He replied, "I can't remember that far back."

Joe Yule Sr. was a heavy drinker, a womanizer, and a neglectful, when not resentful, husband and father. At times he was abusive to both wife and son. The marriage's shaky façade finally crumbled one day when, during a costume change, Sonny came upon his father enjoying a backstage blow job given by a showgirl he was having an affair with. Uncomprehending but understandably alarmed—what was that lady *doing?*—four-year-old Sonny cried out, and Nell came running. Husband and wife separated, eventually divorced, and after a few false starts elsewhere, Nell and Sonny made their way to Los Angeles. (History would repeat itself when, as mentioned earlier, Rooney's second wife walked in on him and a too-young Elizabeth Taylor.)

Now five, Sonny took song-and-dance lessons and auditioned for movie roles while Nell held down jobs managing bungalows, working as a telephone operator, and occasionally turning tricks in the living room of their Hollywood apartment while Sonny supposedly slept. You can imagine the appeal being a part of the stable, non-licentious Hardy family would hold for him a few years later, no matter how make-believe.

By the time he was twelve and a seasoned veteran of knockabout kid comedy shorts, Mickey Rooney, as the boy was now known—he was also a veteran of several career-minded name changes—might have been near the end of the road as a child star. But he began getting good notices in supporting parts in tonier productions, most notably as Puck in a high-profile Hollywood Bowl production of A *Midsummer Night's Dream* and a subsequent film adaptation. At the urging of producer David O. Selznick, MGM offered him a contract.

The good notices and supporting roles continued while Nell made several attempts at providing Mickey with some semblance of a conventional education, at least to the extent required by law. Joe Yule had also settled in California, and was managing to hold down a steady job at a burlesque house in downtown LA. Proving he wasn't an entirely uncaring father, Yule would invite Mickey and his friends to see the shows for free from a stage box. (Burlesque, always more risqué than vaudeville, then meant a bill of strippers punctuated by a comic or two.) "It was a great treat for us horny teenagers to see all those bare tits and asses as they paraded on and off the runway within touching and smelling distance," a friend with vivid recall later told Arthur Marx, Rooney's biographer (and Groucho's son).

My point here, aside from the pleasure of retelling a vulgar anecdote, is not just that Mickey Rooney wasn't Andy Hardy, and hadn't been raised by Judge and Mrs. Hardy; he was, by breeding, something close to an anti–Andy Hardy. *Time* quoted him barking at a studio visitor who wondered whether Rooney resembled the characters he played, "Sir, I am an actor!" The magazine's editors, tickled by such bald presumption coming from a kid, featured the line on their cover.

"He is a handsome but unkempt fellow of sixteen with a ruffled mop of hair that stands on end, shirt open at the neck, and baggy trousers, which he is always hitching up. He looks like a shaggy, overgrown puppy."

That is how Andy Hardy is introduced in the text of the 1926 play that gave him life: *Skidding* by a California writer with the almost impossibly mellifluous name Aurania Rouverol. The work was a comedy-drama about a large middle-class family buffeted by the fast pace and shifting mores of modern life. Judge Hardy and his wife, Emily (or "Mother," as he invariably addresses her), are the central characters, coping with their elder two daughters' romantic upheavals and a corrupt political scheme involving an aqueduct, which threatens the judge's career. (The stage version of Carvel was fixed on the map in Idaho.) You almost surely haven't seen *Skidding*, but if you've seen Ron Howard's 1989 film *Parenthood*, or the subsequent television series, you've seen a more recent equivalent. Family bonds fray but are rewoven more tightly than ever by final curtain. Andy, the youngest child, is on hand mainly to provide comic relief, a caricature of adolescent volatility. His slang vocabulary is a running joke, with Judge and Mother Hardy objecting to his use of outré terms such as "nope," "gee," "heck," and "thing-me-jig." No one has ever cited Rouverol as an original or profound playwright, but if Andy sounds like a stock teenage character, that's mainly because he's since accrued nearly a century's worth of sediment. Within his own otherwise familiar context, he has a certain native vitality.

Skidding debuted in Pasadena in 1926, and two years later made its way to Broadway, where *The New York Times* dismissed it as "a just passable comedy" with "more fidelity to the theater than to life." Still, it ran for over a year. A future movie producer happened to catch it, and eight years later, when he was at MGM, decided that *Skidding* might make "a nice little picture" for the studio's B-movie unit.* Retitled A *Family Affair* when it was released in 1937, the adaptation starred Lionel Barrymore and Spring Byington as Judge and Mrs. Hardy, and Cecilia Parker as the younger of the two daughters, Marian. Another young actor under contract at MGM, Frankie Thomas Jr., had been considered for Andy, but a growth spurt rendered him unsuitably gangly. According to Ann

---

*Among MGM's A pictures that year were its adaptations of Pearl S. Buck's *The Good Earth* and Rudyard Kipling's *Captains Courageous*, both Academy Award nominees for Best Picture.

Rutherford, who would play Polly Benedict, Andy's on-and-off girlfriend, through most of the series, "They thought that having a short Andy Hardy would be a little more amusing and touching." Sixteen-year-old Mickey Rooney, whose full adult height would be reported as anywhere between five feet two inches and five feet three inches (and five feet one inch during his World War II army physical), fit the bill. Moreover, he had previously co-starred with Barrymore, Byington, and Parker in a successful film adaptation of Eugene O'Neill's *Ah, Wilderness!*, so the new picture could be advertised as a de facto sequel—"Stars of *Ah, Wilderness!* Thrill Again," as the posters promised.

Still, *A Family Affair* was made on a B-movie budget ($178,000, or $3.7 million in 2024 dollars) and with a B-movie running time (sixty-nine minutes), destined to fill out the bottom half of double features as a "programmer." The director was George B. Seitz, a steady but unflashy hand whose career had begun in the teens with silent serials like *The Exploits of Elaine*. Expectations were low. But as Rooney later wrote, "A funny thing happened to this little programmer: released in spring 1937, it ended up grossing more than half a million dollars nationwide"—not a blockbuster number, but a nice return on a shrug of an investment.

Reviews ran from unkind to tepid. The *Chicago Tribune* labeled the film "a boob trap," and *Billboard*, which then covered movies, dismissed it as "a harmless concoction, neither very bad nor very good, but just about hitting the level considered excellent by the Legion of Decency." Eight and a half decades later, the picture remains a pleasant enough sit, though it would be of interest only to Barrymore family completists if not for Rooney. Dropped into a film where the rest of the cast affects mid-Atlantic accents and stagy mannerisms, he functions like a wild card, a jolt of modern energy with his brash newsboy's voice and athletic physicality, his shirtless scampering up and down the Hardy staircase, his repeated bellowing into the family's sole telephone. "Holy jumping Jerusalem! A party with girls!" he yelps with disgust when Mrs. Hardy informs him he's expected to escort Polly Benedict to a soiree. When he's dressed in a suit, the wide-shouldered cut on his short frame makes him look not unlike a circus chimp—a presumably intended effect repeated in wardrobe choices throughout the series. As *Time* noted, Rooney would become notorious for his mugging, reaching a horrifying, even-Jerry-Lewis-would-cringe apotheosis with his yellowface performance in *Breakfast at Tiffany's* (1961). But here and in his better moments in the other *Hardy* films, he has a naturalness that you don't often see in 1930s movie performances, even from live wires like Jean Harlow and James Cagney. Rooney claimed to have a photographic memory and not to read his scripts until right before shooting, relying on instinct to feel his way through a scene, often improvising when a director allowed him—a rarity in that era. Playing the new breed of adolescent, he was an appropriately fresh presence, at his best unstudied and occasionally even raw.

An unexpected success demanded a follow-up, and a partially recast sequel, *You're Only Young Once*, reached theaters in December of 1937, just nine months after the first picture's March release. With Lionel Barrymore reluctant to get trapped in a B-movie series (though a year later he would be cast in a recurring role in MGM's *Dr. Kildare* series), Judge Hardy was now played by Lewis Stone. Fay Holden took on the Mother Hardy role, with Cecilia Parker and Sara Haden held over as, respectively, sister Marian and spinster Aunt Millie. (The elder daughter in *A Family Affair*, Joan, disappeared; it was as if she'd been institutionalized and thus, by custom of the day, never spoken of again.) That would be the set cast for most of the rest of the series, along with Rooney. Stone provided a second strong presence, with a calm, often droll demeanor that played nicely as a counterweight to Rooney's jitterbug spontaneity, though Stone—in whom today's audiences might see a bit of Harry Morgan or J. K. Simmons—could also be gruff or stern when a script required. The entire cast conveyed a sense of ease with one another that mimicked the fond give-and-take of a real family. That familiarity was itself a draw: even for their first audiences; the films had a baked-in, present-tense nostalgia, with the same actors, the same sets, the same plot rhythms—the old-couch appeal that TV sitcoms have long thrived on.

Nevertheless, MGM may not have been entirely confident in the Hardys, because the second film hedged its bets by adding a dose of travelogue, with the family vacationing on Santa Catalina Island. Rooney, previously fourth billed, was now third, but, as before, didn't figure on the film's poster, which featured Parker's Marian in the arms of a dubious love interest (a Handsome Harry lifeguard with oil-slick hair who turns out to be married) while Judge Hardy looks on skeptically. The tagline: "I'm seventeen! I'm no baby, Dad—I'm love-wise!" (This was perhaps another hedge, suggesting something more in the vein of *Flaming Youth* than would be delivered.) Still, within his first five minutes on screen, Andy establishes his brash presence by trying to kiss Polly on a front-porch swing, asking to borrow the family car, pleading for a new tennis racket for no particular reason, and disrupting the family's post-dinner quiet by tuning in to a raucous swing band on the parlor radio. On vacation, he falls for Geraldine, a rich sixteen-year-old girl who's cooling her heels on Catalina by herself while her mother gets her fourth Reno divorce. We know she's trouble long before inexperienced Andy because she smokes and drinks and goes by the masculine "Jerry." It's up to Judge Hardy to sit his son down for one of the man-to-man talks President Roosevelt teased Rooney about. "This girl isn't good," Judge Hardy explains, more in sorrow than anger. "I suppose she's a product of the bad features of the age we live in, but that doesn't keep her from being rotten fruit. She'd poison whatever she came in contact with—mentally, morally, and spiritually."

I think we all know what Judge Hardy is getting at. Andy dismisses his father as an "old fogey," but a seed has been planted, and Andy soon realizes that dissipation and tarnished fruit aren't so keen after all; by film's end, he's back to chasing the willing (but not *too* willing) Polly. And thus the template was set: Andy getting in over his head one way or another, sometimes with a girl, sometimes with money, often with both, and then, after a curative dose of paternal wisdom, figuring a way out of his "fix"—until he makes a similar mistake in the next picture.

Rooney finally made the poster and received second billing, after Stone, for the third film, *Judge Hardy's Children*, released in March 1938, which featured arguably the most memorable of all man-to-man talks, when Andy confesses, "I want to kiss all the pretty girls. Do you think I'm normal?"

"Well, yes, Andy," the judge replies, just barely stifling a laugh, "I really believe you are."

This is silly and dated, of course. But it's noteworthy for its time in treating adolescent sexuality with a modicum of seriousness—really, for acknowledging it at all. Andy's concern, however naively expressed, coupled with Judge Hardy's relaxed reassurance, made for an unusually frank and tender moment between a father and son by 1930s movie standards. It was almost as if MGM were trying to reassure America that its sons and daughters would still be okay in a quickly changing world.

I should note that Andy had a de facto counterweight in the Dead End Kids, an elastic troupe that originated with the 1937 film *Dead End*. Adapted from a hit Broadway drama, it was meant to be a hard-hitting essay in social realism, featuring a gang of fast-talking Manhattan slum kids who engage in petty crime, swim in the garbage-strewn East River, and roast potatoes on sticks over an oil drum fire; their primary adult supervision is an impotent beat cop while educational opportunities are limited to lockups in reform school and the occasional tip from an older hood about how to fight dirty. I can't vouch for the film's authenticity, but it seems to provide a glimpse into the kind of feral urban childhoods that reformers had been working so hard to eradicate. Happily, given the movie delinquents' insufferable, possibly exaggerated New Yawk accents, I was grateful that their antics serve mainly as backdrop to a better-enunciated adult melodrama starring Humphrey Bogart, Joel McCrea, Sylvia Sidney, and Claire Trevor. (Nominated for a Best Picture Oscar, the film was further classed up by director William Wyler, screenwriter Lillian Hellman, and cinematographer Gregg Toland, who four years later would shoot

Citizen Kane.) But social realism would soon devolve into schtick: the rowdy delinquents proved popular enough that the young actors, with their edges sanded off and their budgets decimated, continued making movies in various configurations and under multiple guises—the Dead End Kids, the Little Tough Guys, the East Side Kids, and, finally, the Bowery Boys—well into the 1950s, their run ending in post-adolescent slapstick comedies. It was as if the Little Rascals had hung around long enough to go to seed.

Meanwhile, there would be a second and third *Hardy* picture in 1938: *Love Finds Andy Hardy*, released in July, which became the series' most popular installment (I'll return to it); and *Out West with the Hardys*, released in November in time for the holidays. All told, Rooney appeared in eight movies that year, a heavy workload for a seventeen-year-old, surely eased by MGM's practice of dispensing "pep pills" to young performers. It was the first of his three consecutive years as box office champ, during which he also made many well-received and successful non-*Hardy* films, including *The Adventures of Huckleberry Finn* (1939), *Young Tom Edison* (1940), and three "backyard musicals" that paired him with Judy Garland under the direction of Busby Berkeley, which for all intents and purposes were song-and-dance extensions of the Andy Hardy brand (with some of the most elaborate and appalling blackface numbers ever staged).

A postpubescent boy star! Hollywood had exploited the talents of many notable child actors, including Jackie Coogan, who had held his own at the age of five, opposite Charlie Chaplin in *The Kid*, and Shirley Temple, a top draw at five—she had preceded Rooney as Hollywood's top ticket seller for four years straight. But child stars' careers tended to peter out once they hit puberty, as would be the case with Temple, who, after a series of flops, was dropped by Fox in 1940, a budding has-been at twelve. (She landed briefly at MGM, and as a teenager appeared in a few memorable movies in supporting roles, but was out of the business by twenty.) Rooney and contemporary teenage stars Deanna Durbin, Jackie Cooper, and Judy Garland were something new: actors who found fame in adolescent roles. So new to the scene were teen stars that the industry wasn't quite sure what to make of them, lacking even the language to distinguish them from younger performers. In 1939, beneath the headline "Heavy Run of Kid Films," a front-page story in *Variety* reported, "Money-making potentialities of casts topped by moppets currently has the coast film industry agog." Among those "moppets" were Rooney (then nineteen), Durbin and Garland (both seventeen), Cooper (sixteen), Freddie Bartholomew (fifteen), Bonita Granville (sixteen), and Jane Withers (thirteen).

An AP story from the same year, headlined "Hollywood at Last Learning How to Rear Its Children," observed, "Years ago, child stars were not expected to last more than a year or two. When they reached the 'awkward' age they were dropped like a Hank Greenberg drive from a third baseman's glove." What had changed? No one really seemed to know, though an MGM soundman credited Rooney's staying power to the miraculous stability of his larynx: "From twelve to sixteen it is normal for a boy's voice to change but Mickey's has remained virtually at the same level with a minimum of fluctuation."

Reading Rooney's press clips from the 1930s and early 1940s, you get an almost real-time sense of writers and editors struggling with how seriously to take him and his peers. As ingenues, Durbin and Garland didn't fare too badly, but Rooney was treated like a novelty act, written about with equal parts amusement and condescension. He was variously Hollywood's "colossal kid" and "the mighty mite of the screen world," more than once posing for photographers while attempting to shave—an inherently comic conceit, like a picture of a dog seeming to drive or read a book.

Like most teenagers, Rooney was in a hurry to move past adolescence, at least off screen. "People don't seem to realize I'm grown up. They're still pulling that 'kid star' stuff on me," he told a reporter, who described the actor emphasizing his point by "heatedly rising to his full five feet two and a half inches." At the time, in the fall of 1938, he had just turned eighteen. "The way some people talk, you'd think I still played with toys," he complained "bitterly" to another interviewer. When it was pointed out that in fact Rooney had a large alcove off his bedroom with an elaborate electric train set up, he bristled: "For gosh sakes, a lot of men have electric trains for a hobby."

A line from his 1939 studio biography: "He boasts of the fact that he has always worn long trousers."

Gossip columnists liked to tweak Rooney anytime he was perceived as putting on adult airs. These included his taste for stylish overcoats and men's hats (kids were supposed to wear caps); his "Negro valet"; his habit of popping up in nightclubs; the fancy roadster he drove around town (though not to his movie premieres, where MGM forced him to pull up in the beat-up jalopy Andy drove in the films, his mother as his safe, steady date). A movie magazine reported that he was causing problems for the studio with his "growing pains" and "this desire of Mickey's to be a man." He was teased for having a man crush, as we'd call it now, on Clark Gable:

> He has mastered the Gable swagger and always he carries the Gable prop, a pipe—sometimes clenched between his teeth, sometimes flourishing it in his hand. Like Gable, too, he calls all waitresses "Honey" or "Toots." Once someone tried to admonish Mickey on this point: "Don't you think it's out of keeping for a youngster to address grown women like that?" "Who's a youngster?" Mickey wanted to know belligerently.

His romantic life was also subject to inquiry—a burden shared by most celebrities, but one that, because he was underage, was particularly fraught for the star and his handlers. "Is Mickey Rooney in Love?" one movie magazine headline wanted to know, adding: "At seventeen, the Rooney kid is old enough to think about girls—and he does!" Scandal sheets ran headlines such as: "Million Dollar Problem Child" . . . "Mickey the Menace" . . . "The Youngest Wolf in Hollywood?" Rooney, or MGM's publicity department, countered with a fan magazine article under his byline titled "I'm Not Girl Crazy." Elsewhere, he was quoted uttering bromides like "Dames are the bunk as far as I'm concerned" and "Necking's all right, but it ain't necessary."

Those pronouncements were, let us say, insincere. Ava Gardner, his first wife (of eight), met him in 1941 when she was a cloistered eighteen-year-old starlet fresh from North Carolina, just signed to MGM. As she later wrote, "He was incorrigible. He'd screw anything that moved. He had a *lot* of energy. He probably banged most of the starlets who appeared in his *Andy Hardy* movies—Lana Turner among them. She called him Andy Hard-on."

According to Rooney, he got Turner pregnant, her abortion serving as one more MGM perk, alongside the amphetamines; she denied the tale. At any rate, this was a heady time and place to be America's most famous teenager. As he later put it, "I became as cocky a kid as ever cruised the Sunset Strip in his own convertible, exploding with sheer, selfish energy— and pissing off almost everyone around me." That last was no doubt an exaggeration—the people in movie stars' orbit tend to have a high toler-ance for their misbehavior—except when Rooney's skirt-chasing threat-ened the Hardy family honor, and with it MGM's bottom line.

If something as machine-tooled as the Hardy family movies could be said to have an auteur, it would have been Louis B. Mayer—certainly in his own estimation. "I was the daddy of the Andy Hardy films," he declared in 1957, not long before his death. "Daddy" was a telling choice of words, given both the crude, emotional paternalism with which he ran MGM and the more genteel sort that suffused the *Hardy* films. Mr. Mayer, as his stars invariably addressed him, could be a canny, ruthless businessman, acting at times as if he ran a factory that only happened to manufacture movies and movie stars but might have just as easily turned out iceboxes. "The idea of a star being born is bush-wah," he once proclaimed. "A star is made, created; carefully and cold-bloodedly built up from nothing, from nobody. All I ever looked for was a face. If someone looked good to me, I'd have him tested. If a person looked good on film, if he photographed well, we could do the rest. . . . We hired geniuses at makeup, hairdress-ing, surgeons to slice away a bulge here and there, rubbers to rub away the blubber, clothes designers, lighting experts, coaches for everything—fencing, dancing, walking, talking, sitting and spitting."

That was Mayer's filmmaker-as-industrialist side. He could also be nakedly emotional, given to outbursts of anger and sometimes physical violence—he was short but powerfully built, a fist of a man—as well as torrents of sentimental (if manipulative) tears. When it suited him he liked to treat his stars as wards as much as indentured servants. They would be summoned to his large white-carpeted offices for dressing-downs that could devolve into family-style psychodrama. Lena Horne, in trouble for turning down a role, offered a tearful apology (as more experienced colleagues had advised her to), bringing Mayer to tears as well. "You've been a bad girl," he told her between sniffles, "but we'll forgive you." Judy Garland once turned on him for his habit of praising her talent for "singing from the heart" while cupping his hand on her chest to underscore the point. "Mr. Mayer, don't you ever, ever do that again," she finally snapped after his umpteenth feel. "I just will not stand for it." According to her biographer, Gerald Clarke, "Mayer reacted not with anger but with tears, sitting down, putting his head in his hands and crying. 'How can you say that to me, to me who loves you?' he asked, looking so miserable that Judy found herself consoling him."

Like most of the Jewish immigrants who built Hollywood, Mayer had a fierce devotion to a narrow American ideal—a sometimes necessary devotion given periodic anti-Semitic crusades against movie morals. He had been born in Poland in the early to mid-1880s. (Records give conflicting dates.) The family immigrated to the United States in 1887 and then to New Brunswick, Canada, where Mayer's father ran a scrap-metal business, which Louis joined at the age of twelve. Living in Boston as a young man, he began acquiring movie theaters and eventually moved to Los Angeles, where he created his own production company. By 1924, following a confusing succession of musical-chair mergers, common in the early film industry (and continuing on to this day), he was running Metro-Goldwyn-Mayer in partnership with Irving Thalberg, the "boy wonder" producer in his early twenties who tended to creative affairs while Mayer, a decade and a half older, handled the business. Together, they built MGM into the most successful, prestigious, and glamorous of all the Golden Age Hollywood studios. But Mayer tired of Thalberg's taste for high-flown literary properties and expensive costume dramas—"Garbo with the ribbons," in Mayer's dismissive phrase—and wanted to steer the studio in a more populist direction. Thalberg's death from pneumonia in 1936, at the age of thirty-seven, shocked Hollywood—and left Mayer fully in charge and free to indulge his own tastes.

Enter the Hardys. With most movies, Mayer was content to trust his producers and directors once filming got underway, waiting until he saw rough cuts to weigh in; with the *Hardy* pictures, he insisted on watching the "rushes"—the daily screenings of the latest raw footage. He would sit next to Carey Wilson, who produced the films, and pull on Wilson's arm or even punch it whenever something displeased him—Andy forgetting to take off his hat indoors, say—and demand reshoots.

Andy's dealings with Mrs. Hardy were a point of inordinate attention. "That was kind of a quirk with Mr. Mayer," Rooney wrote in his autobiography. The studio head could explode in rage over the most anodyne of offenses to motherhood. In one scene, for instance, Andy returns home at suppertime, glum after finding Polly enthralled by a handsome suitor, notably older and taller than Andy. Moping at the table, he only toys with his food. Mrs. Hardy expresses concern. "I'm not hungry, Mom," Andy says. That earned producer Wilson a tug or a punch from Mayer, who then went off on the picture's screenwriter: "Don't you know a boy of sixteen is hungry all the time? You tell me you were brought up in a good American home—in the kitchen! You lied to me! You've let Andy insult his mother! No boy would tell his mother he wasn't hungry. Change that line!" The scene was reshot with Andy taking pains to compliment his mother's cooking but adding that he just didn't "feel" like eating.

Andy's libido was another vigorously policed precinct. In a *Hardy* movie equivalent to the ritualized moment in a James Bond picture where 007 asks for his vodka martini "shaken not stirred," or introduces himself as "Bond, James Bond," Andy typically responds to being kissed by shouting

"WHOO WHOO!" and crossing his eyes or lifting his legs or both; if you want to be charitable, you could say it was an homage to the wolf characters in Tex Avery cartoons whose eyes bugged out and tongues hit the floor anytime a "dish" walked by. But in one take, according to Scott Eyman, a Mayer biographer, the studio chief felt the hubba-hubba had gone too far even by the normally elastic standard allowed for Rooney's mugging. Mayer hauled director Seitz into his office and lectured him: "George, if you want to get a sex laugh, I can tell you a better one. Let Andy kiss her, then turn around and unzip his fly and take out his prick. That'll get you a wow!" Seitz dutifully reshot the scene, showed it to Mayer, and said dryly, "I hope you'll notice Mickey didn't even reach for his fly."*

Mayer's ambitions for the films had limits; he knew not to fix something that wasn't broken, at one point laying down the edict, "Don't try to make these films any better. Just keep them the way they are." He added, "If you had a stronger director, the films wouldn't be as good." The point wasn't to be distinctive but rather universal. And the formula worked. As he once remarked, taking another swipe at Garbo, this time for her critically adored 1939 comedy *Ninotchka*, directed by Ernst Lubitsch, which earned four Academy Award nominations for MGM, including Best Picture, Best Actress, and Best Director, "*Ninotchka* got everything but money . . . a Hardy picture cost $25,000 less than Lubitsch was paid alone. But any good Hardy picture made $500,000 more than *Ninotchka*."

Maybe more to the point, Mayer, however powerful, would never be Garbo's and Lubitsch's "daddy," not in the way he saw himself as the Hardys'. Someone at the studio once made a crack about a potential

---

*Mayer wasn't the only watchdog where Andy's love life was concerned. Letters to MGM from the Motion Picture Association of America, reviewing scripts in the series for possible violations of the Production Code (which had been guarding screen morals since 1934), make amusing reading: "Please modify the words 'hot stuff' . . . Here and elsewhere, please be sure that the girls are covered adequately in these hula costumes . . . The underlined word in the following dialogue of Andy is unacceptable because of its suggestiveness: 'Hello, there, cupcake!' . . . The expression 'back-alley tomcat' must be deleted . . . The underlined word in Andy's line: 'When I can practically see your lungs?' is unacceptable."

crossover film. The premise was that Andy would get the clap from one of his girlfriends and see Dr. Kildare for a cure. When the joke got back to Mayer, he was outraged and let his executives know that where Andy Hardy was concerned, irreverence had no place at MGM.

Mayer's biggest headache with the series wasn't the occasional lapse of taste; it was the fact that the movies starred a teenager who was much less easy to wrangle than his fictional counterpart. "Was Mr. Mayer happy? He was delirious," Rooney writes of the *Hardy* films' box office. "The only trouble was, Mr. Mayer wanted me to be Andy Hardy off the screen, too, which was pretty unreasonable of him considering that this was the same Mr. Mayer who once tried to put the make on Shirley Temple's mom."*

Rooney remembered a time in 1938 when Mayer called him into his office, only the second time Rooney had been granted an audience. Mayer perhaps intended this to be his version of a man-to-man talk. He complimented Rooney on the success of his films and his reviews, as the actor later wrote:

> "The critics," he said. "They love you. And I must agree with them. I love you, too."
>
> Well, I said, "Thank you very much, Mr. Mayer."
>
> "But—"
>
> I said to myself, "Uh-oh."
>
> "I've been hearing stories around town."
>
> I nodded very seriously, just as I nodded at my father on screen, Judge Hardy . . . "Stories, Mr. Mayer?"
>
> He was taken aback by my tone, so polite, so deferential. "Well," he said. "Yes. I hear—" He laughed with embarrassment over the

*At least Mayer didn't come on to Temple herself the way the musical producer Arthur Freed did when she was twelve and newly arrived at MGM, according to her memoir. Temple's giggle when Freed exposed himself allegedly doomed her tenure at the studio.

silliness of what he was about to say, but he said it anyway. "I hear you've never met a pretty girl that you didn't kiss."

"Kinda like the song, huh? 'When I'm not near the girl I love, I love every girl I'm near'?" I grinned.*

He frowned . . . "Look," he said, "I'm not talking about kissing. I'm talking about fucking."

Mayer went on to tell Rooney that he was worried about the star's image, and pulled out a file of clippings from newspapers and fan magazines.

"You're everywhere. The Palomar Ballroom, the Ocean Park Ballroom, Ciro's, the Cocoanut Grove, the Trocadero. Blondes. Brunettes. Redheads." He pointed at one picture of me holding a glass. "Is this champagne? Champagne?"

Very respectfully (for I was afraid of him), I said, "It's a champagne glass, Mr. Mayer. But it isn't champagne."

"No?"

"No. It's ginger ale." (It really was.)

He grunted.

Rooney was telling the truth: because he was famous for being underage, nightclubs wouldn't serve him alcohol. He compensated by having accomplices bring him shots in the men's room, where he would also sneak cigarettes.

Feeling he wasn't getting his point across, Mayer came around from his desk and got in Rooney's face.

"You like being Andy Hardy?"

"Yes, Mr. Mayer."

"Then," he said, "be—Andy—Hardy."

---

*Rooney's memory may be fuzzy here. He's (mis)quoting a song from the musical *Finian's Rainbow*, which wouldn't premiere until 1947.

The confrontation escalated into a shouting match, with Rooney insisting he owed MGM nothing when he was off the clock and Mayer (who was himself only five feet six inches) bellowing that the star was an "ungrateful runt." Rooney stalked out of the office, and Mayer chased after him, his tone now returning to something more paternal. He took hold of the actor's lapels and told him, calmly but not without menace, "I don't care what you do off camera. Just don't do it in public . . . You're the Stars and Stripes. Behave yourself. You're a symbol."

Like Lena Horne, Rooney promised to be "good," and the two men hugged. "We stood close for a moment more, he looking into my eyes, I into his. We had an understanding. He'd be Uncle Sam. And I'd be the Stars and Stripes."

However crudely or cornily put, Mayer's feelings about the series were shared by a wide swath of the public. Witness the critical reception of the fourth film, *Love Finds Andy Hardy*, released in July 1938. While the first three pictures had received increasingly kind notices, *Love Finds Andy Hardy* was treated as a cultural event, winning raves that read like Pulitzer Prize citations and might even have caused MGM's publicists to fear the movie would be tainted as unbecomingly highbrow. *The Washington Post*: "These simple, yet profound revelations of the workings of a typical American household go beyond the matter of mere entertainment." *Variety*: "As a truly human celluloid document, this picture will take its place alongside of anything to come out of the Hollywood studios this season." The *New York Herald Tribune* published a curious essay that hailed the picture as a milestone in American realism alongside works by Mark Twain, Sherwood Anderson, Sinclair Lewis, Theodore Dreiser, Erskine Caldwell, William Faulkner, and F. Scott Fitzgerald.

The movie may have fallen in comparative estimation since then, but it is still widely regarded as the series' high point. In 1996, a survey of *National Review* readers went so far as to rate it one of the one hundred "best conservative movies" for its contributions to "glorifying the American family," and it is the sole *Hardy* film chosen to date for the Library of Congress's National Film Registry, added in 2000 alongside *Goodfellas* and *Five Easy Pieces*, two very different views of the American family.

And yet, having watched all the *Hardy* films, I can't tell you that *Love Finds Andy Hardy* sits head and shoulders above the pack in terms of wit, profundity, or even quintessential middle Americanness. So why has this one stood out? I don't think it is coincidental that it was the first to give Andy prominence in title, poster, and share of running time (though Stone continued to receive top billing). Another vote in its favor: it has Judy Garland, in the first of her three appearances in the series, bringing more depth and spunk to her scenes than did Andy's usual love interests. (Donna Reed would add something similar to 1942's *The Courtship of Andy Hardy*.)

This was Garland's second picture with Rooney, following a modestly successful 1937 horseracing caper, *Thoroughbreds Don't Cry*. Off screen, they were genuine friends, having attended a Hollywood school for professional children together, and their chemistry on screen is palpable. Garland, not quite two years younger, was herself a child of vaudevillians but a late bloomer compared to Rooney, having not made her first stage appearance until the age of two. The pair enjoyed horsing around on set, sometimes trying to break each other up during scenes. It's telling that Rooney rarely resorts to mugging opposite Garland; it's as if he trusts her to hold the audience's attention—a compliment he rarely extended to other performers. (Lewis Stone was another.) According to Garland, he came into her dressing room at the start of the shoot and told her, "Let's have a sort of pact with each other. Let's never try to steal a scene. Let's work with each other, not *at* each other. That's the way to make a good picture." Their chemistry was troupers' chemistry, mined to its greatest effect in the backyard musicals.

But what truly distinguishes *Love Finds Andy Hardy* is that it brings its hero's libido fully front and center. Whatever homespun values it thinks it's sowing, above all else this is a movie about horny teenagers, and fairly explicitly so in an era when horny adult behavior was highly coded on screen. The plot places Andy in the middle of a love triangle between Ann Rutherford's Polly and Cynthia, a newcomer played by Lana Turner, with the added complication of Garland's Betsy Booth off to the side, pining quietly for him. Scrape away subplots involving Judge and Mrs. Hardy and you're left with something along the lines of a leering 1960s sex farce like *Boeing Boeing* or *Divorce American Style* but played as a juvenile novelty, not all that far removed from *Bugsy Malone*, the 1976 gangster movie with an all-kid cast (led by Jodie Foster) brandishing tommy guns that shot whipped cream instead of bullets.

Following some dull scene-setting with the adult characters, *Love Finds Andy Hardy* opens properly with Andy sitting next to Polly on the Benedicts' porch swing, learning that she'll be away with her family for the holidays and thus can't be his date for the big country-club dance on Christmas Eve. He laments this lost opportunity to take advantage of the club's "swell little places where you can sneak out between dances."

"We're getting too old for that sort of thing, hugging and kisses," Polly demurs, clearly disingenuously, Rutherford's eyes broadcasting the presence of what used to be called feminine wiles.

"I'm never going to be too old for hugging and kissing," Andy counters. "Besides, you didn't act like no ninety years old on the porch last night yourself."

"Why, Andy Hardy! You kissed me last night by force!"

"Well, it's good that way, too," he says sheepishly, though not sheepishly enough.

Andy eventually persuades Polly to give him a goodbye kiss, prompting one of his Pavlovian "WHOO WHOO!"s. (Let's stipulate here that if anyone was truly learning how to be a teenager from this—or learning about gender roles or sexual politics or even simple manners—the lessons could have been better.) Andy and Polly's back-and-forth is played even more broadly than in the earlier films; the pair feel less like a plausible romantic couple than a comedy team. (When Rutherford wanted to, she could match Rooney for ham.) "We were very careful not to be serious with this young-love type of story, and especially to have no suggestion of adult sex about it," the director, George Seitz, told an interviewer at the time. "It must be kept true puppy love." It was, and then some: Andy's boyish eagerness, even compulsiveness, puts his obsession with "hugging and kissing" at but a short remove from a toddler's demands for toys and treats; at times, following kisses, Rooney even giggles and holds his hands between his legs in the exaggerated manner of an adult comic playing a mischievous infant—the sort of act Rooney surely witnessed during his vaudeville days. (Think Joe Besser playing Stinky on *The Abbott and Costello Show*.)

The rest of the plot: Andy's pal Beezy is also leaving town for the holidays. He asks Andy to "date up" his girlfriend while he's out of town "to keep all the other fellas away"—a strictly platonic arrangement that Beezy offers to pay for. His girl turns out to be Cynthia, the haughty blonde played by Turner, then seventeen and evincing much the same languor and lack of personality she would later bring to *The Postman Always Rings Twice* and *The Bad and the Beautiful*. Andy dutifully tries to date her up, but Cynthia doesn't much care for swimming or malts; she only likes necking—to the point where the usually indefatigable Andy starts wearing down, though he perks up when she tells him about the backless evening gown she plans to wear to the dance.

This leads to the inevitable man-to-man sit-down in Judge Hardy's den:

"Dad, I don't understand these modern girls."

"In what way?"

"Well, Polly, for instance. Sometimes she won't let you kiss her at all. But this Cynthia, oh, she'll let you kiss her whenever you want."

"Well, of the two degrees of kissing, which seems the most desirable to you?"

"Well, when you want to kiss a girl and she won't let you, you want to kiss her all the time. But this Cynthia . . . Dad, do you think there's anything wrong with a guy if he doesn't want a girl kissing him all the time?"

The judge doesn't really answer, but he doesn't have to: we already know that Andy is "normal" and that he'll choose the "good" girl over the "bad" one. He always does. But first there are plot complications: Polly comes home early, meaning Andy now has two dates to the Christmas Eve dance. What to do? That's where Garland comes in. Her Betsy Booth is visiting from New York for the holidays, staying with her grandmother right next door to the Hardys. She falls for Andy, but, as was the case between Rooney and Garland in real life, he refuses to see her as anything but a kid-sister type. "I'll never be able to get a man, much less hold him. No glamour. No glamour at all," Betsy pouts, channeling Garland's own insecurities about her standing at MGM vis-à-vis more conventional screen goddesses like Turner. But because she's Garland—and reminding us why she had a much bigger career than most of her rivals—she's then given a song:

> I'm past the stage of doll and carriage
> I'm not the age to think of marriage . . .
> I'm just an in-between

The song is meant to be comic, I think, and Garland begins with a light touch, but by the end she's selling this thin stuff with all the ache she would bring to "Somewhere Over the Rainbow" a year later in *The Wizard of Oz*, finishing the song in tears. She really was too good for the material. On the other hand, inflating emotions adults might see as trivial to epic proportions is almost the definition of an adolescent sensibility, so we should credit Garland with a pioneering portrayal of teen pathos— a pathos multiplied by a hideous dress with puffed sleeves and a Peter Pan collar augmented by ruffles which she wears with saddle shoes, an "awkward age" costume that was surely even more humiliating for Garland than the song. But to whatever extent this film has "meaning," this is where it lies: the serial mortifications of growing up, a theme that would recur in many teen movies to come.

In terms of plot, poor Betsy can serve only as a deus ex machina. She contrives to rid Andy of Cynthia and ultimately squares things with a jealous Polly. For her troubles, she gets to sing two more songs at the big dance.

Love Finds Andy Hardy ends more or less where it began, with another go-round between Andy and Polly, now sitting side by side in his jalopy in the Hardy family driveway.

"Did you like kissing Cynthia better than kissing me?" Polly asks.

Andy fumbles for an answer. "Well . . . it's been so long since I kissed you, I—"

She grabs him, but before they kiss, the camera cuts away to Judge Hardy watching through a window. He at first looks appalled, then smiles indulgently—blessing this union, as it were. The camera then cuts back to Polly and Andy post kiss, he now holding on to his hat.

Polly: "Well, what about Cynthia now?"

Andy: "Aw, Cynthia was just one of the errors of my childhood. But you, Polly! WHOOO WHOOO!" For added emphasis, Andy honks his car horn.

The film then cuts to Betsy, looking on from a window next door, also smiling beneficently—the film's final shot. What to make of this curious fusion of the smarmy and the wholesome? I would venture the ending is meant to reassure us that, as Andy reassures his father earlier in the film, he and Polly are only having "good, clean fun." Surely, with both a judge and a twelve- or thirteen-year-old looking on, there is no danger of passing first base. All the same, the scene feels a little . . . voyeuristic? And Andy's "WHOOO WHOOO!"—is it ejaculatory? Self-congratulatory? Both? I can't help but be put in mind of the final shot of Stanley Kubrick's adaptation of Anthony Burgess's *A Clockwork Orange*, in which the antihero Alex, a sociopathic juvenile delinquent restored to his naturally vicious state after an unpleasant round of forcible behavior modification, imagines himself having wild, triumphant sex in front of an approving crowd of Victorian burghers. "I was cured all right," Alex says in voice-over—just another "normal" teenage boy, at least in his own reckoning. But Kubrick's ending is meant to sting. *Love Finds Andy Hardy* wants us to salute American youth in all its healthy, red-blooded glory. Which, you know, is not a bad thing in theory, however weirdly arrived at.

The picture would be the eighth-highest-grossing film of 1938, bringing in $2,247,000 and, given its low budget, providing a full quarter of MGM's profit for the year.

The understanding between Rooney and Mayer, reinforced by a new studio minder who was assigned to Rooney off-hours, seemed to have worked well enough for a couple years. But his resolve "to be as close to Andy as possible" melted when he met Ava Gardner. "I figured you were a new piece of pussy for one of the executives. I didn't give a damn. I wanted to fuck you the moment I saw you," he later told her, not in Stars and Stripes mode. She, however, was determined to carry her virginity over the marital finish line, and after a few months of frenzied courtship, he proposed.

Mayer was apoplectic when Rooney's minder told him the couple planned to wed. "Tell him he can't," Mayer shouted. "He belongs to MGM. Tell him a married Andy Hardy would break the hearts of all those little girlies out there who want him for themselves. Who knows what that would cost—him, me, the studio?" Mayer then offered his best stab at Judge Hardy–like wisdom: "He should just boff her and get her out of my hair."

It was a tribute both to Rooney's stubbornness and to the leverage his box office prowess gave him that Mayer eventually agreed to the marriage (which lasted only four months before the couple separated over his uninterrupted womanizing).

It was inevitable that he would also have to grow up on screen, though the studio did its best to hold him back. After ten films, Andy had finally graduated from high school in 1941's *Andy Hardy's Private Secretary*. But following a brief attempt to seek his fortune in New York in the following year's *Life Begins for Andy Hardy*, he beat a retreat back to Carvel and treaded water for the next two pictures, still working on his jalopy, still fretting about who to take to country-club dances, still whooping after kisses. As Judge Hardy says to Mother Hardy, "Now remember, Emily, nothing has happened. We've got our boy back." It was true: nothing had happened; the series ground on. It was also remarkably tone-deaf, given

that in real life a world war had happened. Many families with boys Andy's age were not getting them "back."

The hero was finally allowed to become a full-time college man in
the fourteenth installment, *Andy Hardy's Blonde Trouble*, shot in 1943
but not released until the following year. (*Variety*: "Picture fulfills the re-
quirements expected of it.") The movie did passable business, but MGM
had better luck that year with three war dramas, *Thirty Seconds Over
Tokyo*, *The White Cliffs of Dover*, and *A Guy Named Joe*. (The studio's
biggest picture of the year was Garland's *Meet Me in St. Louis*.) There
was beginning to be a perception problem, on screen and off. Rooney
was a famously athletic and energetic performer; he was also a young
man who had already capsized one marriage—in other words, he was
draftable by most any standard, though with MGM's help he had so far
managed to stay out of uniform. That ended when news of his "occupa-
tional deferment" began generating bad press. "I'll do whatever Uncle
Sam says," Rooney vowed in a statement, echoing his fealty to Mayer.
He was finally inducted in June 1944, just as Allied forces were landing
in Normandy. He entertained troops in Europe through the war's end
and into the occupation. Discharged in the spring of 1946, he returned
to MGM to make *Love Laughs at Andy Hardy*, the final film in the
original series.

The Best Years of Our Lives it was not—which might seem an unfair, even snide comparison, but the *Hardy* movie was released only a few
months after William Wyler's masterpiece of postwar disillusionment, so
if the comparison occurred to me, it surely occurred to moviegoers in
1946. Echoing Wyler's film, *Love Laughs at Andy Hardy* opens with its
uniformed hero returning home. But unlike Wyler's scarred and troubled
protagonists, Andy has been left none the worse for wear by his unspecified duty, and so returns to college right where he left off, eager for more
girl trouble. That Rooney was twenty-six and himself a veteran—he now
looked his age and then some, with thickened features and bags under his
eyes—only makes the spectacle of Andy dashing around in a freshman
beanie all the more discomfiting, like running into an old school friend

who's clinging to the past with more eagerness (or desperation) than is called for.

Rooney's career was never the same post Andy. Was he still a leading man or was he now a character actor? Studios and audiences alike couldn't decide or, eventually, much care. But the Hardy family saga heaved a belated last gasp with 1958's *Andy Hardy Comes Home*. MGM, now under new management—Mayer had been forced out in 1951—was interested in revisiting past glories (or mining IP* as we now say). Looking at successful family sitcoms on TV like *The Adventures of Ozzie and Harriet* and *Father Knows Best*, the executives must have thought, *We invented this business!* The new script posited a middle-aged Andy living in Santa Monica and working as counsel for an aerospace company but returning to Carvel on assignment to buy property for a missile plant. He makes a deal for a pristine woodland site owned by his old pal Beezy, but the plan spurs opposition from suspicious townsfolk worried the factory might attract transients, immigrants, and other "undesirables." The twenty-first-century viewer is hard-pressed to choose a side to root for—the military-industrial complex or a mob of bigots?—but the film's sympathies clearly lie with good old Andy.

Rooney, now thirty-eight—and looking more like fifty—was eager to reprise his signature role, and the rest of the old cast was reassembled, minus Lewis Stone, who had died in 1953 (Andy has a moment of silent man-to-man communion with his portrait); and also minus Ann Rutherford, who wasn't interested. Since Polly and Andy were supposed to have married, the younger Mrs. Hardy had to be reconceived as a new character, played by Patricia Breslin, a novice actress whose main qualification was her simultaneous role as the girlfriend of MGM executive Benny Thau, which suggests the level of care taken with the project. Rooney's own son Teddy, then eight, played Andy Hardy Jr. Aside from patrimony, his primary attribute as a screen presence was his apparent lack of acquaintance with orthodontia.

*Intellectual property, for non-Philistines.

The movie was made with the usual B-picture budget and tight schedule. The director, Howard Koch, described the shoot in an interview with Arthur Marx: "It was sad in a way. On the sound stage next door, Paul Newman and Elizabeth Taylor were shooting *Cat on a Hot Tin Roof*, and here's Mickey, who'd been one of the world's biggest stars, and the fellow responsible for keeping Metro in the black all those years when he was a kid, and no one even knew he was alive. Nobody came to the stage to wish us any luck. Nobody sent flowers. Nothing."

Andy Hardy Comes Home isn't as awful as it sounds; in fact, it's as cheerfully mediocre as many of the earlier pictures. The final scene has Andy resettled in Carvel and newly installed as Judge Hardy 2.0. An end title reads: TO BE CONTINUED. It wasn't.

"That kind of fairy tale . . . didn't work for that generation," Koch said. "They wanted to remember Andy Hardy as he was, and they resented his growing old." This was the problem with Andy: as Mayer had insisted, he was as much a symbol as a character, if not more so—and as such, he belonged to another era. The new film tried to acknowledge that by having Andy pull his chin at updated teenage slang like "cool" and "split" and throw out his back while trying to dance to rock and roll. It was sad. Sadder still was the obligatory but half-hearted, almost quizzical "Whoo whoo?" following a flashback featuring old footage of Lana Turner. If Andy had started his life on screen as Hollywood's first modern teenager, he ended it as one of Hollywood's first-generation cringe-inducing dads.

3

REBELS

The career of James Dean has not ended, it has just begun.
  —The Reverend Xen Harvey, eulogizing Dean perhaps more
  astutely than he realized, at the actor's funeral, October 8, 1955

"What's that?" asks Buzz, the toughest, coolest kid at Dawson High, looking over James Dean's Jim Stark, new kid in town and hero of *Rebel Without a Cause*.

"That's the new disease," says Natalie Wood, playing Buzz's girl, Judy.

The new disease. It's a flip line, maybe trying too hard as a simulacrum of hep 1950s teenspeak. And yet it's a key line in Hollywood history, resonating not just in the context of the film's plot—Jim's arrival is the catalyst that sets this fever dream of a film racing—but also the story of its making and reception. Dean was himself a new arrival on movie screens in 1955, the year *Rebel Without a Cause* was shot and released. He had attained the status of incipient superstar with the success of his first film, *East of Eden*, that March. His follow-up would have been hotly anticipated, regardless. But Dean's death in a car accident on September 30, less than a month before the premiere of *Rebel Without a Cause*, linked forever the haunted character of Jim Stark and the doomed twenty-four-year-old who played him. They even shared a name, though that, too, was inadvertent, the character's having been chosen before the actor was cast. But I don't think it's hyperbolic to say that the fusion of role and actor, movie and tragedy, crystalized something enduring in the culture: Dean, who even had the "teen angel" look of a boy too beautiful to live, became an icon—the first and the sexiest icon—of angry, wounded, alienated youth. Rebellious youth. The filmmakers and Warner Bros' publicity department had a big hand in this, but in many ways the picture was itself a new and unpredictable virus released into America's receptive bloodstream.

It's not just that the film was one of the year's most popular, earning a then-impressive $7.2 million ($84 million in 2024 dollars). It was the emotional hold the movie and its star had on young audiences. Martin Scorsese, who I quoted earlier, was twelve when *Rebel Without a Cause* was released. He went back to see it again and again, his identification with Dean's character compounded by the actor's death. "There he was with this new movie. And it was *that* movie, a movie about life and death and about being misunderstood . . . It made for an overwhelming experience."

Bob Dylan turned fourteen in 1955. A high school friend of his told the writer David Hajdu that the adolescent then known as Robert Zimmerman saw *Rebel Without a Cause* four times and bought a red windbreaker like the one Dean wore in the film—a wardrobe choice falling somewhere between affectation and totem. (Just as the singer-songwriter would later adopt the black snap-brim cap favored by a subsequent idol, Woody Guthrie). Elvis Presley was twenty—four years younger than Dean—when the film came out. Its director, Nicholas Ray, recalled meeting the singer several years later: "I was sitting in the cafeteria at MGM one day, and Elvis Presley came over. He knew I was a friend of Jimmy's and had directed *Rebel*, so he got down on his knees before me and began to recite whole passages of dialogue from the script. He must have seen *Rebel* a dozen times by then and knew every one of Jimmy's lines."

A decade and a half of big-type headlines—"War! The Bomb! Victory! Cold War!"—had passed since *Love Finds Andy Hardy*, and Dean's Jim Stark was a very different kind of role model than Mickey Rooney's

Andy, but each seized the zeitgeist with the aid of both luck and design. In the case of *Rebel Without a Cause*, ostensibly about the scourge of juvenile delinquency, it was initially conceived as a "social problem" film along the lines of *Gentleman's Agreement* (1947) and *Pinky* (1949), which respectively examined anti-Semitism and racism, and can today be admired for their good intentions, if not much else. *Rebel Without a Cause* struck deeper and more lasting chords due to Ray's artistry, his empathy with teenagers in general, and with his young cast in particular—and Dean most of all. Much of the film's power is derived from its claustrophobic, overheated feel, the way it captures the anxious, fast-burning intensity of teenage life. In parallel, the movie's sets and locations were by all accounts their own kind of hothouse. Somehow, a volatile mix of personalities, needs, ambitions, desires, and jealousies cohered to make a movie that not only captured the increasing apartness of American teenage culture but also drove it forward, defining romantic alienation for generations to come. It was the type of virus that never leaves a body. Eminem reportedly studied Ray's picture before undertaking his thinly veiled autobiographical movie, *8 Mile* (2002). Bernardo Bertolucci showed it to his cast of young actors in preparation for shooting *The Dreamers*, his 2003 film about the 1968 student riots in Paris.

In a letter to the editor published in *Life* a year after Dean's death, responding to the magazine's report on the actor's growing posthumous popularity ("Delirium Over Dead Star"), a teenager captured the movie and its central performer's appeal as straightforwardly and elegantly as anyone ever has. "I don't believe all the 'to-do' is as morbid as your writer pictured it," wrote Margaret Moran of Cleveland, Ohio. "To us teenagers, Dean was a symbol of the fight to make a niche for ourselves in the world of adults. Something in us that was being sat on by conventions and held down was, in Dean, free for all the world to see."

But if the star performance was the main attraction, that was due not just to Dean's jumpy, anguished charisma but also to the bold and nearly unprecedented way that Ray and his collaborators centered their teenage hero, along with the rest of their young characters. As popular as Andy Hardy had been with teenage audiences, his movies condescended to him; even in his most sympathetic and vulnerable moments, he remained, in essence, an adult's comic construct—his father's son, and MGM's. The cycle of delinquency films that began after the war preferred to keep their subjects at an almost anthropological remove, foregrounding grown-up stand-ins for presumably grown-up audiences—Glenn Ford's rookie English teacher in *Blackboard Jungle*, for example, torn between sympathy and disgust toward his wayward charges. In contrast, Ray's film strove to present adolescence on its own self-mythologizing terms. As Lawrence Frascella and Al Weisel write in their definitive *Live Fast, Die Young: The Wild Ride of Making Rebel Without a Cause*, "The film took teenagers as seriously as they took themselves," offering "a heroic ideal of what being a teen might mean."

This was new. Teenagers before the war were viewed as unruly but harmless. Now, with the winds of postwar prosperity at their back and their tastes increasingly catered to by eager marketers, with a growing sense of power and entitlement and an insistence on being heard—and in some cases a willingness to lash out and act out—the next generation of teenagers were becoming more and more alien to adult eyes, like an occupying force met with a mix of indignation and disbelief—bafflement at the "something in us," whatever that was, which was allegedly being "sat on."

That sense would be captured vividly, though in terms that would soon become clichéd, on the final page of an early draft of the *Rebel Without a Cause* screenplay. This version, like the final film, ends with a tragedy witnessed by a crowd of parents and other adults:

```
A WOMAN turns to her neighbor. She looks troubled,
uncertain, as if she has lived all her life in a
dream, and now finds herself awake in a strange and
foreign land, and she says in a hushed and anxious
voice:
```

                              WOMAN
                    I don't understand it. Children
                    today have everything—and look
                    what happens.

        FADE OUT.

        THE END.

In the spring of 1955, while *Rebel Without a Cause* was being shot in and around Los Angeles, the education editor of *The New York Times,* Benjamin Fine, published a nonfiction book hyping the alleged threat posed by a new breed of teenage hoodlums. It began, as did many sensationalized mid-century books and articles about teenagers, with a series of horrific headlines taken from newspapers around the country. Hubcap stealing was the least of it:

TWO TEEN THRILL KILLINGS CLIMAX PARK CITY ORGIES . . . SCHOOL PILLAGE . . . WHIPPED GIRLS . . . . 22 JUVENILES NABBED IN GANG WAR . . . SLAYING BY THREE YOUTHS BAFFLES EVERYONE INVOLVED . . .

"These headlines and stories shocked and disturbed the people of this country in the year 1954," Fine wrote. "These headlines spoke of the young boys and the increasing number of young girls who are becoming, or who already are, dangerous criminals." Fine cited the nation's attorney general, Herbert Brownell Jr., who in a 1953 speech had claimed, "There is every sign that more than one million children this year will be in trouble serious enough to require the police to pick them up." That factoid gave Fine's book its irresistible title: *1,000,000 Delinquents.* (What a great drive-in picture it could have inspired.) Straying into the same metaphoric woods as Natalie Wood's Judy, Fine called juvenile delinquency "a serious epidemic" and warned, "Unless this cancer is checked early enough, it can go on spreading and contaminate many good cells in our society." Fine added a scary final caution: given that the first wave of the postwar baby boom would crest into its teenage years by the end of the decade, "we may reach the fantastic annual number of 2,250,000 delinquents."*

Fine was an alarmist, but he wasn't an outlier; in fact, he was late to the party. America had been fretting about teenage criminality since the early 1940s, when wartime disruptions—fathers overseas, mothers at work, families on the move, the general intensity and anxiety of life during a mass mobilization to fight a foreign war on two fronts—tore at the fabric of American life. The New York Society for the Prevention of Crime had warned of "the serious menace" to children posed by "these abnormal times." Across the country, Earl Warren, future chief justice of the United States, then governor of California, sounded a similar alert: "Normal family life and living conditions have been dislocated, and as a result youth problems are greater and more complex than ever before."

For those of us who didn't live through the war, these anxieties may not square with the received notion of a self-sacrificing home front that banded together seamlessly to support the war effort, with chipper Boy and Girl Scouts collecting scrap metal and helping their parents tend victory gardens. A 1943 *March of Time* newsreel, "Youth in Crisis," would have made Hitler, Mussolini, and Tojo smile. Over footage of teenagers smoking reefers, burning cars, and jitterbugging with abandon, the usual stentorian voice-over warned that "domestic upheaval and disruption," caused by the war, had confronted kids with "a new spirit of violence and recklessness" and "a profound and unsettling change in their manner of living . . . Freed from parental authority, youngsters are venturing into new and unwholesome worlds." A teen boy is observed at a newsstand buying a presumably unwholesome publication, which the shopkeeper furtively

---

*Make what you will of the fact that that first wave included three future presidents, all born in 1946, who would each, in his own way, prove problematic: Bill Clinton, George W. Bush, and Donald Trump.

pulls from a drawer and tucks into a newspaper. "Boys of this age," the v.o. observed, "just too young to be taking an active part in the war, are all too often finding abnormal outlets for their wartime excitement." Girls of that age, too: "To them, any man in uniform seems a hero. And in towns crowded with footloose soldiers or sailors . . . too many youngsters, thinking of themselves as Victory Girls, believe it is a part of patriotism to deny nothing to servicemen." This last bit was illustrated by a noir-ish shot of a sailor looming over a teenage girl, ready to move in for a kiss, or worse. (The American Sexual Hygiene Society defined the Victory Girl phenomenon as "sex delinquency of a non-commercial nature.")

J. Edgar Hoover provided a statistical underpinning to these frightening assertions and clumsily staged re-creations in a 1943 article, "Youth . . . Running Wild" (ellipsis Hoover's), that he or someone in his employ contributed to the *Los Angeles Times*. According to the FBI director, arrests for rape were up 10 percent over the previous year among boys and young men under the age of twenty-one. For assault, the increase was 17 percent; disorderly conduct, 26 percent; drunkenness, 30 percent. "For girls," Hoover wrote, "the figures are even more startling: 39 percent more for drunkenness, 64 percent more for prostitution, 69 percent more for disorderly conduct, 124 percent more for vagrancy." Hoover fretted that the war had produced "a new 'lost generation,' more hopelessly lost than any that has gone before."

Hoover's numbers were frightening, but he might have had a finger on the scale. Crime statistics from that era, especially where youth crime was concerned, are notoriously unreliable.* The United States Children's Bureau, which also compiled dodgy youth crime statistics (based only on juvenile court cases in a sampling of jurisdictions), disputed that there was a wave of delinquency, and as the FBI itself admitted in a pamphlet,

---

*The FBI compiled its nationwide numbers from voluntary reports offered by local police departments, whose recordkeeping had no consistent methodology. Moreover, the definitions of offenses that kids tended to be rounded up for, baggy charges like "disorderly conduct" or "sex delinquency," were often left to the beholding eye of a cop or magistrate.

its director's *Times* article to the contrary, "We cannot say with certainty whether juvenile delinquency is increasing or decreasing." A series of Senate hearings on home-front issues in December 1943 were inconclusive about whether or not there was a problem. One expert admitted the issue was "an open question," but concluded, "It seems to me that there is a tremendous need for our citizenry to be stirred up about delinquency in this country."

I wonder how much that "need" for people to be "stirred up" may have been psychological, to what extent juvenile delinquency had become an emotional lightning rod—and surely not the only one during wartime, which also saw flare-ups around race and class. Teenagers themselves were still a newish phenomenon with which Americans were just beginning to grapple, and war, of course, is even more disruptive than adolescence. The two made a potent combination, upsetting norms even if some fears were overblown. As the historian James Gilbert writes in *A Cycle of Outrage: America's Reaction to the Juvenile Delinquent in the 1950s*, the war "lifted certain restraints from the behavior of young people," with consequences that many experts feared "might well spill over to disturb the peace for years to come." Hoover, for one, continued to sound the alarm, predicting a new crime wave would surge as home-front punks stepped up to the criminal big leagues in peacetime. "Like the sulphurous lava which boils beneath the slumbering volcano—such is the status of crime in America today," Hoover warned in a 1946 article for *Rotarian* magazine, reaching boldly beyond epidemiological similes.

That was the backdrop that saw *The Amboy Dukes*, "a novel of wayward youth in Brooklyn," embraced as more than just a potboiler when it was published in 1947. The *San Francisco Call Bulletin* deemed it "a warning to parents all over America," while *The New York Times* declared that the author, Irving Shulman, "writes not to shock but to clarify" and praised him for blending "the sociologist's research with the writer's art." Clarifying and researched or not, the fact that the book did shock led it to be hugely popular, selling five million copies and earning a reputation as one of its era's foremost dirty books, thereby providing service for real-life teenagers.*

Set in 1943, *The Amboy Dukes* focuses on a member of the titular street gang, sixteen-year-old Frank Goldfarb. (For reasons perhaps owing to the Anti-Defamation League, the name was Anglicized to Frank Abbott in the paperback.) The boy's once-poverty-stricken family has been bailed out by his parents' new wartime jobs, but at the cost of Frank and his younger sister, Alice, growing up unsupervised in the slums of Brownsville. We meet them one morning getting themselves ready for school. Frank's routine: "He opened the bottom drawer of his dresser, reached back under a pile of underwear . . . took out a packet of three Ramses and put them in his pocket, placed three reefers in his cigarette case, and removed his homemade pistol and five .22-caliber shells." Frank spends the rest of the novel beating up random people, strong-arming prostitutes, smoking dope, selling counterfeit gas-rationing coupons, accidentally shooting and killing a shop teacher with a zip gun, and facilitating the rape of a twelve-year-old girl. Frank has a conscience, though, feeling sort of bad about the girl.

"Where are we making our mistake?" wonders Frank's father. "Now we're working, but our children seem to be getting the wrong thing out of our working," says his mother—an early version of a lament that would echo down the next several decades as American parents tried to square a newfound prosperity with their children's restlessness. Shulman doesn't pretend to offer an answer, ending the novel on a nihilistic note as a rival tosses Frank off a tenement roof to his death. Nearly eight decades later, it retains a power to disturb even amid an otherwise amusing rush of pulpy prose and dated slang. ("You're really reet . . . a high-powered looking babe.")

Naturally, given the strong sales and lurid—but socially important!— subject matter, Hollywood took notice. "I hear rumors that practically

---

*In the 2004 story "Elsie by Starlight," set in the 1950s, John Updike credits *The Amboy Dukes*, alongside *For Whom the Bell Tolls* and *Forever Amber*, as a source for what little sense of "primitive" sexual etiquette his young hero possesses.

every company in the motion picture business has announced a juvenile delinquency story," an MGM executive remarked in 1947. Naturally, one of those projects was *The Amboy Dukes* itself. Early on, Mickey
Rooney, now in his late twenties with his film career beginning to stall,
was reported to be under consideration for a role, though one wonders
if Louis B. Mayer would have agreed to place even his faded Stars and
Stripes in such a raw undertaking. The picture ended up being made by
Universal with a cast of unknown young actors. Retitled *City Across the
River* and released in 1949, it is mostly faithful to the book's spirit and
plot, though with some of the rougher edges sanded down. (There are no
reefers, and the book's explicit rape is now a vague "attack.") Movies then
being held to more uplifting standards than novels, the producers further
perfumed any whiff of exploitation from the source material by bringing
in the political columnist Drew Pearson, author of the widely syndicated
Washington Merry-Go-Round, to provide serious-person ballast. Pearson,
his credibility reinforced by a well-groomed mustache and a declamatory
speaking style honed by years of radio experience, introduces the film sitting behind a solid, respectable desk and speaking directly to the camera:
"To most of us, a city where juvenile crime flourishes always seems to be
a city across the river. But don't kid yourself. It could be your city . . . your
street . . . your house." The movie, once it finally gets going, is memorable
for some evocative location shots of late-1940s Brooklyn (Williamsburg,
Canarsie, and the edge of Prospect Park) and for the first credited appearance of Tony Curtis (billed as "Anthony"), in a supporting role as one of
the Dukes. Curtis is reliably himself; otherwise, the cast seems to have
been divided into competing gangs of over- and underactors; even the
normally wonderful Thelma Ritter, playing a mostly absentee working
mother, is flummoxed by her stilted dialogue.

The movie does follow through here and there on Pearson's promise of sociological context.* There are a few establishing shots of urban

---

*The former Dead End Kids, now Bowery Boys, had long ago given that sort of thing
up, now enjoying escapades such as *Spook Busters* (1946) and *Bowery Buckaroos* (1947).

squalor: a wino resting his head on some kind of slop bucket, a woman eating a big pickle without a napkin. Before he is shot, the doomed shop teacher offers this observation, after his principal tells him he needs to be firmer with Frankie and his friends: "Firm? I can't slug them. I can only reason with them." The very idea spurs him to a bitter laugh: "Might as well reason with a pack of wild animals. That's just what they are—a pack, once they get that gang spirit, that arrogance. Sometimes I think the only solution is to clear out all the people and drop an atom bomb on that whole slum." While the film doesn't endorse that solution, it does commit the sin we now call "othering." The delinquents are indeed across the river; "we" are on this side.

One major change from the novel: the antihero, Frankie Cusack (renamed yet again), winds up in the clutches of the judicial system rather than caroming off a fire escape. The director and co-screenwriter, Maxwell Shane, manages to wring some pathos from the scene as the cops lead Frankie down the stairwell of his grimy tenement, past an immigrant family huddled in their doorway with requisite squalling infant. Over a shot of Frankie being driven away in a squad car, the voice of Drew Pearson returns to remind us we have been watching a social problem movie and not a pulpy melodrama: "Frankie, he'll do his time. And perhaps *with* time, he'll find hope. But what of all the other Frankies? That's the challenge to all of us." *The end.* Any teenage moviegoers who might have found something to identify with in the film, or at least found it entertaining, were surely repelled by this spritz of adult disinfectant. Hollywood had yet to figure out how to speak *to* or *for* this supposedly troubled postwar generation of young people, if it even cared to.

With the new decade, teenage misbehavior would attract even more attention. In 1952, a front-page headline of *The New York Times* declared, in as sensational terms as the paper allowed itself, "Youth Delinquency Growing Rapidly Over the Country." The lengthy article was undergirded by the now-familiar array of troubling statistics: "juvenile delinquency" had

increased by 20 percent in New York State in 1951, and by 10 percent
for the country as a whole. These numbers remained unreliable and to
some extent subjective; the paper noted "youth *seems* to be committing
more serious offenses, like resorting to the use of narcotics and violence."
(Emphasis mine.)

And almost exactly a year later, the *Times* published a much shorter
article on an inside page with the headline "Youth Delinquency Down."
Nevertheless, anxieties about teenage offenders only grew. James Gilbert,
the delinquency historian, writes that the panic "peaked from 1953 to
about 1956," citing public opinion polls and tabulations of magazine and
newspaper articles on the subject. In 1954, Senator Robert Hendrickson,
a New Jersey Republican, addressed a conference on delinquency organized by the Department of Health, Education, and Welfare and painted
the problem in existential Cold War terms: "Not even the Communist
conspiracy could devise a more effective way to demoralize, disrupt,
confuse, and destroy our future citizens than apathy on the part of adult
Americans to the scourge known as Juvenile Delinquency." In his 1955
State of the Union address, President Dwight Eisenhower asked Congress
for $3 million to combat delinquency (a tenfold increase from his 1954
budget).

In the press and literature of the day, there was no shortage of causes
to blame for this crime wave, real or dreamt. The most notorious bête
noire was comic books, demonized by the psychiatrist Frederick Wertham in his bestselling 1954 book, *Seduction of the Innocent*. A prominent
family court judge, quoted in the 1952 *Times* survey, suggested that the
problem might be "the heightened, more startling pace of life," a phrase
which would have been understood by contemporary readers as encom-
passing all sorts of disorienting features of the postwar landscape: growing
prosperity, increased mobility, the Cold War, the nascent nuclear arms
race, the civil rights movement, television—pretty much all of modernity.
Newsweek, under the headline "Our Vicious Young Hoodlums: Is There
Any Hope?," quoted a sociologist's lament: "Biggest problem is that there
doesn't seem to be enough love to go around anymore. There's too much

divorce, too few normal homes, so what can you expect from these kids?" This despite the fact that divorce rates were in decline while the number of new marriages surged.

That delinquency statistics were no more reliable than Joe McCarthy's lists of alleged government Communists didn't ultimately matter; like "Reds," troubled teenagers had become scapegoats in an era of rapid change. Or maybe the panic derived from something more ineffable—a premonition about the shifting balance of cultural power.

During the fall of 1954, amid this climate of fear and unease, Nicholas Ray, then forty-three, began incubating what would become *Rebel Without a Cause*. Though Ray didn't come up with that title, it fit him even better than it did his protagonist. He was a volatile, sometimes reckless man given to tumultuous personal and professional relationships, a heavy drinker and gambler, an occasional brawler, and a onetime Communist Party member with an ingrained antipathy to authority and convention. "It seems to me my most vivid recollections of my life reflect efforts to draw attention to myself," he told a group of students in 1977, two years before his death, at the age of sixty-eight. "While I was preparing the script for the filming of *Rebel*, a schoolteacher from Missouri told me of a remark made by a small-town schoolteacher in Michigan: 'A juvenile delinquent is merely a boy or girl who has fallen out of attention.' Sixty-some years is a long time to be a juvenile delinquent."

Not that he lacked ambition, or the savvy, to maneuver through establishment hierarchies like the Hollywood studio system. He also had a knack for attracting important mentors. One of those, the producer, director, and actor John Houseman, offered a frank yet affectionate portrait of Ray as a raw mess of contradictions: "A stimulating and sometimes disturbing companion; garrulous and inarticulate; ingenuous and pretentious; his mind was filled with original ideas which he found difficult to formulate or express. Alcohol reduced him to rambling unintelligibility; his speech, which was slow and convoluted at best, became unbearably turgid after more than one drink. Yet confronted with a theatrical situation or a problem of dramatic or musical expression he was amazingly quick, lucid, and intuitive with a sureness of touch, a sensitivity to human values, and an infallible taste that I have seldom seen equaled."

Ray grew up in La Crosse, Wisconsin, lost his alcoholic father when he was sixteen, studied haphazardly in high school, graduated next to last in his class, studied haphazardly at a local college, founded a small theater company, and somehow made his way to the University of Chicago in the fall of 1931. There, for a single semester, he studied theater and acting and worked to endear himself to Thornton Wilder, the playwright who was on the school's faculty. Through Wilder, Ray met Frank Lloyd Wright, and after furiously cultivating the architect, Ray joined the Taliesin Fellowship, the high-minded (but money-generating) artists' commune Wright had founded on his Wisconsin estate. Alas, Ray's stint at Taliesin ended in just a few months when he was banished by the imperious architect after a clash over some now-obscure question of aesthetic dogma; or possibly the rub was Ray's behavior, his drinking and/or trysting, with women and sometimes men. However, some lasting good came from the relationship. "I'd say the most obvious influence Wright had on me . . . is my liking for CinemaScope," Ray told *Cahiers du Cinéma* several decades later. "I like the horizontal line and the horizontal was essential for Wright." He would put that affinity to excellent use in *Rebel Without a Cause*'s startling wide-screen compositions.

In 1935, Ray moved to New York, committing himself to the city's roiling left-wing theater scene. He joined a collective, the Theatre of Action—a peer of the more prominent Group Theatre—where he came under the tutelage of Elia Kazan, who directed him in *The Young Go First*, a piece of agitprop meant to expose the "militaristic conditions" that were allegedly undermining the New Deal's Civilian Conservation Corps. Alas, the combined talents of the future directors of *A Streetcar Named Desire* and *Rebel Without a Cause* were not enough to overcome the premise; the show flopped, and the Theatre of Action eventually disbanded. Ray continued to work on various New Deal–funded theatrical

projects, and helped produce a Voice of America radio show for Houseman during the war's early days.

In 1944, Kazan brought Ray to Hollywood as an assistant on Kazan's
first film, A *Tree Grows in Brooklyn*. Ray stuck around for a bit, his most
notable work a writing credit on the Three Stooges' musical *Swing Parade of 1946*. He moved to Los Angeles for good two years later when
Houseman, now at RKO, brought him on. In 1948, he directed his first
film for the studio, *They Live by Night*, but just as quickly imperiled his
career when he started sleeping with the actress Gloria Grahame, the
girlfriend of Dore Schary, RKO's head of production, who had given Ray
his break. The breach (though by some accounts, Schary saw it as a favor)
was compounded by the fact that Grahame soon became pregnant with
Ray's child. Any question of hard feelings became moot, however, when
Howard Hughes bought the shaky studio and fired Schary. Ray's career
at RKO continued; he also married Grahame, and directed her in one of
her greatest performances, as the girlfriend of Humphrey Bogart's possibly
homicidal screenwriter, in *In a Lonely Place* (1950).

It was during the fall of 1954, after he had directed a pair of star-
driven westerns, *Johnny Guitar* with Joan Crawford and *Run for Cover*
with James Cagney—assignments he had taken mainly for "bread and
taxes"—when Ray told his agent, Lew Wasserman, that he was casting
about for a more personally meaningful project. "I really have to want to
do the next one," he said, according to his account in a later interview. "I
really have to believe in it, or feel it's important."

"Like what?" Wasserman asked.

"I want to do a film about kids," Ray replied.

That was, in some sense, familiar territory for him: two of his first
three pictures had dealt with delinquent themes. *They Live by Night* was
a crime drama in which Farley Granger plays a nice boy who keeps getting mixed up in trouble, with predictably tragic results, but not before
he falls in love, marries, and goes on the lam with a naïve small-town girl
played by Cathy O'Donnell (a sweet but complex presence who should
have had a much bigger career). A year later, Ray directed *Knock on Any*

Door, which starred Humphrey Bogart as a tough but compassionate defense lawyer who fails to steer John Derek's slum kid away from a life of crime—the picture tread similar ground to *City Across the River*, released the same year. Ray's film lacks a serious-person preamble, like the one Drew Pearson provided for *City Across the River*, but it does give Bogart's lawyer a classic message-movie thesis statement, disguised as a courtroom summation, when he tries to save Derek's Nick Romano from the electric chair: "Until we do away with the type of neighborhood which produced this boy, ten will spring up to take his place. A hundred. A thousand. Until we wipe out our slums and rebuild them—knock on any door—and you may find Nick Romano."

But Ray wanted to do something different with his new, as yet undetermined "film about kids." He told Wasserman, "I've done stuff with the depressed areas, the misfits. Now I want to do a film about the guy next door, like he could be one of my sons." That was a telling association given that Ray was an inattentive, often-absent, guilt-ridden father of two boys: Tim, his son with Grahame; and Tony, who he had fathered with his first wife, Jean Evans, a journalist. The marriage to Grahame, never stable, had broken up for good in 1951, after Ray returned to their Malibu home one afternoon to find her in bed with then-thirteen-year-old Tony, who was visiting while on break from the East Coast boarding school in which he'd been stashed. The story was soon widely known in Hollywood, in part because Ray himself frequently talked about it.* That he would even notionally conceive *Rebel Without a Cause* with his own progeny in mind was the first of many psychosexual undercurrents that would inform the writing, casting, and direction of the film—and propel it well beyond the puny gravitational field of previous delinquent pictures.

• • •

---

*Tony Ray would end up marrying his former stepmother in 1960. They had two sons of their own, who were thus Tim Ray's half brothers as well as his nephews. As Nicca Ray—the director's daughter with his third wife, Betty Utley, a dancer—once put it, "Some families are fucked up differently than others."

Ray approached Warner Bros. with his vague idea about troubled middle-class kids. From the studio's perspective, there was a lot to like: it was a hot, potentially commercial topic and Ray an important and critically admired director (though not impeccable from a box office perspective). So Warner had him look at troubled-kid projects already under development, including one called *Rebel Without a Cause*, which various screenwriters and directors had been noodling with ever since Warner Bros. had bought the rights to a 1944 nonfiction book with that catchy title. It was a psychologist's case study of his treatment of "Harold," a juvenile offender serving time on unspecified charges in a Pennsylvania state prison. (The book's less catchy subtitle: *The Hypnoanalysis of a Criminal Psychopath*.) This was yet another story of a "slum kid," told through the eyes of a prison psychologist, and Ray insisted he wanted to create an original story about, he would emphasize again, "'normal' delinquents."

His solution was to stay up all night in his bungalow at the Chateau Marmont and, with his secretary's help, crank out a seventeen-page treatment he titled *The Blind Run*. It's a remarkable document, reading at times like an outline for one of the era's conventional delinquent films and at other times more like a feverish draft of a news magazine article on the subject; it even cites the *Newsweek* "Our Vicious Young Hoodlums" piece and a *U.S. News & World Report* cover story, "Why Teen-Agers Go Wrong." There is a wild prologue that could never have been filmed: "A man aflame is running directly Toward Camera . . . A girl, sixteen, stripped to the waist, is surrounded by and being whipped by three teen-agers." Ray then indicates a pause for the requisite sober preamble:

> Jack Warner, Willie Mays, Ed Sullivan, Walter Winchell, or some
> other public figure who is still likely to be in the news six months from
> now, appears and then informs the audience that what they have seen
> has actually happened, that what they are about to see has also hap-
> pened and is happening—and it can happen to anyone here regardless

of age, income, education or profession. This is no sermon, no lecture,
but an invitation into an adventure of today—tonight.

That last note of immediacy hints at the power of the final film. So does
a strange metaphysical sequence in which a young gang leader on death
row appears on the night of his pending execution to give his fellow gang
members a kind of delinquent's version of Jesus's words to his disciples at
the Last Supper. As Ray describes it:

> He talks to them. He hasn't escaped. He's going to die tonight. And
> how he got here is unimportant. And then he just talks—kid to kid—
> beautifully—simply—sometimes humorously about himself—and
> even the parents and the officers . . . begin to understand a little bit.

This is ludicrous, even laughable. But it points toward the wrung-out catharsis of the finished film's final moments, and even more so to the way
the entire picture spreads "a layer of myth over something so real," in the
words of one of its screenwriters, Stewart Stern. (Strictly speaking, Stern
was describing a quality of Elia Kazan's *On the Waterfront*, written by
Budd Schulberg, which Stern had labored to emulate.)

Ray's treatment, more akin to a sizzle reel than a narrative, did have a
few concrete elements that would make it into the finished film, including a knife fight; a potentially deadly driving game (two cars driving at
each other from opposite ends of a tunnel with their lights off—the "blind
run" of the title); and a central trio of teenagers comprising a troubled
boy, a troubled girl, and a second, even more troubled boy. Perhaps most
essential was this authorial aside: "As a matter of approach, it should be
left in mind that the youth is always in the foreground and adults are for
the most part to be shown only as the kids see them." The director knew
from the beginning he wanted to speak to young audiences in ways they
hadn't been spoken to before.

Warner Bros. bit on the treatment and signed Ray to develop and
direct the film, which at some point usurped the title *Rebel Without a*

Cause—but nothing else—from the earlier project. Ray was partnered with a young producer named David Weisbart, who came with the important imprimatur, for Ray, of having edited A *Streetcar Named Desire* for Kazan. (Weisbart's credits as a producer included a handful of westerns and *Them!*, a B movie about giant irradiated ants attacking Los Angeles. *Valley of the Dolls* lay in his future.) Ray and Weisbart brought in the novelist Leon Uris, future author of the bestsellers *Exodus* and *Trinity*, then under contract at the studio, to help Ray shape his ideas and intuitions into a workable script. Insisting the story be credible, the director arranged for Uris and himself to talk to psychiatrists and social workers at Los Angeles Juvenile Hall, attend family court sessions, sit in on interviews with delinquents, and go out with police on "riot calls." In a memo to Weisbart citing the "full cooperation" the project had received from experts—"more than we can use, in fact"—Ray enthused this was evidence "that our approach to the problem is fresh, different, and as realistic as the headlines . . . perhaps more so . . ." (Ellipses Ray's.)

One of the film's key themes began to emerge from Ray and Uris's research: oblivious parents as the reason for the anxiety and restlessness afflicting 1950s youth. "In listening to these adolescents talk," Ray wrote in a making-of piece for *Sight & Sound*, "what they felt, when asked about their families, was a bitter isolation and resentment. All told similar stories—divorced parents, parents who could not guide or understand, who were indifferent or simply 'criticized,' parents who needed a scapegoat in the family." Ray understood these issues all too well, as both a son and a father, acknowledging as much when the studio raised a red flag over a scene in the shooting script where Plato, the disturbed younger boy played by Sal Mineo, finds a check with the note "for support of son" from his absent father. "For some reason the front office at Warners had a strong objection to this," Ray later recalled. "I could only reply that for me it had an equally strong reality, as I have two sons in that situation, and it was an idea drawn only too directly from personal experience."

Uris wrote a long, detailed treatment that began to show some distant relationship to the finished film, but Ray found his take too broad, too conventional, too focused on community and social forces, maybe too 1930s-style agitprop; it didn't get under the characters' skins. The director turned to Irving Shulman, who had helped adapt his *Amboy Dukes* into *City Across the River*. Shulman contributed much to the final film, including the central characters of Jim, Judy, and Plato. Inspired by a news clipping, he also turned Ray's blind run in a tunnel into the "chickie run" sequence, *Rebel Without a Cause*'s most famous scene, in which Dean and a rival drive their cars to the edge of a cliff overlooking the Pacific, the first to leap out of his car before both vehicles hurtle into space being the "chicken." But Shulman and Ray fought over the ending. They agreed that Plato would die, giving the film tragic weight, but Ray, looking for a classical sense of unity, wanted the film to climax at the Griffith Observatory, where the movie's main action begins during a high school field trip and where, in the finished film, Plato is shot by police. Shulman wrote an even more violent and far more melodramatic ending in which Plato, not just disturbed but psychopathic—he has earlier shot and killed a random stranger with a zip gun—finds an arsenal of serious weapons that his absent father has inexplicably left around the house and holes up there like an old-school Warner Bros. gangster, daring the coppers to come and get him. As Shulman's screenplay climaxes, Plato is in the doorway of his house holding a rifle and a hand grenade. Jim and Judy are trying to coax him to give himself up to the police, but Plato panics and begins to take aim. The police fire. Jim is hit in the shoulder, Plato in a "vital area." He then pulls the pin on his grenade, seems momentarily intent on throwing it at Jim and Judy, then turns, tosses the grenade back into the house, falls on it, and dies as the house and he are "blown to bits" while "Judy shelters Jim with her body as the debris rains around them."

I'm dwelling on this draft because it's hard to read that final scene in the twenty-first century and not feel queasy, as if Shulman's pulpy imagination somehow foresaw the epidemics of school shootings and teen suicides across the last three or four decades that have informed more recent teen films ranging from *Heathers* (1988) to *Elephant* (2003) to *The Hunger Games* (2012), which I'll explore in a later chapter. Audiences in the

1950s would likely have been so disturbed by Shulman's scenario as to doom the film at the box office, assuming the ending even passed muster with the Production Code. Perhaps needless to say, Ray fired Shulman.*

Though hardly remarkable by present-day Hollywood gestational periods, where these things are measured by years not months, the development process dragged on long enough that it supposedly got back to Ray that a studio technician had bet a colleague $250, not nothing in those days, that the movie would never be made. His ambition snowballing, Ray kept pushing the project toward something more than just another problem movie about delinquents; intuitively, perhaps, he was goading himself and his collaborators to capture something essential: the "stranger in a strange land" quality of adolescence. As Ray described the film's initial scene inside Griffith Observatory, where the main characters and their classmates witness a planetarium show that dwells on the dwarfing, incomprehensible vastness of space and time (as if teenagers don't have enough to feel self-conscious about): "Flashes of light explode across the sky. And while the other students mock and whisper, Plato suddenly shivers from an awareness of his own solitude."

That description was written after the film was finished. While he was planning it, Ray, as John Houseman observed of him, had a hard time expressing what he wanted, if he even entirely knew. "Nick was in agony, a kind of private hell, at that time. A creative hell. He had a concept and a vision of what he wanted to say, but he had not found a way to say it," recalled Stewart Stern, the third and final writer to shape the screenplay, in an interview years later. "He was almost inarticulate about what he wanted and why he was not satisfied. Through all-night sessions, talking mainly about ourselves, I began to get a picture of what that agony consisted of. Nick, like most artists, is part child. His child talked to my child. His bewildered adult talked to my bewildered adult, and out of the

---

*Shulman managed to negotiate the rights to turn his version of the screenplay into a novel, which was published in 1956 with the title *Children of the Dark*. "RIOT AND REBELLION IN THE DUNGAREE SET" was the paperback edition's come-on.

horns of our private dilemmas, I began to get a picture of what we both wanted to say through a story about children." The project was taking on deeply personal shadings. To Stern, Ray "was a zealot about his subject; and he was consumed with the necessity to do it, and the necessity to do it a certain way."

Stern, who Ray had met at a party at Gene Kelly's—precisely how one imagines 1950s Hollywood worked—was then twenty-two years old. His calling card then was a screenplay for the 1951 Fred Zinneman film *Teresa*, about a teenage Italian war bride struggling with life in the United States. (The star was Pier Angeli, who would have a well-publicized romance with James Dean.) One key change in Stern's drafts of the screenplay—he and Ray would later both claim credit for the idea—was compressing the film's main action into a single twenty-four-hour day, which helped give the film not only the classical sense of unity Ray was striving for but also the heightened intensity of adolescence, as kids themselves experience it. Stern would later say that Ray was after a kind of "poetic excess," a "crazy compactness" that was "typical of young people who are running away from boredom and who are running away from themselves. Their days are stuffed with such incredible drama."

Ray put it more succinctly: "For teenagers, a whole life is lived in twenty-four hours."

More even than his serial screenwriters, however, Ray's most essential collaborator was Dean. The actor came to Ray's attention through Kazan, who had directed Dean's first film, *East of Eden*, which would be released in March of 1955, just as Ray's movie was about to start shooting. Kazan admired Dean's talent but disliked him personally, finding him narcissistic, hypersensitive, mercurial, spoiled, self-dramatizing, show-offy. "This twisted, fidgety kid," is how he introduces Dean in his autobiography. The actor was not unaware that he was a pain in the neck; at times he reveled in it. "I'm a serious-minded and intense little devil . . . terribly gauche and so intense I don't see how people stay in the same room with me. I know

I wouldn't tolerate myself," he admitted, or bragged, in a *Life* magazine profile.

Ray first met Dean sometime in late 1954 at a screening of an early cut of *East of Eden*, when the buzz surrounding the picture already marked Dean as a likely new star. In person, Ray found the actor to be "aloof and solitary," he later said. "We hardly exchanged a word. That he had talent was obvious, but I respected Kazan's skills too much to give full markers to any actor who worked with him." Even Kazan seemed to share Ray's reservations about Dean. "I was totally unprepared for his success," Kazan wrote, grudgingly and perversely (given that he had cast and directed Dean). "We had a first preview at a theatre in the Los Angeles area, and the instant he appeared on the screen, hundreds of girls began to scream. They'd been waiting for him, it seemed—how come or why, I don't know."

Watching today, the "why" is obvious. Cast in *East of Eden* as a World War I–era black sheep, another misunderstood teenage rebel, by way of the Bible and John Steinbeck, Dean is alternately wary, wounded, mischievous, bereft, and, most of all, desperate to be loved. He acted with a spontaneous, almost simian physicality not unlike Brando's—at times, too, he affected a similarly nasal plaint—but he also had a jawline and cheekbones to rival Katherine Hepburn's. He was dangerous yet exquisite.

Ray soon came around to his virtues. As Lawrence Frascella and Al Weisel write in *Live Fast, Die Young*, "Dean's neurotic vitality, his narcissistic sexuality, his contempt for authority were qualities that attracted Ray. They were qualities Ray himself possessed. And they were just what he was looking for in a boy to play Jim Stark." The casting process proved to be a long "sniffing courtship," in the words of one of Ray's biographers. Dean was interested in the part from the get-go, but slow to commit (so much so that the courtship almost went unconsummated when Dean got cold feet just before shooting started and briefly fled to New York). Flush with incipient stardom, he worried that Ray wasn't in the same directorial league as Kazan or George Stevens, who had cast Dean in *Giant* (which would begin production shortly after *Rebel Without a Cause* wrapped). From Ray's perspective, Dean required "a special kind of climate. He needed reassurance, tolerance, understanding." Years later, he compared Dean to a cat: "Maybe a Siamese. The only thing to do with a Siamese cat is to let it take its own time. It will come up to you, walk around you, smell you. If it doesn't like you, it will go away again. If it does, it will stay." Hinting at the contradictions in Dean's personality, Ray described him on another occasion in much less diffident (though still belittling) terms. Dean was an actor, Ray said, who "threw himself upon the world like a starved animal after a scrap of food."

Dean, who would be twenty-four when *Rebel Without a Cause* finally went before the cameras, had been born in a farming town in Indiana. His family moved out west to Santa Monica when he was five or six, but three years later, when his mother died of cancer, his father, a dental technician, sent Dean back to Indiana to be raised by an aunt and uncle. He returned to California after graduating from high school in 1949, eventually enrolling at UCLA, where he studied acting before moving to New York and joining the Actors Studio. He remained largely estranged from his father—Kazan's memoir records a meeting between the two where they barely exchanged a word ("I sensed the father disliked his son")—and he and Ray bonded in part over their shared heritage of difficult, absent fathers. While the script was still in development, they began hanging out together at Ray's bungalow at the Chateau Marmont, where Dean would sometimes bring friends. When Dean went to New York to shoot a television play in December 1954— he had initially made his name appearing in prestige omnibus series such as *Kraft Theatre* and *Robert Montgomery Presents*—Ray followed along, nominally in order to audition New York actors. He ended up chaperoning Dean through days and nights of dinners, walks, movies, and even a trip to the drugstore to buy a bottle of "personal insecticide" for Dean, who claimed not to know how to deal with a case of the crabs. Ray's son Tony, now seventeen and an aspiring actor, began accompanying Dean to late-night pot- and bongo-fueled parties—arguably yet another example of Ray's own lackadaisical parenting and very much an example of the off-screen psychological mirroring and gamesmanship that marked the making of *Rebel Without a Cause*. Ray would even describe his son as "a kind of Plato."

Most importantly, Ray involved Dean in the shaping of the screenplay. One reason Shulman was let go, aside from his disagreements with Ray over the ending, was that Dean didn't connect with him. Stern was hired because he and Dean, only two years apart in age, developed a fast friendship, bonding over a shared offbeat sense of humor. They would take long nighttime drives, swapping stories about their lives, and, for Stern, Dean began to morph into Jim Stark, or vice versa. "Without meaning to use specific aspects of Jimmy's personality, I became infected by it," Stern said. "Nothing he did could surprise me since it was already inside me."

As the writing process dragged on, Ray and Dean would improvise new scenes or dialogue, sometimes by themselves, sometimes with a growing group of young people who were being cast or considered for roles in the film, including a nominal student named Frank Mazzola who was the leader of a Hollywood High gang called the Athenians. In his quest for accuracy, Ray had hired Mazzola as a technical advisor, even giving him an office on the Warner lot. A memo from producer David Weisbart to a studio higher-up detailed some of Mazzola's "services rendered":

> 2/5/55: 2 hours discussing problems and attitudes of delinquents—list of expressions. . . .*
> 3/8/55: 7:00 p.m.–2:00 a.m. with Mr. Ray and Jim Dean, discussing different types of delinquent personalities, then driving Jim to different delinquent "hangouts."
> 3/11/55: 7:00 p.m.–3:00 a.m. with Mr. Ray, Jim Dean and writer going over script and describing dress, manner and dialogue of delinquents.

Meanwhile, *East of Eden* was finally released on March 9, and Dean's performance proved to be the sensation everyone expected, at least with

---

*Among the "list of expressions" that Mazzola helped Stewart Stern compile for a "Juvenile Talk" glossary: "dig," "flip," "nowhere," "too much," "twisted," and "wow."

young audiences if not necessarily critics. Bosley Crowther, the lead film critic at *The New York Times*, dismissed Dean as "a mass of histrionic gingerbread." A week later, as if in penance, the paper ran a respectful if mildly snarky profile of Dean, noting his "flourishing reputation for unvarnished individuality." Asked if his contract with Warner gave him story approval on his films, he replied, "Contractually, no—emotionally, yes. They can always suspend me. Money isn't one of my worries, not that I have any." Regarding Hollywood, he added, "The problem for this cat—myself—is not to get lost." Off screen, too, he had begun playing the antiestablishment hero, setting a template for generations of ostensibly ambivalent young male movie stars to come.

The film's two other leads were far more eager participants, though they, too, were objects of Ray's emotional gamesmanship—and worse, in Natalie Wood's case. She had managed to get her hands on an early version of the script, and later said she wept while reading it: "I felt exactly the way the girl did in the picture about her parents. It was about a high school girl rebelling, and it was very close to home. It was really about my own life." Yes and no. In the film, Wood's Judy is devastated when her father shuns her because he can't cope with her emerging sexuality. In real life, Wood, a star since appearing in *Miracle on 34th Street* at the age of eight, had been groomed by a stage mother who had no qualms about exploiting her daughter's attractiveness. Wood was looking for a movie role to propel her out of juvenile parts—she was sixteen—and lobbied Ray to play Judy, as did her fellow child star Margaret O'Brien, then seventeen. Ray, who had tested Debbie Reynolds for the part, worried that Wood was too prim and mild to play Judy, but they had had several meetings about the film, which had led to a dinner, which, by the time Ray finally granted her a screen test, had led to an affair—at least according to a chronology given by the screenwriter and novelist Gavin Lambert, a friend of both Ray's and Wood's. (He was the director's lover for a brief period following *Rebel Without a Cause* and would write a biography of the star after her death, in 1981.) However physically attracted Wood was to a man twenty-seven years her senior (and she was the youngest of all the actresses he seriously considered casting), she was also drawn to him intellectually, entranced by his ideas about acting and filmmaking and his literary and cultural enthusiasms, feeling she had entered, in her words, "a golden world." As she is said to have told a friend, "All the other guys just want to screw me. He wants to make love *with* me."

Nevertheless, Ray continued to keep her at arm's length professionally, unwilling to commit to casting her, still convinced—ironically, appallingly—that she wasn't mature enough for the role. (When he finally came around, he had her hips padded under her costumes; she was also fitted with a custom-designed push-up bra that would become an industry-wide staple known as "the Natalie Wood.") Ray worried about her acting chops, too. A second screen test helped persuade him, though Hollywood legend has it that his hand was forced by an incident that occurred one night when Wood and eighteen-year-old Dennis Hopper, who had been cast in the movie and with whom Wood was simultaneously having a more age-appropriate fling, got into a car accident after an evening of drinking on Mulholland Drive. Hopper and a third-wheel friend suffered only minor bruises but Wood a concussion. Taken to a hospital, she asked for Ray. When he arrived at her bedside, she pulled him close, and referencing the snide comments of a nurse or orderly, told him, "They called me a goddamn juvenile delinquent. *Now* do I get the part?" It was a good story, and widely repeated, becoming part of the film's mythology, though Ray later claimed that Wood's hospital-bed pitch was a publicity contrivance, designed to explain why she had asked for her adult lover to come to her aid rather than her parents.

Sal Mineo was the only other teenager in the principal cast. He had grown up in the Bronx, starting his professional career on Broadway with a one-line part in *The Rose Tattoo*. After another small part in *The King and I*, he graduated to the role of the musical's crown prince of Siam. (Dark complexioned, he would play Mexican and Native American parts as well.) He was fifteen and had appeared in a couple of films when Ray pulled him out of a lineup of actors because the director thought Mineo looked like his son Tony, "only prettier." Mineo got the part when he and Dean connected while reading scenes and improvising together, the younger actor impressing both star and director with his ability to keep up.

Mineo was gay, though he may not have been fully aware at the time he was shooting *Rebel Without a Cause*. He was infatuated with Dean, however, to a degree that was remarked upon by his co-stars as well as himself. Of Dean, he later confessed, "If he didn't say good morning to me, I'd be a wreck the whole day. If he put his arm around me, that was fabulous." Dean was bisexual, and though no one has claimed he and Mineo had a physical relationship, they did grow close, paralleling the friendship between Plato and Jim, with its strong sexual undercurrents. At one point in the shooting, Dean even told Mineo to "look at me the way I look at Natalie," and the younger actor later described his collaboration with Dean in terms of sexual awakening: "I couldn't understand, couldn't comprehend what was happening. Something was happening to me. I had no idea or any understanding of affection between men. And for the first time, I felt something strong."

Wood, meanwhile, though still sleeping with both Ray and Hopper, was crushed out on Dean, too. They had first worked together a year before on a live *General Electric Theater* broadcast, in which Dean had given Wood her first on-screen kiss. "He was all she could talk about," Mineo said. "Every night for weeks in a row, she went to see *East of Eden*—she must have seen it over fifty times. She even taught me to play the theme song from the picture on the piano." While visiting Dean's apartment, she stole a scrapbook of his, which she then pored over. He was well aware of his hold on her. On one social occasion, he told her that her outfit—peasant blouse, gypsy skirt, chunky jewelry—was "corny," reducing her to tears. He then grinned, prompting an onlooker, the actress Carroll Baker, to observe years later, "He was being deliberately callous and cruel, and he was obviously enjoying his domination of her." There was perhaps an element of retribution, too, since Dean, according to his biographer Donald Spoto, was "exasperated" by his co-star's affair with

Ray and "jealous—not, perhaps, from his desire for either Natalie or Ray, but from a wish to have his director's devotion entirely to himself." No reliable source has claimed Ray and Dean had an affair, but they shared a strong emotional and creative bond—a little bit father-son, a little bit co-conspirators. They talked about forming a production company together.

Somehow—Consciously? Unconsciously? Six of one, a half dozen of the other?—Ray had built a cast bristling with sexual and emotional vectors that paralleled their characters', while he played out his own familial and sexual psychodramas, off screen and on. In Stewart Stern's words, "He was the maypole around whom everyone needy and dependent swirled and danced." Dean was a second center of gravity. As a friend of his told Frascella and Weisel, describing a visit to the film's set, "There was some interesting interaction among the young actors. Everybody knew Jimmy was going to be a superstar. There was terrific competition to be Jimmy's friend among that young group, vying for first position. You could cut the jealousy with a knife."

It is now a cliché to say Hollywood is like high school with money, but in those waning days of the studio system, when Hollywood was more like a factory with sex, the volatile hothouse environment that forged *Rebel Without a Cause* must have felt a lot like high school—maybe a bigger-stakes version of the usual drama club rivalries, romance, and intrigue. It was almost as if Ray, who had been exposed to method acting with Kazan during his New York theater days, had intuitively groped his way toward a form of method filmmaking.

Rebel Without a Cause began shooting on March 25, 1955. That same day, *Blackboard Jungle* opened in theaters. Kids loved it, but the picture divided adult audiences and was condemned in some quarters as exploitative, even irresponsible. The controversy likely helped at the box office, but the movie's notoriety cast a shadow over the production of *Rebel Without a Cause* and would influence its release. Ray and Warner Bros. were determined that their film stand apart.

Blackboard Jungle was written and directed by Richard Brooks, a skilled journeyman probably best known today for *Cat on a Hot Tin Roof* (1958) and *In Cold Blood* (1967). (The executive at MGM who green-lit *Blackboard Jungle* was Dore Schary, Ray's former boss at RKO and his ex-wife's ex-lover.) The picture focused on an idealistic English teacher trying to reach delinquents in a New York City vocational school; it came with perceived authority since it was based on a bestselling novel by Evan Hunter, who had briefly taught at a vocational school for boys in the Bronx. We meet Glenn Ford's rookie teacher during the run-up to the first day of school, played as if it were the tense calm before battle — maybe not surprising given that many of the characters, and presumably much of the audience, were veterans of World War II. Gathering in the teachers' lounge, a cynical old history teacher tells Ford's character and another green recruit, a math teacher played by Richard Kiley, that he's been at the school for "fifteen years and two Purple Hearts."

"Last time I felt like this was when we hit the beach at Salerno," says Kiley's character, a vet like Ford's, who stammers as if he were trying to allay his fears about the enemy's resolve, "These kids — they can't be all bad, can they?"

"No, why?" answers the history teacher. "This is the garbage can of the education system . . . They hire college graduates like us to sit on the garbage can to keep them in school so women for a few hours a day can walk around the city without getting attacked."

The big question: Will Ford's Mr. Dadier* eventually get through to the kids, an admirably diverse student body made up of Black, Latino, and Asian boys, who maybe just need to be engaged with rather than disdained? Anyone old enough to watch the film knows the answer, but first Mr. Dadier has to stop an attempted rape; survive nearly being run

---

*Pronounced French style, as dah-DEE-ay. His class laughs at the fancy pronunciation and starts calling him Mr. Daddy-O — the origin of that form of address, soon adopted by stock beatnik characters in films and cartoons, and possibly by one or two hepcats in real life.

over by hot-rodders; also survive getting jumped in an alley by the gang led by punk Artie West (Vic Morrow, in his film debut); and win the respect of the smartest kid in his classroom, an "approachable Negro" (in *The New York Times*' words) played by a twenty-seven-year-old Sidney Poitier. (Poitier got the part despite refusing to sign an MGM-mandated loyalty oath promising he wouldn't overthrow the US government. Fortunately, Brooks backed him up, advising the actor, "Fuck 'em," according to Poitier's memoir.) Approachable or not, Gregory Miller is angry, well aware of the social and institutional forces stacked against him, and far from a pushover where Dadier's overtures are concerned, giving Poitier one of the meatier roles in his early career. As Donald Bogle describes the performance in *Toms, Coons, Mulattoes, Mammies, and Bucks*, his authoritative history of Black representation in Hollywood:

> He hounds and torments white teacher Ford . . . [Poitier] snarls, acts tough, and displays his virility more effectively than in any other film. "Come on! Come on! Hit me!" he yells to Ford . . . Even before it was fashionable, he was bucking the corroding system. Yet at the same time, Poitier's Miller was an easily hurt, sensitive young man forced to live outside society. He was the classic loner of the 1950s.

In the final reel, the film's tone shifts from combat picture to *High Noon*, with Ford facing down a switchblade-wielding Morrow and no one intervening, until Poitier finally comes to his aid. Today, much of *Blackboard Jungle* is risible, but Ford, Poitier, and Morrow are all excellent, and the picture retains a claustrophobic immediacy, thanks to Brooks's astute framing and staging, the pulpy menace and energy of the movie's violence, and the vitality of the mostly youthful cast. Jazz fans will be legitimately horrified by a scene in which callous punks smash up the Kiley character's collection of rare shellac records by the likes of Bix Beiderbecke.

Critical reaction was generally positive, granting the film its power—and begrudging it its shock value—while hedging bets as to its accuracy.

Bosley Crowther in *The New York Times* was fairly typical, calling the movie "blood-curdling, nightmarish," and "a full-throated, all-out testimony to the lurid headlines that appear from time to time, reporting acts of terrorism and violence by uncontrolled urban youths." But he added, "We suspect it may be challenged not only as responsible reporting but also as a desirable stimulant to spread before the young."

Indeed, the film greeted teenagers with a blast of subversive energy, at least by 1955 standards, though the kids first had to endure an unpromising title card insisting on the filmmakers' absolute seriousness of purpose (no matter what antisocial thrills were promised by the ads): "Today we are concerned with juvenile delinquency—its causes—and its effects. . . ." *Blah blah blah.* Boilerplate out of the way, audiences were hit with the Bill Haley & His Comets song "Rock Around the Clock," playing over the opening credits—widely recognized today as the first use of rock and roll by a Hollywood film and likely many white audiences' first exposure to the art form, however denatured.* There were stories in the press of kids dancing in the aisles as "Rock Around the Clock" played at the beginning and reprised at the end. Worse, and even more frightening for adults, young audiences reportedly cheered the scenes of classroom violence. The film was denounced by the Daughters of the American Revolution, the National Congress of Parents and Teachers, the Girl Scouts, and even the Communist Labor Youth League (no friends of frivolity). The picture had been selected for the Venice Film Festival but was pulled when Clare Booth Luce, then the US ambassador to Italy, threatened to boycott the festival if *Blackboard Jungle* was shown. At the end of the year, the American Legion would declare it the movie "that hurt America the most in foreign countries in 1955" (perhaps offsetting all

---

*In an era when music was heavily segregated by race, rock and roll remained a novelty for most white audiences. Elvis Presley, for one, was still a regional phenomenon in the spring of 1955; he would have his first nationwide hit the following January with "Heartbreak Hotel." Thus, when the white kids in *Blackboard Jungle* express a musical preference, the script has them pipe up for "bop" or Frank Sinatra, while the Black kids are heard harmonizing on spirituals for a Christmas pageant.

the global goodwill Louis B. Mayer believed the *Andy Hardy* movies had engendered). The only people who were unreservedly enthusiastic about *Blackboard Jungle* were audiences, who helped make it one of the year's top-grossing films. It would earn four Oscar nominations, including one for Brooks's adapted screenplay.

That mix of success and sensation had to be reckoned with by Ray and his collaborators. Avoiding any whiff of exploitation had been part of the director's motivation for so assiduously researching his subject and seeking stamps of approval from experts. Warner Bros. may not always have seen the picture in the same light—at one point the studio had pushed Ray to screen-test Jayne Mansfield for the role of Judy, and Tab Hunter had been in the mix for Jim as Dean dragged his heels—but a week into shooting, the studio ordered a switch from black-and-white CinemaScope to color. Ostensibly, this was due to a licensing issue with CinemaScope, but the studio surely didn't mind distinguishing *Rebel Without a Cause* from *Blackboard Jungle*'s gritty black and white. Color signified prestige, which would also help Ray's movie capitalize on Dean's breakout in *East of Eden*, which was not only a reputable literary adaptation, shot in color, but also, and more important, a hit. "We started out making a routine program picture in black and white," Jim Backus, who played Jim Stark's weak but genial father, wrote in a memoir. "It was going to be a picture about teenage kids I thought was going to be sort of *Ozzie and Harriet* with venom. Then the reports started coming in on *East of Eden*, and they knew they had a star on their hands."

Ray's willingness to indulge that star's eccentricities often angered and perplexed veteran members of the cast and crew, a group who felt they'd already seen a lot over the years in the way of movie-star indulgence. "Even Garbo never got away with that," one crew member reportedly grumbled while Dean kept the company waiting for an hour, locked away in his dressing room and psyching himself up to shoot a scene early in the film in which Jim vents his rage and frustration by pounding his fists on a police detective's desk. As Frascella and Weisel recount it, Dean was "drinking cheap red wine, banging on his bongo drums, and listening to Wagner's *Ride of the Valkyries*, which he can be heard humming earlier in the scene." And yet, when he finally emerged, he won the crew over— and earned their applause—when he nailed the scene in one take. Ray: "We rehearsed the scene so Jimmy would be able to hit without hurting his knuckles, but when we began to shoot, it was clear that in the intensity of the scene he was hurting himself. I resisted the temptation to cut, and he continued to play the scene. Tears came, and pain, and the scene was very intense and meaningful. We finished the shot and even changed setups before I took him to the hospital and learned he had broken a knuckle." (Other accounts say the hand was only bruised.)

According to Dennis Hopper, Dean was "the real director of *Rebel*, and controlled every scene he was in"—an observation that should be taken with a grain of salt, given Hopper's antipathy toward Ray over their shared interest in Natalie Wood. That said, in one often-recalled incident, when Ray called "Cut!" at the end of a scene, Dean turned and shouted at him, "I'm the only one who says fucking 'Cut' here!" Ray didn't push back, and it is further tribute to Dean's sway over his fellow actors that in postproduction the film required copious rerecording of dialogue thanks to the vogue for mumbling that permeated most of the cast. But the power dynamic between director and star flowed in both directions. Marietta Canty, the actress who played the housekeeper caring for Plato, recalled of Dean, "When he felt the director wasn't pleased with him, that really hurt him, right in his heart. He would stand there and cry like a baby."

Decades later, Susan Ray, a fourth wife who the director married in 1969 when she was eighteen, described watching *Rebel Without a Cause* for the first time, at her husband's urging: "What was all the fuss about Dean when Dean was so clearly—to me anyway—aping Nick?"

While *Rebel Without a Cause* was in postproduction, the nation's panic over juvenile delinquency seemed to crest, at least where Hollywood was concerned. The Senate Subcommittee to Investigate Juvenile Delinquency had been formed in 1953 and generated headlines a year later by holding hearings in which senators grilled comic book publishers, attractively deplorable targets who tried their best to defend the practice of depicting severed heads, bloody axes, and decomposing corpses on the covers of titles like *The Vault of Horror*. In June of 1955, the subcommittee convened in Los Angeles for three days of hearings on Hollywood's parallel contributions to teenage depravity. The chairman and sole senator on hand was Estes Kefauver, who had made a name for himself five years earlier chairing televised hearings on organized crime. The film industry, having already seen careers shattered and reputations tarnished by congressional investigations into Communists among its ranks, had to be concerned. As *The New York Times* set the scene, "Top echelon studio executives appeared . . . to defend the movies against allegations that excessive violence, brutality and—dare we mention it—sex on screen have reached proportions that constitute a danger to the morals of the nation's youth."*

"Film Men Strike Back at Kefauver" was probably not the headline the senator was hoping for (even if from the hometown *Los Angeles Times*), but the studios' self-serving defenses were effective enough, given the inquiry's flimsiness. *Blackboard Jungle*, for one, turned out to be an elusive target. The subcommittee's counsel, who bore the almost too perfectly yahoo-ish name James Bobo, asked MGM's Dore Schary to "give us your reasons for the production" of *Blackboard Jungle*, which, Bobo noted, "has become rather controversial."

---

*Even in 1955, this was not a new accusation. Jane Addams, the urban reformer and future Nobel Peace laureate, had decried the influence of movies on children in her 1909 book, *The Spirit of Youth and the City Street*: "Is it not astounding that a city"— she was writing about Chicago, where she was based—"allows thousands of its youth to fill their impressionable minds with these absurdities which certainly will become the foundation for their working moral codes and the data from which they will judge the proprieties of life?" It wasn't dubious content alone that Addams found appalling but also the "five-cent theaters" themselves: "The very darkness of the room, necessary for an exhibition of the films, is an added attraction to any young people, for whom the space is filled with the glamour of love making." To her possible disgust, Addams lived just long enough to witness the opening of America's first drive-in movie theater, in New Jersey, in 1933.

"Well, we knew from the start that it would be a controversial film," Schary replied evenly. "It seems to be within the nature of good filmmaking to occasionally make a film that will provoke talk and controversy, if you have a moral conviction that what you are provoking the controversy about is deserving of that attention."

Kefauver, who admitted he hadn't seen *Blackboard Jungle*, may have thought he would score a point when he took over questioning: "Mr. Schary, it was reported in the Memphis paper . . . that some girls went out and burned down the big barn at the fairgrounds for some unexplained reason, and when apprehended they said the reason they did was they got the idea from *Blackboard Jungle*. What could be in the picture that would cause that?"

Schary batted that one away: "Sir, I haven't the faintest idea. There is no fire in the picture; they can't pin that on us."

Jack Warner showed off an equally effective counterpunch when it was his turn to step into the ring for *Rebel Without a Cause*, "which we are just about finished with." He explained that the movie would break new ground in the delinquency genre by showing "the parents are at fault."

Kefauver was skeptical: "We have had some calls saying this is not a good picture, from the viewpoint of influence on young people."

"They must be working from radar," Warner countered, "because I myself haven't seen it put together." This was true: he had been badgering Ray for weeks to show him a rough cut. "You mustn't believe everything you get by call," Warner added.

"I don't believe everything I get by calls," Kefauver said, now on the defensive. "Some of these people seem to know what they were talking about. One or two of them seemed right reliable. I thought I would ask you about it."

"They are not sore they didn't make the picture themselves, are they? Are these competitors?" Warner asked, ending that line of inquiry, before running out the clock.

•   •   •

"Those doubting Thomases who claimed James Dean was a one-shot boy in *East of Eden* are in for a word-eating session. Those lucky enough to see the sneak preview of Nick Ray's *Rebel Without a Cause* for Warners tell me Dean tops his acting in *Eden*."

So declared Hedda Hopper in her column on September 7, 1955, less than two months before the movie's scheduled release date of October 27. Preview screenings had indeed gone well, and a promotional campaign was in full swing, though some of the ads and posters churned out by the studio's advertising department seemed to be selling precisely "the type of film we have tried to avoid . . . brutal and without explanation," as Ray had put in a letter to Jack Warner earlier that summer, thanking him for supporting his vision for the movie (while aiming a barb at the competition).

"LOOK, MA! NO HANDCUFFS—YET!" read one tagline over an image of Dean holding his hands up in front of Griffith Observatory. "THESE KIDS ARE PLAYING 'COPS AND ROBBERS' WITH REAL COPS!" read another. A third had fun with the star's initials:

J.D.
JAMES DEAN!
JUVENILE DELINQUENT!
JUST DYNAMITE!

Those were the obvious selling points for the movie—Dean and delinquency. That didn't change after the actor, an amateur car racer, died in an accident while driving his new Porsche Spyder north from Los Angeles to Salinas for a race. He was on a two-lane highway when, at an intersection, another car turned into his path. He tried to swerve but to no avail (though police determined he wasn't speeding). "I thought he was alive because there seemed to be air coming out of his nostrils," said a friend of Dean's, who had been following behind in a second car. "They told me later he had died instantly. His forehead was caved in and so was his chest."

That was on September 30, less than a month before the film's scheduled release, and the studio very quickly decided not to change its plans
beyond scrapping a line that had appeared in some of its advertising: "The
overnight sensation of *East of Eden* becomes the star of the year!"

Ray was devastated. According to a friend, in the days immediately
following Dean's death, he would cry and keep repeating, "Jimmy is
dead." He had been in London, preparing to screen the film for the British Board of Film Censors, which he finally did two weeks later. "Much
as I love the picture, it's a little like going to a funeral," he wrote to Steve
Trilling, second-in-command to Jack Warner. "The accident was regrettable and tragic and left us all a little numb," Trilling wrote back. But he
had some good news for Ray: "There was general enthusiasm" for the
picture at a Los Angeles press screening. "No noticeable reaction about
Dean—which was our primary concern. We can only hope now that the
public will react in the same manner."

What Trilling and the studio feared was that the tragedy would over-
whelm the film's reception, smother its drama and artistry, turn audiences
away. *Variety* seconded that fear when, in its generally positive review, it
added a cautionary aside about how Dean's death "under real-life conditions of recklessness" lent the movie "a macabre press agent frame." The
fatal chickie-run sequence was now a sensitive plot point, which the *Los
Angeles Times* took note of with a surprisingly glib headline over a review
of the film: "James Dean Cheats Car Death in a Bit of Film Irony."

Taste aside, Warner Bros. needn't have worried. Dean's death was a
force multiplier, especially where young audiences were concerned. As
Stewart Stern later observed, "No one will ever know where the merit of
the movie gained the audience and where the death of an actor gained the
audience." No doubt they both did, impressively: *Rebel Without a Cause*
would prove to be Warner Bros.' third-highest-grossing film released that
year, after *Mister Roberts* and *East of Eden*. Most reviews were mixed.
Critics, being adults, tended to call out the film's simplistic treatment of
the "howling idiot" parents, as *The Nation* described Backus et al., and a
few compared the picture unfavorably to *Blackboard Jungle*. But almost

all praised Dean. After dismissing his work in *East of Eden* for Kazan as "doing a Marlon Brando," *Variety* now hailed the actor as "almost free of mannerisms" under Ray's direction: "As a 'farewell' performance he leaves behind, with this film, genuine artistic regret, for here was a talent that might have touched the heights. His actor's capacity to get inside the skin of youthful pain, torment and bewilderment is not often encountered."

In fact, you encounter it in the film's very first shot, one of the great entrances in American movies. The camera is set low to the ground, on a sidewalk, one of Ray's beloved horizontal compositions. It is night. In the foreground we see a wind-up monkey playing cymbals. We also see some scattered Easter lilies and the wrapping paper they presumably came in. In the background, on the right-hand side of the CinemaScope screen, slightly out of focus, is a white floodlit mansion. On the left, in pointed juxtaposition, is some kind of construction site with a sign reading "DANGER . . . KEEP OUT." Suddenly, Dean lurches into view, lying down on the sidewalk beside the toy. Drunk and grinning, hardly looking like a delinquent in a suit and tie—See? He's not a slum kid—Dean plays with the monkey as the credits are superimposed on the scene, then gently pulls the wrapping paper over the monkey as if it were a blanket, then puts a bow under the monkey's head for a pillow, gives it a tender, parental pat, and curls up alongside it, tucking his hands between his knees like a little boy. As an opening, it's wry, sad, disturbing, and unexpected—still startling in its audacity no matter how many times you've seen the film. It is also thematically succinct, conveying in a single shot Ray's vision of neglectful parents producing teenagers desperate for love and stability, compelled to act out on the streets and parent themselves. The wind-up monkey is a weird touch—what's it doing on the sidewalk?—but as a discarded children's toy, and one with a creepy, manic edge, it's apt.* Dean

---

*The monkey was left over from a prologue, shot but discarded, in which a gang of teenage hoodlums beats up a man who was carrying the toy and the lilies, presumably intended as gifts, on his way to Easter dinner. This was a vestige of an earlier draft of the script set on Christmas Eve, and an even more distant trace of the opening of Ray's *The Blind Run* treatment, with its random, unmotivated violence.

improvised his sidewalk ministrations, more than justifying Eric Rohmer's description in *Cahiers du Cinéma* of his overall performance: "He is like a chrysalis badly folded out of its cocoon. Turned in on himself? A solitude that is suffered rather than willed, a tortured quest for affection." It's all right there in the film's first minute and fifteen seconds.

The scene ends with the sound of sirens and a dissolve to a shot of Dean being led by two cops into a juvenile justice center, where we are introduced to the film's two other principals, Natalie Wood's Judy and Sal Mineo's Plato, and the central trio's emotional conflicts are sketched in maybe too explicitly, with Jim and Judy in particular breaking down and, between sobs, baring psychological scar tissue the way they might in the final reel of a more conventional movie—almost as if Ray wants to get motivations out of the way as fast as possible. It's an odd sequence, schematic in its outlines, theatrical in its conception, yet fluid in its filmmaking as Ray moves among the trio as they interact with officers and parents.

Wood is first seen in a crimson coat with matching crimson shirt, pussy bow, and lipstick—the costume as caught between innocence and self-aware sexuality as the character herself. Ray later described Judy's lipstick as "gauche" and her outfit the marker of a "fifteen-year-old tramp," but perhaps six decades of turbulent fashion history have muted the intended effect; to my eyes, Judy's presentation aspires to sophistication, awkwardly but poignantly. At any rate, her problem is that her father, unable to deal with her budding sexuality, has rejected her emotionally. "He hates me. He looks at me like I was the ugliest thing [in] the world . . . He called me a tramp. My own father!" she blurts through tears to a sensitive detective played by Edward Platt (later the "Chief" on *Get Smart*), who represents the film's single trustworthy adult; not coincidentally, the character's name is Ray. Judy tells him her father couldn't handle her primping for Easter dinner: "He grabbed my face and started rubbing off all the lipstick. I thought he'd rub off my lips, and I ran out of the house." That, she says, is why she was wandering the streets at one in the morning when the police picked her up.

"You weren't looking for company, were you?" Ray asks—before the film board got to it, the screenplay suggested Judy had been brought in on suspicions of solicitation—but he's sympathetic, and Wood, despite the dialogue, does some of her best acting: angry, confused, and wounded all at once, sobbing convincingly throughout. As a child actor, she had long experience crying in front of a camera, but it was a fraught act for her— early on, her mother had resorted to cruel tricks to get her to cry on cue, like pulling wings off butterflies—and shooting this scene at the end of a long day, she couldn't rise to the occasion until Ray started berating her. Horrible—he was her director *and* her lover—but it worked. As Frascella and Weisel note, "The Warners publicity department would later crow that Wood had matched an on-screen record: her prolonged five minutes of crying 'equaled the mark set by Bette Davis in 1948 in Warner's *Winter Meeting.*'"

Meanwhile, on screen, Jim and Plato cool their heels in a waiting area. Accompanied by Marietta Canty's housekeeper, Plato is dressed in a white shirt, tie, and black sweater vest. Canty's character, addressing him by his real name, says, "You're shivering, John. Are you cold?" Jim, noticing, offers Plato his jacket—an action that will be repeated at crucial moments later in the film. Plato declines but can't take his eyes off Jim as he's brought into a windowed room to talk to an officer. "John . . . John . . . ," the officer calls out, trying to get Plato's attention, "do you have any idea why you shot those puppies?" That single line does a lot of work, establishing Plato as not just troubled but seriously disturbed, foreshadowing violence (and provoking laughter from latter-day audiences). Plato's problem is that his divorced parents have abandoned him: his father is out of the picture, except for the check "IN SUPPORT OF SON" we'll see later in the film, while his mother is frequently away traveling. "I don't think it's right for a mother to go away and leave her child alone on his birthday," Plato says, by way of a justification for the puppy slaughter. The housekeeper explains that he got the gun from his mother's drawer, in case Plato's psychopathology needed further underscoring and the plot more foreshadowing.

Jim's parents (Backus and Ann Doran) now show up, along with his grandmother (Virginia Brissac). They're all in fancy evening wear, having been at an Easter party at "the club"—a curious detail since the family has supposedly just moved to town, though their swanky clothes and snooty ambience reinforce the notion that *this* delinquent picture won't be slumming. The grown-ups arrive to find Jim standing on a shoeshine platform, shot from a low angle so that he looms over his visually diminished parents. Still drunk, he maneuvers his father into the chair as if he were seating him on a throne; it's a comic bit of business but it also illustrates Jim's yearning throughout the film for his complacent, ineffective father to assert authority, to figuratively—and several times literally—stand up and be a man. The parents are soon arguing about who or what is to blame for Jim's misbehavior, mom harping, dad placating—"Don't I buy you everything you want?" he pleads to Jim—leading to Dean's famous explosion of angst: "You're tearing me aparrrrrt!!"

Jim then unloads on Mom and Dad to Ray, the detective: "She eats him alive and he takes it. It's a zoo. He always wants to be my pal, you know." But Jim doesn't want a pal, he wants, well . . . "If he had guts to knock Mom cold once, maybe she'd be happy . . . because they make mush out of him. Mush . . . How can a guy grow up in a circus like that?"

"Beats me, Jim," Ray replies, "but they do."

Jim, sensibly, isn't willing to settle for that. "Please lock me up. I'm going to hit someone, do something." Ray suggests he hit the desk. Dean pounds on it, furiously—this is the scene where he may have broken his knuckle—then leans back in his chair with a look on his face that signals something close to sexual abandon, not unlike Bernini's Saint Teresa. (Seriously. Watch it again.) His next line reads like a more existential spin on Andy Hardy's worries about being normal or not: "If I had one day where I didn't have to be confused, where I wasn't ashamed of everything, where I felt like I belonged someplace." It's a primal teenage complaint.

The opening really is an extraordinary sequence, as crucial to the film's effect as the more iconic knife-fight and chickie-run scenes, and the Griffith Observatory climax. In a sense, it serves as Ray's analog to the disclaimers that opened previous delinquent movies, with the sympathetic detective and the textbook nature of the kids' emotional wounds signaling seriousness of purpose in the same way a Drew Pearson does—it's border-line instructional. Indeed, one ironic thing about *Rebel Without a Cause* is that, despite the title, it fills its first reel with . . . causes. At the same time, the performances, all three of the principals' but especially Dean's, turn the sequence inside out. Audiences were used to seeing kids in trouble on screen, but not at a near-operatic scale. If some adult audiences and critics, like Crowther, found that a bit much, it clearly struck a nerve with young people, since being a teenager means *feeling* on a near-operatic scale. The film itself was speaking their language even if the script still had one foot in the more conventional precincts of a prestige problem picture. As the critic Anthony Lane later distilled it, *Rebel Without a Cause* "is not just a portrait of adolescence; it breathes haltingly, with adolescent lungs."

For the rest of the film, the kids are mostly on their own. Jim goes off to school the next morning in a jacket and tie, with a bag lunch and thermos, driving a customized 1949 Mercury coupe with whitewall tires we've already been told his dad bought for him—reminding us again that this is a story about "good" families. At school, we see Plato at his locker, inside of which he's taped a picture of Alan Ladd in what appears to be a publicity shot from *Shane*, released two years earlier. This bit of set decoration has been widely interpreted as a hint to savvy audiences that Plato is gay, reinforced by the fact that while he's combing his hair in a small mirror above the Ladd photo, he sees Jim, who he stares after with a look that very definitely conveys, per Mineo's later words, that "something was happening." But the picture of Ladd as Shane is also a sign of Plato's yearning for a father figure, and a token of the western themes that infuse *Rebel Without a Cause*, *Blackboard Jungle*, and so many other teen movies to come: high school as a lawless territory where civilization is provisional and physical strength and force rule. Another token: later in the film, when Judy asks Plato what Jim is like, Plato, who still barely knows Jim, invents an archetypal western hero: "He doesn't say a lot, but when he does, you know he means it."

The field trip to Griffith Observatory, where Plato is cowed by the vast emptiness of the cosmos, ends in a confrontation between Jim and the gang led by Buzz (Corey Allen), who of course is Judy's boyfriend and who punctures a tire on Jim's car with his switchblade, just to get a rise out of the new kid. "You know something? You read too many comic books," Jim responds laconically—a tart topical joke. Jim doesn't want trouble, but the gang surrounds him and backs him into a literal corner, which Ray shoots from above as if it were the O.K. Corral. When Buzz calls Jim "chicken"—his emotional Achilles' heel—Jim can't help but fight. He's triggered, as we'd say today. The ensuing knife fight can still get your pulse up, even seventy years on, shot intimately with Dean and Allen jabbing at each other with real switchblades that the film's prop crew had borrowed from the confiscated stash at juvenile hall. The sequence was one that had to be shot twice because of the switch to color. The first time around, filming came to a halt when Allen accidentally cut Dean's ear— which presumably pleased Warner's publicity department since it made good copy for the gaggle of entertainment reporters invited to the set that day. "Isn't this pushing realism a bit?" one writer asked Dean. "In motion pictures, you can't fool the camera," the actor replied. "If we were doing this on the stage, we'd probably be able to gimmick it up—but not in a picture. Film fans are too critical these days."

The realism was aided by Frank Mazzola, the gang consultant, who had taught Dean and Allen how to fight. Equally key to the scene's effect are Wood's excited, almost feral reaction shots, her wide eyes ablaze, as the two boys go after each other. Which points up one of the film's flaws: Judy is underwritten and serves mostly as a passive love interest, but Wood makes up for her lack of lines and agency with the lit-from-within intensity of a silent film star. She nearly steals the subsequent chickie-run scene. Like the switchblade fight, this sequence remains tense and visceral, but its single indelible shot is the one with Wood, who has signaled the start of the race, standing dead in the center of the CinemaScope screen as the two cars roar by her, then turning to run and follow the action, her long skirt unfurling behind her, for a split second, like an opening rose—the character's hunger for sensation matched by a sensational shot, a triumph for actor, director, and cinematographer (Ernest Haller, who had won an Oscar for shooting

Gone with the Wind and been nominated for *Mildred Pierce*). Dean gets the film's showiest moments—and he makes the most of them—but Wood, often undervalued as a performer, does so much with so much less.

The lead-up to the chickie-run includes an oft-quoted exchange, as Jim (now dressed in his iconic after-school uniform of bomber-style red windbreaker, white T-shirt, and jeans) and Buzz (in a young hoodlum's more traditional black leather motorcycle jacket) look over the cliff before getting in their cars, staring down into the Pacific's crashing waves:

"You know something? I like you," Buzz says out of the blue.

"Why do we do *this*?" Jim asks. (A reasonable question.)

"You gotta do something, now don't you?" Buzz replies.* Here *Rebel Without a Cause* earns the nihilistic zing of its title. The line feels designed to get a rise out of adults, and maybe a smattering of applause from the kids. But at the same time, it's not hard to imagine an alternative version of the film where Buzz's circular logic is played for laughs; it's the kind of dopey thing MGM might have had Andy Hardy say under very different circumstances. But this is precisely one of the moments where Ray's film takes teenagers as seriously as they take themselves, romanticizing a dumb, self-destructive impulse as somehow defiant.

The two boys rev their engines. Jim smokes a cigarette. Buzz suavely combs his hair, then less suavely puts the comb in his mouth. Wood does her thing. The two cars hurtle toward the abyss. But uh-oh: a strap on the left cuff of Buzz's jacket gets stuck on the door handle and he can't get out, while Jim jumps free at the last second. What follows—a POV shot from Buzz's driver's seat as his car falls toward rocks and waves; a close-up of Buzz screaming, the comb falling out of his mouth; a long shot of the car exploding on the rocks—remains a truly shocking moment in a film whose violence is otherwise tamer than some of its predecessors (or kept off screen, in the case of Plato's puppy killing). "Let's get out of here!"

---

*It's an echo, deliberate or not, of the exchange in *The Wild One*, released in 1953, where Marlon Brando's biker is asked, "Hey, Johnny, what are you rebelling against?" "Whattaya got?" he answers.

someone shouts—venerable wisdom in such circumstances—leaving behind a stunned Jim, Judy, and Plato.

What follows is the dullest part of the film, fifteen or so minutes of plot machinations, plus an unfortunate scene in which Jim goes home and finds his father wearing a frilly yellow apron, literally on his hands and knees cleaning up a broken dinner plate he doesn't want his wife to see. Jim, wanting to go to the police to tell them about Buzz, is desperate for his father's counsel and backing—for a man-to-man talk, as it were. "Far be it from me to tell you what to do," Backus's emasculated dad fumfers, while Mom the harridan shrieks at both. "Dad, you've got to give me something," Jim pleads before grabbing his father by the collar in frustration, throwing him over an ottoman, and storming out of the house, which the camerawork has tilted on its axis.

The three teenagers reunite at a deserted mansion near the observatory. Judy, whose boyfriend died only several hours ago, is now in love with Jim, which might sound as if she's pathologically fickle, and he a callow opportunist, but the relationship plays anyway, given the film's compressed time frame and exaggerated emotions, and this wouldn't be the first or last time a teenager's romantic life experienced major upheaval over the course of an evening. The extended sequence at the mansion, shot at an abandoned pile owned by J. Paul Getty, which had been used for *Sunset Boulevard* five years earlier, is the film's emotional centerpiece. Having fled their homes, the trio are now free to form a symbolic family, fulfilling the desire Plato expressed to Jim earlier in the film: "Gee . . . if you could only have been my father" (a line that scrapes down to the movie's subtext, painfully hitting bone). The three play a game where Jim and Judy pretend to be an adult couple, pointedly childless, and Plato a Realtor showing them a house. They all end up in the empty pool—the same one where William Holden is found floating face down at the beginning and end of *Sunset Boulevard*— giggling like children themselves. It's an affecting scene and the genuine-sounding laughter a tribute, I'd like to think, to the close bonds among the three actors. They end up relaxing in a gazebo with Jim's head in Judy's lap, and Plato at their feet. The younger boy eventually falls asleep, Judy singing

him a lullaby and Jim finally putting his jacket on Plato. It's a powerful tab-
leau, an archetype for a period of life when friendships can have the intensity of family bonds, if not the endurance. (I remember the vague fantasies
my high school friend group used to have that after college we might all
somehow live together in a big house like, I suppose, the Monkees or the
Seven Dwarves.) As Frascella and Weisel write, "It's during this sequence
that *Rebel* taps into its most important new idea: the sense that teenagers
had the power to form a world of their own." James Dean might have been
a catalyst for the passions the film provoked in young audiences, but he was
far from the whole story.

The final act's movement into tragedy—sorry, but no one on screen
or in the audience cares much about losing Buzz—begins when Jim asks
Judy if she wants to go "explore" the mansion. This was an ongoing issue
for the Production Code office, which forbade the suggestion of "an illicit sex affair," but the gentle yet meaningful way Dean says the word
"explore," the slight hesitation before he gets there, and the spark between
him and Wood tells the audience everything it needs to know. (As goofy as
the *Hardy* pictures could be, they countenanced displays of physical lust
in a way that Ray, for whatever reasons, demurs from here.)

While Dean and Wood are off having their second on-screen kiss, three
gang members, including Frank Mazzola's Crunch and Dennis Hopper's
Goon—such exemplary 1950s hoodlum names!—show up looking for Jim,
who they suspect has finked on them to the police. They threaten Plato, un-
wisely, since he has once again swiped his mother's gun. He shoots, wound-
ing Crunch, and then flees on foot up a trail to the observatory, followed
by Jim and Judy, with Plato now shouting, "You're not my father!" All three
wind up hiding out in the observatory, as Ray had wanted, the building
surrounded by police, including the sympathetic Detective Ray, plus Jim's
parents and Plato's caretaker. Plato, crazed, threatens more violence. Jim
tries to talk him down, surreptitiously removing the bullets from his gun.
Wood continues to deliver great reaction shots. Finally, the three emerge,
but the police, mistakenly thinking Plato is about to fire, shoot and kill him.
Dean gets his last big moment, weeping convulsively over Plato, who is still

wearing Jim's red windbreaker, then laughing sadly when he notices Plato's mismatched socks. In the moment, the performance was so wrenching that Mineo would later claim, "In Plato's death scene, I understood what being loved meant . . . I wanted to do that scene over and over."

If *Rebel Without a Cause* posits Jim Stark as an American hero—Ray's careful eye surely didn't miss the implication of dressing Dean in a red windbreaker, white T-shirt, and blue jeans for much of the movie—it's as a new kind of hero: vulnerable and sensitive and tortured, a harbinger of the conflicted antiheroes to come in the films of the New Hollywood in the late 1960s and 1970s. As Plato's surrogate father, Jim is in fact a failure, less Shane than Jack Nicholson's Jake Gittes in *Chinatown*. And yet, in its final moments, Ray's film takes a surprisingly conventional turn, with Jim Backus rather abruptly transformed into the father Jim has always wanted, helping Jim to stand up and draping his own jacket over his son's shoulders—thus capping off two of the film's important motifs. Dad: "I'll try and be as strong as you need me to be." The result is a film that plumbs and even defines teenage angst but concludes with the redemption of a father. A surprising twist, but then again, maybe not, given where, how, and why the idea for it first stirred in its director's imagination.

A year after Dean's death, *Life* published "Delirium Over Dead Star," which began, "The U.S. is currently in the throes of a movie fan craze for a dead man that surpasses in fervor and morbidity even the hysterical mass mourning that attended the death of Rudolph Valentino in the dim past of the movies." According to the magazine, Warner Bros. was receiving eight thousand letters a month meant for the actor, many of which "address Dean as if he were still alive." This was in part evidence of a growing conspiracy theory that the star had survived the crash but was locked away in a sanatorium somewhere because his looks had been destroyed.* The

*The rumor may have been sparked by the car crash that same year that nearly killed Montgomery Clift and left his face in need of multiple reconstructive surgeries.

magazine quoted one such letter: "Jimmy darling, I know you are not dead. I know you are just hiding because your face has been disfigured in the crash. Don't hide, Jimmy. Come back. It won't matter to us." George Stevens, who was still editing *Giant*, called the fan mail "absolutely weird" and "the most uncomfortable stuff I've ever read." Arguably even creepier was the California company producing life-sized busts of Dean cast in plaster and covered in "a plastic called Miracleflesh . . . that looks and feels something like human flesh." A photo showed artisans painting Dean heads by hand—and honestly, they don't look that bad. The company was turning out three hundred a week, selling for $5 apiece; a deluxe version, in bronze, went for $150.

The actor's death also created a vacancy in the Hollywood Pantheon that movie publicists have been trying to fill ever since. Among the young actors dubbed "the new James Dean" at some point, by someone: Anthony Perkins, Lee Majors, Matt Dillon, Sean Penn, Mickey Rourke, River Phoenix, Luke Perry, Johnny Depp, Brad Pitt, Paul Walker. (PS: That was a list that required barely three minutes of googling to compile.)

Though public anxiety about juvenile delinquency had peaked by 1956, at least as measured by media attention, the troubled-youth film continued to be a popular genre; by one count, the 1950s produced sixty such films. The vast majority had at least one thing in common, as Colson Whitehead observed in his 2021 novel, *Harlem Shuffle*. The book's first chapter, set in the late 1950s, mentions an uptown movie theater that "showed these juvenile delinquent and hot-rodder movies featuring angry young white kids. They didn't make movies about their brown-skinned Harlem versions, but they existed, with their gut hatred for how things worked."

More than a handful of the JD movies had something else in common: they starred Sal Mineo, typecast after Plato and earning the industry nickname the Switchblade Kid in films such as *Crime in the Streets* (1956), and *Dino* and *The Young Don't Cry* (both 1957). He had a simultaneous if brief career as a teen pop star, releasing several singles, one of which, "Start Movin' (In My Direction)," made it to number nine on the US charts—an impressive showing for a pseudo rockabilly tune in which Mineo sounds as if he's been ordered to split the difference between Buddy Holly and Vic Damone while singing lyrics like, "I want you to start moooooovin' / Come on, hold me tight / Start movin' in my direction / And let's start our lovin' tonight."

Natalie Wood had a more varied and storied career, though she appeared in two more significant teen movies: opposite Warren Beatty (in his first screen role) in Elia Kazan's *Splendor in the Grass* (1961); and as Maria, in brownface and with her singing voice dubbed by Marni Nixon, in *West Side Story* (also 1961).

Nicholas Ray never topped *Rebel Without a Cause*, artistically or commercially. It shadowed him, too. In 1962, when he directed the biblical epic *King of Kings*, *Time* dubbed it "I Was a Teenage Jesus." "If *Rebel* has been playing for the last twenty years (and it has)," Ray wrote not long before his death, "then it can stand as my epitaph."

Aside from its lasting influence on several generations of stars, directors, moviegoers, and traffickers in kitsch Hollywood iconography, *Rebel Without a Cause* also had a curious corporate afterlife. Warner Bros. had the rights to make a sequel, which thankfully never happened. A memo from 1962 suggests the studio was developing a TV series based on the film, with a teleplay written by Gloria Elmore, whose credits included *77 Sunset Strip* and *Hawaiian Eye*. Thankfully, that never happened, either. But best of all are some memos about a possible musical adaptation. Sonny Burke, an executive at the studio's record label, had apparently been queried for his thoughts. Writing in March 1967 to the producer and director Mervyn LeRoy (who had directed Wood in the title role of a 1962 film version of *Gypsy*), Burke observed, "It seems quite apparent to me that the music for 'REBEL' in all respects should be completely contemporary." He mentioned approaching Paul Simon or the team of Burt Bacharach and Hal David to write a score, but his top recommendation for the job: John Lennon and Paul McCartney.

These two young fellows are as prolific as anyone on the scene today— probably the most standout team to be found! . . . Although I would imagine that they're very expensive, I'd say that they'd be a great buy at any price!

Did LeRoy really need to be told who Lennon and McCartney were? And would Lennon and McCartney have conceivably written music for a *Rebel Without a Cause* musical in 1967? I'd bet not, even at "any price." But they might have been intrigued. Before they were fans of Little Richard, Chuck Berry, and Elvis Presley, the Beatles had been fans of Dean's. Describing his childhood sense of self, Lennon once said, "I'd get in trouble just because of the way I looked; I wanted to be this tough James Dean all the time." Prior to joining the Beatles, George Harrison had briefly played in a band named the Rebels, in honor of Ray's film. But perhaps the group's biggest Dean fan was Stuart Sutcliffe, the art student who played lousy bass for the Beatles in their formative, pre-fame years but was instrumental in shaping the group's early image — Harrison once referred to him as the group's "art director." Lennon said of Sutcliffe, he "was really our leader, and he was really into the James Dean thing. He idolized him. Stuart died young before we made it to the big time" — in 1962, of a brain aneurysm; he was twenty-one — "but I suppose you could say that without Jimmy Dean, the Beatles would never have existed."

That feels more than generous — the group surely would have made music one way or another even if Ray had cast Tab Hunter as Jim Stark — but not without symbolic truth. In early 1967, when their names were floating around Warner Bros., the Beatles were in the studio recording *Sgt. Pepper's Lonely Hearts Club Band*, the album that would cement their place at the absolute center of the decade's cultural universe, where trends in music, film, fashion, and even cars were being shaped by young audiences in ways that would have been inconceivable in 1955. It was an entirely new world, but one for which *Rebel Without a Cause* had offered a febrile preview.

4

FRANKIE AND ANNETTE

The last thing teenagers wanted was a lecture during an evening of entertainment.

—Samuel Z. Arkoff, co-founder of American International
Pictures, dumping on the *Andy Hardy* movies

It's a government of the Teenyboppers, by the Teenyboppers, for the Teenyboppers.

—proposed advertising copy for the 1968 AIP film *Wild in the Streets*

In 1963, as the very idea of authority was increasingly up for grabs in America, an entirely straight-faced book was published with the title *Teen-Age Tyranny*. The authors were a married couple, Grace and Fred M. Hechinger, journalists who specialized in child development and education; he would serve for three decades as the education editor at *The New York Times*. The two had felt tremors beneath the nation's cultural institutions, and they were alarmed: things might soon go very wobbly. "We do not want to be cantankerous," they wrote. "But we strongly believe that . . . American civilization tends to stand in such awe of its teenage segment that it is in danger of becoming a teenage society, with permanently teen-age standards of thought, culture, and goals. As a result, American society is growing down rather than growing up."

The root of the problem, as the Hechingers saw it, was teenagers' growing numbers and attendant economic power, abetted by cowed, noodle-spined, permissive adults. The Andy Hardy cohort's habits and tastes may have been inexplicable, but they were also mostly harmless — minor disturbances in the nursery. Now, with newfound muscle, the young were inflicting their preferences upon their families and the country, and those preferences, lacking the traditional guidance that would have led them to Mozart and Shakespeare, or at least Rodgers and Hammerstein and Herman Wouk, were increasingly drawn to the flashy, the vulgar, the immature, and the irredeemably popular. Rock and roll, as you'd expect, was the primary evil. "This is a creeping disease, not unlike hardening of the arteries," the Hechingers concluded. "It is a softening of adulthood." That was a loaded phrase in an era when *softness* was a quality frequently ascribed to anyone deemed insufficiently muscular when it came to America's long twilight struggle against communism.

It is tempting to poke fun, but the Hechingers weren't entirely wrong about the erosion in adult cultural authority — I'm advancing a similar narrative with this book. And if you want a vivid example of what they believed "American civilization" was up against, Tom Wolfe — reporter, social critic, gadfly in boulevardier's clothing — provided one in an article published in *Esquire* that same year, the piece with which he made his bones as one of the decade's preeminent "New Journalists." It was about Southern California car culture and it was titled "There Goes (Varoom! Va-room!) That Kandy-Kolored (Thphhhhhh!) Tangerine-Flake Streamline Baby Around the Bend (Brummmmmmmmmmmmmmmmm . . . . . . "*

Wolfe's story opens in Burbank, at a "Teen Fair," a marketing event

---

*Note to copyeditors and other attentive readers: yes, that is sixteen m's, a six-period ellipsis, and no closing parenthesis.

that he described as looking like "an outdoor amusement park" with all kinds of merchandisers chasing teenage dollars. At the literal center of it all was a "hully-gully band" and about two hundred kids "doing frantic dances." Wolfe continued:

> If you watched anything at this fair very long, you kept noticing the same thing. These kids are practically maniacal about form. They are practically religious about it. For example, the dancers: none of them ever smiled. They stared at each other's legs and feet, concentrating. The dances had no grace to them at all, they were more in the nature of a hoedown, but everybody was concentrating to do them exactly *right*.

Wolfe also noticed the uniformity of dress and hairstyle for both boys and girls, even the consistency of each gender's silhouette.

> They have created their own style of life, and they are much more authoritarian about enforcing it than are adults. Not only that, but today these kids—especially in California—have *money*, which, needless to say, is why all those shoe merchants and guitar makers and the Ford Motor Company were at a Teen Fair in the first place. I don't mind observing that it is this same combination—money plus slavish devotion to form—that accounts for Versailles or St. Mark's Square. Naturally, most of the artifacts that these kids' money-plus-form produce are of a pretty ghastly order. But so was most of the paraphernalia that developed in England during the Regency.

Two thoughts. One, with the phrase, "They have created their own style of life," Wolfe came within a whisker of coining the term *lifestyle*, in the tribal, performative, consumerist, overused sense of the word as we've known it since the later 1960s. (The term, apparently borrowed from German, dates back to 1915, according to the OED.) And two, while he clearly had a more nuanced appreciation of youth culture than did Grace and Fred M. Hechinger—and even a sneaking respect for it—all three would likely have been appalled by *Beach Party*, if they ever saw it.

The film, yet another artifact from 1963, was of an indisputably ghastly order, but its form was sui generis: the foundational work of a short-lived but lucrative genre devoted to the spectacle of kids surfing, dancing, trying to get lucky, and, one or two wisps of a make-do narrative thread aside, not much else. *Beach Party*: it was the rare exploitation film that delivered on the promise of its title. In essence, it was the Burbank Teen Fair packed up and moved to the sands of Malibu and put in front of the cameras, complete with an adult interloper hoping to make some anthropological sense of the spectacle, played here not by Wolfe but by the movie and sitcom star Bob Cummings, slumming it on the downside of his career.

Beach Party wasn't created by teenagers; it was made by middle-aged men harboring varying degrees of cynicism toward their young target audience. But with its near-complete jettisoning of dreary authority figures such as parents and teachers, along with all their boring expectations, and with its depiction of a sandy, sun-kissed teenage Neverland segregated from almost anything resembling real life, *Beach Party* represented something new and, at the same time, the culmination of a ten-year wave of films made for the teenage market. Produced by American International Pictures, an independent studio trafficking in cheapie exploitation pictures, *Beach Party* wasn't a family comedy like the *Andy Hardy* series, and unlike most juvenile delinquent movies, it didn't feint at social import. Indeed, it punted on even trying to draw audiences over the age of twenty-one; instead, the producers toyed with leaning into the decade's widening generation gap and advertising *Beach Party* and its sequels as "not suitable for adults."

The cast represented another shift in Hollywood norms: while the stars of earlier teen movies had emerged from something like a common if broad show-business culture—Mickey Rooney was a vaudeville baby

and James Dean a Brando acolyte who had studied with Lee Strasberg—
the *Beach Party* stars, Annette Funicello and Frankie Avalon, were products of the new youth culture, the former a onetime TV Mouseketeer, the
latter a singer of syrupy teen pop songs.

Sex was essential to the formula—or, more accurately, essential to
the come-on. In keeping with the leering quality of much early-1960s
movie comedy, from *The Apartment* (1960) to *Boeing Boeing* (1965), the
ads and posters for *Beach Party* and its sequels emphasized shirtless boys
in surfer trunks and girls in bikinis, a style still considered risqué in the
early 1960s. As the ads for *Bikini Beach* (1964) put it, "WHERE THE GIRLS
ARE BARE-ING . . . THE BOYS ARE DARING AND THE SURF'S RARING TO GO-
GO-GO." But while the promise was all kandy-kolored lasciviousness, in
reality the Beach Party movies played more like junior versions of Doris
Day–Rock Hudson tussles than spark and fuel for raunchier descendants
such as *Porky's* or *American Pie*. "The key to these pictures is lots of flesh
but no sex," William Asher, the director of five *Beach Party* movies, told
The New York Times in 1964. "It's all good clean fun. No hearts are broken
and virginity prevails."

Or, as the producer Samuel Z. Arkoff, co-founder of AIP, owned up to
in his autobiography, *Flying Through Hollywood by the Seat of My Pants*,
"We gave the illusion of being daring, but there was a lot of teasing with
no real payoff."

Bait and switch aside, the *Beach Party* movies, and pretty much the
entire run of exploitation offerings that AIP had been cranking out since
the mid-1950s—disposable reels of celluloid like *The Cool and the Crazy*,
High School Hellcats, and *Teenage Cavemen*—were designed to give
young people not what would elevate them, not what their parents or educators would approve of, not what might appeal to the whole family, but
what teenagers themselves wanted. Or rather, what Arkoff and his partner, James Nicholson, thought they wanted. The two guessed right often
enough, since nearly all of AIP's low-budget movies turned a profit. The
pictures were mostly crap, but interesting crap, compelling as artifacts if

not as films per se, notwithstanding a 1979 retrospective at the Museum of Modern Art and the occasional film journal reappraisal. And as artifacts, they were probably inevitable—an algae bloom in the Hollywood ecosystem, fed by the conditions *Teen-Age Tyranny* lamented.

Seventeen, the first magazine aimed specifically at teenagers ("*Seventeen* is your magazine, High School Girls of America—all yours! It is interested only in you—and in everything that concerns, excites, annoys, pleases or perplexes you"), had been founded in 1944. It turned seventeen itself in 1961, and celebrated that self-reflexive milestone with an editorial that contrasted the era of its birth, "a world in which teenagers were the forgotten, the ignored generation," with a new and improved universe where "the accent everywhere is on youth" and "the needs, the wants, the whims of teenagers are catered to by almost every major industry." Two years earlier, the British film magazine *Sight & Sound* had made more or less the same point, but in less upbeat terms, conjuring a sinister figure stalking theaters: "His clothes are comfortable and sexually explicit. His manners, except to barmen, seem abominable . . . He is today's teenager; and for the first time in cinema history, Hollywood has gone down on its knees to him."

That was overwrought, but again, like the Hechingers' fears about a nation bent on dumbing itself down, and like Wolfe's overthought aperçus about the parallels between highly stylized teen dances and opulent Regency knickknacks, it was not entirely wrong.

The 1960s "youthquake," as *Vogue* editor Diana Vreeland dubbed it mid-decade, was the crash of a demographic wave that began forming in 1946 and gathered force throughout the 1950s. Subsequent generations have grown weary of hearing about it, but strip away the mythology—and the clichéd montages with hula hoops and poodle skirts giving way to civil rights marches, the Beatles, and long hair—and the passage of the baby boom through adolescence nevertheless represented a profound change in American culture, one that was unsettling for adults who had to grapple with it in real time. By 1958, when the inaugural boomers were on the verge of turning thirteen, there were already 17 million teenagers in the US (roughly a tenth of the population). The number would swell to 24 million in 1965 (roughly an eighth of the population), just as the oldest boomers began bumping up against adulthood (an unexpectedly low ceiling for all who first encounter it).

In the space of less than two decades, teenagers had gone from inhabiting an indistinct stage of life that no one thought much about to coalescing as a demographic and cultural force that was now the subject of unending hand-wringing, chin-pulling, and, in some quarters, diligent cultivation.

"We have always had pubescents and adolescents," the critic Dwight Macdonald allowed in 1958, in a two-part article on the subject in *The New Yorker*. "But now we have something quite different; namely teenagers—not just children growing into adults but a sharply differentiated part of the population. Nationally, they are a special interest group, like the farm bloc or organized labor. Psychologically, they are as baffling to the lay adult as if they were in the grip of a severe neurosis." He added: "It is true that every older generation worries, and with reason, about its young . . . [But] it does seem that things have gone pretty far this time." His point wasn't so much that kids were weird—maybe kids had always been weird—but that now they and their inexplicable fads and tastes *mattered*. They had economic clout. They had cultural muscle. Adults could laugh at them, but they couldn't dismiss them. And the kids now had swagger; they laughed back.

Reading the popular press of the late 1950s and early 1960s, you get the sense of a generational war fought hand-to-hand across America in homes and high school hallways. From the adult vantage point, the foes were no longer just the juvenile delinquents drinking beers in the park or larger-than-life pied pipers like Elvis Presley and Jerry Lee Lewis—those were merely the shock troops—but teenagers as a phenomenon, as force majeure. "We feel bound to question whether the teenagers will take over the United States lock, stock, living room, and garage," the CBS newscaster Eric Sevareid complained during a 1956 radio broadcast, recycling familiar complaints about kids hogging the family car and television set. (At the time, most homes were limited to one of each, if they had any at all.) A year later, *Look* magazine devoted a special issue to the subject with a tone that fell somewhere between sensational and zoological. "Teenagers," the cover exclaimed. "Why They Go Steady . . . Why They Go Wild . . . Why They Don't Listen." The cover featured a smiling crewcut boy with his arm around his smiling, sandy-haired girlfriend, both kids toothy and attractive enough to be Kennedys, yet seeming to threaten a home invasion. Inside, a fifteen-page special section was titled "A Primer for Parents: How American Teen-Agers Live," as if most parents didn't, well, live with their own children. And in a sense they didn't: parents and teenagers might share a home but not, increasingly, a culture.

Cosmopolitan published its own "Special Teenage Issue" in the fall of 1957. "Are You Afraid of Your Teenager?" one article asked. *Yes* was the implicit answer. Another piece, "The Nine Billion Dollars in Hot Little Hands," spun nightmare scenarios about the growing purchasing power of teens and the attendant hegemony of their likes and dislikes: "It is possible to regard them as a vast, determined band of blue-jeaned storm troopers, forcing us all to do exactly as they dictate."

The $9 billion figure was marketing experts' estimation of the annual disposable income the nation's teenagers had accumulated in 1955, thanks largely to allowances and after-school and summer jobs. (America's gross domestic product that year was $420 billion.) "In many cases they have more uncommitted pocket money than their parents do," one researcher told *Cosmopolitan*. Teenagers were credited not just with driving trends in music, television, and fashion but with influencing their families when it came to less-sexy purchases such as toiletries, appliances, and "even houses." The magazine cited Eugene Gilbert, a once-famous marketing consultant (when that was a cutting-edge occupation) who had been supplying companies like GE, CBS, and AT&T with insights into the teen market since he himself was in high school (class of 1944). According to Gilbert, "Studies have indicated that a youngster who has [coveted] an item beyond his own means will endeavor to persuade his parents to buy it." That such behavior was considered noteworthy captures an America in transition: still adjusting to postwar affluence but not yet reconciled to spoiled children.

In 1958, when Dwight Macdonald interviewed him for *The New Yorker*, Gilbert estimated that in the year since he'd spoken to *Cosmopolitan*, teenagers' income had grown by another half a billion—a figure "quite apart from what their parents spend on them." Granted, Gilbert and colleagues who cast themselves as teen whisperers had a vested interest in hyping kids' economic clout, but the fact that so many in business and the media were listening meant *something* was afoot. All told, by Gilbert's calculation, teens' weekly income had quadrupled since 1944. Decades earlier, teenagers who lived at home might have contributed their income to the family pot; now they bought their own records, clothes, makeup, and, of import here, movie tickets, much of this bounty created with precisely them in mind.

Even in the best of times, all that concentrated spending money would have caught Hollywood's attention, but the 1950s and early 1960s were not the best of times for the movie industry, which was suffering from competition with television alongside the weakening of the studio system. (Thanks to regulatory changes and a growing power shift in favor of stars, the assembly-line dream factories once ruled by Louis B. Mayer and Jack Warner, which had dominated the 1930s and '40s, would crumble altogether by the end of the '60s.) Between the end of World War II and 1960, American movie attendance dropped by half. Filmmakers fought back not just with wide-screen Technicolor spectacle—the eye-popping musicals and biblical epics of the 1950s—but also with more sophisticated adult dramas, enabled by the Production Code's loosening its belt a notch or two. All of that helped, in the sense of keeping a loss from turning into a rout.

Teenagers, with their thick wallets and heavy purses, were a lifeline, as the Dean cult had demonstrated for Warner Bros. But the studio that first seized that lifeline and held on tightest for the next decade and a half was the independent AIP, founded in 1954 by Sam Arkoff, an entertainment lawyer, and Jim Nicholson, a former theater owner. By the end of the decade, even as older "Poverty Row" studios like Republic Pictures and Monarch Pictures were shutting down or selling themselves off, AIP was thriving, producing and/or distributing between twelve and twenty movies a year.

"So you might ask," Arkoff wrote in *Flying Through Hollywood by the Seat of My Pants*,

> Why did AIP succeed and remain prosperous when so many other independents failed? The answer was sitting restlessly in homes across America, neglected by movie studios for years: the teenager . . . the gum-chewing, hamburger-munching adolescent dying to get out of the house on a Friday or Saturday night and yearning for a place to go. The youth whose parents were just as eager to have him or her out of the house for the evening. AIP didn't invent the American teenager, but the big studios lagged so far behind that they might have thought our company did . . . We attracted millions of young people to the movie theaters, and even more often to drive-ins.

There were some five thousand of the latter venues studding the American landscape by 1955, so-called passion pits that for teenagers were a draw in and of themselves, regardless of the offering on screen—which played to AIP's strengths in marketing while mitigating its weaknesses in actual filmmaking.

Arkoff, who was invariably photographed mogul style with cigar in mouth or hand, was born in 1918 in Fort Dodge, Iowa, where his father owned a haberdashery and the family was part of a small Jewish community. (Lacking a synagogue, local Jews celebrated the high holidays in a Knights of Columbus dance hall.) As a boy, Arkoff had the gift of a specific passion: by the time he was in high school, he had a subscription to *Variety* and was regularly cutting classes so that he could keep pace with the crop of new films that swept in and out of the town's theaters each week. "I can always catch up on my math homework," he would tell friends, "but those movies are going to be gone in a few days." That was not hyperbole in a day when films were not yet recycled on broadcast TV, let alone VHS, cable, DVD, or streaming; if you missed *Broadway Melody of 1936* with Eleanor Powell and Robert Taylor at the local Loew's, for all you knew, you had missed it forever.

After serving as a cryptographer during World War II, Arkoff continued his obsessive moviegoing and less-obsessive study habits while not always physically attending Loyola Law School in Los Angeles, where he'd gone not so much for the degree but to be near Hollywood. Even before graduating in 1948, he had begun his life's work, as the producer of an independent TV sitcom, *The Hank McCune Show*. (The eponymous star was an army buddy of Arkoff's.) The series ran on a local station until it was picked up in 1950 for a single season by NBC, which aired it with what is said to have been the first artificial laugh track in TV history. Arkoff always insisted this regrettable innovation was the network's brainstorm, not his, and given his otherwise happy embrace of bad taste, crass motives, and shameless credit-hogging, we should believe him.

His day job as an entertainment lawyer on Hollywood's fringes introduced him to his future partner. Jim Nicholson, two years older than Arkoff, grew up in San Francisco, where he began his career in cinema as a movie-theater usher, working his way up to the projectionist's booth. By the late 1940s, he owned a chain of revival houses in Los Angeles that he branded the Academy of Proven Hits, an odd but memorable name with an implicit rhetorical question: Why waste your entertainment dollar on new, *unproven* pictures?

A health scare forced Nicholson to sell the theaters, and he ended up working for a small distributor named Realart Pictures, which had carved a niche for itself rereleasing dusty old movies with new, grabbier titles. Nicholson had a gift for that. *The Atomic Monster*, for instance, was the more 1950s-ready title he stapled on top of *Man-Made Monster*, a forgotten Lon Chaney Jr. picture from 1941. But there was a catch to that one: *The Atomic Monster* happened also to be the title of a spec script that one of Arkoff's legal clients had submitted to Realart. Arkoff threatened to sue the distributor for stealing the title, despite having a flimsy case because: a) you can't copyright a title; and b) *atomic* was a ubiquitous, all-purpose, virtually meaningless adjective in the 1950s, akin to *artisanal* in the 2020s. Nevertheless, Arkoff managed to wheedle a $500 settlement out of Realart's notoriously cheap CEO, a demonstration of negotiating prowess that so impressed Nicholson he asked Arkoff out to lunch, figuring the lawyer was someone he should know. A friendship developed, and given the one man's flair for showmanship, at least where titles on marquees were concerned, and the other's gift for squeezing money out of people and budgets, the two must have felt Fate goading them to make cheap exploitation movies together. In 1954, they formed what would become AIP with a $3,000 investment.

"It's not easy to start a film company," Arkoff once said. "You have to be needed." He and Nicholson got off to a good start: the first film they distributed, a car-centric noir called *The Fast and the Furious* (which would lend its name and maybe the most threadbare strand of DNA to the twenty-first-century Vin Diesel franchise), grossed a quarter of a million dollars on an investment of $50,000. That deal inaugurated a long relationship with the director and producer Roger Corman, a Stanford engineering grad and student of English literature at Oxford, then just getting his start as a schlock filmmaker. (He would go on to make dozens more films for AIP.) The studio next tried its hand at a few conventional if low-budget westerns, but a pair of latex-monster science fiction movies, *The Beast with 1,000,000 Eyes!* and *Day the World Ended* (another Corman picture), sent into theaters and drive-ins as a themed double feature, gave the company both a distribution model and a sense of where it might gainfully be needed.

Arkoff: "We eventually realized that if we concentrated on movies aimed at the youth market, we might be able to create a lucrative niche for ourselves." And so they did, fusing tried-and-true exploitation elements— Crime! Sex! Unearthly Terror!—with contemporary teenage concerns. As Nicholson, ever conscious of a catchy title's value, explained to *Variety* in 1957, at bottom AIP relied on old movie formulas. "However, we update them by use of modern expressions such as 'Hot Rod,' 'Drag Strip,' and 'Rock 'n' Roll.'" The result was a filmography that would include:

Hot Rod Girl (1956)
Shake, Rattle, and Rock (1956)
Dragstrip Girl (1957)
Rock All Night (1957)
Rock Around the World (1957)
Dragstrip Riot (1958)
Hot Rod Gang (1958)
Ghost of Dragstrip Hollow (1959)

Wringing so many workable titles from so few buzzwords was a worthy achievement in showbiz sizzle-faking. But Nicholson's true masterpiece, and AIP's signal pre–*Beach Party* contribution to American culture, was a title so magnificently brazen it didn't need to be made to cause a stir: *I Was a Teenage Werewolf*. Its notoriety wasn't just because it was among the first films to employ the word *teenage* in its title.* The promise of a lurid horror movie so nakedly targeted to a youth audience gifted the era's scolds with an irresistible fusion of the doubly disreputable—boosted further by an obviously hormonal metaphor in transforming an adolescent hero into a gamey, hirsute, flesh-hungry monster. "At first I wasn't sure I wanted to put my name on the film," Herman Cohen, who was hired to produce it, later admitted. "Then people from *Time* and *Newsweek* and *Life* started calling the office. They'd heard about the picture and wanted to know who was producing it. I didn't want to pass up the publicity. It was

*The very first appears to be *The Flaming Teen-Age*, a 1940s *Reefer Madness*–style scare film about drinking and drugging, originally released as *Twice Convicted*, which in 1956 was rereleased in hopes of latching on to the craze for juvenile delinquent movies, but with some new footage and the new title—perhaps meant to trigger dimming memories of *Flaming Youth*. The director of the added material was Irvin Yeaworth, who would achieve B-movie immortality two years later with *The Blob*.

the title that made them so curious." PS: That might be the most honest interview ever given by a movie producer.

Nicholson later claimed that the inspiration for the title was a crack made by a friend of his teenage daughter's, bemoaning some perceived shortcoming in her personal grooming. Another account places the origin in a meeting where several AIP executives were riffing on memorably long movie titles and somehow the 1951 Red scare thriller, *I Was a Communist for the FBI*, morphed into *I Was a Teenage Werewolf*. Arkoff remembered Nicholson simply presenting him with the title one day in early 1957: "I was stunned. 'My god, it's terrific,' I told him. At the same time, I wasn't sure quite how middle America would react to it over their morning cup of coffee. There had never been a teenage horror movie before . . . For the next few days, Jim and I talked about the title again and again. Should we really use it?" They tested it on some theater owners, who were cautiously enthusiastic. So was Arkoff's wife. "It's a great title," she told him. "But don't you dare use it."

They dared. Shot in seven days for a budget of $82,000, parsimonious even by AIP standards—the "star" was a then-unknown Michael Landon, who received a mere $1,000 for his troubles—the movie made $2 million at the box office ($23.4 million in 2024 dollars). Twenty when the film was shot, Landon comes across as a budget James Dean, with a similarly fine-boned beauty and a French curve pompadour. His character, Tony Rivers, is a seething high school hothead who can't seem to help getting into fights. "I burn easy. People bug me," Tony confesses to a sympathetic police officer. The cop suggests he consult with "a psychologist out at the aircraft plant" who's been "working with the police department helping difficult kids adjust." Tony is rightly suspicious—"What's this 'adjust' kick?"—but the cop insists: "This Dr. Brandon—he's *modern*. He uses hypnosis."

Poor Tony: Dr. Brandon, despite the aircraft plant's seal of approval, turns out to be a mad psychologist searching for a youngster with the "proper disturbed" personality to experiment on. As he explains to his skeptical assistant, Hugo, "Through hypnosis, I'm going to regress this boy back—back into the primitive past that lurks within him. I'm going to transform him, and reveal the savage instincts that lie hidden within. Mankind is on the verge of destroying itself. The only hope for the human race is to hurtle back into its primitive dawn—and start all over again!" On the one hand, this makes no sense. On the other hand, it is more or less the same motivation screenwriters would subsequently provide for several Bond villains and half the baddies in the Marvel Cinematic Universe.

Dr. Brandon's experiments work all too well, regressing Tony into an unconvincingly made-up wolf man, though tribute must be paid to whoever was tasked with applying glycerin to Landon's fangs; his slobber retains a plausibly lupine froth throughout. After attacking two friends, Tony spends most of the movie's seventy-six-minute running time hiding behind scrubland bushes as the authorities hunt for him, until the inevitable fatal confrontation back at Dr. Brandon's office. The most terrifying aspect for viewers in the climate-change era may be the sight of a tinder-dry Southern California landscape threatened by torch-carrying search parties. I suspect young audiences at the time accepted *I Was a Teenage Werewolf* as a hoot, though a couple of mild scares at the end may have provoked a few shrieks and propelled drive-in couples into each other's arms, if they weren't already necking, so in that sense the picture did its job. "For what it is," conceded the *Hollywood Reporter*, "it is a good one."

The movie's success spawned a run of teen horror movies, sublimated and sometimes not-so-sublimated anxiety dreams about adolescent sexuality, which would ebb and flow for decades, most notably with *Carrie* (1976) and the dozens of teen slasher franchises spawned by *Halloween* (1978). In *I Was a Teenage Werewolf*'s immediate wake, AIP hastily assembled *I Was a Teenage Frankenstein*, which arrived in theaters just five months later with the winning tagline "Body of a boy! Mind of a monster! Soul of an unearthly thing!" This time, Nicholson and Arkoff were defying not only conventional taste but also pedantry, as the teenager here was technically a Frankenstein's monster, cobbled together from a young car accident victim and several high school athletes killed in a plane crash. Perhaps this was meant to lure the Dean conspiracy theorists? Whit

Bissell, the middle-aged actor who had played Dr. Brandon, was cast as Professor Frankenstein, demonstrating once again his talent for lending silly expository dialogue a calm, if demented, authority—he could have been Judge Hardy's evil twin. Here the actor got to utter the memorable command, "Speak! I know you have a civil tongue in your head because I sewed it back myself." As Dwight Macdonald wrote of the appeal the AIP horror films held for their target audiences, "The teenage movie goers can thus blame everything on the grown-ups who have created them—a symbolism too obvious to be called Freudian." In this context, Jim Backus in an apron qualifies as understatement.

I Was a Teenage Werewolf's more lasting accomplishment was lending its title's construction to subsequent generations of filmmakers looking for a quick way to convey shock or camp or both. I counted seventy-four iterations of "I Was a Teenage . . ." on IMDb, including features, shorts, TV movies, direct-to-video junk, and episodes of TV series. Among the entries: *I Was a Teenage Mummy*, *I Was a Teenage Bride*, *I Was a Teenage Beatnik*, *I Was a Teenage Apeman*, *I Was a Teenage Sex Maniac*, *I Was a Teenage Zombie*, and *I Was a Teenage Zombie Prostitute*. The working title for *Clueless* was *I Was a Teenage Teenager*, which would have been the perfect capper.

In his history of AIP, *Faster and Furiouser*, Mark Thomas McGee makes the point that, despite the company's creative and shrewd marketing, its films had mainly chased trends throughout the 1950s: the delinquent movies, the rock-and-roll musicals. Even the teen horror movies could be discounted as youth-market riffs on Universal's monster movies from the 1930s and '40s. Arkoff admitted as much in his autobiography: "We followed the young people, really . . . We were not trying to create new areas that young people weren't ready for. We were trying to fathom how far and how fast the youth changes were occurring."

This was true as well of *Beach Party*. One trend Arkoff and Nicholson surely sniffed was the increasing popularity of surf music: the Beach Boys, signed to Capitol Records in 1962, had already had a couple of Top 20 hits, and they were only the most musically accomplished among a number of popular surf rock acts. (*Variety* headline, March 1963: "Teens Take to Surf Sound: Lotsa Labels Get in Swim.") A Hollywood precursor to *Beach Party* was *Gidget*, the 1959 movie about an intrepid sixteen-year-old tomboy who falls in with a group of beach bums and learns to surf while confronting the question: Will Moondoggie, Kahuna, and the rest of the guys ever see her as anything *more* than a mascot? The movie birthed two sequels, *Gidget Goes Hawaiian* (1961) and *Gidget Goes to Rome* (1963). Another predecessor was *Where the Boys Are* (1960), which follows a group of college coeds on spring break in Fort Lauderdale, with not entirely sunny consequences.

In later life, Arkoff would claim improbably virtuous motives for making *Beach Party* and its sequels: "In a sense, Jim Nicholson and I were taking a gamble with the beach movies. After all, there were no beaches in Iowa, Idaho, Kansas, or many of the places our pictures played. But we felt that kids across America needed a change from the films about hot rods and juvenile delinquents." Why, *Beach Party* was practically a public service! In the moment, however, the producer may not have been as rah-rah. Arkoff "hated the idea of the beach pictures," according to their director, William Asher. "He came down and watched the first day's dailies and said, 'This will never work.'"

And yet through some provident collision between calculation and inspiration, it did work. Arkoff, Nicholson, Asher, and their collaborators conjured something not necessarily good but, in its way, original with *Beach Party*. McGee: "They had, at last, created something that was uniquely AIP—a mix of pop music, adolescent romance, slapstick comedy, surfing, dancing, and bikini-clad hopefuls. It was summer without parents. Without jobs. Without anything to get in the way of fun except a gang of over-the-hill motorcycle bums."

That "without parents" is key: AIP had demonstrated commercial cunning in catering to teen tastes, but so had other studios and independent producers. AIP's cannier insight, and perhaps its greatest contribution to the evolution of teen movies, was the gradual sidelining of adults in its films. Arkoff: "We started looking for our audience by removing the element of authority in our films. We saw the rebellion coming, but we couldn't predict the extent of it, so we made a rule: no parents, no church or authorities in our films."

As we've seen, the creators of most delinquent films felt that to justify their racy storylines they needed periodically to pause the knife fights and attempted rapes for speeches by older actors or recognized authority figures about how this sort of youthful mayhem could occur in any town, any family, maybe yours. Even the delightfully sleazy *High School Confidential* (1958) made a pass at respectability. After a lively eighty-five minutes in which undercover narcotics agent Russ Tamblyn infiltrates a school rife with "weedheads" (while lusty Mamie Van Doren, playing his ostensible guardian, confronts a prim teacher with the immortal line, "Don't tell me you never rode a hot rod"), the movie ends with a narrator trying to convince the audience that what they have just seen is not a whiz-bang exploitation picture but "an effective disclosure of conditions that unfortunately exist in some of our high schools today."

Less faux-cautionary teen movies also courted adult audiences to varying degrees, mostly to the films' detriment. *Rock Around the Clock*, quickly released in 1956 after the song's success on the *Blackboard Jungle* soundtrack, is often cited as the first rock-and-roll musical. It featured a creditable—and integrated—lineup of acts, not just the expected Bill Haley & His Comets but also the Platters, the Ernie Freeman Combo, and Tony Martinez. All the same, the main character is a white middle-aged big-band promoter looking for a new sound. You can almost feel the strain of producers torquing their project to make it relatable to middle-aged audiences—and, maybe more to the point, middle-aged studio executives.* Other rock-and-roll musicals tried to split the difference between younger and older tastes by making room for buttoned-down acts such as

---

*The movie connected with at least one teen: Pete Townshend, who was inspired to pick up the guitar—and eventually help form The Who—after seeing Haley in the film. It was revelatory. "Nothing would ever quite be the same," he later recalled.

the Brothers Four or Stan Getz. For her part, Gidget, like so many movie adolescents before her, was at heart an adult's caricature of a contemporary teenager, however sympathetic. In fact, the film was based on a 1957 novel written by a father who had been inspired by his real-life daughter's adventures surfing in Malibu. The book was titled *Gidget, the Little Girl with Big Ideas*, and the movie adopts a similarly paternal, even patronizing tone toward the character; it was the goofy, coltish appeal Sandra Dee brought to Gidget that likely made her palatable to teen audiences. (For contractual reasons, however, Dee was replaced by Deborah Walley in the 1961 sequel, *Gidget Goes Hawaiian*, and she by Cindy Carol in 1963's *Gidget Goes to Rome*—making the role something of a precursor to sitting behind Spiñal Tap's drumkit.)

The *Beach Party* movies flipped adult-centrism on its head. The ethos was "Don't Trust Anyone Over Thirty" (or really twenty), a year before Berkeley free-speech activist Jack Weinberg made the phrase famous. Parents are neither seen nor referenced; teachers and any other authority figures who might sound distracting notes of responsibility, obligation, or toil are also non grata. There are a handful of adults in the film, but they're comic stooges, like the beatnik bar owner, played by Morey Amsterdam, on a break from *The Dick Van Dyke Show*, or the bumbling motorcycle gang leader Eric Von Zipper played by Harvey Lembeck, a former regular on *The Phil Silvers Show*.* Bob Cummings—far from his work with Hitchcock (*Saboteur, Dial M for Murder*), or even his comeback sitcom, *The New Bob Cummings Show*, which had been canceled by CBS after one season—gets top billing as an anthropologist spying on Avalon, Funicello, and the rest of the kids for his study of the mating habits of "post-adolescent surfing societies." He likes to watch, as it were, with the aid of telescopes and a parabolic microphone, until his sexually frustrated female assistant finally gets his attention. Dorothy Malone, who had won a Best Supporting Actress Oscar only seven years earlier for her

---

*Giving his life to his art, Lembeck would die of a heart attack on set while filming a 1982 episode of *Mork & Mindy*.

role in the Douglas Sirk melodrama *Written on the Wind*, took on that thankless role. (As *The New York Times* wrote in a remarkably not-all-*that*-negative review of *Beach Party*, "Miss Malone had better hold tight to that Academy Award.")

Similarly clownish adult roles, mostly male, were a staple of subsequent *Beach Party* movies—"the schlub who didn't understand the kids," in the words of Don Rickles, who played the part in different guises in *Muscle Beach Party* (1964), *Bikini Beach* (1964), and *Beach Blanket Bingo* (1965).* Often, like Cummings's professor, the schlub was both voyeur and neuter. "Just like Dad—but it really isn't Dad so it's all right" is how an AIP executive once perceptively described the part, as ritualized in its way as a commedia dell'arte character. Variations of Dad/Not-Dad were played by some of the era's edgier comics, including Rickles and Buddy Hackett, or older stars on the tail ends of their careers such as Peter Lorre, Boris Karloff, and Buster Keaton. About that last credit: if you are a fan of Keaton's, and you should be, it is depressing to see him near the end of his life—he would die in 1966, at the age of seventy—pear-shaped where he once was hatchet lean and gamely executing dumb slapstick gags, like hooking a girl's bikini top while casting his fishing line or sitting glumly in the background, barely on the clock, while the movie's young principals carry on. I assume he needed the paycheck and hope he made fine use of it. Mickey Rooney, of all people, turns up in *How to Stuff a Wild Bikini* (1965), perhaps the last great AIP title. Playing it more or less straight, he brings welcome energy to his scenes as an ad man trying to exploit the Malibu gang for a promotional campaign. There is an

---

*In his autobiography, Rickles describes sitting next to then–First Lady Barbara Bush at a White House state dinner, during which she displayed a surprising, perhaps aide-assisted knowledge of his career: "I know you were in that submarine movie with Burt Lancaster and Clark Cable," she told him, referencing *Run Silent, Run Deep*, from 1958. "I know you did some *Twilight Zones* and some fine television dramas. But there's one question I've always wanted to ask you, Don . . . Were things so bad that you had to do *Bikini Beach* and *Beach Blanket Bingo*?" Rickles didn't record his response, observing only that "Mrs. Bush is something else."

ouroboros-like irony in the former Andy Hardy playing a smarmy middle-aged buffoon—not a parody of Judge Hardy as much as an insult to the very idea of sagacity. But I have already put more thought into their adult characters than do the *Beach Party* movies themselves.

This minor but thoroughly American subgenre can be tenuously blamed on Italy. In the late 1950s, Arkoff and Nicholson had begun picking up Italian films to fill out their release schedules—mostly sword-and-sandal epics along the lines of *Sheba and the Gladiator* (1959) and *Goliath and the Dragon* (1960). On one overseas shopping trip, they screened a December-May romance set at an Italian seaside resort. They didn't like the movie—the interests of AIP's target audience didn't extend to sex with partners its parents' ages (or at least not until the release of *The Graduate* a few years later)—but the two men sparked to the idea of setting a movie on a beach. They assigned the screenwriter Lou Rusoff, Arkoff's brother-in-law, whose credits included the AIP double feature *The She Creature* and *It Conquered the World*, to come up with something. They brought the script to the director William Asher, whose résumé, mostly in television, included more than half of the 181 episodes of *I Love Lucy*; he had also co-created *The Patty Duke Show*, and in 1964 would dream up *Bewitched* as a sitcom vehicle for his wife, Elizabeth Montgomery.

You don't watch *Beach Party* and its sequels with any sense that their director had a hand, alongside Lucille Ball and Desi Arnaz, in some of the sharpest, most well-rehearsed and carefully staged American comedy ever put on film. (Asher's *I Love Lucy* ledger includes the episode where Lucy and Ethel work in a chocolate factory, the one where Lucy gives birth to Little Ricky, and the one where she does the mirror routine with Harpo Marx.) But the *Beach Party* movies do feel as if the people who made them were enjoying themselves, indulging a certain try-anything silliness and formal playfulness that you could say, if you are being charitable, build on the directorial innovations of Frank Tashlin and Jerry Lewis.

Or not. But Asher, forty-one when he shot *Beach Party*, did give the movies a heart, of sorts. His secret was that he knew something about hanging out on a beach all day, day after day. As he would later say of his involvement with the series, "Well, that was a natural, because I was a surfer from *way* back . . . I had a real connection to the thing." He was raised in Southern California where his father, Ephraim M. Asher, was an associate producer at Universal, with credits that included *Dracula*, *Frankenstein*, and *The Black Cat*. But William's parents divorced when he was "about eleven or twelve," he told the film historian Wheeler Winston Dixon. He and his sister then moved to New York with his mother, Lillian Bonner, an alcoholic actress. "My sister and I were abused terribly by her . . . She beat us all the time. . . . It was just awful. There was no reason for her to do it; she just did." To escape, he dropped out of high school and returned to Los Angeles, where he got a job in the Universal mailroom, though his father couldn't do much for William there, having died of a stroke. After serving in the Army Signal Corps during World War II, Asher found himself adrift in Southern California, trying to make it as a writer and living what he called "a sort of nomadic existence by the sea—surfed a lot, pretty much lived like a beach bum. It was great." Alas, this idyll was interrupted when the new medium of television beckoned with creative opportunities, and he found himself saddled with a career.

By Asher's account, Arkoff and Nicholson had offered him a pedestrian surfing movie that he then transformed into something giddier but also, in its way, pointed:

They had a screenplay . . . that was kind of like the films they'd been making at the time, an exploitation thing, kids in trouble, parent-kid relationships, the generation gap—those kinds of things. And I didn't want to do that. I asked them if they'd do a film based on kids having a good time and not getting in trouble. Where they don't have to make up their minds right away about what they're going to do with their lives. The kids in the beach pictures were right out of high school, a time to be free before they made a commitment. Commitment, as we all know, is difficult because there might be something better down the road. I wanted to use that time and just let them enjoy themselves.

He did, almost to the point of parody: though ostensibly on vacation from "school"—the movie declines to get more specific—the *Beach Party* gang seems to have spent their entire lives on the sand. They were, in their hedonistic way, forerunners of the decade's rising tide of runaways, drop-outs, and flower children, but without regret or consequence, let alone overdoses and STDs.

"It was a teenage dream, the perfect world," Asher continued. "I loved making these films; it was the way I wished I'd lived my childhood . . . I had no parents, so to speak, so there were no parents in the films, because I didn't have the source for it. And nobody ever got in trouble, no matter what they did . . . It was a beautiful dream of what it was like to live in California at the time." In this, as a fortysomething guy who identified with kids at a time when few fortysomething guys did, Asher was like a mellower Nicholas Ray—a Ray with less tsuris and more boundaries.

Asher rewrote AIP's surfing script with a collaborator, Leo Townsend, who he knew from *The Dinah Shore Chevy Show*. But if the director brought some measure of emotional conviction to the material, that only went so far. "We're not being arty-farty here"—that was Arkoff summing up the *Beach Party* philosophy to an *Esquire* reporter who visited one of the films' sets. The producers did agree to a budget of $350,000 for the first picture, lavish by the company's standards, while Frankie Avalon brought rare marquee value to an AIP project. Twenty-two when he was cast in *Beach Party*, he had risen to fame as a singer in the late-1950s "teen idol" era alongside the likes of Fabian and Ricky Nelson, products of a pop-music industry intent on sanding the edges off rock and roll and remaking it in the smoother, milder mold of established pop stars like Perry Como and Andy Williams. Which worked for a few years: Avalon charted a total of thirty-one singles between 1954 and 1962, with two #1 records in 1959 alone, "Venus" and "Why." But he wasn't thrilled with the sappy, strings-soaked music he was making—he had started his show-business life as a big-band trumpet player modeling himself after Harry James—and began chasing an acting career. This worked for a few years, too; a supporting role in John Wayne's prestige passion project, *The Alamo* (1960), served as Avalon's Hollywood calling card before *Beach Party* came along. He didn't surf, but stand-ins for long shots and rear projection for close-ups solved that problem. A product of South Philadelphia, he retained a hint of the street corner in his demeanor and voice, which never registered as convincingly Malibu but did lend him the fast-talking, wise-guy appeal of a budget Tony Curtis.

Annette Funicello wasn't a native daughter of California, either—she was born in Utica, New York, even farther from Malibu spiritually than it was geographically—but her family had moved to the San Fernando Valley when she was four. She became the breakout star on the original *The Mickey Mouse Club*, which ran for four seasons from 1955 to 1959 (and for many more years in reruns). She was twelve when she was picked for the show, supposedly scouted by Walt Disney himself at a dance recital in Burbank. She quickly became the show's most popular cast member, receiving upwards of six thousand fan letters a month by the end of the first season. As one of the older Mouseketeers, she had a pubescent appeal the rest lacked, a selling point for both her and the show—within bounds of good taste, of course. A moderately icky theme song was written for her that captured the tension between exploiting her sex appeal and keeping it off the boil. Titled simply "Annette," it described her as "just a cute preteener" who was "dainty as a dream" while noting that soon enough "they'll give Annette away / to the world's luckiest boy."

That "they" was a reference to Annette's parents, by the way, not the studio. Disney took pains not to give Annette away, keeping her under contract after *The Mickey Mouse Club* folded and casting her as an ingenue in films like *The Shaggy Dog* (1959) and *Babes in Toyland* (1961). The studio also pushed the reluctant teenager into a successful singing career, thanks in part to the aggressive double-tracking of her thin voice—a pioneering example of the now-common practice of using technology to bolster pipeless-but-marketable performers. Her biggest hit was the 1959 single "Tall Paul," about dating a "king-size" boy. ("Tall Paul / He's my all.") Less a song than an adolescent nursery rhyme, it was written for her by the Disney songwriting team of Richard B. and Robert M. Sherman, who would do better a few years later with their score for *Mary Poppins*. Somehow "Tall Paul" reached #7 on the Billboard Hot 100—the first Top 10 single by a female artist to be labeled (either cynically or aspirationally, but for certain inaccurately) rock and roll.

All of this made Funicello an avatar of wholesomeness, a female counterpart to Pat Boone. "It wasn't an act," she wrote in her 1994 autobiography, *A Dream Is a Wish Your Heart Makes: My Story*. "Even in the late fifties and early sixties Hollywood tolerated promiscuity, drinking, and wild partying, and everyone knew who did what. While I wouldn't presume to pass judgment on anyone, that kind of lifestyle didn't attract me. I came home from work each day, sat down to dinner, helped my parents with chores and taking care of my brothers, did my homework, talked on the phone or had a friend over, then fell asleep."

Casting Funicello in a comedy that would advertise itself as risqué (if not quite deliver on that promise) was thus a minor coup for AIP. However, she was still under contract to Disney so Arkoff, in his account, had to get the headman's sign-off: "I told him that there wouldn't be anything that would offend, that it wasn't that type of picture. They were a little wary because it was AIP."

According to Funicello's book, Walt Disney asked for the *Beach Party* script and liked what he read. "It's good clean fun, and I think you'll have fun doing it," he told her, but added, "I do have a special little request."

"Okay," I said, somewhat curious.

"Now, I see in here that all the other girls are going to be running around in bikinis, which is fine. But Annette, I want you to be different. You *are* different. I would simply like to request that you not expose your navel in the film."

"Mr. Disney, that's not a problem. Of course I won't," I replied.

And it wasn't; at least not for me. I wore a bikini around my pool at home, but never in public. So I was happy to comply with Mr. Disney's request.

This wasn't a problem on AIP's end, either. In Arkoff's ungracious recall, "Annette just didn't have the figure to provocatively fill out a bikini."

However peculiar it seems today, the concern over female navel display wasn't unique to Disney. Although the Production Code didn't say anything specific on the subject, its prohibition against "indecent or undue exposure" was long understood to include bared belly buttons, especially women's. Though Ursula Andress had notably broken the taboo a year earlier in *Dr. No*, Arkoff claimed that over two hundred newspapers around the country airbrushed out belly buttons from the ads for *Beach Party*. As for Funicello, she wears a one-piece in *Beach Party*'s early scenes, but midway through the film changes to a modest two-piece with an extremely high waist, presumably intended to cover her navel, which is nevertheless visible in several shots. Whether Disney or Funicello herself ever noticed is unrecorded, but Arkoff claimed that Disney subsequently chewed him out over some mildly suggestive ad copy, yelling over the phone, "How dare you subject Annette to this sort of degradation!" The allegedly offending copy: "When 10,000 Bodies Hit 5,000 Blankets . . ."

It's true that sex provides the plot engine of *Beach Party*—to the extent that there *is* a plot. The picture opens with Funicello's Dee Dee and Avalon's Frankie driving down the Pacific Coast Highway in a yellow jalopy with surfboards in the back and lip-synching the anthem "Beach Party Tonight," with lyrics about "surfing all day and swinging all night" which also provide several weak double entendres for horny high school sophomores to smirk at:

> Got an early start, gonna have a ball
> Gonna ride the surf, yeah, and that ain't all . . .

And so on. Frankie and Dee Dee drive onto the sand and pull up to the house they've rented, right on the beach, for a romantic getaway. "It's just like we're married," Dee Dee says. "Exactly!" says an insinuating Frankie. But surprise: it turns out Dee Dee has invited the whole gang to share their love nest (much of the cast recruited by Asher from among Malibu's surf crowd).

"You know it's more fun with a whole gang," Dee Dee insists.

"Not for what I had in mind," Frankie grumbles (declining uncharacteristically to misread her line as another weak double entendre).

"That's just it, Frankie! I don't trust myself alone with you," she coos, with just the right combination of demureness and not.

Later, Dee Dee tells a girlfriend, "I want Frankie to think of me as more than just a girl."

"Is there something else?" the friend asks.

"Yes!" Dee Dee insists. "A wife!"

"Wife? You're not even a woman."

"But I'm close. And I'm not getting any closer until I'm a wife!"

In the end, however, Frankie, Dee Dee, and their pals seem fully preoccupied by their surfing, tanning, and dancing. Money is never mentioned, none of the principals has a job, school is so remote as to be virtually nonexistent, as is any kind of adult future, despite Annette's gentle mewling about settling down. There are jealousies and romantic rivalries to complicate things and give the movie an illusion of narrative drive. There is also an extended sequence of kids making out on the sand at night. But Frankie's frustration and Bob Cummings's unwittingly smutty anthropological language about "first contacts" with the natives aside, *Beach Party* is as blithe about sex as it is everything else—a world away from the likes of Elia Kazan's *Splendor in the Grass* (1961), in which not having sex with Warren Beatty drives Natalie Wood mad, or *Blue Denim* (1959), a surprisingly frank film for its era featuring a teenage couple who risk their future by seeking out an abortion (though the word is never spoken).

Even *Gidget* spends more time wrestling with her libido than do Dee Dee and Frankie. In that film's opening scenes, Sandra Dee's heroine has no interest in joining her girlfriends for a "man hunt" at the beach, but by the end of the picture, now determined to lose her virginity, she throws herself at the Big Kahuna, an older beach bum played by Cliff Robertson, who ultimately puts on the brakes, leaving Gidget to complain to her mother the next morning, "I'm hopeless . . . I'll probably die an old maid and never have made the step." "The step?" her mother asks. "Aw, Mom, I could perish!" Gidget wails. "Last night, after all these hours of concerted effort, I came home as pure as the driven snow." Surprisingly, Mom isn't alarmed. Rather, like Judge Hardy before her, she's inwardly amused but empathetic, allowing that "a girl does have to become a woman" at some point, but then offering a bromide about true womanhood having more to do with bringing out "the best" in a man than just mere sex. However cringe inducing, the scene is franker and more nuanced than *Grease*'s "Look at Me, I'm Sandra Dee" ("Lousy with virginity") might have led you to believe.

AIP's bet—whether insight or intuition—was that teenage audiences didn't want frankness and nuance, that they wanted to laugh at and nudge each other over a few innuendos and have a good time without having to think through any of the implications. The bet was that they wanted a sex comedy without anything approaching the emotional mess and social freight of sex itself. In a 1969 essay in *Rolling Stone* about teen movies, Richard Staehling criticized the *Beach Party* pictures for their "super uptight sexual overtones," adding, "Never outside *Playboy* has such sick plastic sex been seen." That was meant as a put-down, but sixty-some years later, it speaks to the movies' time-capsule appeal as examples of pop art that are less blunt than a Tom Wesselmann nude, say, or even an issue of *Playboy*, but in their own way just as canny and cheerful about selling sex.

And however "uptight" Frankie and Dee Dee may or may not have been, the movie ends with them more or less where they started: happily in love, her virtue still intact (Funicello's as well), and with the question of marriage raised but now forgotten—in violation of every rule of romantic comedy dating back at least to Shakespeare. It was as if the characters had sensed adulthood lurking out in the ocean's colder depths and, feeling a chill, quickly paddled back to shore.

• • •

Beach Party was released in July 1963. According to Asher, it opened in
only three theaters, including the Astor in Times Square. He and Elizabeth
Montgomery went to check out the lines, but there weren't any: inside
the vast theater sat a mere four ticket buyers. "They had to turn down the
air conditioning," Asher claimed. But Manhattan and other cosmopolitan city centers were never likely territory for *Beach Party*'s relentless sun,
corny gags, and circumscribed naughtiness. AIP persisted with an aggressive advertising and promotional campaign—among the stunts urged on
local theater owners: "A MUST: Any girl showing up at the theatre dressed
only in a bikini . . . is admitted free!"—and the movie found its audience
in smaller towns and suburban drive-ins. An exhibitor in Houston with
multiple drive-ins wrote to Arkoff that the picture was outgrossing Paul
Newman's *Hud*, Jerry Lewis's *The Nutty Professor*, and Alfred Hitchcock's
The Birds. Altogether, it took in $6.4 million at the box office (roughly $64
million in 2024 dollars)—a nice enough figure, though hardly headline
making. But given its budget of $350,000, *Beach Party* was surely among
the most purely profitable pictures of the year. (*Cleopatra*, with Elizabeth
Taylor and Richard Burton, was the box office champ, with gross receipts
of $57.8 million, but its budget had been upwards of $44 million, and it
nearly bankrupted its studio, 20th Century Fox.)

The reviews for *Beach Party* were mostly unkind, but not unfair. *Time*:
"Makes Gidget's Roman misadventures look like a scene from *Tosca*."
Cue: "Puerile . . . Foolish . . . Best that can be said for this opus is that it
kept the youngsters out in the sun." (In 1963 tanning butters had not yet
been replaced by high-SPF sunblocks and warnings about skin cancer.)
Variety, with its eye on the bottom line and no need to impress anyone
with references to Puccini: "While many adults might find it a frightening
manifestation of the culture of our age, *Beach Party* has the kind of direct,
simple-minded cheeriness which should prove well nigh irresistible."

AIP immediately made plans for a sequel. Might Frankie *now* pop the
question? "The first inclination was to grow with the characters," Asher

recalled. "And I said, 'What are we going to grow with? This is a comic strip. They don't have to be a year older. They don't have to be in jobs now. It can be the longest summer on record.'"

The sickening prospect of employment was nevertheless raised by the follow-up, the just-as-good/bad/laissez-faire *Muscle Beach Party*, in order to give Frankie and Dee Dee something to argue about.

She: "You should be making your life count for something more than just the next big wave."

He (perhaps channeling *On the Road*'s Dean Moriarty): "Look, honey, the beach is free and the sky goes straight on up and your life is your own. Isn't that enough? I want it easy and I want it free. I want it without the ropes, squares, bills, or bombs . . . Now you swing with me on that or you don't swing at all."

But once again, where Frankie would have earned a comeuppance for such snotty fecklessness in a more conventional picture—in *Gidget*, even Kahuna comes to see that there's no future in beach bummery—*Muscle Beach*, like its predecessor, ends more or less where it began, Frankie and Dee Dee back in equilibrium, two scoops of vanilla ice cream that never melt. This not-coming-of-age movie's most memorable moment: thirteen-year-old Little Stevie Wonder (as he was then billed) making his first film appearance for a musical number. He is also the only Black cast member of note in the series, although in several films at least one African American can be seen on a board in filler shots of genuine surfers shooting curls and whatnot.

The longest summer on record ended up stretching over three years, with *Muscle Beach Party* and *Bikini Beach* both released in 1964, followed by *Beach Blanket Bingo* and *How to Stuff a Wild Bikini* in 1965; though neither directed by Asher nor set on the sand, AIP's *Pajama Party* (1964) and *Ski Party* (1965) were conceptually Beach-adjacent.* The larger stu-

---

*Some *Beach Party* filmographies also include AIP's James Bond parody, *Dr. Goldfoot and the Bikini Machine* (1965), and the horror spoof *The Ghost in the Invisible Bikini* (1966). As you can see, "bikini" had become the new "hot rod."

dios chased the trend as well, releasing sun 'n' fun quickies like Warner Bros.' *Palm Springs Weekend* (1963), Fox's *Surf Party* (1964), United Artists' *For Those Who Think Young* (1964), Columbia's *Ride the Wild Surf* (1964), and Paramount's *The Girls on the Beach* (1965). The genre garnered at least one adult fan. "I have recently fallen under the spell of teen surfing movies, an enthusiasm I should probably try to pass off as sociological. In fact, they amuse me," wrote twenty-nine-year-old Joan Didion in 1964, in her role as *Vogue*'s film critic. She went on to praise *Ride the Wild Surf* as "a first-rate surfer" before complaining about the movie's female roles: "Let me note in passing the real sexlessness and extreme passivity of these girls, who presumably embody virtues admired by their audience." In that sense, it had all been downhill since *Gidget*.

Asher dismissed the competition. "None of them succeeded because they were making them better," he said, echoing Louis B. Mayer's insight about not ruining the *Andy Hardy* series by improving it. Rival filmmakers erred, Asher continued, when they "put in parents. The reality of parents. What would really happen if kids spent the summer at the beach? Parents would be concerned about the whereabouts of their kids, their behavior, what they were involved in and so on. Our pictures were fantasies."

The genre peaked in 1965, when a dozen beach-party-style movies hit theaters to diminishing returns. As well, a *Gidget* TV series debuted on ABC that fall. Starring Sally Field, and with multiple episodes directed by Asher, it lasted one season. Perhaps not coincidentally, troop levels in Vietnam increased eightfold that same year: young people now had more on their minds than catching waves and dancing the Watusi. For many, it no doubt felt a little too topical when Avalon's absence from long stretches of *How to Stuff a Wild Bikini* (he was filming another AIP movie simultaneously) were explained by having Frankie called up for overseas Naval Reserve duty. A job, at last! In the movie, however, shipping out meant not Southeast Asia and the Viet Cong but the South Pacific, beautiful island girls, and unlucky Buster Keaton wearing a grass skirt as a "witch doctor." And how funny were the jokes to a draft-age boy without a college deferment? (Or to anyone, really?) *Mad* magazine writer Larry

Siegel may have been even more on point than he knew when he had one of the revelers in "Mad Visits a Typical Teenage Beach Movie" exclaim, "Hey, gang! I just heard World War III has started! In respect for the casualties, let's dance slower."

It was "time to move on to a new genre," Arkoff sensed. For AIP, that would be a cycle of outlaw biker movies that were far more violent, graphic, and dark than anything the studio had previously made or distributed, beginning in 1966 with *The Wild Angels*, which starred Peter Fonda, Bruce Dern, and Nancy Sinatra. *Devil's Angels* and *The Glory Stompers* followed in 1967, the latter with Dennis Hopper. AIP also dipped into psychedelia with *Riot on Sunset Strip* and *The Trip* (both 1967, the latter written by Jack Nicholson, no relation to Jim). Regrettably for the studio, it passed on a chance to produce what would prove to be the biggest biker movie of all: *Easy Rider*, starring Fonda, Hopper, and Jack Nicholson, and directed by Hopper, though in fairness, the project might have sounded too squirrelly—perhaps even fatally arty-farty—to turn a buck. (To my mind, it remains one of the most inexplicable blockbusters in Hollywood history.)

At any rate, none of these were teen movies per se, and with so many aspects of American life in upheaval in the late 1960s, with the stakes raised in Vietnam and on campuses and city streets, "the teenager" as an object of cultural fascination was largely elbowed aside by hippies, college radicals, and Black Panthers. On screen as well, the young had new avatars, with two films released in 1967 representing a paradigm shift: Faye Dunaway and Warren Beatty's bank robbers in *Bonnie and Clyde* were like Dee Dee and Frankie with machine guns, going perhaps a bit too far in their efforts to avoid steady paychecks and a mortgage; as the poster put it, "They're young . . . they're in love . . . and they kill people." Dustin Hoffman's Benjamin Braddock in *The Graduate* was Frankie a few years older and with a better education, but still not wanting a job and sunk into anomie so deep that he sleeps with some chick's mom. That film ends with an image of young lovers metaphorically lost when it comes to a future: a boy and a girl (in a wedding gown) on a bus to nowhere, the infatuation slowly draining from their faces as the camera refuses to look away or cut. See what happens when you commit?

Though the *Beach Party* movies had caught the decade's generation-gap zeitgeist earlier than most with their "no grown-ups allowed" fantasies, the concept had blown past its sell-by date faster than even AIP's disposability merchants likely predicted. There was, however, a kind of spiritual sequel to the series—its teen-centrism taken to a logical extreme. Released in the spring of 1968, AIP's *Wild in the Streets* was the story of a twenty-two-year-old rock star named Max Frost who becomes president of the United States after the voting age is lowered to fourteen. Along the way, Max and his followers dose the Washington, DC, water supply with LSD, decree a mandatory retirement age of thirty, and force everyone over the age of thirty-five into reeducation camps—all in the name of creating "the most hedonistic society on earth." (What that seems to mean in the context of this not-very-entertaining film is large groups of people lying around on groovy furniture waiting for an orgy that never happens.) Somehow, Hal Holbrook and Shelley Winters were dragooned into the cast as the latest models of adult schlubs; an actor named Christopher Jones, who had a brief career as the new James Dean of the late 1960s, played Max. The shock ending: Max confronts an even younger antagonist who dismisses him as "old," then turns to the camera and says, "We're going to put everyone over ten out of business."

It was as if AIP had bought the rights to *Teen-Age Tyranny* and rewritten it as sledgehammer satire. Even as a historical artifact, it is close to unwatchable—as sloppy as a *Beach Party* picture, but with bad-acid vibes instead of sunshine daydreams. You will likely feel bad for Winters, who gives the thankless role of Max's sweaty, hysterical mom her best shot; you may be happy to see Richard Pryor show up in a small role—it was only his second film.

In its day, the movie had its fans, including Renata Adler, then a critic at *The New York Times*, who inexplicably deemed it "by far the best American film of the year so far." A very pleased Arkoff later wrote that *Wild in the Streets* was "our biggest moneymaker of the antiestablishment pictures, thanks in part to good timing." By that he meant it premiered two months after Martin Luther King Jr.'s assassination and a week before Robert Kennedy's, and thus, as it rolled into theaters across the country, caught a slipstream of outrage, chaos, and revolt, ultimately pulling in $4 million at the box office. Arkoff could hear a *ka-ching!* over the sounds of screams, gunfire, breaking glass, and sirens.

5

GRAFFITI

American Graffiti is a beach picture, *x* years later. Well done.
—Sam Arkoff, claiming a sliver of credit for one of
the most profitable teen movies ever made

To mark the distance between 1962, the year *American Graffiti* takes place, and 1973, the year it was released, you could do worse than heed the example of Mackenzie Phillips, who was twelve when she played Carol, the movie's youngest character, a junior high school tagalong. Though Carol's clothes—shapeless jeans, an oversize T-shirt with a logo for the surfboard manufacturer Dewey Weber, and, worst of all, braces—mark her as terminally underaged, she wants to be seen as more mature than she is. At the first sign of success, however, when an older male character feigns sexual interest (he's actually trying to get rid of her), she panics and beats a swift retreat back to prepubesence. But that was the movie.

In real life, Phillips was the daughter of John Phillips, the songwriter and former member of the Mamas & the Papas, and the adults she knew encouraged—probably too mild a verb—precocity. *American Graffiti's* casting agent had discovered her onstage at the Troubadour, the venerable West Hollywood rock club, fronting a band made up of fellow junior high school students. "I was a crazy glitter kid, a David Bowie wannabe," she writes in her memoir, *High on Arrival*. She first saw *American Graffiti* at a special screening she attended with her dad. Her outfit that night included teetering six-inch white-patent-leather platform heels, and, in place of her eyebrows, which she'd shaved off, glittery, glam-rock lightning bolts. "We walked down the red carpet and took our seats in the theater," she writes. "My dad gave me a couple quaaludes, and I popped them all at once. All I remember from that first viewing is the opening credits, which started before the ludes kicked in . . . After that, the night is a blur. I was stoned off my ass. Maybe Dad felt guilty about the quaaludes. He kept passing me little silver spoonfuls of coke to help me wake up." She was now thirteen. (According to her memoir, when she was eighteen—and addicted to multiple drugs—her father raped her after she blacked out in a hotel room, which somehow led to a ten-year sexual relationship she describes as consensual.)

That chasm between the comparatively naïve teenage world of 1962 portrayed in *American Graffiti*, preoccupied with sock hops, zit cream, and chrome trim, and the decadence and abuse that marked Mackenzie Phillips's off-screen 1970s adolescence, extreme as it was,* is the film's underlying subject. It would be wrong to call the characters writer-director George Lucas created with co-screenwriters Gloria Katz and Willard Huyck innocents; the film is too wise for canned sentimentality. But these white, mostly middle-class kids move through their world protected by guardrails that would be long gone by 1973.

Like two of his four central male characters, Lucas was himself a member of the high school class of 1962. With *American Graffiti*, he was making not only a personal memory film but also a generational one, a de facto prequel to the likes of *The Graduate* and *Easy Rider*. The mere fact of conceiving a film about teenagers trying to make the most of the last night of summer before some of them head off to college, and setting that night not too long before John F. Kennedy's assassination—catalyst in the popular imagination for a decade of turbulence and revolt

---

*I don't mean to imply that every thirteen-year-old in 1973 did drugs with their parents.

(cue "For What It's Worth," "White Rabbit," and "Purple Haze" on the soundtrack)—created a "before" context that initial audiences understood even without being elbowed by the famous "where are they now?" coda. A ribbon of tragedy was baked into the premise.

Not that *American Graffiti* isn't fun. It is! It's a sharp, well-written, beautifully acted ensemble comedy, with a fantastic if then largely un-known cast, most of whom went on to significant careers. It's got the added fizz of boss cars, period clothes, and a soundtrack carpeted with vintage rock-and-roll hits from the likes of Chuck Berry, Del Shannon, the Platters, and Frankie Lymon and the Teenagers. The picture has an innovative structure, too, interweaving the stories of four main charac-ters (all boys; like most teen movies up to this point, *American Graffiti* shortchanged its girls). But all the same, it's a comedy with a melancholy undertow and a notion that it's shouldering a historical burden—and you don't title your picture *American Graffiti*, and then stick with it even in the face of studio resistance, if you're not making a Statement.

Unlike some artists, Lucas wasn't reticent about interpreting his own work. "Remember, the film is about 1962," he told an interviewer. "A lot of people say it's a '50s movie—the innocent '50s. What it's about is the end of the '50s." In another interview, he expanded on that thought, while conflating the stability of his own childhood with the nation's:

It's about a period of transition in history in America where in one year you had a president that a lot of kids admired, were proud of; you had a certain kind of rock 'n' roll music; a certain kind of country where you could believe in things. You were also a teenager, eighteen years old, going to school, living at home. You had a certain kind of life. But in the next two years, everything changed: no longer were you a teenager, you were an adult going to college or doing whatever you were going to do. The government changed radically, and everybody's attitude toward it changed radically. Drugs came in. Although it had always been there, a war surfaced as an issue. The music changed completely. *Graffiti* is about the fact that you have to accept these

changes—they were on the horizon and if you didn't, you had a problem. You know, the little bough breaks. The willow bends with the
wind and stays on the tree. You try to fight it . . . and you lose. You're
not going to remain eighteen forever.

I'd argue that *American Graffiti* was attempting to do for baby boomers
what the novel and film *From Here to Eternity*, set on an army base in
Hawaii in the months leading up to Pearl Harbor, did for their parents—a
portrait of the not-so-calm before the storm, shadowed by retroactive grief.
Rolling Stone saw the movie that way, too. The magazine, published and
co-founded by Jann Wenner (high school class of 1963), was then only
six years old and still presiding as the counterculture's journal of record.
Its review of *American Graffiti* was written by the critic Jon Landau (also
class of '63 and future producer and manager of Bruce Springsteen). In
Landau's words: "The film is [Lucas's] account of the formative years of
the tribal village . . . I hesitate to call *American Graffiti* a masterpiece . . .
But taken on its own terms, it is a brilliantly original conception of not
just the nature of the past but the roots of the present—a very immediate past and present that readers of this particular magazine should find
extraordinarily significant and moving."
    Baby boomers may not have been the first cohort of young people to
have a sense of themselves as a singular generation, but they were surely
the first to think of and refer to themselves as a tribal village—a self-
dramatizing streak that *American Graffiti* both exemplifies and pokes fun
at. Writing in *Time*, the critic Jay Cocks (class of '62 and a future screenwriting partner of Martin Scorsese's) used similar language to Landau's,
praising the movie for capturing the "tribal energy of the teenage 1950s,
but also the listlessness and resignation that underscored it all . . . Few
films have shown quite so well the eagerness, the sadness, the ambitions
and small defeats of a generation of young Americans."
    Less demographically invested critics also loved Lucas's picture. To
The Atlantic, it was "one of the best American films about adolescents
ever made." (The competition wasn't all that fierce, as we have seen.) In

The New York Times, Stephen Farber called it "easily the best movie of the year so far. Beyond that, I think it is the most important American movie since *Five Easy Pieces*—maybe since *Bonnie and Clyde*." The comparatively unimpressed *Los Angeles Times* hailed *American Graffiti* as merely "one of the most important American films of the year."

And here I need to repeat: the movie is not a dissertation. It's fun, a crowd pleaser, even at times too eager to be loved. Made for $750,000—a bare-minimum budget for a period film with complex logistics involving cars and night shoots on location—*American Graffiti* ultimately took in $112 million at the box office (or $793 million in 2024 dollars—what we now call Marvel money). All told, it was the third-most-popular film of the year, behind *The Exorcist* ($193 million) and *The Sting* ($160 million)—a feat all the more impressive given that the young director's one previous film, a forbidding dystopian drama, had been a flop, and that the only known quantity in his even younger cast was Ronny Howard, as he was then billed, an aging child star who for eight seasons had played Sheriff Andy Taylor's freckled, gee-whiz son, Opie, on *The Andy Griffith Show*. When the Academy Award nominations were announced, *American Graffiti* received five, including Best Picture, Best Director, and Best Original Screenplay. *The Sting* ended up winning in all three of those categories, but still, this was rare and heady territory for a teen movie.

Sam Arkoff's remark in his autobiography that Lucas's movie was "a beach picture, *x* years later" betrays a hint of jealousy, I'd wager, for the film's profits if not its critical standing. He's correct on the surface: *America Graffiti* is about kids doing kid stuff without a care about what adults think, with Chevys and asphalt replacing surfboards and sand. But the difference between *American Graffiti* and what no one at the time called the *Beach Party*–verse is the difference between exploitation and understanding, product and art. Lucas's film is a movie that *likes* and respects teenagers. It treats its kids as normal people with conflicted motivations, not as hormonal goofballs with only one thing on their minds—but also not as tragic victims like the tormented case studies in *Rebel Without a Cause* and *Splendor in the Grass*. *American Graffiti* finds humor in teen social rituals, and in the gaps between how its characters want to be seen and who they really are, but all the same, the movie grants them dignity. Even Terry, nicknamed "Toad," the awkward, overeager junior who tries to hang with the graduating seniors but can't handle his car, his date, or his liquor, is allowed to endure his serial humiliations with good-natured grace, humbled but never defeated.

One key to the movie's success is that Lucas, aside from being a talented, even visionary filmmaker,* was also the first director of a teen movie to have been a postwar teenager himself. As he passed through social way stations in high school, he himself had at one point been a nerd like Toad. He had also haunted auto shops and drag strips with the likes of John Milner, the too-cool guy with the fastest car in town who feels time catching up with him. Eventually, Lucas matured into a Curt Henderson type—the searching, self-doubting, quasi-intellectual ambivalent about college. By Lucas's own account, he had never been a Steve Bollander, the confident, self-satisfied class president with a cheerleader girlfriend, but he had surely known Steve Bollanders. In making his film about these four characters, he once said he had "held a ten-year reunion with myself—or rather with my teenage fantasies . . . *American Graffiti* is how I remember my youth—with four years compressed into one night." Contrast that with the months of research Nicholas Ray conducted to get under the skin of his characters; it's not a put-down of *Rebel Without a Cause* to note that *American Graffiti* feels more organic, more lived in. Both movies are felt deeply, but felt differently.

"I wasn't going to make fun of it," Lucas said in yet another interview, "it" being his own adolescence. (For a filmmaker often thought of as aloof, Lucas once spent a lot of time talking to the press.) He had a fine example of what he didn't want in *Summer of '42*, a big hit released in 1971. Framed as a middle-aged man's reminiscence about the summer he lost his virginity—inexplicably, to a grieving war widow (played

---

*You may not like his movies, but you can't argue against their impact on American film, on the kinds of pictures that get made and the way they get made.

by Jennifer O'Neill, a CoverGirl model with neither more nor less presence than that CV implies)—the picture plays like a dirty version of *A Christmas Story*, the corny but beloved 1983 memory film that was set two or three years before *Summer of '42*. To my taste, both movies hit the jeepers-weren't-we-dopes button way too hard, ostensibly affectionate yet somehow condescending.

Lucas was determined not to look down his nose at his characters or treat them like curios. "I'm glad I was a teenager," he said. "I enjoyed being a teenager. I don't hang my head and say, 'Well, we were just a bunch of dumb kids then.' We weren't; we were just kids, and being a kid is great!"

In its director's telling, he made *American Graffiti* only because Francis Coppola more or less dared him to. But before I can get to that, I have to recount some New Hollywood backstory/mythology . . .

Lucas and Coppola first met in 1967, on the set of Coppola's second movie, *Finian's Rainbow*. This celebrated encounter took place on the Warner Bros. lot in Burbank, where Lucas, then a twenty-two-year-old graduate student at USC's film school, had a six-month scholarship that entitled him to hang out at the studio and observe anything of interest. At the time, with young audience tastes disrupting box office assumptions and studio lots littered with the sad carcasses of failed big-budget musicals and last-gasp biblical epics, there wasn't a lot going on at Warner, aside from *Finian's Rainbow*, an effort to split the difference between old and new by hiring a shaggy young director, Coppola, then twenty-seven, to adapt a dated Broadway musical *and* somehow get Fred Astaire and Petula Clark to make sense together on screen. (Alas, no, they didn't.)

According to Lucas's biographer Dale Pollock, Lucas arrived at the studio on the very day that Jack Warner, the last surviving Golden Age mogul (he had founded the studio in 1923 with his three brothers), "cleaned out his office and left," having sold most of his stake in the company. If true, that stands as an almost too-perfect passing of the torch to the rising generation of so-called movie brat directors, most of whom, like Coppola, Lucas, and Martin Scorsese, were film school graduates (UCLA, USC, and NYU, respectively). According to Lucas, he and Coppola quickly bonded because "we were like the only two people on the set who were under fifty, and we were also the only two people on the set who had beards"—facial hair, the right kind, being an important social signifier in 1967. (Jack Warner's thin, elegant mustache was the wrong kind.)

Coppola, though only five years older, became a mentor to Lucas, or at least a friend, and they made big plans together. *Finian's Rainbow*, released in 1968, was a flop, as was Coppola's next film for the studio, *The Rain People* (1969), and yet, full of boundless, possibly manic enthusiasm, he managed to convince Warner Bros. to fund development for a slate of films to be produced by an independent studio he had set up in San Francisco and named American Zoetrope; Lucas, a co-founder, was the vice president. Coppola's plan was to make the kinds of cutting-edge, even experimental films that, in the wake of *Easy Rider*'s surprise success, were deemed commercial for a miraculous minute or two.

The first Zoetrope picture was Lucas's debut as a director: *THX 1138*, an expansion of his award-winning student short about a man escaping from a futuristic underground dystopia. The feature-length version, released by Warner in 1971, is long on creepy atmosphere and striking production design, with a serviceable clothesline of a plot, but unfortunately not much in the way of characterization—perhaps the inevitable by-product of making a film about a dehumanized society where everyone has shaved heads, wears identical white pajamas, is narcotized, and has a serial number for a name.

So yes: cutting edge, even experimental, but not without a few stray pleasures. Lucas intended the film, in part, as a satire of consumer culture, and it has some witty moments. It also has a cool car chase at the end, zooming through a series of tunnels and prefiguring the drag race that climaxes *American Graffiti*, not to mention Luke Skywalker's swoop through the Death Star's trenches at the end of *Star Wars*, the movie that would turn Lucas into a mogul himself. But *THX 1138*'s true selling points are an early performance by Robert Duvall, his first lead role in a film (though he doesn't get to show much more range as the title character than he did as Boo Radley in his very first picture, *To Kill a Mockingbird*); and a directorial style that plunges the audience headfirst into the film's world, its sights and also, crucially, its sounds, while trusting the audience will find their way. (The movie's pioneering sound design was by Walter Murch, a friend of Lucas's from USC who also wrote the screenplay from Lucas's story.) It's an immersive style Lucas would refine and put to good use in *American Graffiti* and *Star Wars*, but here may have further alienated moviegoers from a film that was never going to be a crowd pleaser.

THX 1138 received respectful reviews when it was released in the US, and a screening at Cannes was well received, but the box office take was suitably grim. Warner Bros., knowing it had a dud on its hands, had soured on American Zoetrope months earlier, canceling the rest of its slate and leaving Coppola deeply in debt. Happily for posterity, he was thus forced to take a paycheck gig writing and directing *The Godfather*, a masterpiece made grudgingly.

Lucas, meanwhile, was casting about for a new project, concerned that his nascent career might already be over. He had been developing *Apocalypse Now*, the Vietnam epic by way of Joseph Conrad that Coppola would eventually usurp, radically rewrite, and direct. But a downer war movie with an English-class pedigree didn't strike anyone as an ideal follow-up to a chilly futuristic muddle. In an interview with author Peter Biskind, Lucas recalled Coppola challenging him: "Don't be so weird, try to do something that's human . . . Everyone thinks you're a cold fish, but you can be a warm and funny guy, make a warm and funny movie."

Coppola wasn't the only one pushing Lucas. His wife, Marcia Lucas, a film editor, told Biskind, "After *THX* went down the toilet, I never said, 'I told you so,' but I reminded George that I warned him it hadn't involved the audience emotionally. He always said, 'Emotionally involving the audience is easy. Anybody can do it blindfolded, get a little kitten and have some guy wringing its neck.' All he wanted to do was abstract filmmaking, tone poems, collections of images. So finally George said to me, 'I'm gonna show you how easy it is.'" As he later put it: "I did *Graffiti* to prove I could do a warm movie about real people." So that became another thing he and Coppola had in common: they both made smash hits through gritted teeth.

The warm and funny movie about real-ish people that Lucas eventually came up with was rooted in Modesto, his small hometown in California's Central Valley. He was born there as George Lucas Jr., in 1944, placing him just outside the baby boom generation, but close enough to be considered a fellow traveler. His father, George Sr., owned a stationery and office supply store, which he expected his namesake to take over one day. By the son's lights, his father was "a very old-fashioned guy . . . kind of a classic small-town businessman who you'd see in a movie." Lucas cast his hometown in similarly generic pop-cultural terms: "Modesto was really Norman Rockwell, *Boy's Life* magazine . . . raking leaves on Saturday afternoons and having bonfires. Just very classic Americana."

Lucas was a lousy student through boyhood and adolescence. He wasn't popular, but he wasn't asocial, either. His passions were comic books and rock and roll, and he amassed sizable collections of both, as well as an autographed picture of Elvis Presley that he hung on his wall. Dale Pollock, his biographer, offers this description of his early high school routine: "Lucas got home from school around 3:00 p.m. and headed right for his room. He got out his collection of 45s and 78s . . . and played them, one after the other, for hours on end. Sitting on his bed, he read comic books, ate Hershey bars, and drank Cokes." Which might not be everyone's idea of a well-spent youth, but it's not bad preparation for conceiving and directing both *American Graffiti* and *Star Wars*.

Lucas got into photography when his father, strict yet also indulgent, bought him a 35mm camera and let him convert a spare bathroom into a darkroom. But true love arrived with an exhaust pipe. "My teenage years, they were completely devoted to cars," he recalled. "That was the most important thing in my life from the ages of fourteen to twenty." His first set of wheels was a motorcycle that he'd race around the thirteen-acre walnut orchard on the outskirts of town, where the family had moved when Lucas was fifteen and his dad's store was flourishing. George Sr. soon bought his son a yellow Fiat Bianchina, a stubby little sedan with a two-cylinder engine that looked like something Jacques Tati's Monsieur Hulot might drive. The hope was that Lucas wouldn't be able to do much damage to himself or others in a vehicle so adamantly non-sporty, but the teenager, who eventually landed an after-school job at a local repair shop, managed to soup up the Fiat. Modesto's rabid car culture had given him the social identity—"a juvenile delinquent of sorts," he claimed—which he had previously lacked. He started hanging out with the Faros, a car club that had gang-like pretensions, though Lucas, in his words, was tolerated "more as a mascot than as a full-fledged member."

However aspirational his cool-kid status, he did develop credibility as a street racer while also piling up speeding tickets, another bona fide. Thinking he might become a professional driver, he began competing in autocross events—races on temporary tracks set up on big empty parking lots—and won a few. Socially, however, he remained more Terry the Toad than John Milner. Alan Grant, a few years older than Lucas and a star on the autocross circuit—a model for the Milner character—later described Lucas this way: "He was always jabbering . . . 'What about this? And doing that?' And you know, we didn't take him very seriously. But we liked him."

Cars provided a literal vehicle for teenage socializing in Modesto thanks to the phenomenon known as cruising: a kind of party on wheels in which kids slowly drove back and forth on the town's main streets, showing off, gossiping, flirting, killing time, holding out hope for action of any sort. One writer refers to the ritual, which had sprung up in Southern California in the postwar years and spread across the country, as "a constantly moving town square." Better yet, cruising meant freedom, not only from parents and other adults—cops were the only grown-ups cruisers had to feign deference to—but freedom even from some of high school's normal social restraints.

Lucas offered this paean to cruising to *Seventeen* magazine after *American Graffiti* came out:

When I was eighteen in Modesto, California, it was the largest city within forty miles big enough to have two high schools, so you didn't know everybody and the only way you could meet girls was to cruise around all night. There were at least a thousand kids who came from all over the valley, from San Francisco, Stockton, Sacramento. We had wall to wall cars! You'd park your car and ride around with other guys. I spent most of my money on gas. In the sixties, the social structure in high school was so rigid that it didn't really lend itself to meeting new people. You had the football crowd and the government crowd and the society country-club crowd and the hoods that hung out over at the hamburger stand. You were in a clique and that was it; you couldn't go up and you couldn't go down. But once you got on the streets it was everyone for himself and cars became the way of structuring the situation. If you had one, it gave you a new position. You didn't have to be president of the class or the toughest guy around; you could just have the neatest car!

This phase of Lucas's life nearly came to as abrupt an ending as could be, three days before he was scheduled to graduate from high school, with that milestone in question due to several gaps and black marks on his transcript. He had gone to the local library in an aborted attempt at writing a last-minute makeup paper. Driving home in his Fiat, he began a left turn into the entrance to his family's property and was T-boned by a speeding Chevy Impala driven by another teenager. Lucas's Fiat rolled three times before slamming into a walnut tree with such force the tree was said to have been knocked back a foot or two. (I was skeptical, but apparently this can happen when an impact partially uproots the tree.) The Fiat was totaled; Lucas likely survived only because the racing belt he had installed didn't do its job and he was thrown clear.* A collapsed lung, a few minor fractures, and a four-month-long recuperation, most of it spent

---

*California didn't require cars to have seat belts until 1964; seat belts became a federal requirement in 1968.

in bed, was not that steep a price to pay, all things considered. Even the officious ticket he received for making an illegal left turn was outweighed by the fact that his high school ended up granting him a pity diploma.

And aside from providing the seed for *American Graffiti*'s final act, his accident changed the trajectory of Lucas's life. As George Sr. told Dale Pollock, "He saw his own mortality." Once recovered, he enrolled at Modesto Junior College, now taking his studies more seriously, especially anthropology and sociology, two subjects that captured his imagination. He also reengaged with photography and began thinking about going to art school. Not previously an avid moviegoer—his viewing habits had been mostly confined to television—he discovered cinema and started traveling as far afield as San Francisco and Berkeley, over two hours away, to catch the art films and foreign movies that would never make it to Modesto.

His passions all seemed to merge when Lucas met the cinematographer Haskell Wexler, a racing enthusiast, through Alan Grant, the autocross star. (Lucas hadn't given up his love of fast cars, though he now mostly photographed them, or filmed them with an 8mm movie camera, another gift from his father.) Lucas had applied half-heartedly to USC film school, expecting he would end up at San Francisco State studying English or sociology. Wexler, who would soon win the first of his two Oscars, for his work on *Who's Afraid of Virginia Woolf?*, encouraged Lucas to think more seriously about USC, where Wexler had connections and put in a good word. Lucas got in, left Modesto for Los Angeles, and never looked back, except to mine his adolescence for material a few years later.

At USC, he found his people—including fellow students and future collaborators Walter Murch, John Milius, and Willard Huyck—as well as his life's work. He had "the calling," as Wexler put it. George Sr. didn't approve of film school, though he paid for it. The father-son relationship was growing contentious, and would provide fodder for the galactic familial struggle chronicled in the string of movies Lucas made after *American Graffiti*.

• • •

His junior college brush with anthropology provided conceptual scaf-
folding as Lucas began reflecting on his high school years for a possible
follow-up to *THX 1138*. "I was always fascinated by the cultural phenomenon of cruising, that whole teenage mating ritual," he would later explain,
perhaps channeling Bob Cummings's professor from *Beach Party*. "It's really more interesting than primitive Africa or ancient New Guinea—and
much, much weirder." Two observations: that quote is from four decades
ago; and the detached, even clinical tone indicates just how far Lucas had
to travel to create a warm and funny movie, even one conjured from his
own childhood.

Determined to make only the films he wanted to make, he turned
down several director-for-hire jobs. Another project he had been incubating was an adaptation of the *Flash Gordon* comic strip. He and the producer Gary Kurtz (who would produce *American Graffiti*, *Star Wars*, and
The Empire Strikes Back) approached King Features, which owned the
rights to the strip, but the syndicate was asking too high a price—and perhaps holding out for Federico Fellini, who was supposedly interested in
the property as well. (On balance, I would argue, we should be happy that
Lucas was forced to dream up his own space opera, and regretful that the
world was denied, for whatever ultimate reason, *Fellini's Flash Gordon*.)

Meanwhile, Lucas approached Willard Huyck, his USC film school
friend, and Huyck's wife and writing partner, Gloria Katz, a graduate of
the rival crosstown film school at UCLA, about collaborating on what
Lucas initially described to them as "a film about the 1950s, a rock 'n' roll
movie." Huyck's qualifications for writing a teen movie included not just
his talent and comparative youth but the fact that he had been rewriting
scripts for AIP. (He and Katz had been introduced at the premiere of AIP's
The Wild Angels, directed by Roger Corman—a movie-brat meet-cute.)
Lucas, Huyck, and Katz drafted several treatments, which demonstrated
that although this new project was intended to be more character driven
than *THX 1138*, Lucas hadn't quit his fondness for "tone poems" and

"collections of images." This table setter, for instance: "An endless parade of kids bombing around in dagoed, moondisked, flamed, chopped, tuck-and-rolled machines rumbling through a seemingly adult-less, heat-drugged little town . . . The passing chrome-flashing cars become a visual choreography."

Lucas eventually interested United Artists in the project, and the studio agreed to put up money for a script, but by this point Huyck and Katz had been offered the chance to write *and* direct a low-budget zombie movie and took it. (*Messiah of Evil* was released to neither acclaim nor much box office six months before *American Graffiti*.) Lucas hired another former USC classmate to write a full script but was unhappy with the end results, which apparently veered too close to an AIP-style hot-rod picture. So Lucas, despite claiming to hate writing—"It's very, very hard for me. I don't feel I have a natural talent for it"—took a stab at the screenplay himself, holed up in a home office and spinning his high school 45s for inspiration.

Music was essential to the film's conception. The intro to one of the treatments is adamant: "American Graffiti is a MUSICAL. It has singing and dancing, but is not a musical in the traditional sense because the characters in the film neither sing nor dance." Now that *American Graffiti* exists, one gets what he meant, but at the time, his insistence on describing the film that way confused studio heads and, once auditions began, members of his cast. Ron Howard, when he first met with Lucas, apologetically told the director that he had no song-and-dance skills, despite having appeared in the movie version of *The Music Man* when he was eight. "That's okay," Lucas responded. "It's a musical in that it's built *around* songs. The songs are playing on the radio. They're part of the atmosphere, the setting for the characters."

What Lucas was after, and what the film ultimately captures, is the centrality of music in teenagers' lives, in this case a generation tethered to their cars' AM radios. The soundtrack, composed entirely of vintage hits—a radical concept in an era when films were still mostly scored with orchestral music—was intended to function a bit like a more atmospheric

Greek chorus, though the songs would all be diegetic (i.e., coming from the characters' car radios or some other source on screen). Lucas would later say that he wrote the screenplay while listening to specific songs over and over, the rhythms of the music affecting the tempos and emotions of the scene, the kind of symbiosis that doesn't usually happen until a film gets into the editing room. The finished picture would include forty-two songs, whittled down from a hoped-for eighty, the licensing fees accounting for roughly a tenth of its $750,000 budget.

Unfortunately, UA passed on Lucas's script, as did most of the other studios in town, including AIP. A draft in the collection of the Motion Picture Academy's Margaret Herrick Library, dated December 1971, hints at why. Though the narrative hews close to the finished film's, aside from being curiously set in 1959 rather than 1962 (the characters briefly discuss Richard Nixon's odds of getting the GOP presidential nomination in 1960), the dialogue in Lucas's solo draft is as stilted as anything he would later force on Anakin Skywalker and Padmé Amidala in the *Star Wars* prequels. For instance, the opening scene, as the four main characters gather in the drive-in parking lot, with Steve and Curt preparing to enjoy one last night of cruising before taking off the next morning for college "back east":

STEVE

This is it! Our last night in
"Turkeyburg." Real world here we
come! You ready?

CURT

All packed. But you know, I kinda
hate to leave. I'm going to miss
tooling around here every night.

STEVE

Well I'm not! This town is lost
in the dark ages. Once I get out,
I'm never coming back . . .

Bad writing aside, another drawback in studios' eyes was the film's unusual structure, which jumps back and forth among the four main characters over the course of one long night—a group portrait rather than the usual close-up on one or maybe two main characters. "When *American Graffiti* was first presented, it was an extremely unusual film. It was very experimental," Lucas told *Rolling Stone* in 1987. "No one used music that way, no one cut movies that way. Now even *The Love Boat* is told that way, but then, telling separate stories and intercutting them was unthinkable . . . I felt it was inherent in the story." From today's vantage point, you could argue that *American Graffiti* not only paved the way for *The Love Boat* but the entirety of peak TV, more or less, from *The Sopranos* on. (Veteran soap opera writers and nineteenth-century novelists might also raise their hands for credit here.)

There was one more thing—the very last thing—that made Lucas's movie a hard sell: the coda that reveals how the four lead male characters spend the rest of the sixties, which in Lucas's early script, aside from date changes, is almost exactly the same as in the finished film. Willard Huyck and Gloria Katz, who returned to rewrite Lucas's draft when they finished shooting their zombie movie, thought this was a bad idea, too downbeat an ending for a fun movie. "We would always take out that 'tag,' and George would put it back in," Huyck said. "Even when it was shot, we said, 'George, we hate it,' and he said, 'Well, we can take it out later.'" Huyck and Katz also felt that if the movie *had* to end that way, it was a mistake not to include what happened to the main female characters. Lucas resisted this as well, insisting the film was really the story of the four boys. Moreover, adding the girls would mean adding a second title card, which Lucas felt would have dragged out the ending and spoiled its punch. "My usual problem of sacrificing content for form," he told Pollock.

By Lucas's happy admission, the Huyck-Katz rewrite was a significant upgrade over his draft: "They didn't change the structure; what they did was improve the dialogue, make it funnier, more human, truer." The characters, he said in another interview, "were cardboard cutouts in my script, non-people. Bill and Gloria made it one hundred percent better."

With a workable script in hand, Lucas's agent took a last shot with Universal, where Ned Tanen, a vice president of film production, had been tasked with putting together a slate of low-budget youth-oriented movies. At the time he was pitched *American Graffiti*, he would have been forty or forty-one, more than ten years older than Lucas but still youngish by the era's studio executive standards. Moreover, he'd been a gearhead in high school and a record executive earlier in his career: he loved cars, he loved rock and roll, and he had an affinity for youth movies. (He would go on to champion or produce *Animal House, Sixteen Candles, The Breakfast Club, Ferris Bueller's Day Off,* and *St. Elmo's Fire.*) Tanen liked the script, and was charmed when Lucas came in for a meeting with a cassette containing a bunch of the songs he planned to use on the soundtrack. He was taken, too, with the film's ambition. "It's about every kid you ever went to school with," he said years later. "It's about everything that happened, or didn't happen to you, or that you fantasize or remember as having happened to you."

Tanen agreed to make the movie for $750,000, with the stipulation that a named producer be brought on board to backstop the film and lend credibility. With *The Godfather* having been released in March of 1972, Coppola's was now the biggest name in Hollywood. Hindsight makes it difficult to picture him as a stabilizing force, but this was a very specific and unusual era. Coppola agreed to produce and the deal was signed.

American Graffiti was shot on a compressed twenty-eight-day schedule, mostly at night, with several small Northern California cities, primarily Petaluma, standing in for the Modesto of 1962. Ron Howard, in a memoir he co-wrote with his brother, Clint, describes Lucas's directorial style:

> Take after take, the only direction that George gave was "Action!," "Cut!," and "Terrific."
>
> I approached him for a word. "George," I said politely, "you're saying, 'Action, cut, terrific' for every take, and then you change angles and say, 'Action, cut, terrific' again."

"Mm-hmm," said George.

"Am I giving you everything you need?" I asked. "Is there something more I can do? Because I'm happy to take some direction."

George matter-of-factly explained, "I don't really have time to direct now. I'm just gathering up lots of footage, then I'll direct in the editing room." He added, "That's why I cast you all so meticulously. It took me six months to find the right mix of people for what I want. And six months to find the right cars."

It was at this moment that it hit me: the cars were just as important to George as the actors. Or rather, they were actors to him, playing characters just as his droids and spaceships would do in the Star Wars movies.

Lucas had indeed gone about casting the film meticulously and methodically. Howard, before he was cast as Steve, was called in for six auditions. He was asked to do improvisations; a chemistry read with Cindy Williams, who would play Laurie, Steve's cheerleader girlfriend; a readthrough of the script with the entire cast; and finally an audition on film, with Haskell Wexler as the cinematographer.* The idea, as Lucas explained to Howard, was to assemble a cast of actors with such collective skill and chemistry that he could essentially ignore them. "He stood 'em up and shot 'em" is how Coppola described Lucas's directorial style. Or as Williams later put it, "He was happy to get whatever he could from us, like a guy on his first date."

Howard aside, for most of the cast the movie was indeed a get-to-know-you. Appearing in their first significant starring roles were Williams; Richard Dreyfuss (Curt); Paul Le Mat (John); Mackenzie Phillips (Carol, the junior high school "twerp" who John is tricked into cruising with);

---

*Wexler wouldn't officially serve in that role on the film but was brought in as a "visual consultant" when Lucas was dissatisfied with footage from the first few nights of shooting: "I wasn't getting the garish look I wanted. Haskell came in and made it look exactly the way I wanted." Wexler would spend the rest of the shoot flying to the set every evening from Los Angeles, where he had daytime commitments.

Charles Martin Smith (Toad); and Candy Clark (Debbie, the "bitchin' babe" who Toad picks up with the line, "Hey did anyone ever tell you you look just like Connie Stevens?"). In smaller but indelible roles were Harrison Ford (Bob Falfa, the hot-rodder from out of town who's gunning for a showdown with John) and Suzanne Somers (the mystery blonde driving a white T-Bird who Curt fixates on). It was a group with a lot of future mileage.

As Howard intuited, the director had "cast" the movie's wheels just as meticulously. Like all smart costuming and set design, the cars chosen for *American Graffiti* serve multiple storytelling purposes, indicating not just the characters' taste or socioeconomic status, but also their personalities, their significance to the film. Jack DeWitt, a poet and novelist who knows far more about early-'60s teen car culture than I do, published a terrific essay on precisely this subject in *The American Poetry Review*. His description of the customized 1958 Impala that Steve bestows on Toad, for safekeeping, at the beginning of the movie:

> It's a pretty car, a typical high school custom of the early '60s. Not highly modified, it is merely nosed and decked . . . with a nice paint job—icebox white with crimson-fogged accents . . . It is a completely conventional car within [customizing circles]. There is nothing about it that suggests any risk or personal vision, yet it is perfectly acceptable, even admirable, because it is done in perfect taste. The car suggests that Steve is all surface with little depth. He makes a good appearance.

Right there, not incidentally, is the "slavish devotion to form" that Tom Wolfe referenced in his descriptions of the kids dancing to the hully-gully band at the Burbank Teen Fair.

By way of contrast to Steve and his Impala:

> Curt, the scholarship-winning intellectual, drives a very unusual Citroën 2CV. This is not an obvious choice. It is not a VW or MG that might connect him to another taste culture—brains or preps. So

completely outside conventional car cultures is the Citroën that it sets
Curt apart as a true individual . . . [It] tells us that, unlike Steve, he will
make his decision on his own.

Back on the streets of Petaluma, there were a couple of minor car-related
mishaps that could have been much worse—a ding or two, automotive
and human, but no one and no vehicle was seriously injured. Otherwise,
the shoot seems to have been as efficient as Lucas could have hoped. The
main hurdle for most of the cast and crew was staying up all night, night
after night. On one occasion, the director was found curled up asleep in
a car trunk. Twelve-year-old Mackenzie Phillips learned to drink coffee,
a comparatively mild vice in her constellation. She had been delivered
to the set without a parent or any other kind of adult guardian. (The producer Gary Kurtz ended up looking after her.) "I didn't really know what
the movie was exactly," she wrote in her memoir. "Was it an educational
movie? An after-school special? . . . It just didn't occur to me that I would
be filming a major motion picture."

She wasn't the only cast member who didn't quite get what the film
was, or was going to be. "We didn't really know what we had when we
were filming *American Graffiti*," Howard wrote. Richard Dreyfuss once
told me he thought it was going to be just another dumb teensploitation
picture; he was happy to have a job.

When the movie was finished—on time and on budget—Universal
didn't know what it had, either. At one point, the studio considered releasing it only to drive-ins or, worse, handing it off to television, which in
1970s media terms was one step above euthanasia. A test screening was
held in San Francisco for a mostly youthful audience. By all accounts, it
went smashingly, the audience laughing, cheering, applauding throughout. It should have been a triumph. But Ned Tanen, the executive who
had green-lit the project, was at the screening, seeing the film for the
first time, and he hated it. "He said it was an embarrassment," Lucas remembered. The director and his collaborators, including Coppola, were
stunned. According to Lucas, an angry Coppola "just blew his top" and

dressed Tanen down: "This poor kid has worked his ass off for you, making a really terrific movie the audience loved, and for no money at all. And you can't even say thank you to this kid, at least for bringing the picture in on schedule." Coppola then pulled out a checkbook. "I'll buy the picture back right now," he shouted. "I'll write a check now. I think it's a great film and I want it back."

Tanen declined to take Coppola up on the offer.* But Universal insisted that Lucas reedit the film and ultimately forced him to trim four minutes, which enraged the director, who had previously endured cuts Warner Bros. had made to *THX 1138* against his will.† "Compromise is one of the worst pains you can suffer," he complained at the time—a sentiment that, while debatable, would drive him, in the wake of *Star Wars*, to build a movie fiefdom all his own in Marin County, four hundred miles north of LA, a move that fulfilled Coppola's dream of independence, if not Coppola's vision for it, or Coppola's own freedom.

While *American Graffiti* was for the most part ecstatically received by audiences and critics, Pauline Kael, at *The New Yorker*, offered a prominent dissent, and at considerable length. She hit the movie hard—and fairly—for ignoring its female characters in the where-are-they-now wrap-up: "For women the end of a picture is a cold slap . . . This is one of those bizarre omissions that tell you what really goes on in men filmmakers' heads and what women—who are, for the first time in movie history,

---

*"That's Francis. Francis does that," Lucas told the journalist Sam Kashner years later. "He would have written them a check for a million dollars on the spot. I mean, he didn't have the million dollars in the bank, but he would've written the check anyway."

†The cuts to *American Graffiti* were restored for rereleases. The trims had included a scene in which a manic used-car salesman tries to buttonhole Toad and a sequence in which Steve, at the high school hop, insults an officious teacher who doesn't realize that Steve has graduated and is no longer disciplinable. The added scenes are schtickier than the rest of the film and don't add much, so my hot take is that Universal was right in the first place.

half the moviegoing audience—bitterly (or unconsciously) swallow." She also pointed out the picture's lack of diversity, though this was perhaps less a criticism of the movie itself than an objection to its reception as a generational statement, all the "tribal village" business indulged in by "middle-class white boys whose memories have turned into pop." It hardly undercuts Kael's point to note that the film's high school hop scene delivers a smattering of Black and Asian extras; indeed, as the teen movie evolved over the next few decades, dances and proms would prove an easy and venerable way to sprinkle mostly white casts with token diversity.

Kael herself saw *American Graffiti* on a teen movie continuum and noted a link between the four central characters and their forebears. "Andy Hardy had all these boys' troubles: he was the runt . . . the popular freckle-face . . . the rash driver . . . and the introspective protagonist. Scared innocence (male division) is standard stuff, and there's no reason Andy Hardy shouldn't be divvied up and set to rock." But she was baffled by why young audiences saw the film as "the sum of their experience."

> Every few years, there seems to be a new movie that young audiences say is the story of their lives; they said it of *Rebel Without a Cause* and again of *Easy Rider*, and even without awarding those pictures any laurels, one could see why. One can also see why they're saying it of *American Graffiti*. But they're demeaning their own lives when they do; they're responding to a national trivia show for youth. It's the peer group view of life.

Was Lucas's film truly guilty of "naïve seriousness" and "pop narcissism," in Kael's words? I think she diagnosed something real, but my hunch is that what she found so rankling was less the picture itself than the naïve seriousness of teenagers themselves, the narcissism of adolescence, the mythologizing that goes on inside the closed circuits of modern high schools. The boys in *American Graffiti* don't have wrenching problems or pathologies, but they have a self-consciousness that rings true, at least when it comes to middle-class teenagers in the second half of the twentieth century. Kael may have felt the movie indulged that, playing up to its audience's blinkered perspective, even to the point of flattery. I feel that way about some of the John Hughes movies. Maybe it's a generational issue. Kael, fifty-three when *American Graffiti* came out, was born in 1919.

To my way of thinking, *American Graffiti* works in part as a gentle satire of teenage self-absorption. One aspect of that is nostalgia—not the audience's nostalgia for 1962 but the characters' own nostalgia for glory days they think have already passed—the almost instant nostalgia that provides the lifeblood of yearbooks. The movie opens with Steve, Curt, and Toad hanging out in the parking lot of Mel's Diner, getting ready for a big night. But Curt is having second thoughts about leaving for college the next morning. "Look, I don't think I'm going to be going tomorrow . . . I was thinking I could wait a year, go to City for a while." Steve remonstrates with him as John pulls up in his bright yellow hot rod (the same color as young Lucas's Fiat). "You want to end up like John?" Steve asks. "You can't stay seventeen forever."

John is presented as the coolest guy in Modesto, a pack of cigarettes rolled up in his white T-shirt sleeve. (How many times had John seen *Rebel Without a Cause?*) He's a few years older—twenty or so, though his age is never given. You might even wonder what he's doing hanging out in a parking lot with three teenagers. Indeed, you might wonder what any of this quartet are doing hanging out together; in the worlds of *The Breakfast Club* or *Mean Girls*, they would belong to four warring cliques. At any rate, John asks what Steve and Curt are getting up to on their last night in town. Curt says they're going to check in on the freshman hop at the high school.

John is incredulous. "That place is for kids!"

Curt: "You got no emotions? We're going to remember the good times."

But John is clinging to the past in his own way. "The whole strip is shrinking," he laments. "I remember about five years ago, take you a couple of hours and a tank full of gas just to make one circuit. It was really something." Even his wheels are a backward glance: as DeWitt points out, John drives "the most timeless car in *American Graffiti*. By 1962, the '32 Ford or 'Deuce,' Ford's first V-8, had been the quintessential hot rod for thirty years—eons in teen culture." Truly, John is a dinosaur: his car is only a year younger than Andy Hardy's 1931 Model A.

John's musical tastes are retro as well. When he's stuck with Mackenzie Phillips's Carol in his passenger seat, the Beach Boys's "Surfin' Safari" comes on the radio, and he quickly turns it off. "Why'd you do that?" Carol asks, gobsmacked. "Don't you think the Beach Boys are boss?"

"I don't like that surfing shit," John snaps. "Rock and roll has been going downhill ever since Buddy Holly died." He's referencing the plane crash that killed Holly, Ritchie Valens, and J. P. Richardson, who performed as the Big Bopper. (Songs by both Holly and Richardson are heard in the film.) John probably doesn't like folk music either, that painfully self-serious Peter, Paul, and Mary shit, another big musical trend in 1962—and he'll surely hate the Beatles and the rest of the British Invasion when they turn up two years later. Pop culture's churn is in part what Lucas was alluding to with his choice of the movie's title, which he insisted on despite moans from Universal.* He told one interviewer that graffiti is "what the movie essentially is." By that he meant something that, like a scribble on a wall, is "glib, funny, immediate." He might also have added "transient"—quickly painted over.

But "Surfin' Safari" aside (along with a second Beach Boys track, "All Summer Long," which closes the movie—an anachronism, since it was released in 1964), most of the songs in *American Graffiti* were already oldies in 1962. Practically the first thing you hear in the movie, following some static and AM radio dial twisting, is an old-style sung station ID that includes the words "super golden," followed by the drum hit that announces "Rock Around the Clock," with the song then playing through

---

*Lucas: "Several people at the studio didn't know what the word graffiti means. They said people would think it was an Italian film or a movie about feet. They wanted to call it *Another Slow Night in Modesto*." Coppola volunteered the even worse *Rock Around the Block*.

the opening credits just as it did in *Blackboard Jungle*, eighteen years ear-lier. Of course, the kids in *American Graffiti* don't think they're living in some innocent golden age; Curt and John, the two most self-aware, are in different ways afraid their trajectories are already trending downward.

When John is getting ready to race Harrison Ford's Bob Falfa, who's rumbled into town in a black '55 Chevy aiming to take John down—a gunslinger looking for the sheriff—he is reassured by a mechanic: "Why the hell do they bother? You been number one as long as I can remember."

"Yeah. Been a long time, ain't it?" John replies, more resigned than boastful. The tragedy of the character—aside, that is, from the fact that he'll be killed by a drunk driver two years later, as we learn in the wrap-up—is that while he's self-aware enough to know his days as king of the road are numbered, he lacks the imagination to do anything about it. He wins the race with Falfa, but only because Falfa loses control of his Chevy and overturns. John was on the verge of losing, and he knows that, too. I'm not claiming Lucas had this in mind, but John's epiphany about his narrowing horizons echoes the era's revisionist westerns and the gener-ally beat-up mood of a nation "weary to its bones," as Paul Simon sang in "American Tune," released the same year as *American Graffiti*, when the nation was fumbling its way through the aftermath of the Vietnam War, not to mention the Watergate scandal, which had come to a boil over the summer, and the oil crisis that would hit while the movie was still in theaters.

Curt is another primary character who spends much of the movie in a nostalgic fog. There's a wonderful moment, apparently Richard Drey-fuss's idea, where Curt wanders alone through the empty school grounds while everyone else is at the hop. He pauses at his old locker and tries to open it, for old times' sake; the combination has already been changed, prompting a rueful smile. Later in the evening, a trio of delinquents take him under their wing. The trio call themselves the Pharaohs, but like the real-life Faros that Lucas hung out with, the group's menace is mostly aspirational. They're in the film as comic relief, as a parody of the 1950s hoods who populated that decade's teen movies; they even drive a chopped 1951 Mercury sedan, Mercurys being the hot-rodders' vehicle of choice through most of the 1950s, thanks in part to the 1949 Mercury James Dean drove in *Rebel Without a Cause*. (The teen movie feedback loop in action.) The Pharaohs' Merc, DeWitt points out, is "a relic" and "no longer in fashion," that being the point because, by 1962, "the Pharaohs were relics themselves." As such, they're foils for Curt's nostalgia. "You want to end up like John?" Steve asked Curt at the beginning of the film. Well, you *really* don't want to end up like the three Pharaohs.

Curt's night ends at a forlorn old radio station on the edge of town with an enounter that propels him to reverse course and commit to college. The station is home to the mysterious, larger-than-life DJ Wolfman Jack, but no one thinks the Wolfman truly operates from such a mundane outpost. One of the Pharaohs says he broadcasts from Mexico with a super-strong signal. "Do you know that he just broadcasts from a plane that flies around in circles all the time?" Carol asks John. (Poor girl: her mother won't let her listen to the Wolfman "because he's a Negro.") Curt walks into the station hoping to dedicate a song to the mystery blonde in the T-Bird and ends up talking to the bearded man in a Hawaiian shirt who's manning the controls while trying to make the most of a broken freezer full of melting popsicles. He's not the Wolfman, he insists. The Wolfman just stops by from time to time to drop off prerecorded shows.

When Curt unloads about his college dilemma, the technician replies, "I can't really talk for the Wolfman. But I can tell you one thing, if the Wolfman was here, he'd tell you to get your ass in gear. Now, the Wolfman comes in here occasionally, bringing tapes, you know, to check up on me and whatnot, and the places he talks about that he's been, the things he's seen. It's a great big beautiful world out there. And here I sit— sucking on popsicles." But as Curt leaves, he sees the DJ on a live mic, and, maybe no surprise, he *is* the Wolfman. It's a *Wizard of Oz* moment— the mythic figure revealed as a modest man behind the curtain—but with the opposite moral to "There's no place like home."

The characters' reversals—Curt now set on leaving; Steve, after a nightlong emotional tug-of-war with Laurie, decides to stay home and postpone college until "next year"—are a bit too neat, but as we've seen, a lot can happen in a teenager's life over twenty-four hours, in film and even real life. Steve's destiny—in the coda we learn he is now "an insurance agent in Modesto, California"—represents the future Lucas himself avoided when he set off for USC, instead of going to work for his father at the office supply store. This was something he obviously felt deeply about, given that escape from a deadening home environment is not only a theme in *American Graffiti* but close to the sum total of *THX 1138*. Young Luke Skywalker, too, spends the first half hour of *Star Wars* moping around in the backwater of his desert planet before Obi-Wan Kenobi and Han Solo arrive to show him the galaxy's bright lights.

Was it an intended irony that the lone character in a film titled *American Graffiti* who survives both the 1960s and Modesto is fated to become "a writer living in Canada"? Audiences at the time understood that to mean that Curt had fled north to avoid the draft, though in hindsight I wonder why he didn't just get a series of student deferments, as so many real-life Curts did. Deliberate irony or not, it was one more touch in keeping with 1973's sour mood.

If you weren't there—I was, having caught the movie on its first run as a fourteen-year-old—it's hard to capture how hard that ending landed in 1973, how startling it was, especially since it's been parodied dozens if not hundreds of times since, most notably in *Animal House*, to the point that a "where are they now" coda has become a youth movie cliché. Milner's tragic death and Toad's presumed death—"reported missing in action near An Lộc in December 1965"—were shocking. Then again, the late sixties and early seventies were an era when heroes and heroines routinely died at the fade-out, in pictures like *Bonnie and Clyde*, *The Wild Bunch*, *Easy Rider*, *Midnight Cowboy*, *McCabe and Mrs. Miller*. In the case of *Love Story*, death was the movie's raison d'etre, and even the crowd-pleasing comedy western *Butch Cassidy and the Sundance Kid* ended with a freeze frame just before the two were assuredly riddled with gunfire. (That's why the twist ending of *The Sting* worked so well: audiences in 1973 were fully prepared to believe that Paul Newman's and Robert Redford's characters weren't faking their deaths.) At any rate, in Lucas's mind, the final title card was essential to the film's meaning, and he was lucky that he was working in an era when you could end a movie on a bittersweet, even tragic note and you weren't committing commercial suicide. (He would help put an end to that with *Star Wars*.)

Lucas wasn't the first creator in the early 1970s to revisit 1950s (or 1950s-adjacent) youth culture with fondness and, in some cases, mortification. Sha Na Na, a doo-wop revival/parody group, had formed in 1969; Jimi Hendrix was a fan and helped get them on the bill at Woodstock, where they were the festival's penultimate act, coming on just before Hendrix himself. Continuing to be taken seriously, the group opened for acts like the Grateful Dead and the Kinks at the Fillmores West and East. In 1971, the high school musical *Grease* debuted in Chicago; the following year, the show, set in 1959, moved to Broadway, where it hung on until 1980—the longest-running show in Broadway history until supplanted by *A Chorus Line*. One of 1971's most celebrated movies was *The Last Picture Show*, set in a small Texas town during the 1951–52 school year. (Though the film foregrounds high school students, I don't think of it as a proper teen movie, since it paints a broader community portrait. But it's a fantastic film, the rare movie where a director shows off everything he can do, and all the style and tricks actually serve the story. If you've never seen it, do yourself a favor and change that.) By 1973, an essayist for *The Atlantic* could praise *American Graffiti* but also note that it had arrived "at the end of a nostalgia boom now too familiar for comment."

Er, no. The writer was laughably wrong about the boom being at an end, as a coast-to-coast landscape still littered with fake 1950s diners will tell you. Fueled in part by *American Graffiti*'s success—and its soundtrack album, which went platinum—the rest of the 1970s saw a surge in backward-glancing pop culture, most notably the long-running

TV series *Happy Days*, which also starred Ron Howard,* and the film version of *Grease*. Henry Winkler, who played Fonzie, the lovable greaser on *Happy Days*, turned down the lead in the *Grease* adaptation, fearing he would be typecast. That was wise: by the time the movie was released in 1978, portrayals of juvenile delinquents had become so stylized that *Grease* plays like an American form of kabuki, with ubiquitous leather jackets, ritualized hair combing, and choruses of boys going "'ey!" But buoyed by John Travolta's charisma and a plausibly perky performance from Olivia Newton-John, the Australian pop star making her American movie debut, the picture became the decade's fifth-highest-grossing film, roughly quadrupling *American Graffiti*'s take. It remains notable for aesthetic reasons as one of the last movie musicals made before MTV changed the grammar of song-and-dance numbers, meaning the director, Randal Kleiser (another friend of Lucas's from USC), lets his camera record the performers the old-school way—in protracted long shots that include their feet, so that you can see them dance, not just move.

A more modest hit, but with arguably greater influence, was *Cooley High*, set in Chicago in 1964 and released in 1975 by AIP, which at the time was nudging its way toward relatively mainstream fare. Marketed as a Black *American Graffiti*—the poster even mimicked the antic illustration *Mad* magazine caricaturist Mort Drucker had created for Lucas's movie—*Cooley High* was written by Eric Monte (co-creator of the sitcom *Good Times*) and loosely based on his experiences growing up in Chicago's Cabrini-Green housing project and attending Edwin G. Cooley Vocational High School. The director was Michael Schultz, also Black, who would go on to make *Car Wash* (1976), a comedy with Richard Pryor and George Carlin, and, less happily, *Sgt. Pepper's Lonely Hearts Club*

---

*The pilot for *Happy Days*, which aired as an episode of the anthology series *Love, American Style*, was shot before *American Graffiti*'s release. The movie's success prompted ABC to commit to making the series, which debuted in January 1974. Lucas was not a fan: "It's a turkey, and a real rip-off. They've done so much to make it look like the movie that people think it's a TV series of the movie. People call me up and say, 'I saw your TV show. It was terrible.'"

Band (1978), a Beatles musical but with Peter Frampton and the Bee Gees substituting for John, Paul, George, and Ringo. *Cooley High's* main characters are once again a loosely knit group of boys. They cut school, hang out, party, neck, get in trouble with the police, groove to the great Motown songs on the soundtrack. "*Cooley High* documents perhaps the last moment in modern American history—1964—when it was possible for young Blacks to see their color as simply one of the components of their personalities," Jack Slater, an African American editor at *The New York Times*, observed at the time. He noted the picture's setting in a northern city before the collapse of the civil rights movement and the rise of Black nationalism, an allegedly prelapsarian place and time akin to *American Graffiti*'s. "To be Black and to see *Cooley High*," Slater continued, "is to see one's vanished innocence—and beauty." The movie is mostly a comedy, but like *Rebel Without a Cause* before it, and *Boyz n the Hood* to follow, *Cooley High* climaxes with a sacrificial death, propelling Monte's stand-in, the aspiring screenwriter Preach (played by Glynn Turman), to flee Chicago for Hollywood, where he will presumably write the movie its audiences had just seen.

In the spring of 1974, with *American Graffiti* still in theaters, a *New York Times* reporter visited Modesto to see what the town's contemporary teenagers were up to. A senior at Lucas's old high school was quoted as saying, "I wonder what they'll remember about us twelve years from now if they make a movie *American Graffiti 1974*? They'll probably say, 'Hey, isn't it tough to live in the seventies with all those rock concerts and dope?'"

That is essentially the plot of *Dazed and Confused*, Richard Linklater's 1993 memory film about his high school career in the later 1970s as a member of the class of 1979. Given the decade's focus on Ghosts of Adolescence Past, it wasn't a big era for movies about the Adolescent Present. Once exception: *Over the Edge* (1979), which offered an excellent portrait of bored junior high students living in a boring planned community who burn down their school—fun, though a bit extreme. Alas, the movie barely got a release, despite introducing Matt Dillon to the world. So to my mind—and I was class of 1976, so I claim unchallengeable credibility here—*Dazed and Confused* is *the* movie that nails the 1970s high school experience. Perhaps appropriately, it also serves as the perfect *American Graffiti* sequel, thematically and spiritually, if not literally.*

Linklater's film, set in 1976, echoes and at times seems to comment on Lucas's, taking place on the first night of summer vacation, not the last, while following a couple dozen characters, rising seniors plus a few freshmen, through the afternoon and into the night and morning of a single twenty-four hours. The kids drive around, get high, look for something to do, hang out at a rec center, and eventually coalesce at a kegger out in the woods by an old light tower. Best embodying the mellow, party-hearty seventies ethos is Wooderson, the genial if vaguely creepy older guy with a loaded Chevelle, a Ted Nugent T-shirt, and too-carefully-coiffed hair. He's played by Matthew McConaughey and serves a similar function to *American Graffiti*'s John Milner. But Wooderson isn't haunted by looming obsolescence. Treading water in life, he is happy to share his weed, beer, and philosophy with teenagers: "You just gotta keep livin', man. L-I-V-I-N." I suppose you could say he's blessed with a complete lack of self-awareness, and that might be this easygoing film's greatest source of tension: whether it means to make fun of Wooderson or accept him on his own genial enough terms. Probably both.

That's one big difference between *Dazed and Confused* and *American Graffiti*: the former bends over backward not to be judgy and insists on stakes so low as to be almost invisible. Most of the characters can't see any further into the future than the next night's kegger, and the movie ends with a few of them driving off into the morning sun—not to attend college back east, or to make it as a screenwriter in Hollywood, but to buy

---

*There is a literal sequel, *More American Graffiti*, released in 1979, which Lucas oversaw as producer but didn't write or direct. It follows most of the characters from the first film over four consecutive New Year's Eves, from 1964 to 1967. It got awful reviews, and I have to confess I've never seen it—an affirmative choice, since I have no desire to see Toad in Vietnam or Candy Clark's Debbie wandering through Haight-Ashbury.

tickets for an Aerosmith concert. As Anthony Lane summed things up in his review for *The New Yorker*, the picture has "scarcely any plot and no perceptible moral, aside from the injunction to 'Eat More Pussy' scrawled on a high-school wall."

Or maybe there is sort of a moral? As the stoner quarterback Randall "Pink" Floyd says at one point, "If I ever start referring to these as the best years of my life, remind me to kill myself"—a perspective that has traveled some distance from Richard Dreyfuss's Curt fiddling sentimentally with his old locker.

According to Linklater, any parallels between his movie and Lucas's were unintentional; he had *American Graffiti* in mind only in the way that anyone making a teen movie in its wake would. "It's kind of the air you're breathing," he told me in an interview. "I love *American Graffiti*, but I didn't have any big statements I felt comfortable making like the way that movie does. That movie says so much. I just felt that for anything near what I considered *my* generation, we didn't want generational statements so much. That'd be reason to roll our eyes. My whole point was, like, nothing happens in my movie. That's the difference between the generations. The other generation felt very comfortable making these big statements. They had bigger stakes, bigger things going on—I would say a war in Vietnam's a pretty good one. Where we didn't have that. Going to get Aerosmith tickets—that felt pitched about right for people of our generation."

In one scene, Linklater has one of his more thoughtful characters expound on what she calls her Every Other Decade Theory. "The fifties were boring," she explains. "The sixties rocked, and the seventies—oh god, well, they obviously suck. So maybe the eighties will be, like, radical"—which got a big laugh in theaters in 1993.

The bit rings true for me. A lot of us growing up in the seventies—and by "us" I confess I mean white middle-class Northern California suburbanites; past that, my expertise mostly fails—did feel we were living in a sucky time. Our older brothers and sisters had had all the fun, excitement, and headlines (and also, to be fair, the repercussions), while we were left with the backwash. But don't just take it from me, or from Linklater. Here's another authentic, unfiltered voice from the era:

> Everything was going great in the sixties. Diseases were being cured. We were winning the space program. Then everything went off balance . . . What has happened to the generation or two earlier that was dedicated to answering all the unanswered questions? For the latter part of the seventies it appeared America gave up asking.

The speaker is the "real" Jeff Spicoli, reading a paper in speech class (likely not his own work), as quoted by Cameron Crowe in his 1981 nonfiction book, *Fast Times at Ridgemont High*—a work, like the film that would be made from it, concerned entirely with the teenage present tense.

6

FAST TIMES

Everything is starting sooner today. When I was fifteen, I was interested
in boys, but it was scary. Now, fifteen-year-olds are going to bed
together. I went through the same things—but when I was sixteen or
seventeen.

—Jennifer Jason Leigh, then twenty, surprised by what she learned
about teenagers in the early 1980s while working in a pizza parlor
to research her role in 1982's *Fast Times at Ridgemont High*

Did the seventies *really* suck? Or was the 1979–1980 school year the best
time ever to be an American teenager? That might depend upon how
you feel about the sorts of mellow bacchanalias depicted in *Dazed and
Confused*. Let's say this: the 1979–1980 school year was in many ways the
freest, most unsupervised time ever to be an American teenager, at least
since the war years and maybe even the days when kids had the freedom
to work sixty-plus-hour weeks in textile factories and coal mines.

A few statistics:

According to annual federal government surveys of high school seniors, teenage drug use peaked in 1979, with 54 percent of seniors admitting to having smoked, sniffed, ingested, or injected at least one illicit
substance within the previous year—and 39 percent within the past
month. This was up roughly ten percentage points since 1975, when the

surveys began. The number would dip in 1980 and continue declining through the decade.

As you would expect, if you were in high school at the time, marijuana was the most popular illicit drug in 1979, having been enjoyed at least once within the past year by 51 percent of seniors, and within the past month by 37 percent. Just over 10 percent of seniors confessed to smoking "daily" (technically defined as twenty or more times in the past thirty days).

Meanwhile, cocaine use had nearly doubled between 1975 and 1979, with 12 percent of seniors in 1979 admitting to having used it in the previous year.

The more venerable pastime of getting drunk, whether on beer, cheap sweet wine, or Mom and Dad's vodka, had ticked up slightly, too: 41 percent of seniors in 1979 admitted to binge drinking at least once in the previous two weeks, up from 37 percent in 1975.

Statistics about teenage sex are more difficult to come by, perhaps because the questions are more fraught, and the answers likely less reliable, but it seems clear that kids were having more and more of it throughout the 1970s, alongside the drugs. Regular surveys by the federal Centers for Disease Control and Prevention found that 56 percent of eighteen-year-old girls in 1980 reported having had "premarital sexual intercourse" at least once, compared to 39 percent in 1970. A different survey found that the number of sexually active eighteen-year-old boys had increased from 55 percent to 64 percent over roughly the same time period.*

Another trend peaked as the decade turned: kids working for pay, with nearly 80 percent of high school students holding down some form of job by the end of the 1970s, a number that would begin a long decline with

*Those numbers would continue to rise, if less dramatically, through the end of the 1980s, with boys and girls achieving rough parity, before teenagers began having less sex in the 1990s, a trend that would continue into the 2020s. Possible factors involved: AIDS, abstinence-only education, Internet porn, and a generation exposed in its formative years to the Starr Report.

the recession of the early 1980s. On the one hand, all these jobs surely infringed on the time teens could devote to drugs and sex. But more work, whether after school or during the summer or both, meant more spending money for drugs, beer, clothes, cars, makeup, movies, records, concerts, and dates. If you catered to adolescents, the 1970s economy wasn't *all* bad.

So, yes, it was a freewheeling time for teenagers, and a fortuitous time to be reporting on their lives, as Cameron Crowe did for his 1981 book *Fast Times at Ridgemont High*, the basis for the 1982 movie. A baby-faced twenty-two-year-old music journalist with long, lank hair and a wardrobe composed almost exclusively of T-shirts, he had enrolled undercover for an entire year at a public high school in San Diego, maintaining an "inconspicuous presence" as a fake student in order to research "a book about real, contemporary life in high school." It was the 1979–1980 school year, and what Crowe discovered, and what became signal themes of book and movie alike, were sex, drugs, and jobs—much as the government poll takers had also found.

Regarding work, Crowe observed a big attitude change in the seven years since 1972, when he had last attended high school as a legitimate student, graduating early that spring. As he would remark in a DVD commentary for the *Fast Times* film: "I was really struck at how everyone had gotten jobs in the . . . years I'd been out of high school . . . *Everybody* had jobs now, and there was this quest to get the money for records, for clothes, all that stuff, and it changed their lives." Most kids worked in fast food, and Crowe discovered a status hierarchy based on employer, with Carl's Jr. at the pinnacle of local prestige; Burger King, Kentucky Fried Chicken, and others occupying a wide middle ground of okayness; and 7-Eleven a netherworld for untouchables. Crowe's aphorism for teenage fry cooks: "A man was only as good as his franchise." In hindsight, he felt he had witnessed the first stirrings of 1980s go-go capitalism, Southern California kids once again ahead of the curve.

Drugs held less allure than may have been true in other parts of the country. (Certainly not in east Texas, judging from Richard Linklater's experience.) "Most of these kids have no time for drugs, not on a large scale," Crowe wrote. "Most of them, when asked, say things like, 'Oh,

I went through my drug period in junior high.'" (There was a smoke-shrouded exception: Jeff Spicoli,* the surfer who was brought to heavy-lidded, red-eyed life by Sean Penn.)

As for sex, Crowe found that his classmates treated it as if it were no big deal—or strove to treat it that way. But sex remained the big deal it has always been. Kids he met were having more of it than previous generations, and they were willing and able to discuss it in more explicit terms, yet seemed no more emotionally ready for it than their elders had been. One day, Crowe overheard a girl say, "I don't want to use sex as a weapon"—a line that made it into both book and film, and for Crowe became a key to understanding the world he had infiltrated. "That [line] was such a big deal for me. It changed the way I wrote the book," he remembered. "The idea was, they're living these young capitalist working man and girl lives and they're also using sex without knowing the emotional weight of it—and it *is* a powerful weapon. And they're even saying, 'I don't want to use sex as a weapon,' not even knowing how much of a weapon it is." It was as if kids had been handed grenade launchers but with no training or even an owner's manual.

That disconnect was the seed for the awkward, painful, funny-sad sex scenes in the film, one of the rare teen movies unafraid to risk turning off young audiences with its frankness. That disconnect is central, too, to the book and film's broader portrait of a cohort left to its own devices and occasionally in over its heads. Adults had been marginalized in *American Graffiti* as well as the *Beach Party* movies—clueless at best, clownish at worst—but their gravitational fields were felt, one way or another. Cruising in George Lucas's Modesto took place in a blocks-long youth bubble, while AIP's surf scene was a full-on fantasyland, like Narnia with bikinis, but the teens in these idylls seemed to know just how far they could push things. A handful of teachers aside, *Fast Times* takes place in an adult-free zone, and the kids act like it. They don't even bother to complain about

---

*The names in book and film were pseudonyms Crowe gave to individual students he got to know. Likewise, Ridgemont High is not the real name of the school he attended.

their parents; it's as if parents don't exist, like in *Peanuts*. Which may reflect one more thing that peaked while Crowe was undercover: America's divorce rate, which had skyrocketed throughout the 1970s as the sexual revolution coursed and pulsed through middle America. I remember a high school classmate of mine summing up the decade's domestic ethos in terms like, *Our parents are too busy dealing with their shit to deal with our shit*. You see that dynamic in *Foxes* (1980), about four teen girls growing up free-range in the San Fernando Valley, where Jodie Foster's character serves as a mother hen to her friends while also parenting, more or less, her floundering single mom (Sally Kellerman).

If teens had spent the decades since Andy Hardy pushing for more and more freedom, the late 1970s may have represented a be-careful-what-you-wish-for moment. In the words of Amy Heckerling, who would direct *Fast Times* from Crowe's screenplay, "It was like a grown-up world but with children playing grown-up parts, and they weren't ready."

In Crowe's words, from the book: "The only time these students acted like kids was when they were around adults."

A certain amount of unsupervised blundering was in keeping as well with the spent tenor of the times—the fraying hammock that was the Ford-Carter years, strung between the upheavals of Vietnam and Watergate and the more material upheavals of the Reagan Revolution. Writing in *The Village Voice*, the movie critic Carrie Rickey (class of circa 1969) cast *Fast Times* in just this light—to her mind unflatteringly. There was "something unacknowledged in this film," she wrote, and that something was "the inherent sadness in being a post-baby-boomer." She went on:

> Talleyrand groaned in 1815 that one who has not lived before the revolution can't know the true sweetness of life; in the *Fast Times* book, the typically postliterate Spicoli articulates the melancholy of having missed living in an optimistic time when there was everything to look forward to and rather pessimistically comforts himself with the tarnished trophies of nostalgia. In the movie, such self-awareness is absent.

You won't find a better example of generational self-regard than the phrase "the inherent sadness in being a post-baby-boomer," and Rickey went on to suggest that *Fast Times* suffered dramatically for taking place in a permissive, "value-free" world, in comparison to older youth pictures, with their politically charged "Oedipal authority conflicts." That's a matter of taste, I suppose. But I'm pretty sure Rickey misread the Spicoli anecdote. She was referring to the passage from the book I quoted at the end of the previous chapter, where Spicoli is reading a paper in speech class about 1960s positivity versus 1970s malaise (to not coin a term). But Crowe strongly implies that Spicoli didn't write the paper himself; he's mouthing someone else's pop history clichés. The truth is, Spicoli doesn't give a shit about the sixties. Doing the bare minimum to keep from flunking is what he cares about here.

That's what *Fast Times* the film is interested in, too: the getting by. The movie is close to singular in the teen movie canon for its focus on the day-to-day grind of kids' lives, hewing about as closely as a scripted feature film could to Crowe's journalistic impulse, and for having no other agenda beyond its observant eyes and ears. It's a comedy, but with such a matter-of-fact approach, especially in its several sex scenes, that it precludes being either exploitative or cautionary. Maybe it helped that it was made in a relatively laissez-faire era, when concerns about what teenagers got up to in the dark were at a low ebb. (Those concerns would return.) Maybe it helped that the movie didn't care too much about plot, stringing incidents together in an easygoing way not unlike *American Graffiti*'s, but meandering over the course of an entire school year and thus lacking the dramatic unity of taking place over a single night and the ticking clock of a morning flight back east for college. Maybe it helped that *Fast Times* was made without the explicit or implicit adult perspective of many previous teen movies, but also without the distancing effect of nostalgia. Maybe it was the old trick of finding the universal in the particular. Whatever. The upshot was a movie made to speak directly to the generation watching it, but with an honesty and good humor that welcomes an adult audience as well—and which, four decades on, leaves the film feeling much less dated than most of its contemporaries. (I'll get to the less fortunate *Sixteen Candles* in the next chapter.)

"It was the world of the teenagers, and you were privy to this world," Heckerling said. "Here's that world they function in, here's what you grown-ups don't see, and that's what was cool about it." And it *was* cool. You could call *Fast Times at Ridgemont High* the coolest anthropological study ever committed to book and film.

Crowe was already a veteran journalist in the summer of 1979, when he turned twenty-two. He had begun writing for *Rolling Stone* in 1972, not long after he graduated from high school at the age of fifteen, having skipped kindergarten and a couple of grades in elementary school. Going on the road with Led Zeppelin, Neil Young, and the Eagles was its own education, a trawl through the Golden Age of Rock Star Debauchery (experiences which became the basis for his autobiographical 2000 film *Almost Famous*).

It was also a Golden Age of Celebrities Being Unguarded in Front of Young Reporters. "It's a shame to see these young chicks bungle away their lives in a flurry . . . One minute she's twelve, the next minute she's thirteen and over the top. Such a shame," a philosophical Robert Plant observed in Crowe's 1975 cover story on Led Zeppelin.

The opener from another 1975 report, on Rod Stewart's last American tour as lead singer of Faces:

> "I hate San Bernardino. Why are you playing *there*?" Tatum O'Neal, the eleven-year-old from *Paper Moon*, chugged from a bottle of Blue Nun and cast a jaded glance toward Rod Stewart. The Face was doing her father, Ryan, a favor by babysitting for the day and they were in a limo on their way to Berdoo. "I can't stand the smell," Tatum said. "It's just the lowest." Stewart chuckled politely and turned to stare out the window.

The conversation eventually got around to music and records. "Faces sessions are still the bloody same," Stewart recounted. "We go in at odd hours drunk out of our minds and piss away money."

To his credit, Crowe soon wearied of the rock aristocracy's excess and posturing. "It's hard to keep from gagging on [David] Crosby's constant paeans to the Music," he noted in a story about Crosby, Stills & Nash's 1977 reunion. An inflection point came while covering a solo Rod Stewart concert. "There was this kind of—I guess the word would be 'sybaritic'— life that was happening backstage," Crowe later observed. "You know, it was like the comfiest sofas and, you know, banquet plates of the finest foods and all that stuff. And I just thought, you know, What's happening in the parking lot? And I went out to the parking lot and that's where I felt rock. That's where I felt the story was that night. That to me felt like the better path to tread as a storyteller. And that kind of stuck in my head." Of course, everyone in the parking lot would have killed to trade places with Crowe, and that passion was part of the parking lot's appeal—and the first glimmer of *Fast Times at Ridgemont High*.

As he wrote in the book's introduction:

> For seven years I wrote articles for a youth culture magazine, and per-haps not a day went by when this term wasn't used—"the kids." Music and film executives were constantly discussing whether a product appealed to "the kids." Rock stars spoke of commercial concessions made for "the kids." Kids were discussed as if they were some enor-mous whale, to be harpooned and brought to shore.

I'll interrupt to point out that this is exactly what Fred M. and Grace Hechinger were warning about two decades earlier in *Teen-Age Tyranny*. Crowe continued:

> It began to fascinate me, the idea of The Kids. They were everywhere, standing on street corners in their Lynyrd Skynyrd T-shirts, in cars,

in the 7-Eleven. Somehow this grand constituency controlled almost every adult's fate, yet no adult really knew what it was nowadays—to be a kid.

As we have seen, this was a question that had been vexing parents, educators, journalists, politicians, and marketers for several decades. Crowe brought his still-coalescing thoughts to a book editor, who suggested he tackle the question head-on: attend high school for a year, pretending to be just another kid himself, and bring back a report.

Crowe himself had graduated from a "strict" Catholic boys school but spent a happy summer school session at his local public high school, Clairemont High, in San Diego. He met with the school's principal and pitched his idea; winning approval proved easier than you'd imagine.

Principal Gray was a careful man with probing eyes. He was wary of the entire plan, and he wanted to know what I had written before. I explained that I had authored a number of magazine profiles of people in the public eye.

"Like who?" he asked.

I named a few . . . My last article had been on the singer-songwriter Kris Kristofferson.

Principal Gray eased back in his chair. "You know *Kris Kristofferson?*"

"Sure. I spent a few weeks on tour with him."

"Hell," said the principal. "What's he like?"

"A great guy." I told him a few Kris stories.

"Well, now," said Principal Gray, "I think I can trust you. Maybe this can be worked out."

It was . . . I started school the next week as a seventeen-year-old senior.

Conditions placed on his reporting were that he not use anyone's real names or the name of the school, which he changed from Clairemont

High to Ridgemont High. (He put nosy readers further off the mark by claiming the school was in Redondo Beach, a Los Angeles suburb 120 miles north of San Diego.) Enrolled as David Cameron, the twenty-two-year-old was "completely ignored" for the first month or so, like any new kid. Eventually he made friends with a girl in his journalism class, who he names Linda Barrett—the character eventually played by Phoebe Cates. She in turn introduced him to Stacy and Brad Hamilton—Jennifer Jason Leigh and Judge Reinhold in the movie. An important social break-through came when "a bunch of us went to see a Chuck Norris film at the drive-in," Crowe later recalled. It was one of those magic nights when you're a kid when bonds form in an instant. The students he wrote about became his friends, or vice versa:

> My entire lifestyle changed that year. I went to malls, to slumber par-ties, to beaches, to countless fast-food stands. I can't remember all the times I left situations to "go to the bathroom" and furiously scribble notes on conversations and facts I'd just heard. Back at Ridgemont, no doubt, some still remember me as the guy with the bad bladder . . . By the end of the school year I had become so accepted that even Princi-pal Gray forgot about my project.

"David Cameron" finally fessed up to his friends/subjects over the sum-mer, and most seem to have been okay with the book, to the extent that they cooperated, and Crowe conducted more formal interviews to cor-roborate his initial notes and impressions. Linda and Stacy even offered to tape a slumber party for him, on the sly, but he responsibly declined. "I told the kids I wouldn't write about things if they felt it was an invasion of privacy. In the end, no one said, 'You can't write about any of this.' In fact, they wanted their real names used, but part of the deal with the school was to change the names."

Aside from his introduction, Crowe wisely keeps himself out of *Fast Times*. Written in the third person, the book's shifting points of view hew closely to its subjects'. "I did not want to become yet another adult writing about adolescence and *the kids* from an adult perspective. This story, I felt, belonged to the kids themselves." The result is funny and occasionally appalling (even to someone who graduated high school only four years earlier) but mostly empathetic and generous—much the same qualities as the film. Indeed, read with the movie in mind, Crowe's book feels more like a novelization, so faithful is his screenplay to its source, even to the point of lifting dialogue. Virtually all the major threads in the movie were present at the start: Stacy's quest to lose her virginity; Linda's ill-informed sexual mentorship of Stacy; Brad's tumble down the fast-food hierarchy after getting fired from his enviable perch behind the grill at Carl's Jr. (All-American Burger in the movie); Linda walking in on him masturbating; nice guy Mark "the Rat" Ratner crushing out on Stacy; self-proclaimed playboy Mike Damone coaching the Rat on how to work "the Attitude" to pick up girls; Damone's assignation with Stacy in her family's pool house; Stacy's subsequent abortion; Brad sinking to the level of working at a 7-Eleven and redeeming himself by foiling an armed robbery with a pot of hot coffee; and Spicoli's yearlong joust with American history teacher Mr. Hand, ending with Mr. Hand showing up at Spicoli's house on the night of the prom to teach him a lesson, literally and figuratively.

The book was published in September 1981, receiving mostly nice reviews. ("Often hilarious . . . always pleasantly amusing." —*The New York Times*.) It had already been optioned by Universal, where Ned Tanen, the young executive who had been instrumental in getting *American Graffiti* made (before he freaked out at its first test screening), was now the studio's president and enjoying the success of another youth-oriented hit with outsized profits, *National Lampoon's Animal House*. Crowe was hired to adapt his own book, under the tutelage of the producer Art Linson, who already knew the journalist, having given him a walk-on part ("Delivery Boy") in *American Hot Wax* (1978), a biopic of the pioneering rock-and-roll DJ Alan Freed—and one more seventies youth movie trafficking in poodle skirts—which Crowe had covered for *Rolling Stone*.

Linson also knew director Amy Heckerling, a twenty-seven-year-old graduate of New York University's film school, who had then earned an MFA from the American Film Institute. She had yet to direct a feature, but her thesis film, a short called "Getting It Over With," was a comedy about a girl trying to lose her virginity in the last eight hours before her twentieth birthday, so *Fast Times* was clearly in her wheelhouse; Linson was confident that, in her words, she could "show the awkwardness" (the sine qua non of any good teen movie).*

Heckerling had the perfect origin story for a teen movie director. A New York City kid—born in the Bronx, raised in Queens—she realized she wanted to be a filmmaker one day in the late sixties when she was a ninth grader at the High School of Art and Design and her class was assigned to write an essay about what they wanted to be when they grew up. "I had always loved movies more than anything—it was just my favorite thing in the world, to watch movies," she remembered, "but I didn't think it was something anybody could actually aspire to be, you know? It's too magical and wonderful, and it came from Hollywood or foreign countries, made by genius men. I didn't think that a person could just say that they wanted to do it, you know. So I wrote that I wanted to be a writer for *Mad* magazine, because I love *Mad* magazine." She changed her mind when a boy sitting next to her, a smart but lazy kid who copied off her during exams, wrote that he planned to be a filmmaker. "And it made me so angry, because I really, really loved movies more than anybody, and why couldn't I do that? And this is the guy who copied off me! But it was he who could say he was going to Hollywood to make movies. I just felt like, wait a minute. You wouldn't be this angry unless you wanted to do it." She knew that there weren't many, if any, women filmmakers, but the boy's presumption was a goad. "I decided if anybody's going to go and do it, I want to. I wanted to do it. He had the confidence. But am I going

*In fact, Heckerling was the studio's second option; the project had first gone to David Lynch, which seems a bizarre choice. But with *Eraserhead* (1977) and *The Elephant Man* (1980) to his credit, he must have had a broadly hip enough profile to strike someone at Universal as a filmmaker kids could relate to. Lynch politely passed. "This is funny," he said of the script, "but it's not my material."

to let that get in my way of achieving or doing anything, the fact that I'm more insecure?"

It was Heckerling who pushed Crowe, as he worked on the script through multiple revisions, to remain faithful to his own book: "I really thought they had been doing a disservice to it. Cameron knew all these people, and in the book he'd recorded very accurately everything that was going on with them, and it was very funny because of that; whereas I felt like Universal were probably trying to make more of a regular teen movie." She lobbied to retain the focus on the kids' working lives and not just "romance and the usual stuff going on at school, sports and all that . . . In the book, they had jobs. They were struggling. It wasn't just like, 'I'm cruising around in my car.' It's like, 'I have a job to pay for this piece of junk.'"

Crowe: "She wanted to give dignity to all these characters. And she kind of showed us all that that is actually the funniest way to present these stories."

It was also Heckerling's idea to "condense" the book's settings and provide the narrative with a second, after-school focal point: "In watching old movies about young people, there was always this sort of malt shop. There was 'The Place.' And I thought, where are these places where they all go?" The answer in the early eighties was a mall, which provided the kids in the film with their workplaces as well as a hangout, with the added production benefit of being a convenient indoor location that wouldn't elicit worries about weather and lighting. (More on mall culture in the next chapter.)

Through the fortuitous, possibly one-in-a-million combination of the studio mostly understanding what was strong about the project while not having much at stake in it—the budget was only $5 million (and that outlay was offset by the prospect of a surefire bestselling soundtrack album being assembled by Irving Azoff, the manager of groups like the Eagles, who had previously produced lucrative soundtracks for the movies *FM* and *Urban Cowboy*)—Universal mostly allowed Heckerling and Crowe to make the movie they wanted to make. It helped, too, that the studio was simultaneously preoccupied with *The Best Little Whorehouse in Texas*, the adaptation of the Broadway musical, now cast with Burt Reynolds and Dolly Parton, which Universal correctly expected to be a big summer moneymaker in 1982. Heckerling and Crowe did receive some pushback over the lack of adults in their movie: the studio wanted more of them, along with an element of *American Graffiti*–like nostalgia—maybe flashbacks to parents' high school years?—to help draw older audiences into theaters. It's hard to believe this of an industry that has so assiduously played to young tastes over the past four decades, but at the time Universal feared that teens alone weren't a large enough demographic to support a film, even one with a reasonable budget.

"That was part of our battle, to convince the studio that young people would actually show up if they had a movie about them," Heckerling said. In fact, the film focuses even more tightly on the kids than does the book, with the only significant adult roles being Mr. Hand, the American history teacher played by Ray Walston, and Mr. Vargas, the biology teacher played by Vincent Schiavelli. Parents were a small presence in Crowe's book, but they vanish altogether in the movie, aside from one glimpse of Stacy's mom wishing her a good night, before Stacy sneaks out to lose her virginity to a stereo salesman in a public park. To Heckerling, the custodial vacuum was very much on point: "We had that one parent have that one line and that almost felt like a violation."

She took care to assemble a cast that, as she put it, didn't look like the forty-year-old "teens" in *Grease*. (That wasn't entirely fair: John Travolta was only twenty-four when the film was released in the summer of 1978, Olivia Newton-John was twenty-nine, and Stockard Channing, who played the "bad" girl Rizzo, was thirty-four.) It wasn't just verisimilitude Heckerling was after: she wanted a cast that looked young enough that audiences would empathize with the characters' struggles: "It had to look like it was all beyond them. They were children experiencing all this stuff too fast."

For that reason, she also avoided casting well-known teen actors. Like *American Graffiti*, *Fast Times* launched multiple unknowns into substantial careers. Jennifer Jason Leigh, who brought a disarming mix of vulnerability, confusion, and sangfroid to Stacy, would go on to become one of the finest film actors of her generation. Phoebe Cates wasn't in her co-star's league as an actress, but playing Linda, Stacy's friend and mentor, she didn't need to be. Judge Reinhold, twenty-four when the movie was made, is the one cast member who registers as too old for his part, though he's affectingly beleaguered as Brad. (Reinhold would more credibly play a police detective two years later in *Beverly Hills Cop*, though at the time he was maybe too young for *that* part.) Forest Whitaker, in his second movie, has a mostly thankless role as a Black football star at the nearly all-white school. Eric Stoltz and Nicolas Cage show up in minor roles playing, respectively, one of Spicoli's stoner buddies and a guy briefly seen behind the counter at All-American Burger. As it happened, Cates and Cage were the only true minors in the cast, and Cage had gotten the part by lying about his age. (Producers are often reluctant to cast minors, when they can avoid it, because of restrictive work rules.)

Fred Gwynne, best known for playing Herman Munster on *The Munsters*, was offered the part of Mr. Hand, but he passed, finding the script too vulgar. The role went to Ray Walston, another star of a wacky high-concept 1960s sitcom (*My Favorite Martian*), who brought a ferocious implacability to the part while serving, in essence, as straight man to Sean Penn's Spicoli.

Penn was twenty and virtually unknown when he was cast, though he had one film in the can, *Taps*, which would bring him some attention. (It was a military-school drama in which he had a supporting role opposite Timothy Hutton and George C. Scott, and alongside an equally green Tom Cruise.) His audition for *Fast Times* was awful by all accounts, including his own—"terrible and flat" he recalled—but Heckerling and the producers saw something in him. In fact, they offered him the arguably more central role of Brad, but Penn insisted on playing Spicoli. The son of a TV director, Penn had grown up in Malibu and attended Santa Monica High, so he knew tons of Spicolis. Like many "New James Deans" before him, and many to come, he committed to the role with performative gusto. A friend told his biographer, Richard T. Kelly, "Sean lived as Spicoli for months. He was driving between Malibu and an apartment in Brentwood, and he was living that life: surfing probably every day, drinking plenty." As actorly sacrifices go, this wasn't in the same league as Robert De Niro's putting on sixty pounds to play Jake LaMotta in the final scenes of *Raging Bull*, but Penn brought with him a method-like intensity previously unknown in teen comedies. "He was a nutty kid, he was funny," Heckerling told Kelly. She described a pre-shoot exercise on location at Van Nuys High School, where the school scenes were shot. The idea was to assemble the cast in a classroom, as if for an actual school day, so they could begin to get comfortable around one another. The director asked each actor to bring in an object to talk about. "Like in English class," she told them, "but in your character. Then we'll just have lunch and hang out." Penn insisted on taking a sideways approach. Heckerling: "Sean comes to me and says, 'I don't wanna do the assignment. I wanna, like, disrupt things. In my character . . .' So we were having this class when Sean and his buddies came in late with Chinese food and started to bother everybody. Then, during lunch, he just kept trying to pull up Phoebe Cates's skirt and generally harassing her and Jennifer. Just being a nuisance. In his character."

Throughout the shoot, Penn insisted on being addressed as Jeff, keeping the rest of the cast at a distance. "His answering machine was 'Jeff,'" Heckerling remembered. "For a long time after the movie, people would ask me, 'What's Sean like?' and I would say, 'Well, I only know Spicoli.'"

According to Crowe, Penn broke character just once, during a cold nighttime shoot at Van Nuys High. Crowe spotted the actor hanging out with Cates, Leigh, and some others at a coffee machine, chatting amiably. "For the first time he sorta dropped his Spicoli thing," Crowe said. "And they were all looking at each other like, 'God, he's not such a bad guy after all.' And you could see Sean realize that he was blowing it for himself, and making friends with these other characters. So he took the cigarette he was smoking and stubbed the lit cigarette out in his palm. Twice . . . And Phoebe Cates goes, 'Auaugh!' They freaked out and scattered."

However exasperating, Penn's commitment paid off in ways both obvious and not. According to Heckerling, "Sean's own vocabulary, the slang he brought to the part, was instrumental" to what we'd now call the movie's virality. "The day we shot the school trip to the hospital where the teacher"— Vincent Schiavelli's biology teacher, Mr. Vargas—"pulls out the human heart [from a cadaver] and Spicoli reacts: I just kept the camera running and said to Sean, 'Just keep doing it, say whatever comes out.' So where the line was 'Bitchin',' Sean would say, 'Gnarly!,' 'Tubular!,' 'Awesome!' . . . a whole list. Finally I said, 'Cut,' and everyone on set burst a gut." For the record, in the editing room, she went with "Gnarly!"

Aside from all-night shoots at the Sherman Oaks Galleria, during which, Heckerling said, her cast "went from looking like teenagers to looking like thirty-year-olds," the production went smoothly. In multiple interviews, she and Crowe have both maintained that any interference from the studio was minimal, which isn't to say nonexistent. According to Heckerling, the first week of shooting took place on location at the house serving as Brad and Stacy's, which involved some "heavy stuff" in terms of the scenes' emotional content. Universal executives, viewing the rushes, were unimpressed. "They wanted to fire me, apparently. I did not know this," Heckerling remembered. "They were concerned that they had asked for a teen comedy and they were getting people crying and having abortions and what was this going to be?" Universal sent John Landis, who had directed *Animal House* and *The Blues Brothers* for the studio, to check up on the shoot; he did, and told the executives to leave Heckerling alone.

Momentarily reassured about the humor, Universal continued fretting over the sex. Heckerling: "This was a constant question people had, if they were noticing us at all, of what we were doing on this movie, which was, like, 'It's too edgy. It's too sexual, but not sexy . . . It should be much funnier and lighter and more pornographic.'" Linson, the producer, pushed to eroticize the school cafeteria scene where Linda teaches Stacy how to give a blow job by demonstrating on a carrot, but the pair's casualness—they're no more self-conscious than if they were practicing eating with chopsticks—is what makes the scene funny. "It was really matter-of-fact for these girls," Heckerling insisted. That was her mission throughout, regarding the sex scenes: "Just keeping things real, with sex the way it really is when you don't know what you're doing yet . . . They wanted to turn it into a cutesy beach movie."

There was one scene that arguably crossed the line Heckerling had drawn for herself: the poolside scene where Linda walks through a sprinkler and, glistening in slow motion, seductively discards her red bikini top. Whether or not one finds the scene exploitative, the movie means to justify the nudity by presenting it as Brad's masturbatory fantasy (scored to the Cars' glossy but insinuating "Moving in Stereo," a perfect musical cue and about as sleazy-sounding as synth-pop ever got). The scene comes up in an interview with Heckerling and Crowe conducted by the actor-director Olivia Wilde—chosen because of her 2019 teen comedy *Booksmart*—which accompanies the Criterion Collection's 2021 release of *Fast Times*. Wilde remarks that Cates's topless scene was shot on the second day of production, and asks Heckerling what it was like directing a young actress in such a sensitive scene so early in Heckerling's very first feature. As Wilde notes, "You knew what it was going to be," but at the same time, "you know you're there to protect her."

"Actually, I wasn't there protecting her," Heckerling responds, with admirable (I guess?) forthrightness. "She didn't want to do it. And I was being the, like, cigar-chomping studio guy going, 'You know, we've got to see your tits. That's what we're paying for. Boys are gonna wanna see that and I want them in the audience and we need it.' And she goes, 'You don't really need it.' I go, 'Yes I do.' That's a hard thing to navigate . . . a tricky part of being a director, and I think particularly for women, 'cause it's like, of course you can empathize with that fear that comes from being vulnerable [as a performer], but you know, I knew what the film needed and it was such an integral part of the—the kind of just the fabric of the film."

However reluctantly, Cates did the scene, and Heckerling was perhaps lucky that a commercial imperative also made creative sense, or at least enough so that she could justify the scene; the nudity adds tension and thus heightens the comic payoff when Linda walks in on Brad. You could even argue that the fantasy of a perfect, topless Linda serves as satiric counterpoint to the two more realistic, uncomfortable, and exposed sex scenes involving Stacy (and which Jennifer Jason Leigh apparently had no qualms about appearing fully nude in)—a reflection of kids' media-fed ideas about what sex is, versus the reality of what it typically is when you're seventeen. You could also argue that as Brad, Judge Reinhold had to give the more embarrassing performance, pretending to masturbate in front of the camera (with the aid of a strap-on dildo not visible below the bottom of the camera frame). He was also saddled with one of the film's few punch lines that doesn't land, calling out, "Doesn't anyone fucking knock anymore?" The actor is left holding the bag, as it were.

That was a pioneering and, all things considered, tasteful example of the boundary-pushing set piece that would become a necessary ingredient in teen sex comedies—the raunchy cousin to what old-school TV writers used to call a "Hey, Marge!" moment, as in a guy on his couch shouting, "Hey, Marge! Come here! You got to see this!" An untoppable peak was arguably hit when Jason Biggs had his way with an apple pie in *American Pie* (1999). But an earlier standard was set by *Porky's*, which went into wide release in March 1982, while *Fast Times* was in postproduction. An independent film picked up by 20th Century Fox, *Porky's* would become the fifth-most-popular film released in 1982, taking in $105 million ($340 million in 2024 dollars), its willingness to "go there" outweighing awful acting and a dumb script about horny high school boys picking a fight with a redneck strip club owner. The "Hey, Marge!" in *Porky's* comes when the boys are peeping on the shower in the girls' locker room via a trio of conveniently unused plumbing holes. When the girls—amused in this fantasy rather than alarmed—discover the subterfuge, one of the boys sticks his penis through the hole as a kind of dare, and said penis ends up in a painful tug-of-war with the mannish girls' gym teacher, whose name is Coach Balbricker (*har*). And that is pretty much all you need to know about *Porky's*, except that it was set in the 1950s and may have represented a last, ignominious gasp of the nostalgia craze for that decade.

A more interesting teen movie development in this period was a series of films that took a genuine interest in girls' sexuality. In *Grease*, for instance, Stockard Channing's Rizzo, self-declared bad girl and leader of the Pink Ladies gang, is as unapologetically interested in having her needs met as any of the movie's guys, with the picture seeming to take a stand against slut-shaming decades before that became an idiom. Rizzo and the Pink Ladies even get what you might call a virgin-shaming number, making fun of Olivia Newton-John's demure Sandy, in "Look at Me, I'm Sandra Dee." Near the end of the picture, Rizzo sings a solo number, "There Are Worse Things I Could Do," which serves as her credo:

I could . . . wait around for Mr. Right . . .
And throw my life away
On a dream that won't come true

So why not have some fun with boys? True, the song is more poignant ballad than brassy anthem, and Channing brings an element of pathos to the character, as in the scene where she's about to have sex in a car and instructs her boyfriend, who's moaning, "Rizzo . . . Rizzo," to call her by her first name, Betty. It's a line that feels as if it were written to be funny but it lands plaintively. The picture's third act flirts with punishing Rizzo by saddling her with an unplanned pregnancy. ("I feel like a defective typewriter . . . I skipped a period.") But the sunny finale gives everyone a happy ending, including Rizzo, who gets to announce that her pregnancy was a "false alarm" while riding a carnival Ferris wheel. *Whee! Never mind! Cue the last number!* (Yes, *Grease* is a musical comedy.) Meanwhile, Sandy has surprised Travolta's Danny by ditching her prim sweater sets and long skirts for skintight leather and a huge perm that makes her look more like a 1980s porn star than a 1950s greaser's girlfriend. So this was . . . progress? I don't want to oversell *Grease*'s sex positivity, but it can serve as a mostly cheerful counterpoint to the shame, guilt, and fear swirling around female sexuality in, say, *Carrie* (1976).

The 1980 summer camp sex comedy *Little Darlings*, starring Kristy McNichol and Tatum O'Neal, was more sensitive and nuanced than its advertising let on. Winking slutscapades were promised by the tagline, "Don't let the title fool you," and the plot was summarized fairly enough by another line used in the ads: "The bet is on: whoever loses her virginity first—wins." *The New Yorker* harrumphed: "A disgusting idea for a movie." But the two heroines—Tatum O'Neal's poor-little-rich-girl Ferris and Kristy McNichol's scrappy, working-class Angel—are in fact ambivalent about their wager, which is a result of peer pressure from their cabinmates, rather than any desire or urgency on either girl's part. Angel "wins," but it proves to be a hollow victory, one that she keeps secret; the act, which takes place off camera, leaves her angry at herself, while her partner, the proverbial cute boy from the camp across the lake, played by Matt Dillon, winds up feeling used. Meanwhile, Ferris lies about sleeping with the dreamy older counselor played by Armand Assante—who is nevertheless a little too slow on the draw when spurning her advances. When her falsehood is exposed, everyone confesses, and it turns out the supposedly seasoned cabinmates who egged on Ferris and Angel are all virgins, too. Moral: *And that's okay!* Surprisingly, all of this is handled with as much tact as the premise and the era's standards of taste allow, and the endorsement of "waiting" in the final reel would make Gidget's mom proud. But give *Little Darlings* credit for treating girls' sexuality, their curiosity and desire, with respect; the movie lives in a world where girls might conceivably want and enjoy sex.

That girls can be horny without being "bad" or crazy or doomed, or all three, is assumed in *Fast Times at Ridgemont High*. In the opening mall scenes, after Stacy flirts with an older "fox," a stereo salesman in his twenties, who's eating at the pizza parlor where she and Linda work, Linda urges her on: "Stacy, what are you waiting for? You're fifteen years old. I did it when I was thirteen. It's not a huge thing. It's just sex." "He was hot, wasn't he?" Stacy responds, warming up to the idea. She ends up losing her virginity to Ron, the salesman, in a public park at night, on the bench in a Little League baseball dugout, Ron throwing himself on top of her with little in the way of preliminaries, Stacy an eager but unsure participant. Heckerling cuts to her point of view looking at graffiti—"DISCO SUCKS," "SURF NAZIS"—on the dugout's roof. The final image in the sequence is a long shot: Ron rutting away on top of Stacy, the dugout surrounded by darkness, emphasizing how fundamentally alone Stacy is during an ostensibly intimate moment. It's a sad scene and hard to watch, but it's not judgmental, at least not of Stacy. Her life hasn't been ruined, nor has she been shamed; she's merely perplexed by an act that she had been led to believe—by Linda as well as, we can infer, magazines and movies and pop songs—would be transformative. And pleasurable.

The next day, at school, she complains to Linda that having sex hurt. "Don't worry," Linda reassures her. "Keep doing it. It gets a lot better, I swear." "It better," Stacy says, not a victim but an informed skeptic. When Ron eventually ghosts her, utilitarian Linda suggests she shrug it off, while enforcing Ridgemont High's code of economic determinism: "What's the matter? He's a stereo salesman. You want to marry him?" (Another character dismisses Stacy in similar terms: "Who is she anyway? She's a waitress in a pizza parlor.")

Stacy's second sexual encounter is with Damone (Robert Romanus), a fellow student who contributes to the local economy as a ticket scalper. A practitioner of studied cool, Damone has been coaching nice boy Mark Ratner (Brian Backer), who takes tickets at the mall's multiplex, on the finer points of romance, a counterpoint to Linda's tutoring of Stacy. Tellingly—and accurately, I believe—the boys' sex talk is far less clinical than the girls', concerned more with Playboy Advisor–style seduction techniques. Damone's bottom line: "When it comes down to making out, whenever possible, put on side one of *Led Zeppelin IV*." Mark has a crush on Stacy and eventually asks her out. But when she invites him into her bedroom and starts kissing him, he panics and flees, leaving Stacy more baffled than ever. (Linda: "What do you care about Mark Ratner? He's an usher at the mall.") She then strikes up an interest in Damone. At her instigation, they have sex in her family's pool house—another awkward, uncomfortable encounter that lasts thirty seconds. "I think I just came," says Damone, clearly not as experienced as he lets on. "Didn't you feel it?" "Yeah, I guess I did," replies Stacy, more a question than an answer.

There's more humor in this scene than in the dugout scene, but the takeaway remains that sex, when you're not entirely sure how to do what you're doing or why you're doing it or what it means to you, let alone your partner—when, in other words, you're a teenager—can be awful. Per the "keeping it real" approach, Heckerling shot the pool-house scene with both actors completely nude, their exposure neither erotic nor romantic but emphasizing their youth and vulnerability; they're like baby seals, but painfully self-conscious.

"My attitude was that I didn't want to say that these are lovely, romantic sex scenes," Heckerling said. "We see a lot of the sort of Hollywood soft focus. You know: follow a hand moving slowly down a body, kind of legs and arms . . . It's like, that ain't how it was for me!" Jennifer Jason Leigh's look of wounded bafflement when Damone abruptly leaves her lying in the pool house speaks worlds; it's as naked, literally and emotionally, as a performer has ever been in a mainstream Hollywood movie.

A momentary glimpse of Robert Romanus's penis earned the film an initial X rating; Universal forced Heckerling to trim it to earn an R. "I said, 'How come if naked women are in movies that I see, it's Rs,' and they go, ''Cause the male organ is aggressive and the female organ is passive.'" Verna Fields, who edited the film (and had co-edited *American Graffiti* with Marcia Lucas), insisted that the X rating was earned only because the characters were teenagers: "Had there been adults in the picture, no way it would have been an X."

One thing not discussed by Stacy and Linda, or anyone else in the film, is birth control. Whether true or not to Crowe's reporting, this is in notable contrast to both *Grease*, where a broken rubber leads to Rizzo's false alarm, and *Little Darlings*, where a subplot features the camp girls stealing an entire vending machine full of condoms from a gas station bathroom. Later, when McNichol's Angel gives one to Dillon's Randy, who seems less than gung ho about it, she tells him, with all due vehemence, "If you forget to put that thing on, I swear I'll kill you. I'm not getting myself pregnant. I'm not ready to take care of some guy's brat. I don't know what's with men—they never come prepared. They think it's the woman's responsibility or something." The screenplay, by Kimi Peck and Dalene Young, is editorializing here, but that was not a bad thing for teen audiences to hear in 1980, or, for that matter, in the 2020s.

When Stacy becomes pregnant in *Fast Times*, the only uncertainty is whether Damone will be able to cobble together his half of the fee for her abortion, and then drive her to the clinic. (Enlisting her parents' help is pointedly off the table.) Her choice to have an abortion isn't questioned; the film treats it as an inevitability. Any lingering regret is due to Damone's not coming through for her. In fact, as the author and academic Lisa M. Dresner points out in an essay about the portrayal of girls' sexuality in *Fast Times* and *Little Darlings*, Stacy's abortion leads not to punishment but a rare moment of closeness between her and brother Brad, who, though she tried to keep him in the dark, figures out where she's gone and picks her up at the clinic when she's done. Brad's asking his sister if she's hungry and opening his car door for her is as close to sentimental as the movie gets.

This was a singular moment in American culture. While teen sex remained a reliable subject, it was treated far less bluntly and honestly in the teen movies that followed—think, for instance, of Tom Cruise and Rebecca De Mornay's glossy coupling on an elevated train in *Risky Business*, like something out of an *Emmanuelle* movie, or the string of crude teen sex comedies about horny boys that *Porky's* inspired. Having an abortion would soon become an all-but-formal taboo on screen. And yet, according to Heckerling, the studio didn't just tolerate the storyline in *Fast Times* but were actively supportive. "The executives at Universal at the time were all pretty young, radical people," she noted years later. "They were the student leaders of political movements at their schools and then went to Hollywood and became studio executives. They wanted to show the edge, they wanted to make these statements, so I was very fortunate."

As Dresner points out, subsequent television heroines, teens as well as adults, including Murphy Brown, Rachel on *Friends*, and Andrea on *Beverly Hills 90210*, saw unplanned pregnancies to term, as did the female leads in the films *Juno* and *Knocked Up* (both 2007). "The times changed extremely quickly right after that," Heckerling observed of the early eighties. "I think of it like when a garage door is closing and someone slides in right at the very last second. Because what was allowed to be shown in terms of sex and drugs and all of that kind of shut down afterwards for a long time." As she put it in another interview, "We just got in ever so slightly before the whole Reagan backlash-y thing."

I should note that while Stacy isn't shamed for her sexuality, she does decide to slow down and give Mark, the nice boy, another chance. She has, I suppose, learned some sort of lesson, in keeping with movie tradition. But I should note, too, that Stacy arrives at this conclusion entirely on her own, without the advice of any parent or other adult sounding board, or even Linda.

"I finally figured it out," she explains. "I don't want sex. Anyone can have sex."

"Yeah, Stacy? What do you want?" Linda asks.

"I want a relationship. I want romance."

"You want romance? In Ridgemont?" Linda is incredulous. "We can't even get cable TV here, Stacy, and you want romance!"

As with *American Graffiti* nine years earlier, Universal didn't know what to do with *Fast Times*. The executives continued to worry the movie wasn't funny enough, and in previews, young audiences didn't react the way the filmmakers expected them to, sitting "in stony silence," according to a report in the *Los Angeles Times*. "They seemed to be a little frightened of the sex," Heckerling said at the time. "I wanted certain scenes to be funny, but to people in their teens, they're too close to home." The director also worried that the test audiences Universal chose in Orange County were more conservative than the general run of adolescents. "You get those cards telling you what people thought and it's like, 'You think we teenagers only have sex and drugs, blah, blah, blah.' Like they were mad at us."

The one thing that everyone agreed worked was Spicoli, and throughout the shoot Universal had urged Heckerling to beef up Penn's part. "Sean was very smart about what he was up to," Heckerling said. "I'd get these edicts from the studio: 'More Spicoli!' And we'd try to figure out stuff to do, but to Sean it just seemed too much. He'd say, 'But that'll step on *this* joke' or 'This will be a repeat of that.' He said, 'I'd rather there be less. I want them to want more of me.' I mean, there are actors in their forties who still haven't figured that out."

Universal's marketing department went through numerous potential ad campaigns, trying to nail tone and selling point. One prospective poster featured a giant hamburger bun filled with joints; another depicted a French fry container bursting with cheerleaders—images that sound like what you might get if you asked an AI program to design a poster for a teen comedy. A third version aped the cartoonist Rick Meyerowitz's by then iconic poster for *Animal House*, itself something of a riff on Mort Drucker's stack of caricatures for *American Graffiti*. Eventually, maybe inevitably, the studio's marketing department settled on an image of Spicoli with a couple of random long-legged girls in short shorts. The trying-too-hard tagline: "At Ridgemont High, Only the Rules Get Busted."

The release was set for August, amid a crowded field of youth-oriented movies. *Porky's* was still in theaters while fresh competition included *Pink Floyd—The Wall*, the pompous and grim movie adaptation of the rock group's pompous and grim double album, and *Zapped!*, an R-rated comedy starring TV teen idol Scott Baio (who played Fonzie's cousin Chachi on *Happy Days*) as a boy with telekinetic powers that he uses to lift girls' skirts and pop open their sweaters. Heckerling suspected her film was doomed: "I was worried no one would see our movie 'cause the cool kids will see *The Wall*, and the horny kids will see *Porky's*, and the teeny bopper girls will see *Zapped!*, and we're just gonna die!"

Audiences could have been forgiven for smelling a dud, even more so because Universal held back on the number of theaters the picture opened in. Crowe: "At the last minute, they cut down the release . . . to virtually a regional release, because I remember somebody said they might like the surfer in California." The reviews were mostly unenthusiastic. ("A slick commercial exploitation!" —*Los Angeles Times*.) Even critics who liked the film gave it mostly backhanded compliments, convinced perhaps by the disreputable genre and cheesy marketing that its pleasures must be guilty ones. "Can there be anything about life in high school, particularly life in a suburban California high school, that the moviegoing public hasn't already seen?" Janet Maslin wondered in *The New York Times*. "Well, maybe there can. A little bit of it turns up in *Fast Times at Ridgemont High*." Pauline Kael seemed taken aback by her own positive reaction: "I was surprised at how not-bad it is. It may fall into the general category of youth-exploitation movies, but it isn't assaultive, and it's certainly likeable."

No doubt she appreciated that Stacy and Linda weren't ignored in the tongue-in-cheek wrap-up (the second time a Universal picture had parodied *American Graffiti*'s ending, after *Animal House*). Kael got what distinguished the film from its predecessors: "*Fast Times* is like the Beach Party movies at a later stage—as if they'd evolved and gained a higher form of consciousness. What makes it appealing (yet may upset some parents) is that the kids rely on one another. They've gained independence from the adults at home. The kids are there to catch each other after the falls, and to console each other—they function as parents for each other."

Fast Times was what used to be called a sleeper hit. Audiences discovered it on their own, by word of mouth, and as they did, Universal expanded its release. Heckerling recalled seeing the film in a theater early on and thinking the audience's response was merely "okay." But several weeks later, "somebody calls and says, 'You know what's going on with your movie?' And I went, 'What?' And they go, 'Go to the theater.' So I go to the theater and everybody's saying all the dialogue. And I was like, Oh fuck. This is like too much happiness at once." *Fast Times* would bring in $27 million at the box office, a tidy and profitable sum, though barely a quarter of the $105 million *Porky's* rang up.

•   •   •

And yet, who remembers *Porky's* anymore? *Fast Times* has survived to become an iconic film mainly on its own merits, but also, I think, because it does capture its odd, in-between time in American culture, poised between revolution and backlash, when teenagers had new freedoms but hadn't quite figured out the attendant responsibilities.

Heckerling would go on to write and direct a second great teen movie, *Clueless* (1995), which I'll return to in another chapter. Crowe would become one of the most significant writer-directors of his generation, with a literate filmography that includes *Singles, Jerry Maguire,* and the autobiographical *Almost Famous.* His first movie as a writer-director, *Say Anything . . .* (1989), is a third great teen movie, though I would have more to say about it in a social history of romantic comedies, which is where I think its heart truly lies. It does provide us with the final panel in a triptych of iconic eighties teen movie musical moments (alongside *Risky Business*'s Tom Cruise in his tighty-whities dancing to Bob Seger's "Old Time Rock & Roll" and Judd Nelson accenting Simple Minds' "Don't You (Forget About Me)" with a raised fist at the end of *The Breakfast Club*). *Say Anything*'s contribution: John Cusack holding up his boom box outside Ione Skye's bedroom window and playing Peter Gabriel's "In Your Eyes." I don't know of a scene that better captures the centrality of music to kids' emotional lives, the way a favorite song or album doesn't just crystalize what you feel but can become a personal soundtrack. Life never seems more like a movie than when you're sixteen or seventeen.

Speaking of which, what did the real kids at Clairemont Hight think of *Fast Times*? According to Crowe, they preferred it to the book "because it allowed them to be heroes . . . It was the movie that cemented the kind of, 'Yeah, that's *us*! That's *our* school!'"

As I mentioned, the film is extremely faithful to the book, although it does eliminate a few less-interesting characters and several incidents. A major difference is the attitude Heckerling's film takes toward Spicoli compared to the book's, which is that of his fellow students, not Crowe's per se. Thus the book's Spicoli is something of an outcast, seen by most kids at Ridgemont as a stoner throwback—a loser, basically, albeit an intermittently amusing one. He in turn finds his peers, as Crowe writes, "so serious, so hung up on their social status." In fact, he doesn't really have friends, or rather, "most of Spicoli's friends were still the junior high schoolers from Paul Revere [Ridgemont's feeder school]. They knew how to have a good time." Which means that while he has some Wooderson and John Milner in him, he's even more pathetic because he's hanging out with kids whose voices might still be breaking. On screen, Spicoli might have come across as pathetic, too, if not for Sean Penn's charisma, but that's the difference between movie stars and civilians. The movie Spicoli launched catchphrases and a vogue for checkered Vans slip-ons (Penn's own contribution to his character's wardrobe). The book's Spicoli is an anachronism with a dim future. When last seen on Crowe's pages, he is being dismissed by one of his classmates: "You just know he's gonna grow up to be a shoe salesman."

It was a perfect put-down for the coming "greed is good" era, and just the sort of insult that could have been delivered by a proto-yuppie villain—or, for that matter, a proto-yuppie hero—in a John Hughes movie.

7

HUGHES

I just don't think sixteen-year-olds are being well served by my
generation.

—baby boomer John Hughes, in 1984,

sucking up to Generation X

He was one of us.

—Molly Ringwald, describing Hughes's relationship with

her and with the rest of his multiple teenage casts

S. E. Hinton began writing her first novel, *The Outsiders*, when she was
fifteen, finishing it when she was sixteen. Like diary entries, her pages
throbbed with feeling—volatile, romantic, nerves exposed. Francis
Coppola's 1983 film adaptation was a game and worthy attempt at capturing the book's vulnerable, openhearted spirit, but to my taste he over-
aestheticized the movie, sealing it in an amber of Technicolor sunsets
with a murderer's row of future stars—Tom Cruise, Rob Lowe, Patrick
Swayze, Matt Dillon, Emilio Estevez—who look like they just flew in
from a Bruce Weber fashion shoot. It was John Hughes who came closer
to capturing Hinton's sensibility with the run of films that began a year
later with *Sixteen Candles*—a far sillier story than *The Outsiders*, and
maybe that helped.

Between 1984 and 1987, and the ages thirty-four to thirty-seven, Hughes would write and direct four teen movies—*Sixteen Candles*, *The Breakfast Club*, *Weird Science*, and *Ferris Bueller's Day Off*—and write and produce two more—*Pretty in Pink* and *Some Kind of Wonderful*. All but the last one were hits—not necessarily home runs but solid singles, doubles, and triples. It was arguably Hollywood's most impressive condensed run since Preston Sturges's string of seven landmark comedies between 1940 and 1944, though Hughes's films varied more wildly in tone, from farce to romantic comedy to talky one-set drama. They varied more in quality, too—as anyone's filmography does in comparison to Sturges's. But given his talents, interests, and sensibility, Hughes was perhaps uniquely qualified to connect with teen audiences. "I don't think of kids as a lower form of the human species," he once told *The New York Times*, sanctimoniously perhaps, but exhibiting the lack of prejudice that gave him a leg up on much of the competition. "What I've realized about this audience is that they like serious," he continued. "What turned around for me is remembering how serious I was at that age." In another interview, he recalled screening *The Breakfast Club* for studio executives who told him, "Kids won't sit through it. There's no action, no party, no nudity." But what the executives had forgotten, Hughes continued, "is that at that age, it often feels just as good to feel bad as it does to feel good."

In hindsight, Universal's worry that teenagers didn't constitute a big enough potential audience to support *Fast Times at Ridgemont High* is inexplicable. The 1980s turned out to be a very good time to be in the business of making movies for and about teenagers. The list of highlights is long—*Fast Times*, *The Outsiders*, *Risky Business*, *Rumble Fish*, *WarGames*, *Back to the Future*, *Heathers*, *Bill & Ted's Excellent Adventure*, *Say Anything* . . . , *River's Edge*—as is the list of lowlights—*Porky's*, *Losin' It*, *Getting It On*, *Goin' All the Way*, *Screwballs*. Some of these pictures made considerably more money than any of Hughes's teen movies, though among all the films discussed in this book, his probably provoked the strongest passions in their initial audiences—with the exception of *Rebel Without a Cause*. But that movie's impact hinged on James Dean's outsized performance (not to mention the live-fast-die-young tragedy of his fatal accident), which masked the many ways in which the film catered to adults. Hughes's movies were lifted by many fine performances, but their connection to their audience was even more about a sensibility: a teenage mindset that seemed not to care whether adults would feel left out—which endeared them to kids all the more. They had that in common with predecessors like the AIP pictures, but those movies were cynical screen fodder. Like most truly great popular artists—and I think Hughes has to rank as one, though I am personally less fond of his films than I imagine are most people reading this—he had a genuine, intuitive feeling for his subject matter, so much so that he himself became a brand, a Walt Disney trafficking in lunchroom hijinks and pity parties. But even that comparison doesn't quite capture what Hughes meant to young audiences in the 1980s and beyond.

There is an entire book devoted to the subject: *Don't You Forget About Me: Contemporary Writers on the Films of John Hughes*, a collection of essays by Gen X novelists and poets who grew up with Hughes. Trying to capture the import of *Ferris Bueller's Day Off*, Steve Almond, a short-story writer and essayist, compares Ferris's friend Cameron's monologue about his cold and distant father, the dad who loves his red vintage Ferrari more than his son, to "those long, wrenching soliloquies at the end of *Long Day's Journey into Night*," then adds: "People will tell you they love *Ferris Bueller* because of all the clever lines, the gags. That's what people need to think . . . But the real reason to keep returning to the film is because John Hughes loved those kids enough to lay them bare, and he transmitted that love to us. Bless him." Almond is not the only writer here who gets churchy. Novelist Lewis Robinson on *The Breakfast Club*: "For a fourteen-year-old kid who was devoted to a certain code of teenage behavior, the movie felt like a sacred text."

When Hughes died in 2009, at the age of fifty-nine, from a heart attack, A. O. Scott, the *New York Times* movie critic, who was seventeen when *Sixteen Candles* was released, strove to capture what the filmmaker had meant to Scott's generation of teenagers. Referencing an older friend who was gorging on Jean-Luc Godard in college while Scott was still in high school, the critic wrote, "I don't think I'm alone among my cohort in the belief that John Hughes was our Godard, the filmmaker who crystalized our attitudes and anxieties with just the right blend of teasing and sympathy. Mr. Godard described *Masculin Féminin*, his 1966 vehicle for Jean-Pierre Léaud . . . as a portrait of 'the children of Marx and Coca-Cola.' [Andrew] McCarthy and [Molly] Ringwald in *Pretty in Pink* were corresponding icons for the children of Ronald Reagan and New Coke." Bringing Godard into it was a bit of a reach, in my humble opinion, as was a subsequent comparison to Ernst Lubitsch, but Scott's effort is telling in itself, and no one should be too hard on a critic forced to crank out an appreciation on deadline for an unexpectedly deceased formative influence. (And dear me, I'm the one who put Hughes in a sentence next to Preston Sturges.)

However beloved, the films are not without widely acknowledged problems. *Sixteen Candles* in particular hasn't aged well, burdened by its appalling caricature of a horny Chinese exchange student named Long Duk Dong (*har*)—the only significant character of color in any Hughes teen movie—and a subplot about date rape that is played for laughs. Words like *fag* and *retard* get tossed around more than twenty-first-century audiences might prefer. Moreover, the movies sprawl tonally. They can be tender yet nasty, acerbic yet corny; they punch up one moment, punch down the next. But that, too, might be part of their appeal: in their contradictions and confusions, they mirror their target audience.

And Scott's line about Hughes's *Pretty in Pink* characters standing in for the children of Ronald Reagan and New Coke is apt. Though not outspoken about it, Hughes was a political conservative; he was also socially conservative, an uxorious family man and a confirmed Midwesterner who felt out of place in Hollywood. His films, despite their feints at anarchy, pay deference to wealth, class, and social convention in a way that was very much in sync with prevailing trends in the 1980s—and which may or may not leave a bad taste in your mouth. *Sixteen Candles*, beneath its sometimes snarky, sometimes subversive, sometimes mean-spirited and racist comedy, is a fairy tale about an upper-middle-class girl being courted by a rich boy who lives in something approaching a small castle and can afford to shrug off the potential trashing of his dad's Rolls-Royce convertible. It's a fantasy, sure, but what's being fantasized about is telling.

Further down the socioeconomic scale, John Bender, *The Breakfast Club*'s "criminal" played by Judd Nelson, is a working-class provocateur who bullies, baits, and sexually harasses Ringwald's "princess"; he's obsessed with her privilege, and when she inexplicably makes out with him at the end of the film, it's unclear whether she does so out of genuine affection or noblesse oblige. Most movies would prompt you to feel for the one poor character, but Hughes, with aid of Nelson's abrasive performance, keeps Bender at arm's length. Meanwhile, Hughes wants us to sneer at the teacher running Saturday detention, not only because he's nasty and small-minded and, of course, the Man, but also because, as he confesses to the school's janitor, he's worried about losing his job and his "$31,000 a year" if he doesn't ride hard on his charges. In some films, that might have been an effort to humanize a teacher in kids' eyes; here it feels like the movie wants us to disdain him for clinging to his lousy public-school salary. He's officious *and* tacky. Similarly, *Ferris Bueller's Day Off* shows its disgust for Jeffrey Jones's vice principal by emphasizing his cheap suit, cheap shoes, and cheap Chrysler sedan; one shot inexplicably, even fetishistically lingers on the car's grille with the Chrysler logo in close-up. (If it's product placement, I don't think the automaker got fair value.*) At the same time, we are meant, I believe, to empathize with Ferris when he complains early in the picture about not having his own car while flouncing around a bedroom graced with a stack of high-end stereo equipment. Satirical intent, if any, fails to register: Ferris is just a normal, if absurdly charismatic, suburban kid who, if you look up

---

*By 1986, Chrysler had rebounded from its 1979 near bankruptcy and government bailout, but the company was still working to overcome its reputation for manufacturing shoddy cars.

the 1986 sticker price, happens to own an $8,000 synthesizer-sampler. (That would be $23,000 in 2024 dollars.) This makes for an interesting contrast with *Risky Business*, shot in some of the same neighborhoods as Hughes's films, which has more cutting things to say about upper-middle-class privilege and carelessness—before the picture is hijacked by Tom Cruise's charisma and transforms into a weirdly feel-good romp about boys running a brothel.

Money is the foreground subject in *Pretty in Pink*, where the "richies" serve as the movie's bad guys and the class divide is tribal and unbridgeable—"the Sharks and Jets all over again," as *Time* put it in a 1986 cover story on Ringwald. (I would add as precursors *The Outsiders*'s Greasers and Socs.) Ringwald's character, Andie, lives with her unemployed, alcoholic single father (Harry Dean Stanton) on the other side of the tracks—literally, as the film is at pains to point out in an early establishing shot. Andie wears vintage outfits that she creatively restyles, resourcefulness that the richies deem hopelessly outré. (In fairness to their snobbery, time hasn't been any kinder to *Pretty in Pink*'s costuming than it has to Long Duk Dong.) When Andrew McCarthy's Blaine, a richie, takes a romantic interest in her, his louche pal Steff, played by James Spader in unstructured linen jackets and sockless loafers—primo 1980s assholewear—dismisses Andie as "your little piece of low-grade ass." Blaine, imbued with McCarthy's usual confounding mix of earnestness and diffidence, dewy eyes and pursed lips, isn't much better. "Don't you think she's got something?" he asks, as if he were a high school Henry Higgins, or maybe a horse trader.

Spineless Blaine eventually backs out of his promise to take Andie to the prom. In the film's original ending, she wound up with fellow poor kid and fashion victim Duckie, played by Jon Cryer, who has been pining for her throughout. But test audiences rejected that ending, booing the screen, legend has it, and a reshot finale has Andie forgiving Blaine after his mumbled, weak apology, followed by deep kisses at the fade. In this case, the audience's conservatism had outstripped Hughes's. Perhaps they were too brainwashed by *Lifestyles of the Rich and Famous* to realize that the entire movie had been telling them Blaine was a creep. Just a few years earlier, Phoebe Cates's Linda or Kristy McNichol's Angel would have told Blaine to fuck off; Gidget and Betsy Booth might have, too, in gentler terms. But the mid-eighties were not an era for questioning phony fairy-tale endings and the material attractions of big houses and nice cars. As one critic observed of Andie, "Keeping with the spirit of the times, she gets to have it all."

Hughes's greatest gift, aside from an ability to bat out screenplays in a matter of days, was knowing what teenagers wanted. He had teenage friends. He understood their lives, or at least made the attempt. He researched *The Breakfast Club* by hanging out at his old high school, talking to kids in the parking lot. (Try doing that today.) His movies connected with young audiences, Richard Corliss wrote in *Time*'s cover story on Ringwald, because "they are about the kids who go see them—not the locker-room sadists, lubricious cheerleaders, and barons of barf who populate the *Porky's* films, but teendom's silent majority of average, middle-class suburban kids . . . His movies are like teen psychotherapy with a guaranteed happy ending."

Looked at one way, *Sixteen Candles* and *Ferris Bueller's Day Off* were potty-mouthed updates of the *Andy Hardy* series, mining the more quotidian dramas of teen life ignored or downplayed by filmmakers aiming at higher (or lower) targets. As Molly Ringwald wrote in a post-#MeToo reconsideration of her work with Hughes, for whom she starred in three pictures: "In synopsis, the movies can seem flimsy—a girl loses her date to a dance, a family forgets a girl's birthday—but that's part of what made them unique. No one in Hollywood was writing about the minutiae of high school, and certainly not from a female point of view."

Hughes's ability to get under teenage skins was almost unprecedented. A *New York Times* critic found this gift "slightly unsettling," noting in a review of *Ferris Bueller's Day Off* that the filmmaker "has the sensibility and vision of an adolescent with the technical know-how and expertise of an adult. The movies that result are uncanny recreations—and celebrations—of a teenage point of view." Nicholas Ray excavated teen angst, and George Lucas nailed high school social rituals, but both did so looking down from adult altitude. Heckerling and Crowe observed their characters' needs, moods, and foibles like affectionate anthropologists. Hughes plunges headlong into the muck.

"One of the great wonders of that age is that your emotions are so open and raw," he once said, meaning it, I think, as a compliment. When Ringwald's Samantha is first seen in *Sixteen Candles*, Hughes is literally and figuratively at her shoulder as she looks herself over in the mirror and despairs, "Chronologically, you're sixteen today. Developmentally, you're still fifteen." Resigned, she adds, "You need four inches of bod, and a great birthday." It's like the "I want" song in a Disney princess movie, or, of greater relevance here, a slightly more explicit take on Judy Garland's "In Between." Hughes isn't poking fun at Samantha or murmuring, nana-like, *Isn't she darling?* The scene is meant to be only as ruefully funny to us as it is to Samantha. He's aided by Ringwald, a gifted enough actress that she can sell the clumsy talking-to-herself conceit and keep the moment from turning cringey, or not entirely. The film remains fully attuned to Samantha when she realizes that her family "fucking forgot" her birthday. "I can't believe this," she huffs, with a titanic eye roll. It's an eye roll we're meant to feel, not smile at, one that defies any condescension to what might be deemed, by grown-ups, an overreaction to a relatively trivial slight. It's not trivial to her, and Hughes honors that.

Similarly, when Matthew Broderick's Ferris Bueller breaks the fourth wall and talks to the audience about the coming end of high school, he's realistic about the disruption that graduation will bring to his life and friendships. Unlike a hacky commencement speaker, he's focusing not on possibility but on loss, and his mantra about savoring the present—"Life moves pretty fast. If you don't stop and look around once in a while, you could miss it"—doubles as a plea to hit the brakes. Hughes apprehends a truth most makers of teen movies ignore: not everyone hates high school, and not everyone can't wait to leave. Popular across all cliques, with teachers and parents eating out of his hands, Ferris is the ultimate senior: he's got high school wired. Who would be eager to give that up, to sail off into an unknown? His day off is a lark, but there's an undercurrent of sadness to the fun, even desperation; Ferris and his friends are like sailors on twenty-four-hour shore leave before shipping off to Guadalcanal.

Hughes's first two movies, *Sixteen Candles* and *The Breakfast Club*, were both shot in abandoned high schools in the Northern Chicago suburbs, reflecting a signal moment in not just Hollywood history but also American demographic trends. With the baby boom having finally passed through its teenage years and its vanguard approaching middle age—the class of 1982 was the last one composed primarily of boomers—cities and towns all over America found themselves with a surfeit of classrooms. The population of kids aged twelve to seventeen had peaked in 1974, at 25.5 million; by the time Hughes was shooting *Sixteen Candles* at Niles East High School, in Skokie, in the summer of 1983, the numbers had dropped by three million.

Thus many communities found themselves deaccessioning schools built to accommodate the now-vanishing herds. At the end of the 1980–81 academic year, according to one study, America was littered with some 6,000 shuttered school buildings. A survey of fifty school districts in Hughes's home state of Illinois found each had closed an average of 2.76 schools in the decade between 1972 and 1982. My own junior high school in Palo Alto was converted into a community center in 1978, five years after I graduated. (Good riddance: it was a grim sorting facility named for Lewis M. Terman, a eugenicist and creator of the Stanford-Binet intelligence test.)

But if the number of classrooms was shrinking, the number of movie screens was growing, and young people, despite making up a shallower pool, were now Hollywood's most reliable audience. In 1977, the Motion Picture Association of America's annual survey of moviegoers found that 57 percent of all tickets had been sold to people under the age of twenty-five; that share subsequently dipped a little but remained at just over 50 percent through the mid-1980s. (It dipped again at the end of the decade but was back to 50 percent by the turn of the century.)

1977 is a landmark year in Hollywood history, the year *Star Wars* premiered and not only attracted a record-breaking audience but also demonstrated that the right movies would bring back young moviegoers for second, third, and even more viewings. (Speaking again from personal experience: I was eighteen when *Star Wars* was released in May 1977 and saw it four, maybe five times that spring, summer, and fall.) More broadly, teenagers on the whole were spending more and more over this period, even as their overall numbers fell. So there was poetry, if not inevitability, in surplus high schools being converted into temporary soundstages.

John Hughes was well aware of these trends; for all the credit he is rightly given for divining the hearts of 1980s teenagers, he was also a former advertising man unafraid to sully himself marketing his pictures. "I think the movie business is in a real serious transition right now," he told *Interview* magazine in 1985. "First there was sound, then color, then television, then cable. Now it's demographics." Hughes may have been overstating the case; search "teenage audiences" in an entertainment press database and you'll see that the power of young ticket buyers is a recurring headline across decades, an evergreen like the political press's "Dems in Disarray."* But there were factors unique to the 1980s that encouraged teen moviegoing.

One was the new centrality of malls as staging grounds for teen socializing. As Amy Heckerling observed, the local Galleria or Fashion Plaza had become a place for kids to see and be seen, the food court replacing the old soda fountain or drive-in, cruising now taking place not in

---

Variety, 1949: "In show biz' perennial quest for the secret of a hit, numerous film producers were pondering this week whether the road to b.o."—box office—"success might not be a direct and conscious appeal to the teenage audience . . . [S]urveys have consistently shown that the teenagers are the most frequent and faithful theatregoers." *Variety*, 1999: "Across the country these days, it's definitely the Stridex-set at the plex. As Hollywood worries itself sick over skyrocketing production costs, teen pics—which are cheap as birdseed for studios—are increasingly the films du jour . . . [G]iven the demos, they have potential to gross huge spitballs of cash."

cars but on escalators and across concourses. "Teenagers in America now spend more time in the mall than anywhere else but home and school," asserted William Severini Kowinski, a journalist, in his 1985 book *The Malling of America: An Inside Look at the Great Consumer Paradise.*

"Everything that was happening, happened at the mall," a Pennsylvania teenager told Kowinksi—a double-edged statement, depending upon how many multitudes were contained, or not, by that "everything." The author Rich Cohen, in a 2023 essay mourning the subsequent decline of malls on the American landscape, described a typical 1982 afternoon at his local mall in Northbrook, Illinois (the Chicago suburb where Hughes had spent his own adolescence a generation earlier):

> You were dropped off at noon and picked up at dusk. In the hours between you were left to roam in the preferred fashion—in a teenage pack. Some started at the Sweet Factory, then spent the afternoon dipping into the candy bag like a wino with a bottle. Some started at the food court with caramel corn or Orange Julius. We all made a point of stopping by the knife store to examine the throwing stars and Bowies.

Not every mall had a bad-ass knife display for kids to press their noses against, but Cohen otherwise captures a fairly universal suburban experience. The Northbrook Court, he writes, "was the first place I experienced autonomy, freedom from parents, teachers, coaches. It's the land of my second birth."

The trend was fine with Hollywood because malls were where Americans of all ages now saw movies. According to statistics compiled by the National Association of Theater Owners, the number of theaters inside or attached to malls and shopping centers had grown from a few dozen in 1970 to more than a thousand by 1980—like the multiplex in the Sherman Oaks Galleria used as a location in *Fast Times at Ridgemont High*—and would continue to grow throughout the decade. They filled a role akin to the drive-in theaters of the 1950s, meeting teenagers where they lived.

Malls don't much figure in Hughes's movies, outside of a scene in *Weird Science* where the heroes get showered with a Slushee from several floors above in an atrium. It's a noteworthy absence, like someone making delinquent movies in the 1950s without any hot rods. Hughes was more willing to exploit another fixture of 1980s teen culture, a new medium that proved a godsend for the movie business. Here's how the trade magazine *Box Office* described this miracle in 1984: "It sounds like a promotion man's dream: a way to put a good hunk of film footage and a throbbing soundtrack into the homes of the teenagers who are the core moviegoing audience. And all for free. That dream is now a reality called 'music videos.'"

The concept of producing short films to promote songs dated back decades—Bessie Smith, Louis Jordan, Lena Horne, Bob Dylan, and the Beatles all made them—but "music videos" became a 1980s phenomenon with the launch of MTV, on August 1, 1981. The channel quickly seized a preeminent place in the culture through symbiosis with acts like Culture Club, Duran Duran, Cyndi Lauper, and ultimately Madonna and Michael Jackson. Hollywood soon took notice. As an MTV executive explained to *Variety* in 1984, "*Flashdance* was the picture that brought all the studios into the music video field." A video for the song "Maniac," from the 1983 film, had begun airing on the channel four weeks before *Flashdance* opened and helped make the movie (with no stars and crummy reviews) into the third-highest-grossing picture of the year, after *Return of the Jedi* and *Tootsie*, while propelling the soundtrack to two weeks atop the *Billboard* albums chart and six-times-platinum sales.

"The target audience for MTV is the same target for pictures. You need the twelve-to-twenty-five demographic," a studio executive told *Variety*. Soon the producers behind any movie seeking that young audience—i.e., most of them, apart from the decade's adult-exploitation pictures like *Gandhi* and *Out of Africa*—were crafting music videos to cross-promote both film and soundtrack. Typically, this would involve cutting back and forth between shots of the musicians and clips from the movies—glorified trailers, disguised as entertainment. In *Ferris Bueller's Day Off*, Hughes inserts a close-up of the hero's bedroom TV playing one of the channel's "moon man" IDs, simultaneously establishing Ferris's cool-teen bona fides and offering abject tribute to one of the era's most powerful gatekeepers.

The quasi-official bard of adolescence for Generation X was himself a card-carrying baby boomer. Born in 1950, a member of his high school's class of 1968, his tastes matured along the classic cultural arc: Howdy Doody to the White Album. He spent his formative years on the same leafy streets as Samantha Baker and Ferris Bueller, having moved from Grosse Pointe, the wealthy suburb outside of Detroit, to Northbrook, Illinois, a well-off but not-quite-as-well-off suburb twenty-some miles north of Chicago, when Hughes was about to start the seventh grade. "I didn't have this tortured childhood. I liked it," he told *The New York Times* in a 1991 interview, the sort of blanket assertion sure to raise a therapist's eyebrow. In a more reflective and literary mood, he would write, in an essay published a year before his death, "I understood that the dark side of my middle-class, middle-American, suburban life was not drugs, paganism, or perversion. It was disappointment. There were no gnawing insects beneath the grass. Only dirt." In the contradiction between those two recollections, in the tension between self-satisfaction and unease, between suburban normality and its discontents, lay much of Hughes's humor.

His father mostly worked in sales—a brief foray into beauty-shop ownership ended in bankruptcy—and the family, while comfortable, wasn't as well off as most of its neighbors, a source, perhaps, of the class anxieties and conflicted longings that inform many of his films. He once recalled, "I knew kids that, in the third grade, would say, 'When I'm eighteen, I'm getting $22 million dollars.'" In another interview, he referenced Steff, the callow, sybaritic snob James Spader played in *Pretty in Pink*: "I had a guy like him haunt me all the way through high school. Money to burn. His older brother had an Alfa, the big, nice one, and parked it outside with the top down in the rain. I would walk by and see the rosewood buckling on the dash. I couldn't understand how kids could live like that. I just wasn't part of that world." Except that he was, at least to the extent that he knew his way around different models of Alfa Romeos and what kind of wood was used for their dashboards.

"What were you like growing up?" Molly Ringwald asked her director in a Q&A between the two of them published in *Seventeen* in 1986. "I was kind of quiet," Hughes replied. "I grew up in a neighborhood that was mostly girls and old people. There weren't any boys my age, so I spent a lot of time by myself, imagining things . . . Life just started getting good in seventh grade, and then we moved to Chicago. I ended up in a really big high school and I didn't know anybody." In those years, he was an aspiring painter as well as a budding writer. He was also a passionate music fan. The Beatles and Bob Dylan "changed my whole life," he told Ringwald, describing the transformation as virtually instantaneous: "Thursday I was one person, and Friday I was another." He started dressing like his idols, assembling a mod wardrobe that made him stand out in a preppy student body. "We had a serious dress code," he recalled in another interview. "I almost didn't graduate because my hair touched my collar. Back then I wanted to be Picasso, Michelangelo, James Joyce, or Bob Dylan. That's where I took my solace. People would make fun of me and I'd think, 'That's okay. Picasso would like me.'" The romance of being a misunderstood outsider, or at least pretending to be one, stayed with him. "I think he always felt like he didn't belong," Ringwald observed years later. "I remember him telling me something like, 'I'm a square peg in a round world.' It sounded like some kind of mantra."

Not that this made Hughes a high school untouchable like Duckie or the various geek characters he wrote for Anthony Michael Hall. "He did not fit in, that's all true—but that wasn't a negative. It's what made him *cool*. He was never isolated. He was never made fun of, or chastised, or ignored," a close friend of Hughes's from high school told Susannah Gora for her excellent history of 1980s teen movies, *You Couldn't Ignore Me If You Tried*. (Gora's subtitle, *The Brat Pack, John Hughes, and Their Impact on a Generation*, is yet more tribute to how large these films loomed for their initial audiences.)

In an interview included on the DVD of *Ferris Bueller's Day Off*,

Hughes describes the dynamic among Ferris, his girlfriend, Sloane, and his mopey best friend, Cameron, as "this classic third-wheel situation, which I was always in." Hughes, however, was the first wheel: "I always had my girlfriend . . . and some guy in the back seat going, 'What are we doing?'" In their *Seventeen* interview, Ringwald asked him which of his characters were most like him. He cited Ferris as well as Samantha—and Allison, *The Breakfast Club*'s artsy-spooky "basket case," played by Ally Sheedy. Blend the three and you get a portrait of an odd, sensitive, but self-confident and popular kid.

Two more adolescent obsessions point more directly toward the filmmaker Hughes would become. In junior high school, he began writing jokes and mailing them to comedians like Rodney Dangerfield and Phyllis Diller. He scored at least one hit with Dangerfield. A friend told Susannah Gora that he and Hughes were watching the comedian on *The Ed Sullivan Show* one Sunday night at Hughes's house when all of a sudden, "John starts to freak out and says, 'Those are my jokes! Those are my jokes! The ones I sent him!'" Writing freelance jokes for comics was a discipline Hughes would maintain into his twenties. The writer David Kamp gained access to some of Hughes's archives for a posthumous profile in *Vanity Fair*:

> [Hughes] was relentless, serially pestering the comics with sheaves of gags, neatly typed up on onion-skin paper. He tailored his jokes for each comedian's voice—e.g., for Dangerfield, "I know a guy who's so kosher he wouldn't let his son join the ham-radio club," and for Diller, "My husband thinks my measurements are 34-26-34-HIKE!"

Corny gags reflected one facet of Hughes's developing aesthetic. Opposite that was his preoccupation with the movie *Doctor Zhivago*, released in 1965, the year Hughes turned fifteen. He told Ringwald, "I saw *Doctor Zhivago* every day from the day it opened until the day it left the theater. The usher would say, 'Hiya, your seat's ready.' And I just sat there glued to the screen." Surely Hughes was being hyperbolic about seeing

David Lean's three-and-a-quarter-hour film every day (though he made the claim in other interviews as well). But if you peppered that picture's swooning romance with a fusillade of one-liners, you might end up with a tone very close to *Sixteen Candles'*.

Ferris Bueller's anxieties about life after high school may have had their roots in Hughes's experiences at the University of Arizona. He felt out of place in a big southwestern party school where the social life was dominated by fraternities and sororities, and was further alienated by flunking a creative writing class, a subject he rightly felt was a strong suit. "Enormously homesick and . . . completely displaced"—his words—he dropped out and returned home to marry the aforementioned high school girlfriend, Nancy Ludwig, in 1970. He was twenty, she was nineteen. Unlike most people who a) got married in the 1970s and b) went into show business, he would remain married until his death.

But Hughes was done with college. Having already decided he wanted to become some kind of writer, and get paid for it, he had continued mailing jokes to comedians, and was by now having some success at it. But while freelance gag writing was and is a thing—it's how Woody Allen started, too—scattershot paydays at $5 to $10 a joke only went so far. Unhappy making ends meet with a series of factory jobs, Hughes parlayed his facility for one-liners into a copywriting gig at a local ad agency, launching a meteoric career that soon landed him at Leo Burnett, the most prominent of Chicago's ad agencies. His most memorable achievement was a campaign for Edge shaving gel, a Space Age advance in men's grooming, in which an announcer demonstrated its efficacy by scraping "an ordinary credit card" across a handsome model's face, one half of which has been shaved using Edge, the other with some unnamed competitor's antiquated foam. The credit card barely makes a sound traversing the close, smooth Edge cheek, while scratching like a beat-up old LP across the Brand X cheek. Beneath its cool reserve, the spot had all the verve of an old medicine show stunt, attention-getting and effective.

Not content merely to become Don Draper, Hughes began moonlighting as a contributor to the *National Lampoon*, the humor magazine launched in 1970 by former editors of the *Harvard Lampoon*. It soon became a humming engine of American comedy, powering an off-Broadway revue and a syndicated radio show, with writers and performers who would form the nucleus of the first cast and writing staff of *Saturday Night Live*, among them John Belushi and Chevy Chase. A bigger and more lucrative brand extension was the movie *National Lampoon's Animal House*, which, with Belushi in its most memorable role, became the highest-grossing comedy in Hollywood history upon its release in 1978.* The script was co-written by one of the magazine's founding editors, Doug Kenney, who went on to co-write *Caddyshack*, before falling off a cliff in Hawaii and dying at the age of thirty-three.

The magazine originally had a druggy, countercultural ethos, but its satire could be just as vicious toward its own generation's sacred cows as toward, say, Spiro Agnew and Kate Smith. The tone could be savage and deliberately, even gleefully offensive, but also eggheady, anarchic, and surreal. Tits and ass had always been part of the formula, but after the founding editors cashed out in 1975 and a core of early contributors moved on, the magazine leaned into its puerile side, the satirical persona now more locker-room towel snapper than stoned Ivy Leaguer or profane Jesuit. While the *Lampoon* had never been what would now be called politically correct or woke — a point of fierce pride — minorities and "foreigners" were more and more the butts of jokes. As Ellin Stein writes in her history of the magazine, *That's Not Funny, That's Sick*, it had become less clear whether the writers were "mocking small-mindedness or embodying it." Or maybe it *was* clear. P. J. O'Rourke, a longtime staffer who became editor in chief in 1978, told *Newsweek* that same year, "We take the stance of the white, educated, upper-middle class." In truth, that was always the magazine's makeup, but it had once had the good taste to be embarrassed by it. Now, O'Rourke claimed, "Our comic pose is

---

*That title would be taken six years later by *Ghostbusters*, another film generated by the *Lampoon-SNL* nexus. It was supplanted in another six years by *Home Alone*, written and produced by Hughes.

superior. It's says, 'I'm better than you and I'm going to destroy you.' It's
an offensive, very aggressive form of humor." It was as if the *Lampoon*
was already gearing up for the Reagan years.

That was the magazine Hughes started writing for in 1977, juggling
assignments with his day job at Leo Burnett. Two years later, he quit the
agency and joined the *Lampoon*'s staff full-time, though he remained in
the Chicago suburbs, where he and Nancy were now raising two young
sons. That rootedness may have been his secret weapon as a writer, and it
helped connect him to O'Rourke, a fellow Midwesterner who had grown
up in Toledo. The pair became "real tight," as one colleague put it. In a
tribute to Hughes written after his death, O'Rourke claimed the two men
never discussed politics per se—though Hughes was at least nominally a
Republican—but bonded over a shared resentment of a prevailing cultural ethos that looked down on middle-class middle America, the "pinko"
disdain for suburban strivers. Maybe the best summation of Hughes's so-
ciopolitical outlook was his own passing observation, made to O'Rourke:
"You remember the line in *The Graduate* where the party guest tells the
Dustin Hoffman character, 'I just want to say one word to you. Just one
word. Plastics.' That was 1967. If the Dustin Hoffman character had gotten into plastics, he'd be a millionaire by now, instead of riding on a city
bus with a crazy girl in a wedding dress."*

Perhaps in the spirit of "it takes one to know one," O'Rourke and
Hughes didn't refrain from poking mostly gentle fun at middle-class
mores and myopias, as when they collaborated on a special project for the
magazine, an elaborate and detailed-down-to-the-last-agate-type-notice
Sunday newspaper parody, *The Dacron Republican-Democrat*, which
came complete with color comics, sports, travel stories, obituaries, a
"Living Life" section, another devoted to "Entertainment . . . Also, the
Arts," and an advertising circular for the big Swillmart store ("Where
Quality Is a Slogan") down at the Corngate Plaza. (This was a sequel of

---

*Very possibly true. I once researched the question and people who went into plastics
in the late 1960s generally did quite well for themselves.

sorts to the *Lampoon*'s 1964 high school yearbook parody that O'Rourke and Doug Kenney had collaborated on.) Sample headlines from the "Sunday Week" magazine insert: "Dacron's Illegal Aliens: Will They Both Be Deported?" and "A Mouthful of Courage: One Woman's Battle with Breath Cancer." One of Hughes's presumably more offhand contributions, a single personal ad amid a dense page of classifieds, was a minor masterpiece of comic concision, an epic poem of humiliation in a mere thirteen words: "Karen. HAPPY VALENTINE'S DAY even if no boys sent you any cards. — Dad." It could have served as a pitch for a companion film to *Sixteen Candles*.

Unsurprisingly, many of Hughes's *Lampoon* pieces focus on adolescence. They're a mixed bag. A magazine parody, *Savvyteen*, with features like "Dear Pretty Person . . ." and "A Clean Tongue Is In!," deftly satirize the way the beauty industry and magazines like *Seventeen* exploit—and fuel—teenage girls' insecurities; it was the rare *Lampoon* feature that evinced some interest in women's lives. Other pieces, like "How to Tell What Girls Are Like Under Their Clothes" (self-explanatory) and "Lore of the Firecracker" (a celebratory field guide to childhood explosives) are depressing examples of a once-fearless magazine now pandering.

Arguably most germane to Hughes's future as a filmmaker, more so even than his short story "Vacation '58"—which became the basis for *National Lampoon's Vacation* and its three sequels—were a pair of twinned first-person sagas, "My Penis" and "My Vagina," published five months apart, which read like Kafka, if Kafka wrote the letters in *Penthouse*. In the former piece, a teenaged girl wakes up one morning with male genitalia. In the latter, gender and bits are reversed:

> I was a sixteen-year-old guy with a box! I had a damn ugly, hairy woman's privates and it was gross and sickening, and I was so pissed off I wanted to punch it right in the face!

Neither piece is funny, and both weirdly end with sexual violence: the girl with a penis forces her boyfriend to blow her, and the boy with a vagina is gang-raped by his friends (and must spend the money he was saving for skis on an abortion). But leaving aside whatever else those choices might say about Hughes, they do provide striking early examples of his ability to channel a teenage mindset; it's not just any writer who could devote ten thousand words across two stories to obsessing convincingly over the shock and novelty of having sex organs. Whatever else they are, "My Vagina" and "My Penis" are, in tandem, a feat of sustained adolescent self-loathing.

When the success of *Animal House* led to a gold rush for more *Lampoon*-branded screenplays, Hughes, already known as a workhorse, proved to be one of the few staffers who could not just bat around movie ideas, however dubious, but then also complete a script, a competent one, in timely fashion. Matty Simmons, the magazine's publisher, now a budding mogul, assigned him a comic sequel, *Jaws 3, People 0* (a bad idea but a pretty good title), followed by an adaptation of the illustrated how-to book *The Joy of Sex* (not quite as unlikely as it sounds, given Woody Allen's success a few years previous adapting *Everything You Always Wanted to Know About Sex*). Neither of those came to anything, but *National Lampoon's Class Reunion* was made, released in 1982, and ignored. ("The screenplay, by John Hughes, is a lot more vulgar and dopey than it is genuinely comic . . . Still, it's reasonably cheerful." — *The New York Times*.)

Hughes was also hired to adapt his "Vacation '58," a nostalgic/acerbic story about a Midwestern family's disaster-plagued cross-country trip in a new, soon-to-be-battered Plymouth station wagon. With Chevy Chase as the hapless paterfamilias, the story now set in the present, and with its darker corners scrubbed and lit, *National Lampoon's Vacation* was released in the summer of 1983 to not-quite–*Animal House* levels of box office, but with a good enough return on investment to eventually spawn three sequels. And that was only Hughes's first Hollywood success that summer; less than a month after *Vacation*, he had a second hit with another dad-centric, sitcom-style comedy: *Mr. Mom*, his first original screenplay independent of the *Lampoon*, spun from a stretch of afternoons he spent at home caring for his two sons after morning bouts of writing. Not that he was pleased with what ended up on screen. "*Mr. Mom* was pretty badly butchered," he told *Film Comment*'s Jack Barth, adding (perhaps still in "My Penis/Vagina" mode), "I just got raped on that project." Nevertheless, the picture, directed by Stan Dragoti and starring Michael Keaton, was the year's ninth-highest-grossing film, followed by *Vacation*, which Harold Ramis had directed, in the tenth spot.

Hughes had found his medium, if not quite his comfort zone or his richest subject matter. He would later say, "I wasn't very happy as a [screenwriter]. I got bounced off *Mr. Mom* and *National Lampoon's Vacation* for shooting my mouth off a little too much. One director said to me, 'If they fire you, we make the movie. If they fire *me*, we don't.' So I thought I'd better become one of those director people."

Hughes would become famous in Hollywood for his ability to bash out scripts in marathon writing sessions, fueled only by coffee and cigarettes. With an eye to writing something he himself could direct, he dashed off what would become *The Breakfast Club* over two days in the summer of 1982. "I'm a very disciplined writer, because of my background in advertising," he once explained (as if discipline were all there was to it). "When I get a good idea," he continued, "I can't wait to read it myself, so when I write, I write sixteen hours a day. I have enormous concentration. I don't take a break until it's done." He added—trigger warning for fellow procrastinating writers—"If I'm on a roll, and I finish a script at 3:00, I'll start another at 3:02."

One impulse behind *The Breakfast Club* was that Hughes thought a play-like film set in a single confined space with a smallish cast would be an easy lift for a first-time director. He got a deal with the record label A&M, which was trying to branch into film, but preproduction jitters and some further thought—how do you make a film about five kids stuck in detention cinematic enough to hold an audience's attention?—convinced him he should cut his teeth on something more conventional, so he whipped up *Sixteen Candles* and Ned Tanen, now the former head of production at Universal who you will remember from *American Graffiti* and *Fast Times at Ridgemont High*, brought it to his former studio, where he now had a production deal. Universal ended up hiring Hughes to direct both screenplays.

He later said that writing about teenagers came naturally to him because their concerns were familiar to him. "My wife and I were ten years younger than every other [parent] in our neighborhood, so I was surrounded by teenagers," he told *Premiere* magazine. He had also befriended the children of older colleagues at his ad agencies, and even used them as sounding boards. A friend's teenaged daughter "listened to my script idea for *Sixteen Candles*, liked it, and encouraged me to write it." Another friend's teenaged son gave him the title for *The Breakfast Club*, a nickname for morning detention at the kid's school. Hughes later befriended Ned Tanen's teenaged daughter, Sloane (and gave her name to Ferris Bueller's girlfriend). "He was interested in my life in a way that most adults aren't, interested in the little minutiae and details," Sloane Tanen told Gora. "He was an observer, but you never felt like you were being studied. It felt like he was a contemporary."

As Hughes himself said to Ringwald in their *Seventeen* interview, "I can walk up to a seventeen-year-old and say, 'How do you get along with your friends?' and he'll say, 'Okay.' You ask a thirty-five-year-old the same question and he'll say, 'Why do you want to know? What's wrong? Get away from me.' All those walls build up."

He was adamant that he would never condescend to young audiences, once mockingly imitating a rival teen-movie impresario: "Well, they like sex a lot, and they like dope. We'll put that together, and they love those video things, and they like cars because they're always in cars."

Moreover, Hughes never lost touch with his own inner teen, perhaps to a fault. "I think he's still trying to be popular at school," Jon Cryer told *Time* for its Ringwald cover—joking, but maybe not. "I don't think he had really ever gotten over certain aspects of his adolescence," Mia Sara, who played Sloane in *Ferris Bueller's Day Off*, told Gora. Colleagues frequently described Hughes as "a big kid." Said one, "It's like he channeled teenagers." Said another, "He was just totally on their level, totally 'got' them." Sartorially, he split the difference between high school and creative class professional, with floppy clothes, big sneakers, and a carefully tended mullet lent gravitas by the kind of heavy but clear-framed glasses an architect or a book editor might have worn in the eighties. Contemporary profiles inevitably compared him to the proverbial hip young teacher "that the kids have always confided in," to quote but one example, from the *Los Angeles Times*, in 1986.

Like an adolescent, he himself could be deeply loyal, and he grew close to some of his young stars, meeting them on their terms. He and Ringwald bonded over music and exchanged mixtapes. "It was really sweet and kind of . . . *teenage!*" she recalled decades later. "I spend time with kids, and it isn't condescending time, like, 'Gee what are you nutty kids up to today?'" he told one interviewer, describing Anthony Michael Hall as "a friend of mine. He happens to be sixteen and I don't pay any attention to that. I'm sure people who see me rolling around the floor laughing hysterically at some ridiculous thing that he's said will think that there's something wrong with me, but I do consider him my friend." Hall returned the affection, later saying Hughes was his best friend during the years they worked together. But at the same time, the director was also moody and easily bruised, and not quick to forget a perceived slight. He eventually dropped both Ringwald and Hall for reasons they claimed they never quite understood. In that, too, he resembled a teenager.

Let's get *Weird Science* out of the way. It's about two nerds, Hall and Ilan Mitchell-Smith, who somehow use a 1980s home computer to create their idea of a perfect woman, in the form of British model Kelly LeBrock. Even Hughes dismissed the picture as "a mess," made only because he was in a filmmaking "feeding frenzy—bang bang bang, let's go!" (Nice work if you can get it.) The movie is memorable for LeBrock's unexpectedly winning performance in a preposterous role, and for a painful, interminable sequence where the trio visits a blues club and Hall's character drunkenly does a "jive talk" voice for what feels like fifteen minutes. It wasn't the worst movie I watched while researching this book, but it was in the running.

Now we can discuss the canon.

The idea for *Sixteen Candles* came to Hughes, he would say, while he was looking at actors to cast in his aborted first run at *The Breakfast Club*. He became infatuated with Ringwald's headshot and, as she recalled it, "decided to write another movie around the character he imagined that girl to be." That girl, Samantha, turned out to be a close to quintessential sixteen-year-old: eager, hopeful, sullen, exasperated (in no particular order). Her older sister's wedding, taking place the next day, is the reason her family has forgotten her birthday. Her parents are well-meaning but clueless; her younger brother is a precocious, wisecracking brat—a stock character, though with more of an edge than his TV sitcom counterparts, as when he overhears that the older sister has gotten her period on the eve of her wedding. "Should make for an interesting honeymoon, huh?" he smirks. He was played by Justin Henry, only a few years removed from being the youngest ever Oscar nominee, at eight, for his role in *Kramer vs. Kramer* (1979).

More humiliation: Sam's grandparents are in town for the wedding. Grandma takes a look at her chest and exclaims, "Fred, she's gotten her boobies!" Grandpa: "I better go get my magnifying glass." "They're so perky!" chirps Grandma, reaching out. Cut to: Sam, behind her slammed bedroom door, with another eye roll: "I can't believe my grandma felt me up."

That's Samantha's home life. At school, she answers a friend's written sex test (*Have you ever touched it?* "I don't think so") and pines for Jake Ryan, a dreamy senior boy who is improbably fond of sweater vests. He has the usual blond girlfriend, Caroline, whose nude, perfectly proportioned body is appraised by an intimidated Sam and an unintimidated camera in a gratuitous girls' locker room scene. Meanwhile, Sam has to fend off Anthony Michael Hall's nerd character who has the hots for her and won't take no for an answer, even after she dismisses him as "a total fag." She eventually relents to the extent that she gives him a pair of her panties so he can win a bet with his geeky friends, a development that I feel confident in saying would never, ever happen in real life, and yet somehow didn't cause Hughes to lose his audience.

Like so many other memorably compressed teen movies, most of the action in *Sixteen Candles* takes place across a single night, including a high school dance and a subsequent rager at Jake's house. Four decades later, it's hard to remember why the movie once seemed so fresh. I think it was the mix of caustic, sometimes mean-spirited, *National Lampoon–*style humor—for instance, a series of sight gags about a girl in a back brace played by a then-unknown Joan Cusack, and, of course, Long Duk Dong—with sincere if minor-key melodrama. Samantha's problems aren't huge, but they feel that way to her, and the movie not only honors that but amplifies it. Ringwald's performance is essential to the effect; here, and in her other movies with Hughes, she has an awkward grace that's always watchable—she's half duckling, half flamingo—with a face that betrays her every fleeting emotion, though her specialty is an expression with lips slightly apart that lies somewhere between a grimace and a pout. Resting "whatever" face. Pauline Kael wrote in her review of *Sixteen Candles* that Ringwald radiated a "charismatic normality," which is exactly right. There's a scene during the dance where, thinking she's embarrassed herself in front of Jake, Sam flees the gym, runs down a hall, stops and pounds her fist on a fire hose case, then sinks to the floor with a look of anguish and confusion on her face to rival James Dean's at the height of his "You're tearing me apart!" powers, but minus the howling. She's Dean Lite, which isn't a bad thing.

Hall, too, gives his character a self-aware vulnerability beneath his pestering bravado that renders his potentially tiresome geek bearable, even appealing, and gifts the comedy an inch or two of depth. (Hughes knew the young actor because he appeared in *Vacation*.) As evidence of the character's lowly status, no one ever bothers to use his name, which is apparently Ted. In a quiet scene where the two characters briefly let down their facades in *Breakfast Club* mode, he confesses to Sam, ruefully, "I've never bagged a babe. I'm not a stud." The fact that the confession is so unnecessary is funny, but underneath the humor is a sympathetic nod to the performative nature of high school.

But there's so much that's so wrong with this movie, and not just Long Duk Dong or the subplot about Samantha's panties. There is also the serial humiliation of Caroline, Jake's girlfriend. At the party, after getting her hair caught in a door, she passes out while Jake and Ted have a late-night heart-to-heart in the family kitchen. It turns out Jake has been harboring a parallel crush on Sam all this time. But when Ted chivalrously questions whether his intentions are honorable, Jake responds, "I can get any piece of ass I want. Why, I've got Caroline upstairs passed out. I could violate her ten different ways." He ends up making a deal with Ted, who still has Samantha's panties: "Give me those and I'll let you drive Caroline home . . . She's totally gone. Have fun!" This is the movie's Prince Charming: facilitating the date rape of his girlfriend. The next morning, Ted and Caroline wake up, disheveled, in Jake's dad's Rolls-Royce convertible, which Jake has inexplicably allowed Ted to drive.

                              TED
              Did we, uh . . . ?

                            CAROLINE
              Yeah, I'm pretty sure.

                              TED
              Did I enjoy it? I mean, of course
              I did. Did you?

                            CAROLINE
              You know, I have this weird
              feeling, I think I did.

I think that last line is intended as a grace note.

The movie then leaves Ted and Caroline behind, moving on to preparations for the wedding. Ginny, the bride, has taken four muscle relaxers to deal with her period; as wasted as Caroline was the night before, Ginny can barely make it through the wedding, heading off to her honeymoon with her dress predictably caught in the car door. For a movie often celebrated for centering a teenage girl, *Sixteen Candles* has a wide misogynistic streak.

Samantha, passive and reactive through most of the movie, has barely interacted with Jake. But now, in more traditional Prince Charming mode, he shows up out of the blue at her sister's wedding and whisks Sam back to his house to celebrate her birthday. *Finally.* Sitting on a table with a birthday cake and sixteen lit candles between them, he tells her, "Make a wish." "It already came true," she responds, and then they lean in for a kiss, somehow not burning their chins, while the Thompson Twins' "If You Were Here" swells on the soundtrack. (Hughes, who had a good ear for pop hits, was lucky to be making films during the vogue for synthheavy "new romantic" groups, whose brooding sonic melodrama fit his movies to a tee.)

I hope I am not being guilty of presentism when I note with some surprise that critics and audiences took all this in stride—for the most part. (I include myself in that, a twentysomething fan of the movie when it came out in 1984.) Janet Maslin in *The New York Times* called *Sixteen Candles* "a cuter and better-natured teen comedy than most, with the kinds of occasional lapses in taste that probably can't hurt it in the circles for which it is intended." Kael similarly wrote, "It's less raucous in tone than most of the recent teen pictures; it's closer to the gentle English comedies of the forties and fifties." And I suppose it *was* gentler and better natured than, say, *Risky Business* (which has its own problems with misogyny) or *Porky's* (which has its own problems with misogyny *and* racism). *Sixteen Candles* ended up taking in $24 million at the box office, the thirty-seventh-highest-grossing movie of 1984—a success if not quite an unqualified hit. With a modest budget of $6.4 million, no one took a bath.

The Breakfast Club was a harder sell and a bigger hit, taking in $46 million on a budget of only $1 million (smaller cast, one location), after it was released in February 1985, just nine months after *Sixteen Candles*. Unfolding like a combination kitchen-sink drama, group therapy session, and TV bottle episode, the movie locks its five main characters in their high school library for Saturday detention. (The setting is not quite as dreary as it sounds, given the library's very 1980s neon accents.) The quintet are more or less strangers, each slotted into a rigid role due to the strictures of high school culture as well as the needs of Hughes's screenplay: Ringwald's "princess," Ally Sheedy's "basket case," Judd Nelson's "criminal" or "rebel," Emilio Estevez's "athlete," and Anthony Michael Hall's "brain." By the third act, souls and secrets have been bared amid shouting and tears. Critics cited all kinds of predecessors: Gene Siskel called it "a thoroughly serious teenage version of *Who's Afraid of Virginia Woolf?*" Pauline Kael, less admiring, compared it to *A Chorus Line* "without the dancing." I was put in mind of the stereotypical World War II–combat picture with the Italian kid from Brooklyn and the Okie and the Ivy League lieutenant all crammed together in a foxhole. In this, *The Breakfast Club* occupies a spot in film history as the first teen movie to codify a vision of high school as composed not just of types or social classes but tribes, which, aside from passing volleys of cruelty, keep to themselves. There was no more teenage monoculture (if there ever had been).

The picture opens portentously, with the anthemic chug of Simple Minds' "(Don't You) Forget About Me" (written for the movie and famously reprised at the end). On screen, a title card quotes lyrics from a different song, David Bowie's "Changes," white letters on black, including the line about "these children that you spit on / as they try to change their worlds."

The title card then loudly shatters, like a glass window blown in by an explosion, setting an apocalyptic mood for an otherwise pedestrian setup sequence with parents dropping their kids off at the school on a Saturday morning.

These wintry, stone-faced adults, we will learn in the *Rebel Without a Cause* manner, are the root of all their children's problems, possibly excepting some of their fashion choices. Mom and Dad demand too much, or love too little, or both at once. Estevez's Andrew is in detention because he brutally hazed a younger kid in the locker room in an effort to prove his competitive fire to his drill sergeant of a father. (Andrew imitating dad: "You've got to be number one . . . Your intensity is for shit . . . *Win! Win! Win!*") Hall's Brian is in detention because a gun was found in his locker after he failed shop and, fearing his parents' reaction, contemplated shooting himself. (Mightn't therapy have been a better course of action than detention?) Allison, the Ally Sheedy character, retreats behind bangs, smeary kohl eyeliner, a black sweater the size of Connecticut, and self-consciously weird behavior like throwing lunch meat over her shoulder. Her parents ignore her and possibly don't even know she's in detention— which really, she isn't. She's only present, she finally confesses, because she "didn't have anything better to do."

Judd Nelson's Bender, puller of false fire alarms and product of an abusive home, is the angry pot-stirrer, provoking and insulting everyone, though devoting most of his energy to needling Ringwald's spoiled Claire, whose infraction was skipping school to shop. ("I can't believe you can't get me out of this," she whines to her dad at drop-off.) Inevitably, Bender's needling is sexual. First off, he demands to know if Claire is a virgin: "I'll bet you a million dollars that you are. Let's end the suspense. Is it gonna be a white wedding?" When "sporto" Andrew stands up to him, he sneers, "Do you slip her the hot beef injection?" (Hughes tended to overwrite his teen slang.) Later, when Bender is under a desk, hiding from the vice principal with the $31K salary, Hughes includes a shot from Bender's perspective looking straight up Claire's skirt—making *The Breakfast Club* the second Hughes film in a row in which Ringwald's panties make a cameo. Bender then puts his head between her knees, with Claire's startled reaction, flinching but not wanting to give him away, played for laughs.

A body double was used for the under-the-desk shots, but the sequence still made Ringwald uncomfortable. As she wrote years later in *The New Yorker*:

> Even having another person pretend to be me was embarrassing to me and upsetting to my mother, and she said so. The scene stayed, though.

What's more, as I can see now, Bender sexually harasses Claire throughout the film. When he's not sexualizing her, he takes out his rage on
her with vicious contempt. (If I sound overly critical, it's only with hindsight. Back then, I was only vaguely aware of how inappropriate much
of John's writing was, given my limited experience and what was considered normal at the time. I was well into my thirties before I stopped
considering verbally abusive men more interesting than nice ones.)

Ringwald is right: Bender's harassment of Claire is relentless and hard to
sit through. Aren't there other ways Hughes could have chosen for Bender
to express his anger? If the movie doesn't exactly approve of his abuse, it
doesn't condemn it, either. And ultimately, he's rewarded: for reasons that
neither screenplay nor performances can explicate, Claire makes out with
him and gives him a diamond earring. Was there an element of authorial
wish fulfillment to both the abuse and the snogging? "I didn't have any
fondness for Claire as I wrote that character," Hughes told *Premiere*. "It's
fairly difficult to find sympathy for a character that in high school would
basically have poked me in the forehead and said, 'Get lost!'"

In further deference to last-act conventions, Claire gives Sheedy's Allison a makeover, wiping away the kohl around her eyes, banishing her
baggy black sweater to reveal the frilly pink sleeveless shirt beneath, and
sweeping her hair out of her eyes with a pink hairband and Madonna-style
lace bow. It's an awful misstep that even many of the movie's loyalists acknowledge. (Several generations of goths have surely felt betrayed.) "I think
we probably should have left her alone or tried something less drastic or
more original," Sheedy admitted; she at least talked Hughes out of having
Claire doll up Allison even more with her conventional arsenal of lipstick,
eye shadow, and rouge. Nevertheless, the movie celebrates the character's
cover girl turn by having her catch Andrew's eye. The scene could be a
knowing riff on the old movie cliché of a mousy librarian or secretary taking off her glasses and unpinning her bun to expose the bombshell who's
been hiding beneath, but that would be a different picture. Hughes plays it
straight—conventional prettiness as a character reveal.

The two pairing-offs make for another fairy-tale ending, even more improbable than *Sixteen Candles'*. But audiences might have soured on the movie had it ended on an earlier, more realistic note, where Brian says, "I was just wondering, what's going to happen to us on Monday, when we're all together again?" Will they hang out, or even acknowledge one another in the hallway? "You mean are we still friends?" Claire asks. "You want the truth? . . . I don't think so." The question hangs over the rest of the film. Hughes once said, "There's no way I'm going to end a movie on a negative note," and he doesn't here; but beneath *The Break-fast Club*'s humor and catharsis lies something unsettling, not entirely banished by the making over and making out, not even by Judd Nelson's iconic, defiantly raised fist in the final freeze frame—an all-purpose "fuck you" to the world. It feels good in the moment, though.

Another question hangs over the movie, or rather, it's Allison's response after Andrew blurts out, "My god, are we going to be like our parents?"

"It's unavoidable. It just happens," she replies matter-of-factly. "When you grow up, your heart dies." Hmmm. Do those of us who have aged into adulthood, however awkwardly, agree? I can't put it better than Pauline Kael did in her review of *The Breakfast Club*: "Young audiences have always been suckers for this kind of flattery." True: it worked for *Rebel Without a Cause*, too.

The funny thing is, if I can pull back for a moment, once upon a time, kids *wanted* to grow up. Andy Hardy did: much of the films' humor derives from him straining to take on adult responsibilities, whether a car payment or a date with a big-city sophisticate or a potential marriage proposal. James Dean's Jim Stark is desperate for his father to tell him how to be a man, while "You can't stay seventeen forever" is one of *American Graffiti*'s most resonant lines. Now we have comedies about aging boys (mostly boys, like Will Ferrell or Seth Rogen or Paul Rudd or Pete Davidson, but sometimes girls, too, as in *Bridesmaids* and *Trainwreck*) dragged into adulthood against their will—*Kicking and Screaming*, to cite the title of Noah Baumbach's

1995 film about reluctant, newly minted college graduates. You could argue the cycle began with the slob comedies of the late '70s and early '80s that came out of the *Lampoon-SNL* nexus: *Caddyshack, Stripes, Meatballs,* even *Animal House,* where John Belushi's character, Bluto Blutarski, is in his seventh year of college with no diploma in sight. You could argue the cycle stretches even further back, at least as far as Huck Finn and his refusal to allow Aunt Polly to "sivilize" him.

Yet it's hard to imagine an earlier point in history when a rich and powerful man in his midthirties could blithely tell a newspaper interviewer, as Hughes did in 1986, "I don't feel as if I've grown up, not entirely." The eighties were a signal decade in this regard: the decade when baby boomers began to reach middle age — no fun for most of us, but an extra-rough transition for a generation that was encouraged to see its youth as a cardinal virtue. A pop diagnosis emerged: the Peter Pan Syndrome, which was the title of an influential self-help book (subtitle: *Men Who Never Grow Up*) published in 1983. "It slowly dawned on me," wrote the author, Dr. Dan Kiley, a clinical psychologist who treated students and young married couples, "that an alarming number of young men *weren't* coming of age. Something was wrong." Kiley claimed to have seen "a dramatic increase in the problem. And there's every reason to expect it to get worse in the coming years." However quantifiably true or not that was — had the one million delinquents alleged in the fifties become one million cases of arrested development in the eighties? — it clearly *felt* true to many readers: *The Peter Pan Syndrome* spent months on the *New York Times* bestseller list and ultimately entered the vernacular. It was part of the ethos that animated the worst movie Steven Spielberg ever made, *Hook,* in which Robin Williams, playing a middle-aged Peter Pan, must return to Neverland and rediscover his inner child in order to become a better father. My point here is that Hughes wasn't the only baby boomer in the 1980s, and especially in 1980s Hollywood, who viewed aging as a narcissistic wound. The fact that more and more of this cohort were now occupying executive suites may have added a wishful affinity to the very real marketing and distribution reasons for the decade's surge in teen movies.

•   •   •

Despite his intense identification with kids, Hughes was no Nicholas Ray; no one has ever suggested he crossed the boundaries that Ray did with Natalie Wood. But Hughes did become emotionally involved with his young casts in ways that many of them ended up feeling burdened by, particularly Ringwald and Hall. While shooting *The Breakfast Club*, Ringwald later admitted, she and Hall, the two members of the cast Hughes had worked with before (and the production's only true minors), "were sort of viewed as the teacher's pets. John would take us to concerts and invite us to his house." According to Judd Nelson, who was twenty-five, Hughes "babied" and "coddled" the two; the older actor said he used his resentment over that to fuel Bender's anger.*

Hughes and Hall had bonded on the set of *Sixteen Candles* over a shared sense of humor. "I remember the joy of making John laugh," Hall told Gora. The director was impressed by the young star's ability to improvise and took Hall under his wing, sharing insights into the filmmaking process and hosting him at the Hughes family home, where the two would watch Abbott and Costello and Laurel and Hardy movies and talk comedy shop. "I think it's probably fair to say that I was a muse of sorts for him," Hall said.

Ringwald, too. "I've been called his muse," she wrote, "which I believe I was, for a little while." One producer likened the dynamic between director and star to that of a father-daughter, or even an older brother–younger sister. Some accounts make the relationship sound more like a mutual crush. According to *Rolling Stone*, the two shared "a 'Secret Pleasures Record Club,' wherein they entrusted the name of their favorite Top Ten song to one another." Hughes would set Ringwald loose on his vast, eclectic record collection, gushing, "She always picks the most interesting cuts. She's so hip—she gets it before everybody else does."

---

*As minors, Ringwald and Hall were further distinguished from their *Breakfast Club* co-stars by their restricted hours on set.

The downside of Hughes's ability to channel his inner adolescent was a concomitant moodiness and easy-to-bruise vulnerability. "His was a heavy heart, deeply sensitive, prone to injury—easily broken," Ringwald wrote in a remembrance after his death. "Most people who knew John knew that he was able to hold a grudge longer than anyone—his grudges were almost supernatural things, enduring for years, even decades."

Ringwald and Hall had a brief romance during the *Breakfast Club* shoot, and their director "did not like it at all," she told David Kamp. She was surprised and disappointed that Hughes didn't direct *Pretty in Pink* himself, instead bringing on Howard Deutch, a first-time director who, as an editor, had cut trailers for some of Hughes's movies. When Hughes did visit the set, she felt he ignored her. Ringwald: "It was very hurtful, and it still hurts."

Was her romance with Hall the reason for her falling-out with Hughes? Was it her interest in working with other directors? Was there even really a falling-out? "I don't really know myself," Ringwald told Gora. "John felt really, um, hurt by things and by people."

Hughes took offense with Anthony Michael Hall after the actor turned down roles in both *Pretty in Pink* and *Ferris Bueller's Day Off*. He, too, was interested in working with other directors—he had a long series of discussions with Stanley Kubrick about taking the role in *Full Metal Jacket* (1987) that ultimately went to Matthew Modine—and, as his mother, Mercedes, later said, Michael, as the actor was known to family and friends, was worried about "getting pigeonholed more than he already was." That did not go over well with the man he had called his "best friend." "John Hughes would not accept it," Mercedes Hall remembered. "He would not give him his blessing. Michael tried reaching out to him, calling him, and Hughes never responded . . . I said to Michael, 'He's a grown man. You're half his age and he couldn't acknowledge what you were doing and just move on.'"

Ringwald wondered if the problem was ultimately that she and Hall, like most all teenagers, had needed independence from a parental figure, even from one as intent on being a cool dad as Hughes was: "I wanted to grow up, something I felt (rightly or wrongly) I couldn't do while working with John. Sometimes I wonder if that's what he found so unforgivable. We were like the Darling children when they make the decision to leave Neverland. And John was Peter Pan, warning us that if we left we could never come back."

Peter Pan is an overused metaphor, not just on self-help shelves, and not just in relation to middle-aged men. However, I think it's not only apt here but gets at the real power of Hughes's teen movies and the hold they have on audiences. Ambivalence about growing up ripples through all the films, not just *The Breakfast Club* and *Ferris Bueller's Day Off*, and it was clearly something Hughes felt keenly. I remember my own high school years as suffused with what I think of as present-tense nostalgia. There was a kind of glorious, focused melancholy in the awareness of our collective ticking clock—a good example, I think, of what Hughes meant about how, for teenagers, feeling bad can feel good.

There's a remarkable, even weird moment in the *Seventeen* interview between Ringwald and Hughes where he confesses, "I wrote *Pretty in Pink* the week after we finished *Sixteen Candles*. I so desperately hate to end these movies that the first thing I do when I'm done is write another one. Then I don't have to feel sad about having to leave and everyone going away. That's why I tend to work with the same people. I really be-friend them. I couldn't speak after *Sixteen Candles* was over. I returned to the abandoned house"—an empty home had been used for some of the film's interiors—"and they were tearing down your room. And I was just horrified because I wanted to stay there forever."

Hughes is grieving the transitory nature of filmmaking with the same over-the-top ache that might propel a senior to fantasize about never graduating. Do we ever have friends who are closer, or feel closer in the moment, than our high school friends? For many of us, they form the surrogate families that enable us to begin separating from our families of origin. A film's cast and crew can very much form a surrogate family, too, especially on location shoots, which Hughes's productions in the Chicago

suburbs were. But production intimacy, like teenage friend-group intimacy, can be evanescent.

The sense of an expiration date underscores the *Breakfast Club* line
about your heart dying when you grow up, and it's implicit in the way that
Sixteen Candles, *Pretty in Pink*, and *Some Kind of Wonderful* all center on
rites of passage, whether a sixteenth birthday or a prom. But change looms
especially large in *Ferris Bueller's Day Off*, which takes place in the spring
of the hero's senior year, graduation just a couple months away. Ferris is a
cool customer, but his anxiety about the future is what motivates him to
fake illness, play hooky, and drive into Chicago with girlfriend Sloane and
pal Cameron, who Ferris arm-twists into liberating his father's extremely
rare 1961 Ferrari 250 GT California Spyder. (There were only fifty-six ever
made; the film used replicas.) Ferris always gets his way; he has an incipient
master of the universe's sense of entitlement, which is played for laughs but
never questioned. The kids bullshit their way into a snooty restaurant for
lunch; visit the Chicago Museum of Art to grok Seurat's *A Sunday After-*
noon on the Island of La Grande Jatte; flirt with vertigo on the observation
deck of what was then the Sears Tower (now Willis Tower); attend both a
Cubs game at Wrigley Field and the Von Steuben Day parade on Dearborn
Street, where, at the latter, Ferris drives the crowd wild by jumping on a float
and lip-synching to recordings of Wayne Newton's "Danke Schoen" and the
Beatles' "Twist and Shout." (How Ferris knows "Danke Schoen" and why
the crowd is driven wild by a random teenager lip-synching golden oldies
are questions the movie, admittedly a fantasy, does not answer.)

But these escapades are haunted. At the parade, while Ferris clowns
around, Cameron and Sloane have the following exchange, about "the
future":

                          CAMERON
           I don't know what I'm going to do.

               SLOANE (long pause)
            College?

```
                        CAMERON
             Yeah, but to do what?


                  SLOANE (another long pause)
             What are you interested in?


                     CAMERON (smiling)
          Nothing.


                        SLOANE
             Me neither.
```

They both laugh. But later, in one of his asides to the audience, Ferris lays out his and Cameron's futures, as he sees them, with brutal frankness: "We're going to graduate in a couple months. And then—we'll have the summer. He'll work and I'll work. We'll see each other at night and on the weekends. Then he'll go to one school and I'll go to another. Basically, that will be it." He mentions that Sloane still has another year of high school, and says he wants to marry her (maybe the movie's most unrealistic daydream of all—*I'll always love the person I love at seventeen!*— though Hughes did marry his own high school sweetheart). Then Ferris lowers the boom on his friend:

> Cameron has never been in love, at least nobody's ever been in love with him. If things don't change for him, he's going to marry the first girl he lays, and she's going to treat him like shit, because she will have given him what he has built up in his mind as the end all, be all of human existence. She won't respect him. 'Cause you can't respect somebody who kisses your ass. It just doesn't work.

It's a bleak moment for a film that most people remember as a lark, and I'm not even going to attempt to parse Ferris's philosophy of male-female relationships. According to Matthew Broderick, the picture's first cut trended even darker, more sober and introspective, delving even further into "that fear of what happens when you reach a stage in life where you're at the top of the world in high school, but what comes next?"

It's a question that may have resonated as profoundly for a soon-to-be-middle-aged writer-director-producer of teen movies as for a high school senior. Maybe Hughes was in a pissy mood because he'd been unable to bond with his new cast the way he had with Ringwald, Hall, and some of his other actors. "That didn't happen with *Ferris Bueller's Day Off*," Mia Sara recalled. "I didn't really understand why he wanted to be friends." She added, "There were more experienced actors involved, and they weren't up for that 'Let's all hang out and be kids' kind of thing." At eighteen, Sara was the youngest central cast member, but she had already co-starred opposite Tom Cruise for director Ridley Scott in the fantasy film *Legend* (1985). Broderick, twenty-three, was a genuine star, having won a Tony as the lead in Neil Simon's *Brighton Beach Memoirs*; with *WarGames* (1984), he also had a hit movie to his credit. Alan Ruck, who played Cameron, was even older, just two years short of thirty; he and Broderick came to Hughes as a kind of package, close friends who had co-starred in *Biloxi Blues*, Simon's sequel to *Brighton Beach Memoirs*. Jennifer Grey, twenty-four, who played Ferris's jealous younger sister, had a thinner résumé, but having grown up in Manhattan as Joel Grey's daughter, she hardly needed Hughes as a BFF, especially once she and Broderick began dating during the production.

Hughes now found himself in the uncomfortable role—the *adult* role—of boss more than ringleader. "I don't think—socially and on a personal level—it was easy for him, or as satisfying," Sara said. At one point in preproduction, he complained bitterly to Broderick, "You don't seem *into* it." But Hughes and his more seasoned cast figured out how to work together, and the result was his most successful movie to date, with $70 million at the box office—the tenth-highest-grossing film of 1986.

I think it's Hughes's best movie, his most entertaining and least dated, and also the one that most adroitly captures the contradictory nature of his teenage sensibility: blithe yet melancholy, smug yet sensitive, worried about the future yet unable to see past the end of its nose. That latter quality is, I think, especially prominent in the film's emotional climax, when Cameron, in the midst of deciding he's finally going to stand up to his overbearing, unloving father—"My old man pushes me around. I never say anything. He's not the problem. I'm the problem. I've got to take a stand."—accidentally sends the Ferrari crashing through the window of his dad's sleek, International Style garage and plunging into a ravine. I guess this is satisfying in a symbolic sense, with Cameron destroying his father's midlife phallic plaything—and in the nonsymbolic sense, it's fun to see kids total an expensive car. But Cameron seems to think that this will lead to a breakthrough in his relationship with his father, that he will finally be *heard*. Maybe. It's a fantasy a teenage boy might entertain, or a movie about a teenage boy made for teenage boys, but good luck in real life. As it happened, Ruck would bookend his career (to date) playing Connor Roy, the oldest and largely ignored son of another monstrous father on the HBO series *Succession*. When Connor, in a rare honest moment, says calmly, not angrily or bitterly, "I've learned to live without love. That's my superpower," this seems the destination where Cameron was more likely headed, too. But it's very much the epiphany of someone nearer the end of his life than the beginning.

"People keep asking me when am I going to *grow up* and make *adult* movies," Hughes once remarked. "I say, 'Grow up? Adult movies?' What am I supposed to do? Pat the kids on the head and say, 'Thanks, kids. It's been great, but now I'm going to make grown-up movies'?" He shook his head no.

That was in 1986, the year *Ferris Bueller* was released. But he did move on. "I had shot enough high school hallways, and I thought, I should rest this," he recalled years later. "All those people I had worked with had grown up." His last teen movie was the perfunctory *Some Kind of Wonderful*, basically a *Pretty in Pink* rewrite with the sexes reversed: Eric Stoltz as the boy from the wrong side of the tracks, Lea Thompson as the rich girl, Mary Stuart Masterson as the funky sidekick/competing love interest. Once again, Hughes handed his script to Howard Deutch to direct. It grossed a feeble $18.5 million when released in February 1987.

If part of the problem was that the picture felt like—*was*—a retread, a bigger issue may have been that teenagers' share of the moviegoing public was now contracting, beginning with a 20 percent drop in 1985 alone, according to *Variety*. The suspects: VCRs, video games, home computers. Before decade's end, the trade press was rife with articles about movies "growing up" again. "About half of the thirty highest-grossing films of 1987 were aimed at adult audiences, a ratio that would have been unthinkable just five years ago," the *Los Angeles Times* reported in 1988. "Nearly everyone in the industry concedes that the median age [of audiences] has gone up dramatically in recent years."

1988 was also the year Hughes released his penultimate film as a writer-director: *She's Having a Baby*, an autobiographical comedy-drama about a young married couple living in the Chicago suburbs, which I'm not quite sure counts as a grown-up movie, given its limitations, but it is definitely a movie *about* growing up. Kevin Bacon's Jake is an aspiring novelist who pays the bills by working at an advertising agency. Elizabeth McGovern's Kristy has no discernable interests or personality beyond the actress's soft prettiness; she's less a character than a narrative device, an obstacle deployed to focus Jake's anxieties about monogamy, paternity, mortgage payments, and lawn care. He fears being devoured by "the jaws of responsibility." (A case of something *dentata*?) Jake's ambivalence is driving him and Kristy apart, until the titular pregnancy alters the equation. There's a crisis in the delivery room, but all ends well—and a near tragedy is apparently just the nudge Jake needs to become a man in full, though the movie wraps up so quickly it's hard to say for sure. A moral more consistent with the bulk of the film is a crotchety grandfather's observation early on: "People don't mature anymore. They stay jackasses all their lives."

She's Having a Baby grossed only $16 million—a flop that wounded Hughes, given that the film was so personal. (The credits cite Nancy, his

wife, as "inspiration.") He would spend most of the rest of his career writing and producing the kinds of formulaic family comedies that had gotten him started as a screenwriter, including his most successful picture
of all, *Home Alone*, directed by Chris Columbus, which earned almost
half a billion dollars upon its release in 1990. Also on Hughes's ledger:
Beethoven, *Baby's Day Out*, and *Dennis the Menace*.

Off and on over the years, according to Matthew Broderick, he and
Hughes discussed doing a *Ferris Bueller* sequel, with Ferris taking a second day off, maybe from college or his first job. But nothing took hold of
their imaginations—and just as well. The whole point of Ferris and Andie
and Bender and Samantha and the rest of Hughes's characters is that
they live a true teenage dream, existing forever in the now, defiantly *not*
moving on. The frame freezes with Bender's fist in the air, and Monday
morning never comes.

8

BOYZ, CHER, KIDS

I wasn't going to let some fool from Idaho or Encino direct a movie
about living in my neighborhood.

      —John Singleton, writer-director of *Boyz n the Hood*, staking his claim

In 1984, the African American movie critic Armond White published
an essay in *Film Comment* on the lack of Black representation in American movies. It was a deficit he sensed was beginning to change, albeit in
clumsy, two steps forward, one step back fashion. On the plus side were
recently minted stars like Richard Pryor and Eddie Murphy and new films
with predominantly Black casts such as *Purple Rain* and *A Soldier's Story*
(both 1984). But in White's view—hard to argue with—while Hollywood
had from time to time chosen to exploit Black culture and performers,
its films had rarely granted Black characters full, messy, nonsymbolic,
non-token humanity. It remained a *now you see them, now you don't* conundrum. "The problem is satirized in *Fast Times at Ridgemont High*,"
White wrote, recalling the scene early in the film where a little white kid
is surprised to see the school's Black football star, Charles Jefferson, at the
Ridgemont Mall. "Wow, does he really live here?" the kid asks, incredulous. "I thought he just flew in for games!"

    It's a funny scene; maybe people in Beverly Hills also thought Eddie
Murphy just flew in for shoots. But White might be giving *Fast Times*

too much credit on this point. The movie pokes fun at the way his white classmates view Forest Whitaker's Jefferson as an exotic figure, inspiring fear and awe in equal measure. When he asks Damone about tickets to an Earth, Wind & Fire concert, Damone struggles to maintain his cool; his sweaty stammering implies he's never scalped tickets for an R&B act before and may not have a connection. But at the same time, the film treats Jefferson much the same way the white kids do. He's a stock character: the big, scary, angry Black jock everyone treads lightly around. To White's point, though, he's at least *there*, on screen. And kudos to Amy Heckerling, who had the eye for talent to cast Whitaker in his first significant movie role.

At the time White was writing, teen movies had done no better by performers and audiences of color than had any other mainstream Hollywood genres. "Representation" typically consisted of a couple of Black students seen in passing in an opening montage of kids arriving at school. Non-white kids might also be glimpsed in crowd scenes at football games, pep rallies, or proms, like the handful of Black and Asian dancers at the hop in *American Graffiti*, or the lone Black girl attending *Pretty in Pink*'s prom. A Black surfer can be seen riding the waves in second-unit shots in *Beach Party*, but he isn't part of "the gang." Long Duk Dong gets significant screen time in *Sixteen Candles*, but that is not a plus.

The two most prominent exceptions to the rule were *Blackboard Jungle* and, of course, *Cooley High*. One person who saw the latter during its initial release in 1975 was the future writer-director John Singleton, who was seven at the time. His mother took him. As he later told an interviewer, she teared up when Cochise, the high school basketball star with a scholarship to Grambling, dies at the end of the movie, beaten by some thugs who mistakenly believe he turned them in to the police. "I looked at my mother," Singleton remembered, "and said, 'Why are you crying?' And she said, 'Because it's such a good film.' So I start thinking, when I get to make a movie, I got to make people cry. I got to make them feel something."

Singleton was only twenty-two in 1990, a few months out of film

school, when he began shooting *Boyz n the Hood*, his autobiographical
first film about growing up in Los Angeles's South Central neighborhood.
It covered similar ground to *Cooley High*: the challenges for Black teenagers coming of age amid poverty, gangs, and racism in de facto segregated neighborhoods, along with the obstacles confronting teenagers of
all races and classes, like figuring out sex and navigating conflicts between
individual ambition and loyalty to friends and family. Both films shine
in particular during extended, almost documentary-like scenes of kids
just hanging out, being themselves, and having fun on their own terms,
capitalizing on the performers' seeming ease with one another—a kind of
Black American neorealism.

But where *Cooley High* was a modest if influential success, *Boyz n
the Hood*, released a decade and a half later, in 1991, was a sensation,
one of the most significant films of its era. Partly this is due to the fact
that *Boyz n the Hood* is a better written, acted, and directed film; partly
this is due to the fact that the Hollywood establishment and white audiences in general were readier to embrace a film about Black kids. Many
reasons for that embrace were good, not least the rise of hip-hop as a
cultural and commercial power. "I couldn't rhyme. I wasn't a rapper. So
I made this movie," Singleton himself once said. As well, there was Spike
Lee's example as one of the most talented and original writer-directors of
his generation, and Hollywood's dawning, not entirely altruistic realiza-
tion that it should embrace Black filmmakers and audiences. Just a year
before, *House Party*, a raucous comedy written and directed by Reginald
Hudlin and starring the rap duo Kid 'n Play, had been a sleeper hit for
New Line Cinema, grossing $20 million. (At the time, African Ameri-
cans were punching above their weight at the box office, accounting for
25 percent of tickets sold while making up only 12 percent of the total
population.)

But some factors that fed Singleton's movie's crossover success were
less heartening, including a media fascination with gang culture and drug
dealing amid a historic peak in crime rates. Moreover, *Boyz n the Hood*
would be released just four months after the videotaped beating of Rodney

King had sparked one of America's cyclical reckonings (or not) with racist policing. Worse was a less-well-remembered incident that also made
headlines at the time: Latasha Harlins, a fifteen-year-old South Central
girl, was shot in the back of the head and killed by a local grocer after she
put a bottle of orange juice in her backpack; the grocer, a Korean emigré,
accused her of shoplifting, and after a brief scuffle, fired the fatal shot,
but witness testimony and security camera footage demonstrated Latasha
had money in her hand, intending to pay for the juice. (The grocer was
convicted of voluntary manslaughter but sentenced merely to probation
and community service.) In a tragic but very real way, the shooting and
beating helped set the table for the picture's reception. "It felt like South
Central was the center of American culture then," the author and cultural
critic Touré would later write. "*Boyz* was the cinema's answer to the music
made by N.W.A. and the news around the continuing story of Rodney
King."

For some audiences, Singleton's movie was an urgent bulletin, "not
simply a brilliant directorial debut, but an American film of enormous
relevance," to quote Gene Siskel. It addressed what was considered a national crisis, reminiscent in that way of *Rebel Without a Cause* and *Blackboard Jungle*, and made with a sense of earnest mission that had been
largely absent from teen movies ever since. Echoing a 1950s problem
movie, *Boyz n the Hood* even opens with a title card alerting us that what
we're about to see is important:

> One out of every twenty-one Black American males will be murdered
> in their lifetime. Most will die at the hands of another Black male.

What follows, the movie's first shot, is a close-up of a STOP sign, a symbolic exhortation alerting us that we are in the hands of a recent film
school graduate, for good and ill. "There are subtler, more polite movies
around," David Ansen wrote in *Newsweek*, "but none made out of such
a heart-stopping sense of urgency." In the *Amsterdam News*, New York's
leading African American newspaper, Abiola Sinclair put it more starkly:

"*Boyz n the Hood* is a primordial scream. The sound of the soul in agony." Singleton, Sinclair continued, "has recorded this scream brilliantly, lovingly, painstakingly, note for note."

For some Black audiences, the film served as an affirmation. Ice Cube, the rapper and former member of N.W.A., who co-starred in the movie, grew up not far from Singleton, in the city of Compton; he recalled his reaction upon first reading the script: "Damn. They're actually going to make a movie about how we grew up. I didn't know how we grew up was even interesting enough to be a movie."

The writer-director Barry Jenkins was raised across the country from Singleton, in the projects of Miami's Liberty City neighborhood. He was eleven when *Boyz n the Hood* came out, as he told *The Hollywood Reporter* in a 2019 remembrance following Singleton's death, from a stroke, at the age of fifty-one: "I was aware of John Singleton even before I knew I wanted to be a filmmaker. I was just a kid going to the multiplex, seeing movies like *Coming to America* and *Die Hard* and *Terminator 2*. And then one day I walked into a theater and saw *Boyz n the Hood* and thought, 'Holy shit, that's my life! This is about my world!' I literally remember saying, 'I didn't think you could make films like this.'" The experience helped set Jenkins on the path to co-writing and directing his own time-skipping, coming-of-age story, *Moonlight*, the Oscar-winning Best Picture of 2016. Jenkins himself was nominated as both director and screenwriter, as Singleton had been for *Boyz n the Hood*, when he was both the first Black director honored and, at twenty-four, the youngest of any.

Oscar nominations were only the capper for *Boyz n the Hood*, which had premiered at Cannes, received generally terrific reviews, and earned $57.5 million after having been made for only $5.7 million—for the year, Hollywood's best return on investment. It was also yet another presciently cast teen movie, following in the steps of *American Graffiti*, *Fast Times at Ridgemont High*, and *The Outsiders*, full of mostly unknown young actors who would go on to significant careers: Cuba Gooding Jr., Angela Bassett, Regina King, Nia Long, Morris Chestnut. For Laurence

Fishburne, the character Furious Styles, father to Gooding Jr.'s Tre Styles, was arguably his most significant role since he had played a teenage soldier in *Apocalypse Now*, twelve years earlier. (He was only twenty-nine when he played Furious.) Ice Cube was a well-known commodity as a rapper, but *Boyz n the Hood* launched him on a prolific film career that would see him star in and produce the franchise-launching comedies *Friday* (1995) and *Barbershop* (2002) as well as family films like *Are We There Yet?* (2005).

Singleton was a cinematic omnivore who referred to himself as "the first Black movie brat,"* in honor of the film-schooled generation of seventies filmmakers like George Lucas, Martin Scorsese, and Francis Ford Coppola. He told one interviewer the two men he admired most were born on the same day: his father and Steven Spielberg. He told another interviewer, "What Toshiro Mifune was to Akira Kurosawa, Ice Cube is to me." He quite consciously saw *Boyz n the Hood* in a lineage of teen movies, referring to it in a *Playboy* interview as "my *American Graffiti*, my coming-of-age story. I wrote about what I knew: the streets, friends who fell off from gangbanging and from being in the wrong place at the wrong time and getting shot." In another interview—Singleton was a great, uninhibited talker (and self-promoter) in those days—he dismissed the ambitions of his white classmates at USC who "come out of school and all they want to make is that John Hughes teen-angst movie, you know?" Their problem, as he saw it: "They don't have anything to say, because they never had any worries in their life outside whether or not they were going to get their dick wet. You know what I'm saying?"

Armond White also a saw a huge divide between *Boyz n the Hood* and the Hughes films: "In the former, Black teens see life in terms of survival; in the latter, white teens see it in terms of fun." That's not wrong, but it robs both Singleton and Hughes of their complexity. I think Touré better

---

*NYU film school graduates Spike Lee and Ernest Dickerson, among other of Singleton's elders, might have had something to say about that claim.

captured the ways in which *Boyz n the Hood* was in dialogue with its predecessors (and successors): "In many ways it's the basic American teenage coming-of-age story that we know well from movies like *Risky Business* and *The Breakfast Club*. Can our heroes navigate the last year of high school and make it to college?" Touré cited several of the film's subplots, including Tre's efforts to lose his virginity and study for the SATs, then continued: "They must do this while surviving one of the most dangerous neighborhoods in the country . . . It's as if the sweet, internal explorations of *Ferris Bueller's Day Off* and all those big questions about *Who am I becoming?* were taking place in *The Hunger Games*."

One significant difference between *Boyz n the Hood* and the previous few decades' worth of teen movies is that it features a father who is not only a significant character but also, and even more unusual, neither buffoon nor bully. In that, Singleton's was perhaps the first teen film since *Rebel Without a Cause* to argue for a strong paternal presence, and among the few since the *Andy Hardy* pictures to offer a genuine one. Perhaps fantasizing about the parent-free worlds in the *Beach Party* movies or *American Graffiti* or *Fast Times at Ridgemont High* was a privilege for young white audiences? "My film has a lot of messages in it," Singleton observed (accurately) in the movie's press notes, "but my main message is that African American men have to take responsibility for raising their children, especially their boys. Fathers have to teach their boys to be men." That's almost exactly how Tre's single mother, played by Bassett, puts it when she hands off her son to Fishburne's Furious Styles during the film's extended prologue: "I can't teach him how to be a man. That's your job." Furious, despite a name that sounds as if it were cribbed from a Blaxploitation script, stands as a paragon of old-fashioned masculinity: disciplined, honorable, coolheaded, quietly competent, capable of justified violence when pushed; in an earlier era and different setting, he could have been played by Gary Cooper. On the teen movie fatherhood spectrum, he's at the opposite end from Jim Backus's fumbling, emasculated dad in *Rebel Without a Cause*, and Singleton lays on the symbolism almost as heavily as Nicholas Ray did: where Backus wore an apron,

Singleton has Fishburne roll a pair of big steel stress balls in one hand; there's also the long-barreled Colt Python Magnum revolver that he keeps in the house and fires at a midnight intruder. In guiding and teaching his son—the film periodically hits pause for lectures and homilies—he's got a lot of Judge Hardy in him, too. At one point, he tells Tre, "Any fool with a dick can make a baby, but only a real man can raise a son." Judge Hardy wouldn't have put it that way, but he would have approved of the sentiment.

Indeed, as radical as Singleton's movie felt at the time—radical as an act of cultural assertion—its perspective was in many ways entirely conservative. *Time* noted approvingly that the movie carried the "reassuring message that parental love and guidance can still rescue Black youths from drugs, gangs, and the despair of the inner city." Fans included California's Republican Governor Pete Wilson, who said one Sunday morning on *This Week with David Brinkley*, "I think everyone in America should see the film *Boyz n the Hood*. In that movie, a strong father makes a difference for his teenage son . . . What that movie says is that we need a strong father and that welfare is no suitable replacement for that." In fact, the film doesn't address welfare; that was Wilson straining to score political points on a topic that would become a campaign issue the following year, when presidential candidate Bill Clinton vowed to "end welfare as we know it." But whatever Singleton thought about the governor's plug, it surely didn't hurt his film at the box office. Despite some violence in theaters during the film's opening weekend, which panicked a few theater owners and generated an abundance of media coverage, the film was so widely embraced that Nordstrom screened it for the department store's Washington, DC–based workforce as a diversity training exercise.

The New York Times Magazine published a profile of Singleton and other young Black filmmakers on the summer weekend *Boyz n the Hood* opened. The writer was Karen Grigsby Bates, a novelist and journalist, and she opened her piece with a visit to Singleton's newly purchased house in Baldwin Hills, an upscale Black neighborhood in LA:

The house itself, with impressive views from each oversize window, is mostly unfurnished, testament to a recent windfall and a lack of time to spend it. Singleton . . . lives alone, except for an albino cat who floats down the stairs to greet him.

"That's White Boy," Singleton says, stooping to rub the cat behind his translucent ears.

The metaphor is irresistible: at the moment, John Singleton, a twenty-three-year-old Black man, has the notoriously insular and mostly white Hollywood establishment purring.

One of the most grimly effective motifs in *Boyz n the Hood* is the near-constant presence of police helicopters, never seen but heard on the soundtrack and, at night, running their searchlights across the urban landscape—it lends the movie an oppressive, dystopian feel, a Los Angeles not so far removed from the Manhattan of *Escape from New York*. Singleton was surely aware of how directors like Coppola and Oliver Stone used the rhythmic thumping of rotors and blades to conjure dread in their Vietnam films. But more than just a trick in his director's tool kit, the sound was something he had lived with. "I've heard the copters all my life," he once said. "It's an incredible kind of psychological violence. It makes you not think in terms of the future, because who knows if you'll be around. So you say, 'Not next year. Not next week. I'm going to get mine *now*.'"

He would seize his opening Hollywood opportunity with precisely that ferocity. He wrote *Boyz n the Hood* while he was still an undergrad at USC. Stephanie Allain, a future producer, was working at Columbia as a script reader when Singleton came in for a meeting. Ostensibly, he was there to interview for Allain's job. (She was being promoted.) She remembered, "John just wanted to talk about *Boyz n the Hood*. He was not interested in the reader job. He just wanted to get into a studio to talk about his script and the movie that he was going to direct. He was the most confident neophyte I'd ever seen." Allain agreed to read the screenplay, though for some reason she had to bug Singleton's agent several times before he finally sent it over. According to Allain, she was sobbing when she finished it and told herself, "That's why I'm here—to get this movie made."

The catch was that the studio wanted the project, but not with Singleton attached as director. He was offered $100,000 for his script—roughly a quarter of a million in 2024 dollars—but turned it down, a nervy move for a poor kid fresh out of film school. As he later recalled, "One reason I got to direct *Boyz n the Hood* is because I said, I'm not gonna let anybody else do it. I don't give a fuck whether or not you want to do the movie or not. I'll walk out of here right now and go back to my life. Either I direct or I step. I could be a schoolteacher. I don't give a fuck.'"

Columbia remained wary but grew convinced after Singleton directed several test scenes. With Allain's backing, along with the producer Amy Pascal and the studio's president, Frank Price, Singleton got not only a deal to direct his script but also a three-year contract to develop further films. The stubbornness wasn't simply careerist. "It's my story, I lived it," he told *The New York Times Magazine*. "What sense would it have made to have some white boy impose his interpretation on my experience?"

Like his character Tre, Singleton, who was born in 1968, had lived with his mom in Inglewood, a mostly Black and Latino city just south of LA, not far from Los Angeles International Airport. His parents weren't married, and shortly after his mom became pregnant, his father was drafted and sent to Vietnam; Singleton never knew them as a couple. Like Tre, he moved to South Central to live with his dad when he was eleven or twelve. "My mother was a smart enough woman to know that she couldn't do it all. She let me live with my father so that I could learn responsibility. There's only so much a young woman can show a young man, you know."

Like Furious, Singleton's father was a mortgage broker who commanded respect in the neighborhood. "All the kids looked up to my father because he was known to be that dude who knocks people out," the director once said. As he told *Playboy* in a 1993 interview:

That scene in *Boyz n the Hood* where the father shot at the burglar actually happened. A guy broke into my father's house. My father had these mirrors up in the living room. He plastered them on the wall just so he could see, from the bedroom, a reflection of anyone who walked in the living room, who jumped through a window. He saw the guy and he got his Magnum out—this is in the late seventies. He had it halfway loaded and stuff. He got up to the hallway and just as he clicked it, the guy ran. My father fired on him, but . . . didn't hit him.

He told me later, "Hey, this ain't like *Starsky & Hutch*." The cops came and one—black or white, I don't remember—said, "You should've got him—that would've been one less nigger we would've had to worry about."

That line is in the movie, too, given to a Black cop. Furious then gives him a withering look. "Something wrong?" the cop asks—a challenge. "Yeah, it's just too bad you don't know what it is," Furious replies, pointedly addressing the cop as *"brother."*

South Central was a rougher neighborhood than Inglewood, and by Singleton's account it grew rougher still: "When I was little, you could fight with somebody, kick their butt, and then you could still become friends. But after crack and the gangs took it over, it all changed. If you beat somebody up and kicked their ass, they'd go get one of their friends with a gun and come back and shoot you." He got into trouble, but not much: "My parents didn't have a lot of money. I used to steal little stuff, like candy, toys, and *Players* magazines, but I never got into anything too rough." He told *Time* that the closest he came to inflicting any violence himself was in the seventh grade: after a bully tried to take his money, Singleton brought a box cutter to school the next day and threatened to cut the bully's throat. "He never asked for money again."

Singleton knew kids who were in gangs, who were injured in fights, including someone killed in an alley near his house—a death echoed in *Boyz n the Hood*'s pivotal third-act shooting. He had a close friend, nicknamed Fatbacc, who was in a gang and would become the basis for

Doughboy, Ice Cube's drug-dealing character. But if Singleton himself had joined a gang, or even gotten close to one, "my Pops would've kicked my ass."

At times he discounted his ability to tread a relatively straight and narrow path: "I guess I was a lucky kid. If I did something bad, I never got caught. And if I did something good, everybody noticed." One thing that helped: he had a passion. "The cinema saved me from being a delinquent," he once said. The romance began at an early age: his mom's apartment in Inglewood sat next to a drive-in theater: "From the time I was born, I looked out the window and there was this seventy-foot screen with movies on it." By nine, he had decided he would be a director when he grew up. "I used to make movies when I was in elementary school," he told *Ebony*. "I was like taking a book and flipping the pages of that book and making little animated movies. I had everybody in class doing that. Back then, it wasn't cool using your mind. But I made it cool."

After he moved to South Central, he and his friends would take the bus up to Hollywood Boulevard to see movies at the Chinese and Egyptian theaters, ornate old palaces left over from the 1920s. "We loved the characters and the stories but were like, 'There's nobody in these movies who looked like us.' So we spent all of our time on the bus talking about the movies that we could make." He called himself "a child of *Star Wars*, *Raiders of the Lost Ark*, and *E.T.*," but he also had headier tastes, seeking out films by Coppola, Scorsese, Orson Welles, François Truffaut, Akira Kurosawa, John Cassavetes. For Singleton, like a lot of Black filmmakers, the release of Spike Lee's first film, the independently made *She's Gotta Have It*, in 1986, was revelatory—what a movie could be, who it could be about, who could make it.

According to Singleton, there were also not a lot of people who looked like him when he enrolled in an undergraduate screenwriting program at USC. "I was angry in film school—I always had a shield up. I was one of the only Black kids there, so I couldn't be caught slipping." Already he was exhibiting the preternatural self-confidence that would allow him to stare down Columbia over directing *Boyz n the Hood*. When classmates said he was full of himself, he embraced it. "Hey, I was going to school with a bunch of rich kids who all had uncles in the film business. I had to act cocky. I couldn't fail. I had to practically hypnotize myself into thinking I was going to be a success."

He was, winning one of the school's Jack Nicholson Scholarship in Writing grants two years in a row. While still in school he signed with CAA, then the most powerful agency in Hollywood by leaps and bounds, which surely didn't boost his peer group popularity. "John wasn't a better writer and a better director than everybody in the class," one of his professors said. "But what he had was more original material. This is one of the things that's so hard to get students to do, to write from reality, material that they know."

He also had drive, which helped him earn a series of real-world internships, including stints on the sets of Arsenio Hall's talk show and the CBS Saturday morning series *Pee-wee's Playhouse*. At the former, when Ice Cube was a guest on the show, Singleton bent his ear about this great script he had written, and how there was a great part in it for the rapper—and then asked for a lift back to his dorm. At *Pee-wee's Playhouse*, Singleton first met Fishburne, who played Cowboy Curtis on the show. As the actor remembered it, Singleton had no qualms about pestering Paul Reubens, the performer behind Pee-wee. Fishburne: "Every day, John would go up to Paul and ask, 'Have you read my script yet?' Paul would say, 'Oh, I'm so sorry. I haven't had the time.' It turned out it was the script for *Boyz n the Hood*. John started talking to me about it. I said, 'Look, when it's ready, send it to me.'"

Two years later, with the Columbia deal in hand, Singleton sent Fishburne the script. "I was really blown away by it," the actor said. "I turned the last page, and I was in tears." The studio wanted a different actor for Furious, but Singleton once again held firm and got his way.

True to his word, he also wanted Ice Cube for the part of Doughboy, but the rapper, a year younger than Singleton, shrugged the offer off. As he recalled his perspective years later in *Vanity Fair*, "I'm trying to be the best rapper in the world. I'm not thinking about acting. And my manager was like, 'Yo—somebody wants to put you in a movie! Here's a script.'" Ice Cube never bothered to read it—he claimed the screenplay never left the back seat of his car after he tossed it there—but when he agreed to audition for Singleton, he realized the pushy film student he'd driven back to a dorm was entirely serious, about both the film and casting him. "Oh shit," he thought, Singleton "was for real. He wasn't lying. He's going to do this movie. This kid is no bullshit." By his own admission, Ice Cube's audition was "terrible." But Singleton told him, "Go home and read my script. I'm going to give you one more shot because they"—the studio—"don't want to hire you, and I'm dying inside. I know you're good. I know you can do it." Ice Cube agreed, once he finally read the script. "I know these characters back and forth," he thought. "I can play any of these guys . . . They were all people I grew up with and knew."

Singleton's instincts were borne out: Ice Cube brought a wounded bravado to the role, a mix of menace, vulnerability, and charisma, which makes the film's climactic revenge killing, when Doughboy shoots an already wounded rival at point-blank range, all the more chilling, because the life seems to have drained out of Doughboy, too. The performance comes to dominate the film, overshadowing Cuba Gooding Jr.'s Tre not unlike the way Robert De Niro's volatile Johnny Boy tugs Scorsese's *Mean Streets* away from Harvey Keitel.

However inexperienced an actor, Ice Cube was at least a professional musician who had been in front of audiences. Others Singleton cast had no performance experience whatsoever, but the director was looking for personalities as much as acting chops. Redge Green, a kid from South Central who was paralyzed below the waist, showed up at the casting office in his wheelchair and told Singleton, "I actually got shot in my legs. You got to put me in this movie." Singleton gave him a role as one of Doughboy's hangers-on, alongside Dedrick D. Gobert, an Inglewood native, who played Dooky, notable for the pacifier either in his mouth or hanging around his neck in most scenes—a symbolic prop almost as heavy-handed as the opening STOP sign, but also sad and a little creepy. That these casting choices worked so well was tribute to Singleton's instincts as a filmmaker and contributed to the neorealist vibe. "It played so well," he said, "because they were all from similar backgrounds."

Gooding Jr. was the rare member of the younger cast who came from a more traditional show-business background: his father, Cuba Gooding Sr., was the lead singer of the Main Ingredient, a mellow soul vocal trio best known for the 1972 hit "Everybody Plays the Fool." Twenty-two when he was cast in *Boyz n the Hood*, Gooding Jr. had been working steadily as an actor for several years, most notably with small parts in the film *Coming to America* and on the TV series *Hill Street Blues* and *MacGyver*. Columbia wanted a name actor in the central role—one can easily imagine an alternate-universe *Boyz n the Hood* starring Malcolm-Jamal Warner from *The Cosby Show* or *Fresh Prince*–era Will Smith (or perhaps even Prince himself)—but Singleton liked Gooding Jr., and after enduring repeated screen tests, the actor got the part. "And every fucking time I came back, I wore that gold-and-black Cavaricci shirt with black Cavaricci pants that are on the poster to this day," Gooding Jr. said, recalling his youthful conception of a fashion-forward ensemble, which he also wore in the movie.

American Graffiti and *Cooley High* were elegies for their creators' high school years. *Boyz n the Hood* was, too, but where the earlier films looked back from a decade's distance, Singleton was only four years removed from high school when he began preproduction on his movie, an auto-biographical film but one made very much in the present tense.

Unlike the 1950s, when the government and media preoccupation with delinquency wasn't reflected in crime statistics, the 1980s saw a broad surge in youth crime that justified many of the decade's more upsetting headlines. Juvenile crime rates, as compiled by the FBI, had risen across the country, alongside adult crime rates, from the mid-1960s to the mid-1970s, plateauing for a decade, and then nearly doubling between 1987 and 1994, the peak year for arrests of minors accused of violent crimes. Juvenile murder arrests had begun surging even earlier, increasing more than 150 percent between 1985 and 1991. All forms of teen crime were up: rape, robbery, burglary, car theft, weapons and drug violations, even quaint, old-school standbys like "disorderly conduct" and "loitering."*

In 1989, under a headline touting "Fears That the US Is Breeding a Generation of Merciless Children," *Time* seemed almost nostalgic for *Rebel Without a Cause*–era outrages, wondering why "delinquents of this generation do not content themselves with stealing hubcaps and breaking windows."

What had gone wrong in the post-Eisenhower years? *Time* had some thoughts:

> The experts argue that too many families are broken, too many schools and communities are crumbling, too many drugs are available for children to acquire a sturdy sense of mercy or morality to guide their behavior.
>
> Into this vacuum, the circuits of popular culture transmit images of brutality without consequences. Children play video games in which they win points for killing the most people. They watch violence-packed cartoons. They listen to songs titled "Be My Slave" and "Scumkill." Or they are baby sat by vastly popular movie videotapes like *Splatter University* and *I Spit on Your Grave*. Says sociologist Gail Dines-Levy of Wheelock College in Boston, "What we are doing is training a whole generation of male kids to see sex and violence as inextricably linked."

I should note that the above was written in response to the "Central Park Jogger" case, in which six Black and Hispanic teenagers were arrested in New York City for the rape and beating of a white female runner, an

---

*While FBI juvenile crime statistics remained dependent on local police departments' reporting and classifying arrests and were thus less than definitive, just as they had been in the 1950s, the numbers were certainly indicative of larger trends. Moreover, the steep increase in juvenile arrests wasn't driven by demographic factors, as the total number of teens in the US remained fairly steady throughout the '80s and early '90s.

investment banker, who was left in a coma. National news, it became one of the most sensational, widely publicized crime stories of the decade, prompting a screed from developer and casino owner Donald Trump, published as a full-page ad in the New York *Daily News*, demanding the return of the death penalty in New York State. "I recently watched a newscast trying to explain 'the anger in these young men.' I no longer want to understand their anger," the future president wrote. "I want them to understand our anger. I want them to be afraid." He fondly recalled an incident from his childhood when, he claimed, he and his father had seen New York cops literally throw a pair of delinquents out of a diner. It was the beginning of his rebranding as a thuggish billionaire pseudo-populist.

Five of the six boys were eventually convicted and spent between six and thirteen years in prison. But as you likely know, in 2002 a serial rapist and murderer who was already in prison confessed to the Central Park case. DNA and other evidence supported the confession, and the "Central Park Five" were now the "Exonerated Five," their convictions overturned. I mention this as a reminder that one should approach sensational stories about juvenile delinquency and teen depravity with a degree of skepticism, especially when it comes to sensational stories about Black and Brown teenagers. That said, the crime wave that surged through the US from the late 1980s to the mid-1990s was real, and juvenile crime played a significant role. The true Central Park rapist was himself a teenager when he brutalized the jogger, and just two months after that attack, *Time* duly noted that "sexual violence by adolescents transcends racial and class lines" after five white teenagers were arrested in suburban New Jersey for sexually assaulting a mentally handicapped girl.

The era's moral panics over violent video games and untoward rock and rap lyrics notwithstanding, gang membership was a credible driver of teen criminality. If one was to believe a 1998 report from the Justice Department's Office of Juvenile Justice and Delinquency Prevention, the rolls of "youth gangs" in the US had swollen in the years since 1980, from more than 2,000 gangs with some 100,000 total members, to more than 31,000 gangs with roughly 846,000 members in 1998. That latter number would nearly equal the entire population of today's Charlotte or India-napolis and exceed San Francisco's.

There was a street arms race, too. Forget switchblades and brass knuck-les. Forget even "normal" guns. "As recently as ten years ago, say gang members, the deadliest arms you could lay your hands on easily were sawed-off shotguns," reported *The Economist* in 1994. "Now automatic and semiautomatic weapons are de rigueur." And someone wielding an AK-47, say, and spraying bullets from the passenger side of a moving car, was far likelier to hit more than just his designated target, assuming there even was one. If the shooter was as young as thirteen—not unheard of (ar-rests of thirteen- to fifteen-year-olds for murder nearly doubled between 1982 and 1992)—the carnage might be even worse. By one estimate, half the victims of "gang-related homicides" in Los Angeles County in 1987 were innocent bystanders.

The murder of one particular bystander, a twenty-seven-year-old Asian American artist named Karen Toshima, who was shot in the head by a twenty-year-old gang member gunning for a rival, attracted outsized attention in 1988. What made her killing newsworthy, aside from her race and sex, was the location: a sidewalk in upscale Westwood Village, one of LA's rare pedestrian-friendly neighborhoods, full of movie theaters and restaurants. As the *Los Angeles Times* put it, the killing hit the city "in its living room."

"There were 387 gang-related killings in Los Angeles County in 1987," *The New York Times* reported, "but it was not until terror spread to the mostly white Westwood area near the campus of the University of California at Los Angeles a week ago that Angelenos began to take no-tice." That, of course, was when *The New York Times* and other national media also began to take notice, and the *Times* should have modified "Angelenos" with "white." Black Angelenos angrily noted the police and media attention generated by the Toshima case—as compared to the rela-tive lack of the same when, to cite one example raised at the time, a nine-year-old Black boy had been caught in the crossfire of a drive-by shooting while swinging in a playground. The future US congresswoman Maxine

Waters, then a state assemblywoman representing a swath of South Central, addressed a community meeting: "We are tired and we're not going to take it anymore. We are tired because our babies cannot play in the front yard because they might be shot."

LA was deemed "the gang capital of America" by both criminologists and journalists, with an estimated six hundred gangs with seventy thousand members. The two biggest and best-known gangs, the Crips and the Bloods, were soon "household names across America," as *The Economist* put it. For a 1988 NBC News special titled *Gangs, Cops & Drugs*— introduced on screen with the sharp report of a gunshot and the network art department's best stab at a graffiti-style logo—anchorman Tom Brokaw donned a bush jacket to ride along in LA police cruisers and interview several Crips drinking forties in front of a liquor store. Introducing one man to the audience, Brokaw explained that "after fifteen years on the streets, Bitter Child is considered an original gangster, or OG." Brokaw then asked him, "Why is it important to be a member of this set?" (*Set!*)

"This is me," Bitter Child replied. "This is where I grew up. This is my roots here."

Brokaw: "It's pretty dangerous, though, isn't it?"

Bitter Child: "Just living is dangerous."

He wasn't wrong. The number of LA County's gang-related homicides jumped from 387 in 1987 to 452 the following year—and 771 in 1991, while *Boyz n the Hood* was in theaters. Depending on the year, gang murders during the period would account for between 30 and 40 percent of the county's total homicides. (The total numbers would peak in 1995, then plunge by half by decade's end, as crime rates fell across most of the country.)

Teenagers were victims as well as victimizers, twice as likely nationwide to be crime victims than a hypothetical average American, according to Justice Department figures from 1995. *JAMA*, the Journal of the American Medical Association, reported in 1996 that over the previous decade, the homicide rate had nearly doubled among "persons fifteen through twenty-four," from 12 percent of all deaths in that age group to 21 percent.

And to a point made in Singleton's film, a disproportionate number of those endangered were African Americans. In the 1995 crime survey, 44 percent of Black teens (versus 22 percent of white teens) answered yes to the question, "Do you ever worry that you might be the victim of a drive-by shooting?" As the academic and author Michael Eric Dyson wrote not long after *Boyz n the Hood*'s release, "Most chillingly, black-on-black homicide is the leading cause of death among Black males between the ages of 15 and 34. Or, to put it another way . . ." Dyson then quoted the opening title card from *Boyz n the Hood* about how one in every twenty-one Black males would eventually be murdered, most "at the hands of another Black male." Dyson continued: "These words are both summary and opening salvo in Singleton's battle to reinterpret and redeem the Black male experience."

I can't speak to Singleton's success at achieving those ambitions, or whether he himself would have claimed them in those terms, but it's undeniable that he was swinging for the fences, aiming to write and direct the Great American Movie every bit as much as Coppola was, say, with *Apocalypse Now* or Michael Cimino with *Days of Heaven* or Lee with *Malcolm X*, a year later, albeit Singleton was working on a much smaller budget and a shorter leash. What's unusual about *Boyz n the Hood* is that at times it is exactly as didactic as Dyson makes it sound (and Singleton, too, in many interviews), and yet it has a vitality that transcends its intermittent sloganeering.

The opening is a perfect example. The title card's statistics are underscored by the impressionistic sounds of a gang shooting: angry voices, screeching tires, gun blasts, screams, shouts, a police dispatcher, sirens, helicopter, a child's voice saying, "They shot my friend. They shot my brother." Then the STOP sign—and in case we miss his point, Singleton dollies in on it, a Spielbergian move that shows off both his ambition as a filmmaker and his heavy hand as a messenger. He then cuts to a long tracking shot of four elementary school kids, two boys and two girls, wearing brightly colored backpacks and walking to school past garbage and stray dogs. A subtitle gives the time and place: "South Central Los Angeles, 1984." This is a prologue to the film's main action. The kids, one of whom is ten-year-old Tre, talk about homework and school—typical stuff, the young actors easy and natural, the mood light even if the setting is bleak.

Then one kid asks, "Y'all hear the shooting last night?" (Presumably the same one we've just heard on the soundtrack.)

"Yeah, I heard it," says another. "I got under my bed."

"Man, you a scaredy-cat."

"I ain't afraid to get shot."

"Both my brothers got shot and they alive."

"They lucky."

The boy who isn't Tre asks, "Y'all want to see something?" He leads the other three into an alley and past some posters of a smiling Ronald Reagan promoting his reelection (which, Singleton's camera pauses to observe, have been riddled with bullet holes). The kids duck under yellow crime scene tape and find some bloodstained garbage that they poke at with their feet.

"What happened?" a girl asks.

"What do you think?" the boy snaps. "Someone got smoked. Look at the hole in the wall, stupid."

The girl snaps back: "At least I can tell my times tables."

It's a telling retort: they may live in a war zone, but they're still kids, and math looms large in their lives alongside murder. In just a couple minutes of screen time, Singleton establishes a world and its life-and-death stakes. Just as efficiently, he then establishes his somewhat regressive view of parenting by having Tre move in with his father, who right off the bat teaches him a lesson in responsible manhood by forcing him to rake leaves in the front yard. The block is otherwise inhabited, as far as we can tell, by feckless single mothers, including a drug addict who lets her toddlers wander into traffic. "I know you think I'm hard on you," Furious tells Tre. "I'm trying to teach you to be responsible. Your friends across the street don't have anybody to show them how to do that. You gon' see how they end up, too."

The friends across the street are Doughboy, the wised-up, even cynical character later played by Ice Cube, and his half brother, Ricky, an immature high school football star who, in the eventual person of Morris Chestnut, is like a five-year-old in the body of Barry Sanders. When the film jumps from its prologue to its early-1990s present, Doughboy has just gotten out of "the pen" and claims that he wants to keep his nose clean, though he carries a gun and it's mentioned several times that he still "slings rock." His blue wardrobe and Detroit Tigers cap imply he's also become a Crip, though formal gang affiliations are never mentioned; neither, for that matter, are the words "gang," "Crip," or "Blood"—a politic dodge, perhaps, like the absence of the word "Mafia" in *The Godfather*. Anyway, we get the idea.

Doughboy and Ricky's single mother, Brenda (Tyra Ferrell), does everything she can to aggravate this classic bad brother/good brother dynamic, dismissing Doughboy as a "fat little fuck" who's "never going to amount to shit" while doting on Ricky, to the point of allowing his girlfriend and their toddler son to live under her roof. It falls to Cuba Gooding Jr.'s Tre to be the neighborhood role model, holding down an off-screen job at a clothing store; dating a nice Catholic girl who, like Annette Funicello's Dee Dee before her, is saving herself for marriage (she relents); and parroting his father's wisdom, as when Ricky briefly considers enlisting in the army. (Tre: "What are you, a damn fool? . . . You belong to them! The government! Like a slave or something.") Fortunately, Ricky's prowess as a running back will land him a scholarship at nearby USC—as long as he can score at least 700 on his SATs. Both he and Tre are seen studying for and then taking the test, making *Boyz n the Hood* one of the rare teen movies, alongside *Risky Business*, that deals with the college admissions process, however fitfully. Fans of *Cooley High*, where Chochise doesn't live long enough to enjoy the basketball scholarship he's earned to Grambling, will surmise Ricky's fate, too, once he and Tre set off on foot to run a grocery store errand just as the postman (Singleton, in a cameo) happens to be making a delivery. "Ricky, baby, your test scores!" his mom calls after him, waving an envelope, her words hanging in the air like an ominous chord.

Though *Boyz n the Hood* is haunted by death, the film depicts little violence; when it does come, it shocks. On an earlier evening, Tre, Ricky, Doughboy, and their friends have exchanged heated words with some rival "punk motherfuckers" dressed in red, after their leader, named Ferris, bumps into Ricky. A girl in a pink satin jacket out of *Grease* speaks one of the movie's most resonant lines, "Can't we have one night with no fights or people getting shot?"—a plea that Doughboy honors with a not very nice, "Shut up, bitch." He then simultaneously defuses and escalates the conflict by drawing his gun. The rival group retreats to their car, where Ferris fires an automatic weapon in the air, sending everyone scattering. The beef won't end there.

Ricky and Tre are returning on foot from the grocery store errand when they're spotted by Ferris and his gang, cruising South Central in a bright red Hyundai Excel. The two boys flee through an alley and tiptoe along the top of a cinderblock wall, thinking they've shaken their pursuers. Ricky then seals his doom when he stops to scratch off a lottery card, the test-score envelope waiting at home not being portent enough. It's another moment that encapsulates Singleton's strengths and weaknesses, the melodramatic flourishes offset by rising tension, dread, and, finally, tragedy, when Ricky is gunned down by a succession of shotgun blasts. As Brenda, Tyra Ferrell summons a bruising portrayal of maternal grief when Ricky's body is brought home, her convulsive sobs given a counterpart on the soundtrack by the wailing of Ricky's toddler son.

When Doughboy and his friends set off in his green 1963 Chevy Impala* convertible to avenge Ricky, Tre defies his father and joins them, leading to some anxious intercutting between the boys cruising for their rivals and Furious at home with the stress balls, the stakes raised even higher by the bassist and composer Stanley Clarke's tense yet mournful

---

*Like Richard Dreyfuss's Curt in *American Graffiti*, Tre is distinguished from his peers by driving a European nerd car, in this case a vintage VW bug convertible.

score. The audience knows nothing good is going to come at the end of this night, and Tre eventually realizes that, too. "Let me out," he says simply, through quiet tears, a mix of anger, grief, frustration, despair evident on his face—the cycle of violence's toll. It's Gooding Jr.'s best moment in the film. In an interview, Singleton said the entire sequence was inspired by the intercutting between baptism and murder at the climax of *The Godfather*; he then quotes that film's ending when Tre comes home and Furious, seemingly more disappointed that his son went out in the first place than relieved that he came home, shuts his bedroom door in the boy's face. While the death of an innocent spurred reconciliation between son and father in *Rebel Without a Cause*, here it divides.

Meanwhile, Doughboy finds Ferris and his group at a fast-food restaurant. Singleton drags out a final spasm of violence to the point that the audience's reflexive thirst for revenge and catharsis dissipates, leaving only horror and disgust. Nor does Doughboy take much pleasure in the chore—which is exactly what the killing feels like. The next morning, drinking a forty, he wanders over to Tre's porch, complaining, "I ain't been up this early in a long time." He's rattled by a newscast he watched, that was preoccupied with some overseas hot spot while ignoring local violence. "They had all this foreign shit, but they didn't have shit on my brother, man," he tells Tre, then offers a virtual thesis statement: "I started thinking, man. Either they don't know, don't show, or don't care about what's going on in the hood." This epiphany is interrupted when the block's crack-addicted mom walks up, asking, "Doughboy, you got some blow, got some rock?" and he orders her to "Get the fuck out my face. And keep them goddamn babies off the street."

When Tre asks if they "got" Ferris, Doughboy gives him a hard stare, then confesses, "I don't even know how I feel about it, neither, man. Shit just goes on and on, you know. Next thing you know, someone might try and smoke me. Don't matter, though. We all gotta go sometime, huh? Seems like they punched the wrong clock on Rick, though, man." The two exchange hugs, and Doughboy walks back to his house, pouring his forty out on the asphalt, perhaps in resignation.

The now-requisite *American Graffiti*–style title card announces: "The next day Doughboy saw his brother buried." Then, as Ice Cube literally disappears from the screen, like David Hemmings in the last shot of Michelangelo Antonioni's *Blow-Up* (1966; Singleton learned from the best), a second sentence: "Two weeks later he was murdered." On the plus side, we learn that Tre will end up at Morehouse College, the all-male HBCU in Atlanta, with girlfriend Brandi "across the way" at sister school Spellman.

In Singleton's world, sheer survival is a form of defiance. And as with Curt in *American Graffiti* and Preach in *Cooley High*, getting out proves to be the best revenge.

Not everyone loved *Boyz n the Hood*. One of the few outright negative reviews came from *The New Republic*'s stodgy Stanley Kauffmann (who found it necessary to inform his readers that "Hood means neighborhood"). He dismissed Singleton's movie as "in its form . . . just one more old-time bad-neighborhood picture," perhaps an update on the earliest Dead End Kid movies. He wasn't altogether wrong about that; the movie's hokier conceits always stood out against its naturalistic tone. On the other hand, the familiarity of the plot and the movie's underlying conservatism may have helped the harsher aspects of Singleton's vision go down more easily for some moviegoers. In *Toms, Coons, Mulattoes, Mammies, and Bucks*, Donald Bogle makes a salient point about the movie's appeal to white audiences: given its focus on "violence and conflict within the Black community" rather than "racism directed at African Americans . . . the white audience may have felt it was left off the hook," Furious's lectures about gentrification and the hidden forces behind the drug trade notwithstanding.

Singleton received criticism for the movie's treatment of its women characters, none of whom, with the possible exception of Angela Bassett's Reva Styles, is given enough screen time to blossom into a full character. During a party scene, a girl asks Doughboy, "Why is it that every time you talk about a female you got to say bitch, ho, or hootchie?" His response:

"'Cause that's what you are." It's a laugh line, but the movie doesn't really offer a counterargument.

The contrast between Furious's steady guidance and the inattention of the movie's single moms struck some critics as a slap at "the efforts of present and loyal Black women who more often prove to be the head of strong Black families," as Michael Eric Dyson put it.

Singleton defended himself in *Playboy* (not the best look): "Those motherfuckers who say *Boyz n the Hood* is misogynistic are the same people who give good reviews to films that have Black women who are maids and prostitutes. This movie was about guys—boys—who eventually survive to be men. It was in the title, you know. But at the same time I can say that all the women in the movie were well-rounded and like real people. They weren't like the Black women you see in all these other movies." That's a low bar Singleton set for himself—ironic, since it was the high bar he set with the movie's best moments and deepest characterizations that drew the criticism.

The biggest hitch in *Boyz n the Hood*'s release was out of Singleton's and Columbia's control. "Gunfire and pandemonium broke out at movie theaters around the nation Friday night at the opening of an urban drama with an anti-gang message," *The New York Times* reported during the movie's first weekend on screens. Upwards of thirty-three people were injured in shootings, stabbings, and other violence, including three audience members who were wounded at a multiplex in Universal City. Much, but not all, of the violence was gang related. One man was killed at a theater in Riverdale, Illinois, a small, largely Black village outside Chicago. A seventeen-year-old boy in Minneapolis who was shot in the neck died a few days later. A California man was left paralyzed by a shooting. (He and another shooting victim separately sued Columbia over the film's marketing, which they alleged encouraged violence; both lost on First Amendment grounds.)

Reactions to these incidents, which generated headlines nationwide, were compounded by the fact that five months earlier, the release of *New Jack City*, an inner-city crime thriller, directed by Mario Van Peebles, had prompted similar if less widespread violence, including a shooting at a New York theater and what the *Los Angeles Times* described as a "riot" in Westwood, when teenagers were told that the movie was sold out after waiting patiently in line for hours.* "A Bad Omen for Black Movies?" asked a headline in *Newsweek*—a seemingly rhetorical question.

On the other hand, the magazine pointed out that 1991 had seen the release of enough movies by Black directors *without* gang content that they could serve as a de facto control group. "Between *New Jack City* and *Boyz n the Hood*, five Black films opened without problems." One senses a missing "miraculously."

The New York Times offered an even more patronizing dispatch:

> There was no trouble where many had expected it to be the worst—at the Baldwin Hills Theater, which lies at the edge of the gang-torn Los Angeles neighborhood where John Singleton's drama of growing up in the ghetto was set. All weekend, long orderly lines of young Blacks waited to get into the theater, then quietly absorbed its message of the values of family, school and hope.

Singleton was forced to hold a press conference defending his film, telling reporters, "I didn't create the conditions under which people shoot

---

New Jack City had been the year's best return on investment—made for $8 million, it earned $47 million at the box office—until it was eclipsed by Singleton's film. Though very different movies, the two pictures were lumped together as so-called hood movies, a genre that also drew in Matty Rich's *Straight Out of Brooklyn*, released in January, Ernest Dickerson's *Juice*, which would come out the following year, and, a year after that, *Menace II Society*, written and directed by Allen and Albert Hughes, twenty-year-old twins who offered an even grimmer take on life in South Central. Singleton seemed to object to the company. "I didn't write some new-jack shitty Black exploitation film," he once said. "I wrote a film about people from my neighborhood who are strong and gritty."

each other. This happens because there is a whole generation of people who are disenfranchised." Asked what he would say to kids who shot up theaters, he replied, "There's a certain segment of the population that wants you to do what you're doing to each other. But we don't have time for that." Other defenders of the movie pointed out that gang films by white directors, including Walter Hill's *The Warriors* (1979) and Dennis Hopper's *Colors* (1988) had also sparked violence. Less than a year earlier, a shoot-out involving five teenagers during a screening of *The Godfather Part III* on Long Island had left one person dead and three wounded.

You didn't have to be a racist to be upset by movie theater violence— *Ebony* noted that "Black-on-Black violence" had blunted the "euphoria of [a] record number of Black-oriented films"—but it's fair to say the media reaction reflected broader fears of Black teenagers and their enthusiasms which, periodic moral panics aside, had by now mostly dissipated for white teenagers and their enthusiasms. (All of America was now on the side of Elvis Presley's hips.) Surely adding to anxieties was the fact that hip-hop had begun showing signs it would soon dominate pop music the way rock and roll once had—i.e., white kids were now listening.

Despite some calls to pull *Boyz n the Hood* from theaters nationwide—which Singleton dismissed as "artistic racism"—only eight theaters canceled their bookings. The film actually expanded to 920 theaters, up from 829, for a lucrative and uneventful second weekend, sending it on its way to profitability and its multiple Oscar nominations.

All told, 1991 would see the release of nineteen films directed by African Americans. That was out of some 400 films released in America that year, so in terms of overall share—4.9 percent—it was still paltry. But as Warrington Hudlin, who had produced his brother Reginald's *House Party*, told *Variety*, the first two years of the 1990s would feature more Black-directed films than the entire previous decade. "The frenzy for Black product . . . has become so great that Black film properties may be to the '90s what the car phone was to the '80s: every studio executive has to have one," *The New York Times Magazine* observed.*

In the spring of 1992, Singleton was back at work on his second film, *Poetic Justice*, an awkward road romance starring Janet Jackson as a poet named Justice and Tupac Shakur as a mail carrier. ("Think of the worst possible reason that John Singleton might have had for calling his new movie *Poetic Justice*," began Anthony Lane's review in *The New Yorker*.) The director and his cast and crew happened to be shooting on location in Simi Valley on April 29, 1992, the day a jury in that city acquitted four white LAPD officers in the beating of Rodney King. En route back to his set from lunch as the news broke, Singleton took a detour to the courthouse, where he gave an impromptu press conference on the steps. "The judicial system feels no responsibility to Black people—never has, never will," he told a crush of reporters. "They had a chance to prove the system works and they messed it up."

He returned to the set and managed to finish the day's shoot, even as he and his colleagues followed the growing violence in South Central as best they could, on radios and portable TVs, many not knowing if their families and homes were in danger. Over the next three days, sixty-six people would lose their lives. According to a *Los Angeles Times* tally, thirteen were aged twenty or younger, including three fifteen-year-olds, one Black, one Hispanic, one white, all killed by gunfire. According to the paper, the Hispanic boy's death "may have been gang-related," and thus deemed ancillary.

---

*How did that work out? It's not entirely an apples-to-apples comparison, given the vast changes over the last three decades in the way movies are made and distributed, and how many are made, and what even constitutes a release, but according to UCLA's annual Hollywood Diversity Report, in 2022, the percentage of theatrically released films made by Black directors had nudged up to 5.6 percent, with another 4.5 percent attributed to "multiracial" directors. For Asian and Hispanic directors, the percentages were 5.6 and 1.1 The numbers were generally somewhat better for streaming films: 9 percent for Black directors, 5.5 for both Asian and Hispanic directors, and 3 percent for multiracial directors.

•   •   •

One more coda: Three years later, Dedrick Gobert, the young actor from Inglewood who played Dooky, the kid with the pacifier, was shot and killed following an argument with some Bloods-affiliated gang members over an illegal street race in which Gobert's car had been cut off. Descriptions of the confrontation sound not so different from initial "fuck you"s with Ferris's crew, which lead to Ricky's death in *Boyz n the Hood*. Gobert was twenty-two. Another man, nineteen, was also killed, and Gobert's sixteen-year-old girlfriend was wounded and paralyzed from the neck down. Gobert had also had a part in *Poetic Justice*, and would make a posthumous appearance in Singleton's third film, the college-set *Higher Learning* (1995). A twenty-two-year-old gang member was eventually arrested and convicted for Gobert's murder and sentenced to death; as of this writing, he remains on California's death row.

Okay, a final coda (as promised by this chapter's title):

As mentioned previously, the late 1980s and early 1990s were generally not a robust time for teen movies, studios feeling the genre had turned obsolescent in the mid-1980s, when kids began spending less time in theaters and more time at home, or friends' homes, playing video games and watching movies on VHS. In many fields, minorities and women get their first shots when the business in question is in decline, which is perhaps why Singleton and Hudlin got to make their movies when they did. Or maybe their projects were seen not as teen movies per se but as Black movies, which, in that fleeting moment—the era of the New Black Aesthetic, as the author and screenwriter Trey Ellis has characterized it, when Black artists were asserting their creative independence across all fields—might have been a plus.

Movies foregrounding white teenagers wouldn't make much of a stir at the box office or in the zeitgeist until the summer of 1995, when the Jekyll and Hyde of teen movies, *Clueless* and *Kids*, were released within weeks of each other. The former, a sleeper hit, marked Amy Heckerling's return to the genre, after directing the sequel *National Lampoon's European Vacation* (1985, from a script co-written by John Hughes), along with a pair of major hits that Heckerling herself wrote, *Look Who's Talking* and *Look Who's Talking Too* (1989 and 1990), which starred John Travolta and Kirstie Alley as the harried parents of wisecracking babies voiced by Bruce Willis and Roseanne Barr. For *Clueless*, Heckerling hatched the thoroughly nonintuitive idea of transposing the plot of Jane Austen's *Emma* to a contemporary Beverly Hills high school. It's a wonderful confection, its lightness buoyed by Alicia Silverstone's comically precise effervesence as Cher, the well-meaning but blinkered heroine. (Were this book to pass out honors, its homecoming queen and king would be Silverstone's Cher and Sean Penn's Spicoli.)

The movie opens with a series of establishing shots, *not* at school but with Cher and her friends out shopping, partying at a resort pool, and driving the wide streets of Beverly Hills in Cher's shiny white Jeep. As she notes in a voice-over: "So, okay, you're probably going, *Is this, like, a Noxzema commercial or what?* But seriously, I actually have a way normal life for a teenage girl. I mean, I get up, I brush my teeth, and I pick out my school clothes." Which, her wardrobe being so vast, she does with the help of a computer program—an amusingly implausible aid for even the most spoiled fashionista in 1995. But aside from such sharp (albeit affectionate) satire, and Heckerling's animating insight that fashion and decorum among the privileged could be as prescribed in twentieth-century Beverly Hills as in Regency England, *Clueless* is at heart a terrific romantic comedy. It's larded with great lines, as quotable as *The Big Lebowski*. One is especially relevant here, reflecting the devolution of teen idols across decades. A male friend of Cher's shows her a leather jacket he has just bought and wants her opinion. "Is it James Dean or Jason Priestley?" he asks.

Also noteworthy: *Clueless* depicted the most integrated high school in a mainstream teen movie since *Blackboard Jungle*, with Cher given a best friend, Dionne, played by the Black actress Stacey Dash. As Cher explains in her opening voice-over, "Dionne and I were both named after great singers of the past who now do infomercials." Some bonds transcend race.

Years later, Heckerling denied she had intended to diagnose any significant cultural shift in the thirteen years between *Clueless* and the far less sugary *Fast Times at Ridgemont High*: "It wasn't so much that I felt like the lives of teenagers had changed; it was a different tone, it was a different world. One was extreme reality [while] *Clueless* of course is a comedy of manners based on a book from the 1800s and translated into a much more gentrified and happy and colorful world of the '90s, which was not the real world. I mean, we shot in a high school* where there had just been a shooting, and we painted the walls and changed people's clothes and what it looked like. What I was showing was not the reality of the place."

Clueless took in $57 million at the box office—a big enough hit that Heckerling's conceptual brainstorm became a formula of sorts. Alongside Baz Luhrmann's *Scarface*-inflected *Romeo+Juliet* with Leonardo DiCaprio and Claire Danes, which came out the following year, *Clueless* launched a vogue for classic plays and novels repurposed as teen comedies, among them *10 Things I Hate About You* and *She's All That* (both 1999), reworkings of *The Taming of the Shrew* and *Pygmalion*, respectively; *Get Over It* (2001), a riff on *A Midsummer Night's Dream*; and further down the line, *Easy A* (2010), which borrowed from *The Scarlet Letter*. There were dramas, too, including *Cruel Intentions* (1999; taken from *Les Liaisons Dangereuses*) and *O* (2001; *Othello*). Of course, *West Side Story* had beaten them all to the punch.

Kids, more of a succès de scandale than an outright hit, also begins with a voice-over. Seventeen-year-old Telly (Leo Fitzpatrick) is seen seducing a girl who looks thirteen, and might even be twelve, then ignoring her repeated protests—"It hurts"—once he gets on top of her. Having his way, he rhapsodizes to himself (and us), "Virgins. I love 'em. No disease. No loose-as-a-goose pussy. No skank. No nothing. Just pure pleasure." Telly is

---

*Ulysses S. Grant High School in Van Nuys, a half-hour-or-so drive from Beverly Hills.

the charmless central figure among a group of Manhattan teenagers who we spend a long twenty-four hours with as they get high, drink malt liquor, hang out in Washington Square Park, beat someone up for no reason, call one another "nigga" (though they're mostly white), and talk about sex in the most boorish terms possible. The movie's slender thread of a plot— not even a thread, really; more like one lone fish bone in a sour, watery stew—involves Jennie, one of Telly's earlier conquests (Chloë Sevigny, in her movie debut), who learns that she, and thus Telly, are HIV positive. (The movie was conceived in 1993, precisely when HIV diagnoses were peaking in this country, though not generally among straight white teens.) Will Jennie find Telly and warn him off before he seduces another barely postpubescent virgin? She sort of tries, not that she seems much to care by the end. The movie rewards her for her efforts by having her pass out on a couch at a party and be raped by Telly's best friend.

If I sound censorious, I guess that's because I am. *Kids* is not only repellant—which, in fairness, is its intent—but to my mind pointlessly so. (*Boyz n the Hood* might have turned out similarly if Singleton had been in thrall to Pasolini rather than Spielberg.) The first-time director, then-fifty-two-year-old photographer Larry Clark, and the first-time screenwriter, Harmony Korine, who was nineteen when he wrote *Kids*, claimed that nearly everything in the film was based on behavior they had observed, and I don't doubt them; taken scene by scene, much of the picture is effective. It wants to be an art-house version of something like *The Amboy Dukes*, and it hits that target. Most critics were respectful; many were bowled over. My problem with *Kids* is that the movie is so relentlessly nihilistic, so overdetermined, that taken as a whole it feels canned, its unyielding darkness the obverse of another picture's sentimentality, cooler and nastier but phony all the same. There is a proudly cynical species of adolescent mindset that sees the world as irredeemably awful—I know, having flirted with it myself—so *Kids* does capture a genuine sensibility; you can believe it was written by a nineteen-year-old, but its director could have given it some shading, some depth. One thing that might have helped: while drawing a bead on predatory boys, Clark and Korine could have allowed their girls to be more than sitting ducks.

So, two pictures: one as bubbly as movies get, the other a big bad bummer: one poking fun at a genuine blitheness in its times, the other trying so hard to be a slap in the face that you could laugh it off (after a shower). There's a kind of poetic symmetry in their releasing not quite side by side in the summer of 1995, as Bill Clinton's first term was nearing an end. It's a period that, in hindsight, feels like a historical lull: crime was now falling; the economy was humming; the US was at peace; web browsers were a novelty; most Americans had never heard of Al Qaeda and couldn't find Afghanistan or Iraq on a map (not that they necessarily could today); Russia was a fledgling democracy; Donald Trump was a bankrupt casino owner. As for teenage lives: social media meant dialing up an AOL chat room; sharing pictures with friends first required a trip to the one-hour-photo kiosk; and in most high schools an "active shooter" was a kid who took too many three-pointers on the basketball court.

For much of America, this was the nap before all hell broke loose, though maybe a more fitful one than is often remembered.

9

THE PLASTICS

Not every girl is miserable. There are actually genuinely happy
girls. . . . I don't come across them very often, but they do exist.

—Rosalind Wiseman, in her bestselling nonfiction
book *Queen Bees & Wannabes*, 2002

Mean Girls, released in 2004, is the first teen movie of the twenty-first
century to earn an indisputable spot in the canon. For one thing, Tina
Fey's tart, smart screenplay is as witty and quotable as *Clueless*'s, but with
a refreshingly nasty bite. For another thing, its titular trio, known as the
Plastics, are as iconic as any screen predecessors, outfitted in coordinated
baby-doll pink tops, short tight pink skirts, stripper heels, Breck Girl hair;
any movie can dress villains in black, but it takes skill and imagination
to weaponize pink. And one more thing: this is yet another teen movie
with a killer cast of mostly unknowns who went on to have significant
careers (Lindsay Lohan, Rachel McAdams, Amanda Seyfried, Lacey
Chabert, Lizzy Caplan). Moreover, *Mean Girls* has had a substantial afterlife, generating a TV remake in the guise of a nominal sequel (2011's
Mean Girls 2), an okay Broadway musical adaptation (which arrived in
New York in 2018 with a book by Fey and music by her husband, Jeff
Richmond, and ran for two years, shuttered prematurely because of the
Covid pandemic), and, in 2024, an okay movie adaptation of the okay

musical—meaning that *Mean Girls* has ascended beyond the merely canonical to the hallowed realm of franchisedom. Though the original film has not (as of this writing) been added to the Library of Congress's National Film Registry—unlike *Love Finds Andy Hardy*, *Rebel Without a Cause*, *American Graffiti*, *Fast Times at Ridgemont High*, *The Breakfast Club*, *Ferris Bueller's Day Off*, and *Boyz n the Hood*—its status as a cultural landmark was confirmed in 2020 when Pillsbury released a limited-edition *Mean Girls* Toaster Strudel with two kinds of filling: strawberry; and strawberry and cream cheese. Both came with packets of pink icing of indeterminate flavor profile.

These accomplishments are all the more remarkable given that the original *Mean Girls* debuted in an unprecedentedly crowded market-place, released on the tail end of a several-year stretch when teens were enjoying one of their periodic moments in the sun, their cultural swagger at a zenith not seen since the early '60s. One reason for this was that there were once again more of them: from a post–baby boom nadir in 1990, the population of American teenagers had begun steadily rising, and by 2002 the total number of twelve- to seventeen-year-olds had hit 25 million, matching the mid-1970s peak, give or take a few hundred thousand kids.*

Of course, the US population as a whole had grown by almost half across the nearly three decades between the mid-1970s and 2002, so teens represented a smaller percentage of the population than they once had—8.6 percent in 2002 versus 12 percent in 1974. Nevertheless they constituted a massive market, with $94.7 billion worth of spending money in 2003, according to *The New York Times*. Two years earlier, *Ad Age* had pegged the number even higher: $155 billion. Either way, highball or lowball, there was more money than ever to be made selling things to teenagers. *Mediaweek* estimated that their aggregate spending had more than doubled since the late 1980s.

*That 25 million has proven to be a plateau, the number holding steady into the mid-2020s, with minor fluctuations.

But alas: how much effort it took to snag those dollars! If you look through *Ad Age, Mediaweek,* and similar trade publications from the turn of the century, you find article after article complaining about what one writer called the "elusive art" of selling things to new-model teenagers, "choosy" spenders who too often circumvented the best-laid plans of marketing professionals and branding experts. "Kids' trends and habits change quickly, and they easily tire of the same old thing," *American Demographics* reported in 2001. Worse, the magazine noted, "kids can easily tell when they're being marketed to." They were delightfully avid consumers, but they were also sphinxes.

At a 2003 gathering billed as the "inaugural" What Teens Want conference, organized by *Billboard* and its sister publications *Adweek* and *The Hollywood Reporter,* attendees listened raptly during a panel as a Santa Monica High School student explained her arcane musical tastes: "I like Floetry this week. Last week it was India.Arie. Next week it will probably be something else." Heads nodded; notes were taken. The CEO of a youth apparel company complained in his keynote address about what he called "consumption ADD" among teens, citing a hypothetical boy with unfathomably eclectic tastes who might wear skateboard sneakers, listen to rap, and play football video games. Other speakers had essentially thrown up their hands and, as one advised, decided to trust "our intuition." Whether that was a frightening or liberating prospect, or just disorienting, was unclear.

Not being a marketing and branding professional, I am free to wonder whether turn-of-the-century teens—millennials, as they are now known—were in fact flightier than their forebears. (Were there not boys with eclectic tastes in the 1960s who might have worn surfer jams, listened to Motown, and liked baseball?) Or maybe the issue was more that baby boomer and Gen X marketers were surprised, even wounded, to find contemporary teenagers just as flummoxing as their own parents had found them, once upon a time? I would also note that, judging from my own ventures into retail spaces during this period, many brands seemed capable of cracking the teenage consumer code. I can report having seen

Abercrombie & Fitch, Sephora, Claire's, and American Apparel outlets thronged with young consumers in the early 2000s.

Hollywood had taken notice. As implied by the several film festivals' worth of teen comedies and dramas inspired by classic literature in the wake of *Clueless,* kids had returned to movie theaters by the turn of the century. In 1999, according to the MPAA, 31 percent of all movie tickets sold in the US were bought by twelve- to twenty-year-olds, roughly double their percentage of the population. Nearly half of twelve- to seventeen-year-olds claimed they were "frequent" moviegoers, meaning they went to a theater at least once a month, compared to 28 percent of people eighteen and older who said the same. It surely helped boost attendance that they had so many teen movies to choose from—and not just works inspired by Shakespeare, Austen, or Shaw, or even Philip Roth. (The 1999 teen sex comedy *American Pie,* in which Jason Biggs's character violates the titular dessert, owed an obvious debt to *Portnoy's Complaint.*) There were dramas for jocks (*Varsity Blues, Friday Night Lights*) as well as cheerleaders (*Bring It On, Bring It On Again, Bring It On: All or Nothing*); modern fairy tales starring Anne Hathaway (*The Princess Diaries, Ella Enchanted*); more sex comedies (*The Girl Next Door, American Pie 2*); and even an unlikely historical satire in which Kirsten Dunst and Michelle Williams inadvertently insert themselves into the Watergate scandal (*Dick*). The cycle probably should have ended with the inevitable pastiche genre parody, *Not Another Teen Movie* (2001), which takes place at John Hughes High and riffs witlessly on most of the films referenced in this paragraph as well as earlier classics. (I didn't last much past the first scene, a reverse homage to *Sixteen Candles,* in which the heroine's entire family not only remembers her birthday but barges into her bedroom to celebrate while she's masturbating to a Freddie Prinze Jr. picture.)

Beyond MTV, there was an ever-more evolved and elaborate media universe catering to teens, as well as to their younger "tween" siblings (generally defined as eight- to twelve-year-olds, a demographic that researchers had begun slicing and dicing in the 1990s). Two newish kid-centric cable channels, Nickelodeon and Disney Channel, were minting promising young stars and then plugging them into awful show after awful show with the industrial efficiency of the old studio system (along with, we have since learned, some of the old abusiveness). As in that earlier era, some of these stars would graduate to substantial adult careers while others would become famous cautionary tales, and some would achieve both. Included in these rolls were the Disney Channel alumni Ryan Gosling, Britney Spears, Justin Timberlake, Christina Aguilera, Hilary Duff, and Shia LaBeouf, and the Nickelodeon alumni Kenan Thompson, Melissa Joan Hart, Nick Cannon, and Amanda Bynes.

Aiming at a slightly older audience was the WB, a broadcast network that launched in 1995. (It later rebranded as the CW after a sort-of merger with its rival upstart network, UPN.) The WB had floundered for its first few years, programming edgy sitcoms modeled after shows like *Married . . . With Children*, which had established the Fox network a decade earlier. But the WB found its niche in the late nineties with the breakout hits *Buffy the Vampire Slayer*, based on the 1992 movie about a high school girl doing exactly what the title promises, and *Dawson's Creek*, an earnest mix of after-school special and teen soap opera. The network soon had a full schedule of series aimed at teens (*7th Heaven, Charmed, Felicity, Smallville*, and *Gilmore Girls*) and can claim to have launched, or helped launch, Sarah Michelle Gellar, Alyson Hannigan, Seth Green, Michelle Williams, Katie Holmes, James Van Der Beek, Keri Russell (also a Disney Channel vet), Chris Pratt, and Rose McGowan.

Standing outside this teentainment complex with their own shop—Tesla to Ford and GM—were Mary-Kate and Ashley Olsen, the identical twins who had begun their show-business careers when they were nine months old, sharing the role of an infant on the ABC sitcom *Full House*; by the time they turned eighteen, they had built (or had built for them) what is frequently described as "a billion-dollar empire" based on direct-to-video movie, fashion, beauty, and fragrance lines, and even bedding.

Naturally, there was a parallel resurgence of teen pop. *Billboard*'s Hot 100 was now top-heavy with acts like Spears, Aguilera, Brandy, Mandy Moore, Jessica Simpson, Avril Lavigne, and the boy bands NSYNC and

Backstreet Boys, performers machine-tooled with a precision that had rarely been seen since Annette Funicello was coerced into warbling "Tall Paul." Servicing this renaissance was a new ecosystem of youth magazines, which included *Teen People* (launched in 1998), *Cosmo Girl* (1999), *Teen Vogue* (2000), and *Elle Girl* (2001), alongside the now-venerable *Seventeen*, *YM*, and *Teen*—one more speculative bubble in an era renowned for them. You will have noticed that all these titles were aimed at adolescent girls, adolescent boys being notoriously averse to magazines and other media that target them overtly, as boys per se. The publishers of *MH-18*, a teen version of *Men's Health*, learned this when they launched that title in 2000 and saw it fold after five issues, the target audience probably ignoring it for *Vibe* or *Rolling Stone* or *Maxim* or even regular *Men's Health*, if they were reading magazines at all.

Vanity Fair celebrated the youth renaissance on its May 2003 cover, a fold-out that featured, in order, Amanda Bynes (then seventeen), Mary-Kate and Ashley Olsen (sixteen), Mandy Moore (nineteen), Hilary Duff (fifteen), Alexis Bledel (twenty-one—*oops*, but she played a high schooler on *Gilmore Girls*), Evan Rachel Wood (fifteen), Raven-Symoné (seventeen), and Lindsay Lohan (sixteen). On the evidence of latter-day TikTok homages, the issue was a cultural landmark for millennials—not quite their Woodstock, but maybe their Woodstock '94?—despite a cringe-inducing cover line that read: "It's Totally Raining Teens! And It's, Like, So a Major Moment in Pop Culture."* Inside, photographer Mark Seliger's twenty-page portfolio of the "hottest teen and tween stars" included the nine cover girls plus many more teen queens and even a handful of boys, among them Shia LaBeouf, Bow Wow, and Aaron Carter.

In an accompanying essay, James Wolcott wrote, "To some prunes and professional mourners, *Vanity Fair*'s salute to the talent, potential,

---

*Confession: I bear some responsibility for this, as I was then an editor at the magazine, where my duties included co-writing and editing cover lines. I can't recall if I myself came up with "It's Totally Raining Teens!," but I was undeniably in the room where it happened.

good looks, mass appeal, and bankable power of Hollywood youth will be seen as another sign of the end of civilization, like Paramount's decision to make *Grease 3** . . . dying bubbles from a society drowning in the kiddie pool." That was Wolcott going after a strawman with tongue-in-cheek hyperbole; in the decades since *Teen-Age Tyranny*, the vast majority of American adults now trembled in fear at being caught on the wrong side of any youthquake, or even youth tremors. Wolcott cited an even better reason for *Vanity Fair*'s interest: the estimate that teens had a collective $155 billion burning holes in their pockets and handbags. Even a magazine that routinely featured long-dead members of the Kennedy family on its cover couldn't ignore that.

What was genuinely new, Wolcott observed, was that boys were now taking a back seat to girls on screens and on the charts, as evidenced by the female-male imbalance in the magazine's portfolio, as well as the preponderance of girl-centered movies and TV series I mentioned above. As Wolcott flatly stated, "Girl power propels tween-teen culture," in contrast to an earlier generation's run of movies "fueled by the marriage of testosterone and gasoline," which had reigned from *Rebel Without a Cause* to *American Graffiti*. "Girls now seem to have more poise, daily agon, and purchasing power."

Variety agreed. In a 2004 article about the state of teen movies, *Variety* pretty much ignored boys altogether, citing young girls as the one "demo" of moviegoers that was not only reliable but still growing. Boys, echoing their avoidance of magazines aimed at them, were perfectly happy watching the same action and horror movies that people in their twenties

---

*This was a project that first surfaced in news reports in 2000, with Justin Timberlake and Britney Spears, then a couple, supposedly slated to star. By some accounts, it was derailed by that year's Screen Actors Guild strike; by other accounts Paramount came to its senses and remembered that its first stab at a sequel, 1982's *Grease 2*, with a then-unknown Michelle Pfeiffer and a mostly-unknown-even-now Maxwell Caulfield, had been a huge flop, and that no one in the intervening two decades had been clamoring for a completed *Grease* trilogy.

and thirties liked, whereas teen girls would turn out for movies about teen girls. The problem, as is so often the case in Hollywood, was that a profitable trend had turned into a glut. *Variety*: "Last year, the teen [girl] comedy was a must-have on every studio's development list. Cheap, color-ful, and easy to market, they were the cinematic equivalent of shopping at Target. In the last five months, half a dozen of these movies have un-spooled, with more on the way. When they work, execs are thrilled." But a series of recent flops had made clear that "not all prepubescent divas were created equal." Among the duds and disappointments: *New York Min-ute*, an attempt to see if the Olsen twins could sell movie tickets and not just DVDs and floral tops; *Chasing Liberty*, a teen rom-com with Mandy Moore as a president's daughter who falls for a dreamy motorcycle-riding Secret Service agent; *The Prince and Me*, a modern-day Cinderella story that starred Julia Stiles instead of Anne Hathaway; *Confessions of a Teen-age Drama Queen*, a comedy that featured Lindsay Lohan butting heads with Megan Fox over the lead in a school play; and *The Lizzie McGuire Movie*, an unacknowledged remake of *Gidget Goes to Rome* spun-off from Hilary Duff's Disney Channel series.

"Studios can reap wins if youth pix are savvy, sexy," *Variety* offered, concluding that what teen audiences wanted was, in essence, what most audiences wanted: good movies. The trade's leading example of a savvy, sexy winner? *Mean Girls*, which had been released just a few weeks earlier.

In its original incarnation, *Mean Girls* builds on the anthropological eye that George Lucas brought to *American Graffiti* and Cameron Crowe and Amy Heckerling to *Fast Times at Ridgemont High*. It is also, I am almost 100 percent certain, the first teen movie adapted from a bestselling nonfiction advice book for parents. That work was *Queen Bees & Wan-nabes: Helping Your Daughter Survive Cliques, Gossip, Boyfriends, and Other Realities of Adolescence* by Rosalind Wiseman—a "thought leader on leadership, culture, conflict, and young people," according to her website. In the book, published in 2002 (and updated in 2009 and again in 2016), Wiseman paints what she calls "girl world" as a ruthless, snub-or-be-snubbed doomscape where survival depends on near-military-level discipline: "The common definition of a clique is an exclusive group of girls who are close friends. I see it a little differently . . . I see them as a platoon of soldiers who have banded together to navigate the perils and insecurities of adolescence. There's a chain of command and they operate as one in their interactions with their environment. Group cohesion is based on unquestioned loyalty to the leaders and an us-versus-the-world mentality." Elsewhere, she describes a girl-world dynamic where its denizens serve as a kind of Stasi, "conducting surveillance on who's breaking the laws of appearance, clothes, interest in boys, and personality." To be sure, those laws "are based on what our culture tells us about what constitutes ideal femininity." But Wiseman then lets the beauty-industrial complex off the hook: "Who is the prime enforcer of these standards? The movies? The teen magazines? Nope, it's the girls themselves."

At the time her book was published, Wiseman led a nonprofit called the Empower Program, through which she taught classes in schools around the country, from middle schools to colleges, with a cirriculum that encouraged girls to be nice, or at least nicer, to one another. *Queen Bees & Wannabes* was an extension of that work, addressed to parents, and its view of girlhood can feel bleak to the point of hopelessness. Wiseman quotes one "anonymous queen bee" who asserts, "I'm never mean to people without a reason." This interviewee was twelve.

We all know from lived experience that middle school and high school girls can be mean to one another for many, many "reasons"—some if not most of which barely merit the designation, at least as adults not named Caligula understand it. (PS: boys can be mean to one another, too.) But the familiar scent of moral panic was in the air given that *Queen Bees & Wannabes* was only one of five books devoted to mean girls wholly or in part that came out during the first four months of 2002—roughly, a new book on female bullying every three weeks. The competition:

- *Woman's Inhumanity to Woman* by Phyllis Chesler
- *The Secret Lives of Girls: What Good Girls Really Do — Sex Play, Aggression, and Their Guilt* by Sharon Lamb
- *Fast Girls: Teenage Tribes and the Myth of the Slut* by Emily White
- *Odd Girl Out: The Hidden Culture of Aggression in Girls* by Rachel Simmons

Wiseman's and Simmons's books made the *New York Times* Best Seller list, and the two authors appeared on Oprah and various morning shows. The other books got plenty of attention, too. *The New York Times Magazine* took note on its cover, with an image of a miserable teenage girl stuck with pins like a voodoo doll. In the accompanying story, "Girls Just Want to Be Mean," the journalist Margaret Talbot paraphrased Simmons, writing that it was "time to pull up the rock and really look at this seething underside of American girlhood." Or as Simmons herself put it in *Odd Girl Out*, "Beneath a facade of female intimacy lies a terrain traveled in secret, marked with anguish and nourished by silence." How secret and how silent were up for debate: *Heathers* and *Are You There God? It's Me, Margaret.*, to cite two very different cultural milestones, had touched on these issues, and Laura Ingalls tussled plenty with prairie mean girl Nellie Oleson in the Little House books, and on the 1970s TV series. The 1994 bestseller *Reviving Ophelia*, in which the psychologist Mary Pipher detailed the cultural pressures that led to increased rates of depression and anxiety in high school girls, had done spadework on the subject a decade earlier. Nevertheless, fairly or not, female bullying was the young century's "Teenage Crisis of the Moment," or so *The Washington Post* declared.

There was backlash, too: *Newsweek* ran a cover story that spring under the rubric, "In Defense of Teen Girls: They're Not All 'Mean Girls' and 'Ophelias.'" Inside, the magazine praised what it insisted was a silent high school majority of so-called gamma girls — not alphas or betas, just "kids who may not be 'popular' but aren't losers either," which was not intended as damning with faint praise. The magazine profiled one such sophomore at a high school in El Cajon, California: "Tall and athletic, with a smile that renews itself every time she speaks, the fifteen-year-old is comfortable in her skin, if not crazy about all the freckles." She was evidence, the magazine promised readers, "that a teenage girl in 2002 can be emotionally healthy, socially secure, independent-minded and just plain nice . . . Yet you'd never know such a species existed, given the current media flurry over two bestselling books about teenage 'mean girls.'"

In her *Times Magazine* cover story, Talbot ascribed the new focus not to moral panic, or media exigencies, but to Finnish social scientists. As she explained, "For years, psychologists who studied aggression among schoolchildren looked only at its physical and overt manifestations and concluded that girls were less aggressive than boys." But this assumption had begun to shift in the early 1990s thanks to a study of middle school girls led by Kaj Björkqvist, a professor of psychology at Abo Akademi University in Turku, Finland, which found that girls, in Talbot's summary, were "just as aggressive as boys, though in a different way":

> They were not as likely to engage in physical fights, for example, but their superior social intelligence enabled them to wage complicated battles with other girls aimed at damaging relationships or reputations—leaving nasty messages by cell phone or spreading scurrilous rumors by e-mail, making friends with one girl as revenge against another, gossiping about someone just loudly enough to be overheard. Turning the notion of women's greater empathy on its head, Björkqvist focused on the destructive uses to which such emotional attunement could be put. "Girls can better understand how other girls feel," as he puts it, "so they know better how to harm them."

Rosalind Wiseman brought to the problem not a Finnish researcher's expertise but the evangelism of a reformed sinner. Attending private middle school in Washington, DC, she herself had run with "a very powerful, very scary group of girls who were fun to be with but who could turn on you like a dime." So could she, confessing to Talbot, "When I was in eighth grade, I spread around a lie about my best friend, Melissa . . . something that made her sound slutty. She confronted me about it, and I totally denied it." Wiseman added, "I was really a piece of work."

Perhaps that was why she seemed to take a perverse relish in Queen Bee cruelties. In one passage from the *Times Magazine* piece, Talbot expresses doubt to Wiseman that girls actually engage in three-way phone calls, a trick Wiseman describes where one girl calls a friend and gets the friend to dish about a third girl, who, unknown to the friend, is secretly listening in. But after some girls in one of her Empower classes admitted that they did indeed make three-way calls, Wiseman laughed and said to Talbot, "Haven't I told you girls are crafty? Haven't I told you girls are *evil?*"

You may remember that there is three-way phone calling in *Mean Girls*, as well as nasty-message leaving, scurrilous rumor mongering, slut-shaming—all the things that Talbot, Wiseman, Simmons, and the rest were writing about. Tina Fey had happened to read Talbot's *Times Magazine* article while casting about for a screenplay idea, and it is a credit to her comic imagination that, by her account, she "immediately" saw the potential: "This was something I [felt] that I could write about . . . It was about girls. And it was nasty and violent. And that appealed to me."

It struck a personal chord, too. As she told *Cosmo Girl* two years later, while publicizing the finished movie:

> I admit it: I was a mean girl. I had a gift for coming up with the mean-est possible thing to say in any situation. I ate weaker girls for breakfast. I could sniff out who would take my insults and not fight back. And I was a big behind-the-back girl: I'd spend hours analyzing what some girl did or wore and why it was so jackass.
>
> Why? Well, at my high school—a huge public school in a suburb of Philadelphia—there were a few girls who were kind of "famous."

Everyone knew who they were dating and what parties they went to. They weren't the prettiest girls or the ones with money. They were just randomly anointed. I was an honor student and I was in a ton of activities—the newspaper, the drama club, the tennis team. My friends and I didn't really date or go to cool parties, so we made jokes about those who did. To be honest, we felt kind of rejected, and when you don't feel confident about yourself, you may look for flaws in somebody else to make you feel better.

Looking back, I can see the mean-girl thing for what it is: a waste of energy. It's like eating a huge bag of cheese curls. In the beginning, you're like, "This is fun. Tasty!" Then the whole bag is gone, and you feel disgusting. Nothing good has come of it.

In the spring of 2002, Fey was the head writer at *Saturday Night Live*—the first woman to hold that position—and also the co-anchor of the show's Weekend Update segment. She brought the notion of adapting *Queen Bees & Wannabes* to her boss, SNL producer Lorne Michaels, who agreed it held promise, with one caveat: "Can they also still have cool cars and cool clothes?" With Fey's assent, he took the project to Sherry Lansing, then running Paramount, who was also interested, and a deal was struck to option Wiseman's book.

"It was kind of a bonehead thing to do on my part for my first screenplay—to try to adapt a nonfiction, nonnarrative book," Fey admitted. "I had to make up the whole story. I mean, it's not *Chinatown*. But just to keep a story moving forward was new to me." She initially intended that the central character be a teacher, a sort of Wiseman stand-in—not unlike the math teacher Fey eventually played in the film. You can imagine a version of that movie, a comic all-girl *Blackboard Jungle*. But Fey soon realized the richer material involved the girls themselves. The heroine instead became a student, Cady (pronounced "Katy") Heron, the proverbial new kid at school. But Cady, played by Lindsay Lohan, is not only new to North Shore High, she's new to high school, period, and teenage American mores in general, because she has previously been homeschooled by her zoologist parents in the African veldt. This backstory was a terrific device, allowing the audience to see the usual lunchtime rituals and gym class humiliations through Cady's eyes as if observing the curious behaviors of a new species at the watering hole, though it led to another boneheaded move on Fey's part: she wanted to title the movie *Home Schooled*, but Lansing sagely insisted on *Mean Girls*.

The project came together quickly and made it to theaters in just twenty-six months, a Hollywood split second, following Fey's initial brainstorm. The director was Mark Waters, who had directed Lohan in the 2003 hit *Freaky Friday*, which launched her as a teen star with a gift for comedy—five years after Disney's 1998 remake of *The Parent Trap* had launched her as a child star with a gift for comedy. On screen, she conveyed an instant likability, even innocence, that was perfect for Cady and helped give *Mean Girls* emotional ballast even in its sillier and more contrived moments.

Off screen, Lohan, who was only seventeen when the movie was released, was already turning up in nightclubs and paparazzi photos. Tabloid headlines had her drinking, drugging, dancing on tables, and cat-fighting with Hilary Duff over Aaron Carter (the pop star and younger brother of Backstreet Boy Nick Carter). These were the kinds of adventures that would make her one of the 2000s' more reliable generators of tabloid headlines and unflattering paparazzi shots, overshadowing her considerable talents as an actor, and leading as well to serial stays in rehab, multiple run-ins with the law, several short stints behind bars, and a longer acquaintance with an ankle monitor.

It surely didn't help Lohan's future emotional equilibrium that a not-insignificant portion of the reaction to *Mean Girls* focused on her chest. The most egregious example was a profile by Mark Binelli in *Rolling Stone*, published a couple months after the movie came out. The lead:

> Lindsay Lohan has been eighteen for just under a week when she tells me her breasts are real. I did not ask (gentlemen never do), though my reporting (discreet visual fact-checking, a goodbye hug) seems to

confirm her statement. Lohan fields queries about her breasts in most interviews, which is probably why she decided to preemptively address the issue. "My little sister reads that stuff," Lohan says. "She called me up one day and was like, 'I heard you got that Pamela Anderson thing.' It's just so retar—" Lohan stops and glances at her assistant. They smile at each other in an inside joke sort of way. "Stupid," Lohan continues.

This was written for the magazine's annual Hot List issue, which featured Lohan on the cover mussing her hair and smiling wickedly above the line "Hot, Ready, and Legal!" Binelli continued:

> There comes a time in the life of every teenage girl who works for the Disney Corp. when that girl realizes she has suddenly—how shall we phrase this?—"broadened her appeal" . . . For Lindsay Lohan—or, more accurately, for Lindsay Lohan's breasts—the tipping point came somewhere after the 2003 remake of *Freaky Friday* . . . Suddenly, this year, it became socially acceptable to note that the redheaded child actress was hot.

Personally, I find such observations cringeworthy enough to have retrospective sympathy for Walt Disney's anxieties regarding Annette Funicello's navel.* Of course, this was *Rolling Stone*, a magazine read by the teenage boys who weren't buying *MH-18*. But even a female reporter for *The New York Times*, Jennifer Senior, brought up Lohan's boobs in an interview with Fey, noting that when she had seen *Mean Girls* the "people in front of me, to the left of me, and behind me were obsessed with her breasts." Senior felt this was not only a distraction but subverted the film's meaning, since Lohan's character "is supposed to represent this triumph

---

*Lest I be accused of hypocrisy on the frequently conjoined subjects of bad writing and the male gaze, I confess I once described Keira Knightley as a "sexy tomboy beanpole" in a movie review. Apologies to all concerned.

of substance over style, but she's so voluptuously rendered, so provoca-tively dressed." Fey blamed Lohan's own wardrobe choices, "because Lindsay is seventeen and wants to wear the foxiest clothes in the trailer. We used to have to beg her and say: 'Please, you're still nerdy in this part. You can't be that gorgeous yet.'"

Viewers who manage to focus on the film itself may be surprised to learn that, aside from the fact that Fey had to invent an hour and a half's worth of plot out of whole cloth, the finished movie otherwise reflects its source material with unexpected faithfulness. Take the scenes where Cady's new friends, goth Janis and "too gay to function" Damian (Lizzy Cap-lan and Daniel Franzese), provide her with a map to help navigate the lunchroom, spatially and socially. As Janis explicates clique topography, table by table: "You got your freshmen . . . ROTC guys . . . preps . . . JV jocks . . . Asian nerds . . . cool Asians . . . varsity jocks . . . unfriendly Black hotties . . . girls who eat their feelings . . . girls who don't eat anything . . . desperate wannabes . . . burnouts . . . sexually active band geeks . . ." Wise-man's book features a map just like Janis's, drawn from group labels given to her by two anonymous sixteen-year-old girls from different parts of the country. The kids' real-word typology is as snarky as anything Fey came up with: "model United Nations boys . . . unpopular party kids and ecstasy & acid users (mostly juniors) . . . hacky-sack-playing kids . . . football & 'easy' girls . . . attitude girls . . . sophomore girls that judge." Whether in film or real life, tribal affinities had been ever more thinly sliced across the two decades since *The Breakfast Club*.

At the center of the *Mean Girls* lunchroom, seated side by side by side as if surveying the scene from the head table at a banquet, are the Plastics. "They're teen royalty," Damian explains. "If North Shore was *Us Weekly*, they would always be on the cover." The trio: anxious busybody Gretchen (Lacey Chabert), vacant Karen (Amanda Seyfried), and Queen Bee Re-gina George (Rachel McAdams, an actress who, while witheringly funny here, has otherwise enjoyed a career of making nice, even bland charac-ters interesting). Regina practices a delicious, calculating form of bitch-ery, as when she compliments Cady on being "really pretty," to which the ingenuous Cady replies, "Thank you," prompting Regina to pounce: "So you agree? You think you're really pretty?" In the moment, McAdams projects the volatile, disorienting menace of Joe Pesci, in *Goodfellas*, asking "What do you mean I'm funny?" It's exactly what Wiseman has in mind when she describes a Queen Bee as a "girl whose popularity is based on fear and control . . . Think of a combination of the Queen of Hearts in *Alice in Wonderland* and Barbie." (Historical note for younger readers who may be confused by references in this paragraph: people used to aspire to be on the covers of print magazines such as *Us*, and the Barbie doll was not always considered a positive role model for girls.)

Regina first deigns to notice Cady when a boy named Jason pesters her with a supposed "lunchtime survey for new students."

> JASON
> Can you answer a few questions?

> CADY
> Okay.

> JASON
> Is your muffin buttered?*

> CADY (*confused*)
> What?

> JASON
> Would you like us to assign
> someone to butter your muffin?

> CADY (*really confused*)
> My what?

*The Production Code that had forbidden Andy Hardy from referencing a girl's "lungs" had been dead for decades, but Paramount, eyeing a PG-13 rating over an R, forced Fey to rewrite this question from the original "Is your cherry popped?" It's a matter of taste, but the new line strikes me as even raunchier—"evocative in a dirtier way," as Fey put it.

                    REGINA
Is he bothering you? Jason, why
are you such a skeez?

                    JASON
I'm just being friendly.

    GRETCHEN (*to Jason, whisper*)
You were supposed to call me last
night.

                    REGINA
You do not come to a party at my
house, with Gretchen, and then
scam on some poor innocent girl
right in front of us three days
later. She's not interested. (*To
Cady*) Do you want to have sex
with him?

                    CADY
No thank you.

                    REGINA
Good. So, it's settled. (*To
Jason*) You can go shave your back
now. Bye, Jason.

        JASON (*slinking away*)
Bitch.

    That didn't come from Wiseman. But after Regina invites Cady to
join the Plastics at their lunchroom table on a trial basis, Gretchen gives
a short speech explaining the clique's strictly enforced code of conduct,
which, aside from the often quoted opener—"On Wednesdays we wear
pink"—is lifted almost verbatim from *Queen Bees & Wannabes*, where it
is attributed to a fifteen-year-old girl identified as "Gabrielle":

We have rules about what we wear. You can only wear your hair up (like in a ponytail) once a week. You can't wear a tank top two days in a row. You can only wear jeans on Friday and that's also the only time you can wear sneakers. If you break any of these rules, you can't sit with us at lunch.

As Gretchen, Lacey Chabert probably gives a better line reading than Gabrielle did, but if there is such a thing as found comedy, this is it, though Fey left some money on the table. Gabrielle in the book continues: "Monday is the most important day because you want to look your best—it sets the tone for the rest of the week. So wearing something like sweats on a Monday is like going to church and screaming 'I hate Jesus!' when you walk in the door." (Twenty years later, Gabrielle, now in HR, outed herself to *Washingtonian* magazine. Denying any intent to ostracize or punish, she described the dress code as a cute bonding exercise among pals who just "wanted to wear skirts on the same day. We made up all kinds of random songs and fake clubby things. We weren't the mean girls by any means." She cited *Grease*'s Pink Ladies: "What made them friends? They had the jackets, it was a thing"—one more example of the teen movie hall of mirrors.)

Wiseman's book offers a detailed taxonomy of girl-world hierarchies, with, of course, the Queen Bee at the apex. Gretchen, the movie clique's second-in-command, encompasses two roles in this schema: "Sidekick" and "Banker," the former what you think, the latter a keeper of secrets and dispenser of gossip. Damian fills in Gretchen's backstory, which is all Fey: "She's totally rich because her dad invented Toaster Strudels." (Thus the sixteen-years-later tie-in with Pillsbury.)

Though Amanda Seyfried's Karen lacks an obvious counterpart in Wiseman's taxonomy, she does fill a venerable comedic slot: the dumb blonde, and Seyfried plays her with a deft blend of spaciness and snap timing. (Karen, surveying the crowd at a party: "You know who's looking fine tonight? Seth Mosakowski." Gretchen: "Okay, you did not just say that." Karen: "What? He's a good kisser." Gretchen: "He's your cousin." Karen, explaining patiently: "Yeah, but he's my *first* cousin.")

A shout-out as well to Amy Poehler as Mrs. George, Regina's mother, so desperate not to offend her daughter and the rest of the Plastics that she's ceded all authority. Here she is introducing herself to Cady: "I just want you to know, if you need anything, don't be shy. Okay? There are no rules in this house. [*Winks.*] I'm not like a regular mom. [*Winks again.*] I'm a *cool* mom. Right, Regina?" Regina: "Stop talking." A female Peter Pan with Styrofoam breast implants, Mrs. George could be one of the overly deferential mothers condemned by Margaret Mead back in 1951, after a further half century of devolution; she's the "softening of adult-hood" Grace and Fred M. Hechinger warned about, taken to its logical, embarrassing, but savagely funny conclusion: parent as sycophant.

The not-*Chinatown* plot has Cady becoming the fourth Plastic, ostensibly undercover, at the behest of Janis and Damian. But as Elvis Mitchell noted in his *New York Times* review, in her new role Cady "has a genuine taste for it, the trap of all double agents." Cady eventually usurps Regina's throne, Regina enacts revenge, and the picture climaxes in a melee that seems to involve the entire junior class of girls, followed by an encounter group session led by Fey's math teacher and drawing from the classes Wiseman taught, with the girls apologizing for their cruelties to one another.

```
                    KAREN
         Gretchen, I'm sorry I laughed at
         you that time you got diarrhea
         at Barnes & Noble . . . And
         I'm sorry for telling everyone
         about it . . . And I'm sorry for
         repeating it now.
```

But neither the movie's weak life lessons nor its meandering plot are really the point: the social observations and the jokes are, and it's a tribute to Fey, and to a lesser extent Wiseman, that the jokes and social observations are, at their best, one and the same. As *Teen Vogue* reported in 2018, *Mean Girls* is also one of the rare high school movies, along with *Clueless* and *Bring It On*, which passes the Bechdel test. (Do two female characters have a conversation at some point about something other than a man?) Aside from Damian (a high school version of the heroine's gay best friend in so many adult rom-coms), there is one other semi-significant male character, Aaron Samuels (Jonathan Bennett), a cute former boyfriend of Regina's, who Cady develops a crush on, but he's more a plot device than someone the movie bothers to care about—a sweet, floppy-haired MacGuffin.

Reviews were generally positive—*The New York Times* rated *Mean Girls* "tart and often charming," while *Seventeen* enthused that "claws have never been sharper"—and the movie took in $86 million at the US box office, great numbers for a cheap teen comedy with no big stars. A further $44 million in ticket sales from overseas was maybe even more impressive, given that comedies don't often travel well and that this one in particular mined a deep and peculiar vein of contemporary Americana.

Fey, having sat through the movie with numerous test audiences, had a nuanced perspective on audience reactions: "Adults find it funny. They are the ones who are laughing. Young girls watch it like a reality show. It's much too close to their real experiences so they're not exactly guffawing."

A dissent came from Anthony Lane, writing in *The New Yorker*. While he conceded that the movie's sharper lines and observations promised something with "truer and more piercing aim than most teen comedies," much of the rest of it, he felt, comprised "just another teen movie (why do pretty maids always have to be photographed in a row, in silky slow motion?) . . . I would be more amused if the topic of rich material girls had not been worn to a thread elsewhere. It is all very well to satirize perfect white females, but if you're sick of their attitudes, why single them out as protagonists in the first place? What happened to the Asian nerds? Or the unfriendly Black hotties? Or the tired teachers? Why can't we see a movie about them?"

It was a fair point, and one that Fey addressed in the 2024 remake by integrating the Plastics and others of the movie's cliques, though Cady and Regina, the two central roles, remained white. The new movie also trimmed some homophobia and slut-shaming. What the update added, aside from so-so songs that don't do much to advance the plot or inform the characters, are social media and an embarrassing viral video. In that light, the 2004 film feels as distant as *Sixteen Candles*. Aside from some mild flip phone action, there's virtually no technology in *Mean Girls*; in a pivotal scene, it's almost touching to see Regina enacting her revenge by tossing incriminating photocopies—physical sheets of real paper!—all over the school's hallways.

Here is Wolcott again, in his *Vanity Fair* article, offering a time-capsule glimpse of state-of-the-art teen tech, circa 2003, as he observed various young stars during the magazine's photo shoot:

> Wired up the wazoo with cells, pagers, Blackberrys, iPods, and portable CD players, they are children of the hive, human nodes within a constant hum and flux. For the young idol on the go, the cell phone must be as quick-draw accessible as a gunslinger's six-shooter and aesthetically nifty. Even keener is the cell phone with "a freakin' camera on it," to quote [Shia] LaBeouf, who showed us a picture of himself with Vanessa Williams at a Laker game. Others had pictures of their friends filed so that, when a pal phoned, his or her face would pop up on the little screen and they could make believe they were talking to the pest in person.

How judgy that passage read in 2003, how quaint today. As we are all aware, the human nodes have since grown ever more connected, the hum and flux ever more constant. (I realize that as a point of grammar, "constant" is an absolute, like "perfect," so can't be intensified, but I stand by "ever more constant" as lived experience.)

On April 30, 2004, the day *Mean Girls* debuted in theaters, the first iPhone was three years distant. But twelve weeks earlier, on February 4, Mark Zuckerberg had launched the website he designed to allow Harvard students to connect with one another—TheFacebook.com. By the end of April, it had expanded to several other colleges, including Stanford and Yale. By the end of the year, it had a million users, all over the country. In September 2005, it was opened to high school students. Meanwhile, that spring, the first video had been uploaded to YouTube.

Didi (2024), written and directed by Sean Wang, is set in the summer of 2008 and captures the changed landscape—seemingly a lifetime away from *Mean Girls*, four long years prior. The hero of Wang's autobiographical film is a thirteen-year-old Taiwanese American growing up in a Bay Area suburb (not far from mine!), now enabled by so many shiny, seductive ways to miscommunicate with friends, crushes, the world. I imagine that for millennials, the movie's flip phones and glimpses of old-school Facebook and MySpace pages, stuttering YouTube videos, and AOL Instant Messenger interfaces provide the same dopamine hits of recognition that boomers got from the chromed-up cars and golden oldies in *American Graffiti*.

At the beginning of this chapter, I claimed that *Mean Girls* is the first canonical teen film of the twenty-first century, but maybe it would have been more apt to call it the last great teen film of the twentieth century.

10

BELLA AND KATNISS

We've all had the experience of being [teenagers] and feeling everything is life and death. You know, 'I have nothing to wear today, I'm going to kill myself.' What's wonderful about this story is that everything actually *is* life and death.

—Melissa Rosenberg, screenwriter of all five *Twilight* movies

The first quarter of the twenty-first century seems to have been an especially confusing time to be a teenager—quite an achievement!—and I don't think I say that simply because I am now almost half a century past my own high school graduation.

Take sex.

The journalist Nancy Jo Sales begins the first chapter of her 2016 book, *American Girls: Social Media and the Secret Lives of Teenagers*, with a dismaying but, she would have us believe, representative anecdote. The central figure is Sophia, a thirteen-year-old growing up in Montclair, New Jersey (an upper-middle-class suburb that happens to be home to an inordinate number of journalists, writers, and other intellectual class laborers). Sophia's story begins with a text:

SEND NOODZ

The boy sent the message in the middle of the day, when she was walking home from school. He sent it via direct message on Instagram . . .

Sophia stared at her phone.

Wait what??? she responded.

No answer.

She continued along the empty streets . . . She had heard of boys asking girls for nudes before, but it had never happened to her. This was her first time. She didn't know how to respond, or whether she should respond. Should she be outraged? Shocked? Her first reaction was: "I was like, *Whoa*, he finds me attractive?"

She wondered if he liked her . . . She heard her phone ding . . . It was the boy, responding to her message:

I really need this 'cause I have to win a bet I won't show anyone, he wrote.

The boy did not explain to Sophia how he proposed to win his bet without showing off her pictures, and you will be relieved to know that she did not send him any. In the end, she replied with a succinct lol—which might strike you as an altogether too cheerful and good-sportish response. It might even strike you as a sad response. Sales recounts texts and DMs that other girls she spoke to had received from would-be suitors: "Wanna fuck?" "Nice hair do you do anal?" Does *lol* still suffice? "You want to laugh but sometimes you feel sick," a sixteen-year-old in Louisville said.

"Hypersexualization is ubiquitous, so visible as to be nearly invisible: it is the water in which girls swim, the air they breathe," writes the journalist Peggy Orenstein in *her* 2016 book on this same subject, *Girls & Sex: Navigating the Complicated New Landscape*. Between them, Sales and Orenstein interviewed a cross section of nearly three hundred girls from all over the country; "eye-opening" was an adjective common to the generally positive reviews of both women's books. Orenstein's subjects "talked about feeling both powerful and powerless while dressed in revealing clothing, using words like *liberating, bold, boss bitch* and *desirable*, even as they expressed indignation over the constant public judgment of their bodies. They felt simultaneously that they actively chose a sexualized image—which was nobody's damned business but their own—*and* that they had no choice."

"You want to stand out," one girl confided in Orenstein. "You want to attract someone. So it's not just about being hot, but who can be the *hottest*. One of my friends has gotten to the point where she's practically naked at parties."

"The incessant drumbeat of self-objectification," Orenstein writes, pressures girls "to perform rather than to feel sensuality." She quotes a high school senior from Northern California:

> I'll be hooking up with some guy who's really hot, and we'll be snuggling and grinding and touching and it's cool. Then things get heavier and all of a sudden my mind shifts and I'm not a real person: it's like, *This is me performing. This is me acting.* It's like, *How well am I doing?* Like, *This is a hard position, but don't shake.* And I'm thinking, *What would 'she' do? 'She' would go down on him.* And I don't even know who it is I'm playing, who that 'she' actually is. It's some fantasy girl, I guess, maybe the girl from porn.

Boys, having learned about the finer points of sex not from *The Amboy Dukes* or page 27 of *The Godfather* but from however much Pornhub they care to consume, apparently expect the fantasy girl, too. "I do think porn changes how guys view sex," a nineteen-year-old college student told Orenstein. "Especially with my first boyfriend. He had no experience. He thought it would happen like in porn, that I'd be ready a lot faster and he could just, you know, *pound.*" Said another girl, "They think they're supposed to do this hammer-in-and-out thing and that's what girls like. They don't realize, 'Dude, that does *not feel good.*' It's all they know. It's what they see."

So that is one side of the equation: teenagers growing up in a porn-saturated, hypersexualized world. The other side of the equation: study after study claiming that kids have been having less and less actual sex across the last three decades. According to the Centers for Disease

Control's biannual Youth Risk Behavior Survey, the number of high school students who said they'd "ever had sex," meaning intercourse, declined from 54 percent in 1991 to 38 percent in 2019* (followed by a further, possibly temporary plunge to 30 percent in the pandemic year of 2021). "In other words," as Kate Julian, a journalist and editor, put it in a 2018 *Atlantic* article titled "Why Are Young People Having So Little Sex These Days?," "In the space of a generation, sex has gone from something most high school students have experienced to something most haven't. (And no, they aren't having oral sex instead—that rate hasn't changed much.)"

Not only are fewer kids having sex, but even those who are are having less of it: according to the CDC, 9 percent of high school students said they'd had sex with four or more partners in 2019, down from 18.7 percent in 1991. As you'd expect, teen birth rates are also down, having declined steadily, minus a few short-lived upticks, from a peak in 1991.

Another way to look at these statistics: thirty years ago, on average, Gen X high school students were losing their virginity in the spring of sophomore year; average Gen Z students now lose their virginity a full twelve months later.

The people whose jobs require them to explain these trends are divided about the causes. The fear of contracting HIV has surely played a part, as has the vogue in some parts of the country for abstinence-only sex education and social rituals like virginity pledges and purity balls. Easy access to pornography presumably diverts some of the energies that were once expended at drive-ins and on basement rec room couches. Helicopter parenting limits opportunities for experimentation, as is perhaps its point; so, too, do schedules crowded with extracurricular activities and homework. As Kate Julian wrote—glibly, but surely with some truth—"It takes idle hands to get past first base, and today's kids have a lot to do."

---

*With minor statistical variations, the 2019 percentage was true across nearly all demographics: for boys as well as girls, straight kids as well as LGBTQ kids, and all ethnic groups with the exception of Asian American teens, 11 percent of whom said they had ever had sex.

Sales and Orenstein are both careful to note that they are discussing qualitative rather than quantitative issues, but that wasn't the message that readers necessarily took away. Parents could be forgiven for assuming the worst given that the news media in the 2000s and 2010s were full of hair-on-fire reports about degrading incidents and crimes involving teenagers, sex, alcohol, and cell phone cameras. Almost as upsetting were stories about alleged fads like color-coded sex bracelets, which supposedly revealed which acts a girl was willing to perform, and so-called rainbow parties involving lipstick and oral sex.* And then there was the more pervasive menace of "hookup culture," a trend-piece staple for two decades and counting. An early and pungent example is a Tom Wolfe essay from 2000, titled, as if it were a message in a bottle to whoever might survive the fall of our own Roman Empire, "Hooking Up: What Life Was Like at the Turn of the Second Millennium: An American's World":

> Meanwhile, sexual stimuli bombarded the young so incessantly and intensely they were inflamed with a randy itch long before reaching puberty. At puberty, the dams, if any were left, burst . . . In junior high school, high school, and college, girls headed out in packs in the evening, and boys headed out in packs, hoping to meet each other fortuitously. If they met and some girl liked the looks of some boy, she would give him the nod, or he would give her the nod, and the two of them would retire to a halfway-private room and "hook up."

---

*Rainbow parties first came to mainstream attention on a 2003 episode of *The Oprah Winfrey Show*. An *O Magazine* journalist explained to Winfrey and her audience, "A 'rainbow party' is an oral sex party . . . 'Rainbow' comes from all of the girls [putting] on lipstick and each one puts her mouth around the penis of the gentleman, or gentlemen, who are there to receive favors, and makes a mark on a different place on the penis, hence the term rainbow." "Are rainbow parties pretty common?" Winfrey asked, looking dumbfounded. "I think so," said the journalist, "at least among the fifty girls I talked to. This was pervasive." The cutaways to aghast audience members were priceless. A 2005 YA novel titled *Rainbow Party* sparked even more media alarm, with an article in *The New York Times* asking, "Are These Parties for Real?" The answer, according to most journalists and researchers who looked into it more than cursorily, was no.

In common with most authors, Wolfe's writing about youth did not get better as he aged. (Go back to chapter four and reread his all-neurons-firing account of the 1963 Teen Fair.) But Wolfe's was the sort of report that led Kathleen A. Bogle, a sociologist at La Salle University who studies teenage sexuality, to tell *The New York Times* in 2009, "I give presentations nationwide where I'm showing people that the virginity rate in college is higher than you think and the number of partners is lower than you think and hooking up more often than not does not mean intercourse. But so many people think we're morally in trouble, in a downward spiral and teens are out of control. It's very difficult to convince people otherwise." Bogle would continue to try, co-authoring a 2014 book titled *Kids Gone Wild: From Rainbow Parties to Sexting, Understanding the Hype Over Teen Sex.* As one critic summarized the book: "It's not that every report of a girl giving oral sex to a bunch of hockey players is false. It's that the degree to which this is happening is often exaggerated and sensationalized, according to the kids themselves."

So are the kids themselves over- or undersexed? The answer seems to be both, which is not necessarily a contradiction and might even be an explanation. At any rate, it strikes me as no wonder that teenagers, and especially teenage girls, were primed, beginning in the mid-2000s, to respond to an epic high school romance steeped in sexual attitudes more in keeping with the turn of the previous century. It must have come as a relief.

Writing in *Time* in 2009, following the releases of *Twilight* the bestselling book, in 2005, and *Twilight* the blockbuster movie, in 2008, when the giddy crowds who packed novelist Stephenie Meyer's book signings had metastasized into screaming mobs who went bonkers whenever the stars Kristen Stewart and Robert Pattinson were trotted out on a stage or red carpet, the author Lev Grossman offered an astute take on the story's appeal: "Beatlemania is the comparison that everybody makes, but *Twilight* is more like the Beatles in reverse. Beatlemania was a reaction to the buttoned-down, sexually repressed pop culture of the 1950s. *Twilight* is a reaction to the reaction—it's a retreat from the hedonistic hookup culture that the sexual revolution begot. Nobody hooks up in *Twilight*. Meyer put sex back underground, transmuted it back into yearning, where it became, paradoxically, exponentially more powerful." Powerful enough that the four main *Twilight* novels have sold more than 160 million copies worldwide; the five films made from those novels have taken in more than $3 billion at the global box office.

Appropriately, the Twilight Saga (the franchise's official descriptor) began with a dream. Meyer, the dreamer, was then a twenty-nine-year-old housewife living in Phoenix, raising three sons with her husband, an auditor at an accounting firm. "In my dream," she later recounted, "I can see a young woman in the embrace of a very handsome young man, in a beautiful meadow surrounded by a forest." Essentially, she was dreaming up the generic cover for a generic romance novel. But there was a twist: "Somehow I know he is a vampire."

Meyer wasn't yet a novelist, or any kind of writer, but "for fun" she jotted down the scene. "When I got done I was so interested in the characters that I wanted to see what would happen to them next. And so, I just wrote and let whatever happened to them happen." Once enough things had happened, she went back, found a starting point, and wrote forward to the midpoint meadow scene. Within three months, she had a five-hundred-or-so-page manuscript, and less fecund novelists reading this must surely be weeping.

The result was *Twilight*, the story of a normal seventeen-year-old girl and the 103-year-old immortal who loves both her and her blood type. Not sure of who the audience for this might be, Meyer sent the manuscript to multiple agents, some of whom handled books for adults, some of whom specialized in the young adult (YA) market. When a YA agent responded positively, *Twilight* became a book for teens. (That sounds arbitrary, and it is, but this type of slotting is not uncommon in publishing.) When an editor at Little, Brown Books for Young Readers read the manuscript on a cross-country flight on a Friday, and made a preemptive bid the following Monday, Meyer became the proud owner of a $750,000 three-book deal—for a trilogy that would become a quartet.

The publisher knew it had a commercial property on its hands, but nevertheless underestimated the appeal. *Twilight* was published in October 2005, with an initial printing of 75,000 copies—an ambitious though not outrageous run. A slow-burn success, the book sold well enough that the second volume, *New Moon*, received a first printing of 100,000 when it was released eleven months later. By the time *Eclipse* was published in August 2007, the series had acquired an obsessive fandom big enough to nip at the heels of those devoted to *Harry Potter* or *Star Wars*; a million copies hit the market, and *Eclipse* did exactly that to *Harry Potter and the Deathly Hallows*, knocking it off the US bestseller lists even though that book had been published only two and a half weeks earlier. (I should note, however, that J. K. Rowling's book had already sold 8.3 million copies in only its first twenty-four hours of release.) Meyer's finale, *Breaking Dawn*, was greeted on August 2, 2008, with Potter-style midnight release parties, a print run of 3.7 million copies, and an impressive if not Potter-level 1.3 million were sold in the first twenty-four hours.

For the purposes of discussing plot and theme and so forth, I'm going to conflate the novels and their faithful film adaptations, the latter more like brand extensions than movies with inner lives of their own. The premise of the first *Twilight* installment is fairly simple (and the core dynamic holds steady through most of the series, even as the plotting can feel simultaneously convoluted and static). Isabella Swan, who goes by Bella, has moved from Arizona, where she was living with her mother, to a small town called Forks (a real place) in the rainiest, woodsiest, gloomiest corner of Washington State. Bella's dad is the taciturn local police chief; they get along perfectly well but aren't close, so Bella is essentially on her own, which, along with the spooky-forest setting, lends the story a fairy-tale undercurrent. She tries to put a good face on things, but she doesn't like the weather and she's bored by small-town life.

The only thing at her new high school holding any interest is the spectral presence of the Cullens, five "chalky pale . . . inhumanly beautiful" teenagers, the adoptive children of a local couple. Aloof like any worthy cool kids, they keep to themselves in the cafeteria. Bella and Edward, the most inhumanly beautiful Cullen of all, meet-cute-ish when she's forced to sit next to him in biology lab and he seems agitated by her presence, even repulsed. Circumstances and the push-pull of romance novel conventions keep throwing them together. As Bella narrates one encounter (in a representative sampling of Meyer's prose):

> We were under the shelter of the cafeteria roof now, so I could more easily look at his face. Which certainly didn't help my clarity of thought.
>
> "It would be more . . . *prudent* for you not to be my friend," he explained. "But I'm tired of trying to stay away from you, Bella."
>
> His eyes were gloriously intense as he uttered that last sentence, his voice smoldering. I couldn't remember how to breathe.

Once she regains neuromotor function, Bella takes to the Internet for some cursory sleuthing and figures out that he is a vampire, as are the rest of the Cullen family. (More formally, a "coven.") When she confronts him—the meadow scene of Meyer's initial dream—he confesses both his true nature and his own desperate love for her. But here is the catch: not only is Edward a 103-year-old immortal in the body of a seventeen-year-old hottie, but if he gives in to his attraction for Bella, his passion will almost surely get the better of him and he will drink her blood and turn her into a vampire herself. *That's* why he was acting so weird in biology lab! He was fighting the urge to chomp down on her neck! "I've never wanted a human's blood so much in my life. It's you. It's your scent," the movie Edward tells Bella (rewriting dialogue from the book). "You're like a drug to me. You're my own personal brand of heroin." But the Cullens are good vampires in that they've forsaken human blood and only dine on forest animals. Edward likens their self-imposed dietary restrictions to giving up meat for tofu: you're less satisfied but you get used to it.

This, then, is the crux of *Twilight*: Bella loves Edward and wants to have sex with him; he loves her and wants to have sex, too, but must restrain himself for her own good. Even were he able to control his thirst for her blood during lovemaking, we are told that his superhuman vampire strength might literally break her. Fortunately, because he became a vampire back in 1919 (his vampire "father" saved him from succumbing to Spanish flu by making him immortal), Edward is an old-fashioned lad and believes in waiting until marriage. The books and films thus create a kind of fantasy safe space where sexual desire, especially female desire, is acknowledged and even tacitly celebrated, yet also held in check for the good of all—with the twist that here it's the boy who hits the brakes, acting as guardian of virtue, rather than, per usual, the girl. In a bedroom scene in the film, Edward breaks off from an increasingly passionate kiss by hurling himself across the room (a vampiric skill), recoiling from further intimacy "like a distraught Victorian," as *The New York Times* critic Manohla Dargis put it.

"I'm stronger than I thought," Edward reassures himself.

"I wish I could say the same," Bella says with a sigh, looking thoroughly dazed.

"I can't ever lose control with you," he vows. Cue audience shivers. They then lie together chastely in bed, she falling asleep while he, who never sleeps, watches over her. In fact, so protective is Edward that he drives a Volvo station wagon, one of the safest if least-sexy cars on the market—another sacrifice for virtue's sake. John Milner would gag.

Given the Twilight Saga's atypical levels of responsible teenage behavior, it is not surprising that the parents come off as—dare I say it?—likable. Bella's mother, now living in Florida with her beau, is a free spirit while her father is tight-lipped and emotionally distant (as police chief, he's also alarmingly oblivious to all the bloody supernatural doings out in the woods, even as bodies pile up), but Mom and Dad both love Bella and have her best interests at heart. Edward's "foster parents," Carlisle and Esme Cullen, are calm and levelheaded even when faced with danger. Moreover, they have the good taste, relaxed style, and abiding savoir faire that so often comes with a vague but substantial fortune. For Bella, the coven serves as an aspirational family, the cool parents and siblings she (and surely many audience members) wishes she had.

Meyer added some evil vampires to the mix for menace and invented a chiseled teenage werewolf to serve as an alternate love interest–cum–third wheel (sparking the Team Edward vs. Team Jacob face-offs that divided a generation's worth of slumber parties). But it's the sexual tension between Bella and Edward, the longing and self-denial, which drives the series. You can understand the appeal of this updated lemonade-on-the-veranda court-ship to an oversexed/undersexed generation, and not just girls. A boy who told Nancy Jo Sales that he owned "a scoring average higher than Kobe Bryant's" also confessed that he longed to live "when you had to go knock on the door and ask the dad for permission." Which at one point Edward more or less does, formally introducing himself to Bella's father.

"Like American culture itself, *Twilight* is both lascivious and chaste," the critic and journalist Sarah Seltzer has observed. Meyer found a way to transform the impulse behind virginity pledges, purity balls, and abstinence-only sex education into something erotic and dangerous. The critic Christine Seifert, writing in *Bitch* magazine, memorably labeled *Twilight* "abstinence porn." It's instructive, too, to look at *Twilight* in the tradition of teen horror, which has traditionally been awash in conflicted notions about sex. Movies from *I Was a Teenage Werewolf* to *Carrie* treat the teenage body as an object of fear and disgust, while slasher films like the *Friday the 13th* and *Nightmare on Elm Street* series delight in the bloody punishment of sexually active teens, even turn it into sport. By those standards, the *Twilight* novels and films are sex positive.

Vampire stories have their own sexual undercurrents — or not really "under" since the lust for blood and the biting of necks and attendant ex-change of bodily fluids are but the most diaphanous of metaphors, barely a negligee. The vampire, most often a he, is traditionally a libertine and seducer. Meyer's stroke of genius was to make her lead vampire an avatar of self-sacrifice and bodily temperance. But at the same time, Edward is entirely red-blooded, as it were. He has all the manners and nobility (and alabaster pall) of Ashley Wilkes, but with Rhett Butler's pheromones and knowing smiles. In fact, he's pretty much the perfect boyfriend, aside from being undead and subsisting on forest animals.

However strategic Edward's restraint was on Meyer's part, it was also informed by her devout Mormon faith. "When my editor wanted premarital sex in my story, I explained that I won't write that," she told an interviewer.

Marital sex was not in her authorial wheelhouse, either: Bella and Edward finally tie the knot in *Breaking Dawn*, but Meyer skips over the consummation with a discreet line break. This disappointed her randier readers, who compensated by writing their own explicit fan fiction, much of it focused on Bella and Edward's honeymoon on a secluded tropical island off the coast of Brazil. But for other fans, *any* sex, even wedded, even discreet and off-page, was divisive. Within days of *Breaking Dawn*'s publication, Goodreads was filled with complaints that the book was "anticlimactic" and/or "gross." On a *Twilight* message board, someone complained, "The sweep and scope of a grand love affair was gone. The brilliantly innocent eroticism that took our breath away was also gone."

I can't venture an opinion pro or con on Bella and Edward's lovemaking, but I very much like the oxymoron "innocent eroticism." It captures Meyer's achievement.

Meyer's books had first been optioned for film by Paramount, which misunderstood their appeal, reportedly commissioning an action-oriented screenplay that diverged from the novel, recasting Bella as a track star, and climaxing with a Jet Ski chase. Perhaps the impulse was to broaden the story's appeal by getting Bella out of Pacific Northwest wear and into a bathing suit? The project quickly went into turnaround. Summit Entertainment, established in the 1990s, had found a niche investing in other studios' films, including *Vanilla Sky* and *Mr. & Mrs. Smith*, and occasionally producing its own, most notably *American Pie*. But following a billion-dollar investment from a group of backers in 2006, the company had grown more ambitious. An executive noticed that Meyer's novels had a passionate online fan base and decided to buy the rights from Paramount.

Sales of the books hadn't yet exploded, so initial expectations for the movies were allegedly modest—which, according to Catherine Hardwicke, who directed *Twilight*, is why she got the job: "Why do you think they hired a female director? If they thought it was going to be a big blockbuster, they wouldn't have ever hired me, because no woman had ever been hired to do something in the blockbuster category." All those passionate online fans, the studio worried, "could just be 400 girls in Salt Lake City blogging about it," in Hardwicke's words. Summit viewed *Twilight* as akin to *Sisterhood of the Traveling Pants*, another film based on a YA novel with a primarily female fan base that had been cheap to make and had returned a decent profit for Warner Bros. with a global box office of $42 million in 2005.

Hardwicke's calling card as a director was *Thirteen*, her first film, released in 2003, a teens-today shocker set in LA—a descendant of *Foxes*, a cousin to *Kids*, though not as bleak as the latter and better acted. Evan Rachel Wood, in her first major film role, at fourteen, is introduced in pigtails and clinging to nerdy friends, but she covets a faster lane. Enter new best friend Evie, the woefully unsupervised "hottest girl" in junior high school, played by Nikki Reed, also fourteen. Within a few minutes of screen time, Wood's Tracy is getting her tongue pierced, wearing thongs, huffing nitrous oxide, French kissing the twentysomething lifeguard next door, and failing seventh grade. To the extent the film has a plot, it's perfunctory. To the extent the film has a message, it's the venerable one about the wages of poor parenting. What makes the movie work are terrific performances from Wood, Reed, and Holly Hunter, as Tracy's beleaguered single mom, abetted by Hardwicke's gift for capturing the giddy release of misbehavior, whether the kids are getting high and playing in sprinklers or looking for more grown-up trouble at night on Hollywood Boulevard.

"My god, there is so much stuff going on with kids that we don't know about," Hardwicke told the *Los Angeles Times*. She knew about it because she co-wrote the script with Reed, an ex-boyfriend's daughter

who Hardwicke had known since Reed was five and who she had remained close with following her breakup with the dad. The genesis for
the film came when Reed was in sixth grade and Hardwicke noticed that
she had begun dressing provocatively and sulking—more or less normal
adolescent behavior, but Hardwicke sensed a brewing crisis. Rather than
running for the hills, she chose to remain a friend, suggesting various
activities she and Reed might do together. They decided it would be fun
to co-write a script.

"We both thought it would be a teen comedy; it didn't turn out that
way," Hardwicke later said. "We decided the real stuff was more compelling than any wacky thing we could make up. We just wrote about the real
stuff she and her friends were going through." At the time, Hardwicke,
a native Texan who had a degree in architecture from the University of
Texas and had also studied film at UCLA, was a very busy production designer. Among her credits: Richard Linklater's *The Newton Boys* (1998),
David O. Russell's *Three Kings* (1999), Cameron Crowe's *Vanilla Sky*
(2001), and Lisa Cholodenko's *Laurel Canyon* (2002). With financing
from independent producers, she shot *Thirteen* on a tight twenty-four-day
schedule with a budget of $2 million—or a third of the $6 million budget
for production design alone she had to play with on *Vanilla Sky*.

Her second film as a director, *Lords of Dogtown* (2005), was about the
evolution of skateboard culture in the 1970s and based on a documentary,
Dogtown and Z-Boys (2001). Her third, *The Nativity Story* (2006), starred
a sixteen-year-old Keisha Castle-Hughes as a fourteen-year-old Virgin
Mary (opposite Oscar Isaac as a thirtysomething Joseph). So when Hardwicke was approached to direct *Twilight*, she had as solid a grounding in
teen cinema as anyone since John Hughes. But her previous features all
hewed to some semblance of reality, whether contemporary or biblical.
Twilight offered a big leap forward in scale as well as potential silliness.

When Hardwicke read Meyer's novel, however, she found something
she could connect to: "The author had created this very strong sense in
the novel that obviously many people responded to, of first love, ecstasy,
and yearning . . . I wondered if that intoxicating first love could be put on

screen—as a filmmaker could I create that 'drug' that she created, we've all felt, or at least most people at a certain age have felt. I saw that as an extreme challenge."

To that end, she discarded the script she had inherited from Paramount. Hardwicke realized that what makes Bella such an appealing heroine is not that she's a track star or aces on a Jet Ski, but rather that she's average—in the novel Meyer has the character describe herself as "absolutely ordinary." She is perhaps a little smarter and more observant than her peers, but also self-conscious, unathletic to the point of being clumsy, lacking in any particular passions (aside from, eventually, Edward). The new girl in town, she is something of a loner, aloof from friend-group drama. Perhaps most importantly, she is rigorously unglamorous, having zero interest in clothes, makeup, shopping—which must have further endeared her to a generation of girls exhausted by posing for selfies.

Kristen Stewart is, of course, far from ordinary—but movies need movie stars, and her recessive charisma works for Bella. A meme that circulated about Stewart in the *Twilight* films, "FIVE MOVIES, ONE EXPRESSION," is funny but not, I think, fair. She can hold a screen without doing a lot, and her default sullenness helps an ultimately ridiculous story keep one foot sort of on the ground. It's an effective and watchable performance, with perhaps a less emotive echo of Molly Ringwald in her John Hughes movies. Staying true to the spirit of the novel, Hardwicke and her costume designer dress Bella down in T-shirts, hoodies, and parkas—she surely has the dullest wardrobe of any major female character I've discussed in this book, the antithesis of *Clueless*'s Cher—but at the same time, when she walks into biology class for the first time and catches Edward's attention, Hardwicke is not beneath hiding a fan off screen to blow her hair alluringly and add a touch of Pantene commercial glamour.

Stewart was seventeen when *Twilight* was in production. A Los Angeles native, she grew up around the entertainment industry—her father was a stage manager for TV shows, her mother a script supervisor—and had made her film debut at the age of nine as "ring toss girl" in *The Flintstones in Viva Rock Vegas* (2000). She came to Hardwicke's attention by way of her affecting, natural performance as a teenager who falls for Emile Hirsch's doomed wanderer in Sean Penn's 2007 adaptation of *Into the Wild*.

Twilight was Stewart's first starring role. The male lead, Robert Pattinson, was a twenty-two-year-old Londoner who had dabbled in modeling and singer-songwriting before turning to acting. Then best known for playing the doomed golden boy Cedric Diggory in *Harry Potter and the Goblet of Fire* (2005), he was one of three possible Edwards who Hardwicke brought to her house in Venice to read with Stewart. "When Rob and Kristen met, all of us could tell there was a very strong chemistry there," the director recalled. "You know, just electricity. It was very intense." She had the two actors perform the I-must-control-myself-with-you kissing scene "about three times," on her own bed. More sparks. "When everyone was gone," Hardwicke said, "Kristen was like, 'You have to cast Rob.'" Pattinson was offered the role the next day, buoyed not just by his chemistry with Stewart but by Summit's modest expectations for the film, a blessing that allowed Hardwicke to cast two more-or-less unknowns "rather than a famous movie star from the Disney Channel or whatever," as she put it. In her mind, she was directing one more indie movie, only with a slightly bigger budget and some special effects. For the most part the studio agreed and left her alone. "We just made it, and really in a personal way," she said later.

Meyer's fans weren't as laissez-faire as Summit, scrutinizing the production's every move, not least the casting. Stewart was generally received favorably, despite having committed the sin of confessing ambivalence about the role. "It's just surreal to be a crucial part of a machine like this," she told *Entertainment Weekly* before the film's release. "I'm sort of the vessel. The book is what it is because of these girls' obsession with [Edward] through me. If I wasn't right, I'd be persecuted and put on a cross."

Pattinson wasn't so lucky. Though to anyone's eyes he was a perfectly attractive young man, he wasn't in tip-top physical shape and was prone, moreover, to feckless grooming and dishabille. (According to Hardwicke, he had shown up for his audition with "wacky bangs" and a "messy" shirt.) He was not, in other words, *inhumanly beautiful*.

"When Rob was announced, people had a meltdown on the internet," Hardwicke recalled. "People said horrible things. There were a few pictures of him by the paparazzi that were in London, walking out of a club, not having shaved, looking like a slob. I said to Rob, 'As soon as we get your look down and your photos [in character] out, I know you're going to be good. You just have to have faith. This happens to a lot of actors.' One day he came to me and said, 'I got this email forwarded to me about how revolting I am.' I said, 'Rob, you cannot read these things. Don't torture yourself.' And he said, 'I didn't. My mother forwarded me that.'"

Fans grew less restive after Meyer publicly endorsed Pattinson. But there was another online eruption when the two leads were featured in an embrace on an *Entertainment Weekly* cover five months before the movie's release. With Stewart's shoulders bared and Pattinson wearing what looked like an unbuttoned pirate shirt, the image suggested a swashbuckling romance more than the paranormal sort. Of even greater offense was Pattinson's fluffy, Kennedy-esque haircut and—worse still—a patch of fur visible on his chest. "Horrible," wrote one message board dissenter. "He looks like a hairy powdered donut."

Earlier teen movie stars like Mickey Rooney, James Dean, and Molly Ringwald had committed, even lunatic fans but they didn't have to deal with the blast furnace attention of contemporary "fandoms," in which collective passions, enabled and unleashed by social media, foster a sense of ownership and entitlement. Stewart and Pattinson were among the first. (Facebook was four years old in 2008, when *Twilight* premiered, Twitter was two, and five-year-old MySpace was only just beginning its decline.) At least outwardly, the scrutiny perturbed Stewart more than Pattinson. Complaints sent her way tended to focus on her sometimes moody public demeanor. "I do wish that people would focus more on the work, and I can't say that I don't take it personally," she told *The New York Times*, accompanied by "a deep sigh." She continued: "What really kills me—it really rips me up—is when people think I'm abrasive, inconsiderate, or ungrateful because I don't go outside in a bikini and wave to the paparazzi. Come on!"

Pattinson's look as Edward was eventually redeemed by a floppy pompadour—James Dean by way of a boy band—and his (and his trainer's) achievement of a chiseled, depilated, marble-smooth torso. In the film, he wears the exaggerated makeup of a silent-movie idol: painted white face with bright red lips and darkened, exaggerated eyebrows; at the same time, his wide-set eyes lend him a vaguely feline look. Like Dean and so many subsequent teen idols, he's almost as pretty as he is handsome. Sexy, but not too sexy, safe but not too safe, he was ideal first-crush fodder.

To say that the fans ultimately took to him would be an understatement. Here is an account of his appearance at a mall in King of Prussia, Pennsylvania, written by the late *New York Times* columnist David Carr, who clearly relished describing the reaction when the actor stepped onto a riser in front of more than one thousand "mostly teenage girls":

> In collective pitch, frequency and volume the sound would make a shuttle-launching seem demure, a Jack White guitar solo retiring, a jackhammer somehow soothing. To reach into history, it may have approached Beatles-at-Shea-Stadium loud, replete with the weeping, swooning, and self-hugging, and only the ambient flutter of cell-phone cameras and furious texting by way of modern update . . .
>
> "What is with all the screaming?" Mr. Pattinson asked when he came out. He absently ran his hand through his hair. Pandemonium ensued. He tugged at his white T-shirt in response, ever so nervously. Oh boy. Then he laughed good-naturedly at the absurdity of it all. The smile was just a bit too much. A girl in a "Team Edward" shirt fell into the arms of her friend. "I can't stand it!" she said.

Mind you, this was a week before the movie's release. The *Twilight* cast was on a tour of malls co-sponsored by Hot Topic, a clothing and accessories chain pitched toward teens with a rock-and-roll sensibility. At an earlier stop in San Francisco, there had been such a crush a girl had broken her nose.

"The connection that I am an actor playing this character is sort of skipped," Pattinson told Carr. His Edward works wonders on Stewart's Bella, who spends much of the first movie staring at him, lips apart, across the high school lunchroom and parking lot. He reciprocates: *Twilight* is a movie built on staring, which is appropriate, I suppose, for a film about sublimated desire. Stewart gives the more naturalistic performance. Pattinson is more mannered, his sangfroid studied but effective; at times he seems to be channeling Luke Perry's Dylan McKay from *Beverly Hills 90210*, yet another in the long line of sensitive, brooding, misunderstood pretty boys descended from Dean's Jim Stark—which suggests that 103-year-old Edward has at least kept up with teen culture. A different movie might have profitably explored the existential dilemma of having to repeat high school across nine decades—how many times has Edward had to read *The Grapes of Wrath* or learn to solve quadratic equations?—but that might have struck too literal a note for a heady paranormal romance.

The two actors took their roles almost as seriously as Dean might have, reportedly spending hours on set debating the implications of the story—what would it *feel like* to be a vampire or a girl in love with one? Complaining that Summit should have known what it was getting when it hired "actors who aren't Disney kids," Stewart told *Entertainment Weekly* (*Twilight*'s de facto house organ), "We were like, 'We're going to play this for real,' and the studio was like, 'But it's fun. Lighten up!'" Pattinson, she would claim in a later interview, had an "intellectual approach that was combined with 'I don't give a fuck about this, but I'm going to make this sing.' And I was like, 'Ugh, same.' And, whatever, we were young and stupid and, not to say that we made it so much better, but that's what it needed, and anybody playing those parts needed to feel."

Whatever the mix of chemistry, skill, focus, and fuck-it attitude, the leads make the romance work on screen—they also became a couple in real

life for a year or two—which is of course essential to making the movie
work as a whole, and even more so than with most love stories; given that
this one has vampires, *something* has to be believable. The production's
modest scale and Hardwicke's indie-inflected direction help, too; you feel
like she's capturing scenes on the fly, which keeps even the supernatural
business tethered to life on earth (a few clumsy special effects aside). The
movie, especially in its early scenes, almost convinces you it's a story about
two normal kids, one of whom might be a vampire, but don't judge. The
tone shifts, though, becoming myopic and even a little queasy once the
film leaves high school behind and heads deeper into the forest, literally and figuratively, a shift that mimics the swoony, woozy, consumptive
rush of first love—just what Hardwicke intended to capture. I don't want
to overstate the case for *Twilight* as a film, but you have to admire the
skill of everyone involved in creating such an effective picture given the
limitations—a significant one being that the screenplay gives Edward no
real reason for falling in love with Bella beyond her scent, though in fairness, many adolescent romances have been born of less, even if those relationships tend to be measured in months or weeks, rather than eternity.

As with most presold franchise films, *Twilight*'s critical reception was
beside the point. *Variety* dismissed it as a "disappointingly anemic tale of
forbidden love" that would nevertheless enjoy some "serious B.O. bite"
thanks to its "built-in femme fanbase." (The trade paper conceded Pattinson was "every inch the deadly dreamboat.") Elsewhere, the movie
received mostly positive if patronizing reviews. Manohla Dargis called
it "a deeply sincere, outright goofy vampire romance for the hot-not-to-
trot set." David Denby, writing in *New York*: "A genuine love story might
be difficult for a young audience to handle, but this fantasy is blissful
madness—an abstinence fable sexier than sex." The picture even drew
notice from the *London Review of Books*: "In accordance with the adage
about the rubbishy book making for the better movie, *Twilight* the film
is great." It grossed $69.6 million on its opening week in North America,
then a record for a film directed by a woman.

Hardwicke's reward was getting booted from the sequel, ostensibly because of—the usual—creative differences, which may even have been the truth. But "one insider" leaked to Nikki Finke (the caustic and relentless showbiz journalist whose website, *Deadline Hollywood Daily*, was a source of terror and schadenfreude in the entertainment industry across the 2000s and early 2010s) that Hardwicke was "difficult" and "irrational," which, the source admitted, "doesn't mean anything when you're talking about a filmmaker because they all are, but still . . ." That "but still" does a lot of work here, more or less proving Hardwicke's assertion, once *Twilight* had proven itself, that Hollywood would not trust women with big franchises.

Summit's choice to direct *New Moon* was Chris Waitz, who, like Hardwicke, had prior teen movie credibility, though not of the sort most Twihards, as fans labeled themselves, approved of. "I understand that," Waitz said of the enusing outrage. "I directed *American Pie*. I would be worried too." And, well, yes: it was an alienating move, inviting the male director of a comedy about having sex to helm a female-centered romance about not having sex. Waitz did come with a prior franchise movie on his résumé, having directed a 2007 adaptation of the first novel in Philip Pullman's *His Dark Materials* trilogy, *The Golden Compass*. Alas, it had flopped, stifling planned follow-ups. *But still* . . . he was Summit's choice.

He delivered a glossy, capable picture that managed to feel more conventional than Hardwicke's movie, even as the storyline grew ever nuttier and more gothic. This time, Bella runs off to Rome to save Edward from a coven of campy, overdressed, supercilious aristocrats who are charged with enforcing the code of vampiric law—a creepy crew who would fit right in at Dan Brown's Vatican. Still straddling two worlds, and two genres, though ever more awkwardly, the film also expects us to care at least somewhat about Bella and her friends' pending graduation from high school.

To my mind, the most interesting thing about *New Moon* is its opening, in which Bella dreams that Edward is now with some wizened old lady who turns out to be . . . Bella! This nightmare has been brought on by the fact that she is about to turn eighteen while he, cursed or blessed, will remain an eternal seventeen. "You're not going to want me when I look like a grandma," she tells him, daring to peer even further into the future than did Ferris Bueller. Edward scoffs, but perhaps not convincingly. Given teenage revulsion if not denial at the thought of aging, this might be the scariest moment in the entire series. It certainly raises the stakes. (That is not a pun. Vampires in the *Twilight* universe are killed not by driving a stake through their hearts but by wrenching their heads off like twist caps.)

At any rate, *New Moon* doubled *Twilight*'s opening-weekend gross, and ended up taking in $296.6 million at the North American box office, and $709.8 million globally. I have not much to say about *Eclipse* (2010, directed by David Slade) or *Breaking Dawn—Part 1* and *Part 2* (2011 and 2012, both directed by Bill Condon), except that they all made a ton of money, too, and that Edward keeps refusing to have sex with Bella until they finally get married in the first *Breaking Dawn*. For that, the film adds a minute or two of PG-13 nuzzling to Meyer's discreet line break. Bella wakes up the next morning with the most satisfied glow this side of Scarlett O'Hara's famous fiddle-dee-dee after being hauled up the stairs and raped by Rhett Butler. But he has nothing on Edward Cullen: the bed is broken and the room in shambles; later, we spot bruises on Bella's limbs—all of which is taken from the novel. "For a human, I can't imagine it gets any better than that," movie Bella tells her husband, apparently liking the rough stuff.

One hopes all the young people in the audience, as well as the not so young, took all this with more than a grain of salt. (Especially the boys dating the girls Sales and Orenstein interviewed.) At any rate, if sex in the Twilight Saga proves to be problematic, it is also not without consequence: Bella becomes pregnant straight off the mark and nearly dies in childbirth, saved only by Edward finally sinking his teeth in and turning her into the vampire she's yearned to become throughout four movies. More disturbing: she then names their daughter Renesmee (reh-NEZ-may), a portmanteau combining the names of the baby's grandmothers, Renée and Esme—proof, if more is needed, that teenagers should not become parents. Nevertheless, the saga ends on an ostensibly happy note, with all the bad vampires defeated and Bella and Edward and Renesmee united for eternity in paunchless, wrinkle-free youth.

Contra *American Graffiti*, maybe you *can* stay seventeen forever? Adult *Twilight* fans may wonder how one goes about maintaining a marriage for eternity when ten or twenty years can be work enough.

The Hunger Games series—the books and movies that succeeded *Twilight* as the preeminent life-and-death YA blockbusters—ends on a similar note. In the final frames of *The Hunger Games: Mockingjay—Part 2* (as the concluding film is formally known; the producers followed the lead of *Harry Potter* and *Twilight* by splitting the last novel in two for the movies), the heroine, Katniss Everdeen, is briefly glimpsed in honeyed summer sunlight as a mother and a romantic partner, picnicking photogenically with her family. As played by Jennifer Lawrence, Katniss is as young and beautiful as Bella, but romance for her has been more of a side dish than a narrative raison d'être. Her virginity has not been at issue, and sex barely a concern. In fact, the *Hunger Games* films might be the least-libidinous teen movies ever to come out of Hollywood.

"I don't write about adolescents. I write about war for adolescents," Suzanne Collins, the author of the novels, has said, closing the door on hormones and such. I think this is both true and not. Yes, the series is about war, as well as politics, propaganda, media manipulation, and power in most of its manifestations. But when you create a futuristic dystopia organized around a televised blood sport in which teenage gladiators are forced to fight to the death, you have either wittingly or unwittingly created a pretty nifty metaphor for high school—the battlefields of *The Breakfast Club* and *Mean Girls* made literal. (In fairness to hardworking teachers, principals, and other professional educators, I'll refine the comparison: a metaphor for how high school can *feel* for its most vulnerable and volatile constituencies.) Furthermore, when one of those teenage gladiators, the heroine of your series, becomes the indispensable figure in overthrowing a repressive government, retaining her moral compass even as some of her closest allies succumb to power's corrupting temptations, you have catered to your target audience's bent for grandiosity. I agree with David Denby, who wrote of the first *Hunger Games* movie in *The New Yorker*, "Maybe the reason for its success is simple: it makes teens feel both victimized and important." Just like real life!

You can measure that success in the obvious ways. The books, which have sold more than 100 million copies worldwide, are ranked #1 on Goodreads' list of best YA dystopian novels (as of 2024), ahead of the *Divergent* and *Maze Runner* series, as well as #1 on the website's list of dystopian novels in general, ahead of *1984, Brave New World, Fahrenheit 451,* and *The Handmaid's Tale.** As for the movies, the first took in $152 million on its opening weekend in North American theaters, substantially more than the inaugural *Twilight* and *Harry Potter* movies ($70 million and $90 million, respectively). All told, the first *Hunger Games* made $407 million at the domestic box office, putting it among the top fifty all-time highest-grossing movies, just behind its first sequel, formally known as *The Hunger Games: Catching Fire,* which made $425 million. The box office receipts for the next two, *The Hunger Games: Mockingjay—Part 1* and *The Hunger Games: Mockingjay—Part 2,* tailed off, perhaps because audiences had wearied of producers splitting franchise finales in half, but not to worry: no one took a bath, especially when global box office is included.† And as of 2024, the first two films fall just outside the top 100 on the list of most popular films of all time, when box office dollars are adjusted for inflation; the only teen movies to make the top 100 are *Grease, American Graffiti,* and the original *West Side Story,* a murderer's row (and, unexpectedly—at least to me—two musicals and one self-described wannabe).

A less obvious way to measure the *Hunger Games'* success is by how

---

*Perhaps another key to the trilogy's popularity: it also tops Goodreads' list of "Books That Were Better Than I Thought They Would Be."

†I have largely refrained from including global box office figures in this book, since they only became a significant part of studio revenue in the 1990s.

open to interpretation the books and films have proven—almost as elastic as the Greek myths Collins drew on. (Reread Theseus and the Minotaur.) Perusing the extensive academic literature devoted to the series, I have learned that *The Hunger Games* is a parable about the dangers of big government and thus an inspiration to young Republican activists, but that it is also a parable about the dangers of income inequality, pitched to the Occupy Wall Street crowd. Or . . . the tale might be an allegory of the American Revolution . . . or of Christian love and sacrifice . . . or of the twenty-first century's cutthroat college admissions derbies and ruthless job markets. It might be free-market propaganda. It might be a veiled criticism of the Global War on Terror (entering its second decade when the first *Hunger Games* film hit theaters in 2012). The heroine is an American frontier archetype, descended from James Fenimore Cooper's Natty Bumppo and the loners played in movie westerns by John Wayne and Clint Eastwood—unless, what with her lethal prowess and indifference to male suitors, she gives a proud feminist middle finger to "heteronormative expectations."

The Hunger Games could be about some or many or all these things at once: pop art that lands big isn't always easy to parse—or necessarily coherent at all. People can see what they want to see in *The Hunger Games*, even the commentator on the Stormfront, a neo-Nazi website, who hailed Katniss as a "Hitler figure, a veteran, a reluctant hero, an idealist."

On second thought, him we'll ignore.

The books and films—I'm again conflating the two into one IP schmear—are set in the totalitarian nation of Panem, the backstory of which is never fully detailed, but blame a vaguely apocalyptic event followed by a civil war of some sort. As the first installment opens, the rich and corrupt Capitol rules over twelve outlying districts, some poorer than others, with the poorest of all being District 12, which appears to be what's barely left of Appalachia. Its sullen, hard-bitten, mostly white citizens—in the films they appear to have stepped out of a Dorothea Lange portfolio—are forced to mine coal to keep the Capitol's furnaces or whatever burning. District 12 is where we first meet Jennifer Lawrence's sixteen-year-old

Katniss, who is out in the woods hunting game for food with her bow and arrows, accompanied by Gale, her hunky hunting partner and potential love interest (Liam Hemsworth). Katniss's father has died in a mining accident, and she is now the main provider for her mother, rendered seemingly catatonic by widowhood, and her beloved younger sister, Prim, short for Primrose. Life is bleak in District 12; bellies are often empty.

And that is the upbeat part of the premise.

The Capitol exerts control over the districts by holding an annual Hunger Games in which two teenagers, a boy and a girl, are chosen by lottery from each district, twenty-four in total, and sent off to the Capitol as "tributes" to kill one another. But first, in preparation, they are given dubious mentors and dressed and styled in the decadent fashion of the Capitol, where the fanciful, brightly colored tailored clothes look like they were designed by Alexander McQueen, working in fondant. The tributes are then paraded around in televised spectacles and forced to submit to interviews with an unctuous blue-haired host played by Stanley Tucci. All this is meant to drive interest in the Games, which begin when the tributes are tossed into a wooded, high-tech arena, which has been stocked with weapons and booby traps—it looks to be as big as a decently sized state park—and told they must fight until only one is left standing, the then-lauded victor. Targeted firestorms and genetically modified beasts with sharp teeth move things along. Lasting for days, the slaughter is broadcast nationwide, with cameras in every corner of the arena—a Super Bowl, Academy Awards, and Taliban-style public execution rolled into one. It looks to be the high point of the Panem calendar.

In summary: *The Hunger Games* is a tonal mishmash. Tasked with ensuring the center holds is reluctant heroine Katniss, stoic by nature, defiant when pushed—and possessed of an interior life not much in evidence of the page, thanks to Lawrence, who can convey nuance and complexity even behind steeled eyes and clenched jaw. (Picture Clint Eastwood as a teenage girl, but not in a disturbing way.) Katniss's big troubles begin at the annual District 12 "reaping," as the tribute lottery is called. Twelve-year-old Prim, a sweet waif with the look of an instant goner, is chosen, but noble Katniss volunteers to take her place. The male tribute is Peeta Mellark, the comparatively privileged son of the local baker who once, in an act of chivalry seen in flashback, threw a starving Katniss a burnt loaf of bread in a rainstorm. (The names of Collins's characters don't roll off the tongue quite as smoothly as J. K. Rowling's.)

Whisked off in a high-speed train, Katniss seems more irked by having to play dress-up for the Capitol than she is by the impending bloodbath; in her resistance to fashion and primping, she is, like Bella Swan, a refreshing role model for young female audiences. Another source of irritation for Katniss: Peeta's confession, while being interviewed on TV, that he has a crush on her. *Ick.* But it's a strategy, he later explains, to help them both survive in the arena by drawing on the audience's sympathy, and the question of whether his ardor is feigned or real is a major subplot of the first film and book, as is the question of whether Katniss might be able to dredge up parallel feelings for him.

But this incipient romance is complicated by the fact that the actor who plays Peeta, Josh Hutcherson, has a pleasing affect but not much else; he is the actorly equivalent of a good corn muffin. And what about poor, stolid Gale, left back home despite being played by a Hemsworth brother and forced to watch this will-they-or-won't-they unfold on TV? Regardless of the actors' chemistry or lack thereof, it's hard to care about a love triangle when two dozen kids are spearing and hacking away at one another, and it is not even clear how much Collins and the novels' adaptors want us to care, or whether this dollop of teen soap opera has been added for the same reason perfunctory romances often clot thrillers: someone assumed readers and moviegoers wanted it.

How Katniss will survive is what drives the narrative, since we know due to the laws of franchise publishing and filmmaking—and the existence of sequels—that she *will* survive. A secondary, meta source of suspense: How will the plot maneuver Katniss through this kill-or-be-killed gauntlet without having her lose her moral authority, and the audience's sympathy? The answer: she only kills people who deserve it, like the arrogant, Aryan-looking tributes from the more favored Districts 1 and 2, who are bred and trained for combat and serve as Panem's version of the mean-girl cheerleaders and nerd-torturing jocks of more traditional teen movies.

As mentioned above, *The Hunger Games* can be seen as a kind of Grand Guignol spin on high school. (So much for the early twentieth-century reformers who thought universal secondary school would be a salutary achievement.) I enjoyed the critic Laura Miller's description of the series as "a fever dream allegory of the adolescent social experience," in a 2010 *New Yorker* essay on teen dystopias:

> Adults dump teenagers into the viper pit of high school, spouting a lot of sentimental drivel about what a wonderful stage of life it's supposed to be. The rules are arbitrary, unfathomable, and subject to sudden change. A brutal social hierarchy prevails, with the rich, the good-looking, and the athletic lording their advantages over everyone else. To survive you have to be totally fake. Adults don't seem to understand how high the stakes are; your whole life could be over, and they act like it's just some "phase"! Everyone's always watching you, scrutinizing your clothes or your friends or obsessing over whether you're having sex or taking drugs or getting good enough grades, but no one cares who you really are or how you feel about anything.

That's the thing about Panem: its parents are *the worst*. Katniss's poor mother is barely present—a husk. Peeta's mother, briefly glimpsed, appears to be a horror, as he he relays to Katniss, "You know what my mother said? She said, 'District 12 might finally have a winner.' But she wasn't talking about me. She was talking about you." (Now *that's* an underminer.) In the Capitol, Katniss and Peeta meet monstrous symbolic fathers: Tucci's Caesar Flickerman, whose energetic condescension toward the tributes, and barely disguised sadism, seems inspired by a *Wonderama* host; and, most crucially, President Coriolanus Snow, played by an insinuating, disdainful Donald Sutherland sporting lush silver facial hair in the manner of a Martin Van Buren or Rutherford B. Hayes. He justifies the Games as "a pageant of honor, courage, and sacrifice" meant to reinforce the bond between Capitol and formerly rebellious districts. He has his reasons: "This is how we remember our past. This is how we safeguard our future." The logic doesn't track, even in context, but kids likely hear a variant of the old parental boilerplate:

Someday you'll thank me for this.

What kind of childhood would lead you to dream this up? Suzanne Collins's father was a career air force officer, who for a time taught military history at West Point and dragged his kids to battlefields across the US and Europe, where he would lecture them about the scope of fighting and casualties.

"He felt it was his responsibility to make sure all his children had an understanding of war, about its costs, its consequences," Collins recalled. Her own youthful passions included Edgar Allan Poe, Greek mythology, and gladiator movies, especially *Spartacus*, all three hours and seventeen minutes of it. Collins: "Whenever it ran, I'd be glued to the set. My dad would get out Plutarch's *Lives*"—Plutarch is one of two sources for what we know about Spartacus the historical figure—"and read me passages." You might wonder whether Collins could have *not* written *The Hunger Games*.

Plot twist: After earning an MFA in dramatic writing from NYU, Collins spent the early years of her career turning out scripts for anodyne children's television programs, eventually rising to become the head writer on *Clifford's Puppy Days* for PBS Kids while gaining early experience catering to teenagers on the Nickelodeon shows *Clarissa Explains It All* and *The Mystery Files of Shelby Woo*. When *The Hunger Games* was published, she was simultaneously working on the animated Nickelodeon series *Wow! Wow! Wubzy!*, which stars a character who appears to be half cat, half Lego brick. As the theme song explains, "Wubzy lives in a tree! / He likes to play play play! / He's got a bendy tail / And he likes it that way!" You have to admire the versatility of a mind that could jump back and forth between Wubzy and Panem.

As with the *Twilight* series, work on a film adaptation of *The Hunger Games* began before the books really took off. Lionsgate, a small studio that had bought the rights from an independent production company, brought in the writer-director Gary Ross to adapt the movie with Collins, along with another writer, Billy Ray. Ross had received Oscar nominations for his screenplays for the comedies *Big* (1988) and *Dave* (1993), and had written and directed *Pleasantville* (1998) and *Seabiscuit* (2003)—a nice filmography full of literate and even sweet movies, but one that does not necessarily shout, or even whisper, *This is the man to direct* The Hunger Games. Ross had pursued the movie after his kids, fans of the book, persuaded him to read it; Lionsgate evidently felt he had the chops to make the teen carnage palatable and, not incidentally, earn a PG-13 rating.

Every up-and-coming young actress in Hollywood circa 2010 seems to have read for the part of Katniss. Happily, I guess, many of the also-rans ended up starring in teen dystopias of their own: Hailee Steinfeld and Abigail Breslin, who would both find their way to *Ender's Game* (2013); and Saoirse Ronan, Shailene Woodley, and Chloë Grace Moretz, who would respectively star in *The Host* (2013, based on Stephenie Meyer's first post-*Twilight* novel), *Divergent* (2014, plus two sequels), and *The Fifth Wave* (2016).

Jennifer Lawrence, then nineteen, essentially auditioned for the part by getting an Oscar nomination as Best Actress for *Winter's Bone* (2010), her first starring role, in which she played a gritty young backwoods heroine very similar to Katniss, though here fending off adult meth heads rather than adolescent gladiators.

As with Twihards and Robert Pattinson, the *Hunger Games* fandom picked Lawrence apart. Some complained she was too old and blond to play Katniss. (Collins isn't big on physical description, but she does mention that Katniss has dark hair and "olive" skin.) Some complained about her physicality, echoed in Manohla Dargis's review of the finished film: "A few years ago Ms. Lawrence might have looked hungry enough to play Katniss, but now, at 21, her seductive, womanly figure makes a bad fit for a dystopian fantasy about a people starved into submission."

I pause here to note an unfortunate thread connecting Natalie Wood's hips to Annette Funicello's navel to Lindsay Lohan's breasts to Jennifer Lawrence's figure. With all due respect to Robert Pattinson's chest hair.

A second prerelease controversy, even more dismaying than dissections of Lawrence's womanliness, centered on the thirteen-year-old Black actress Amandla Stenberg, who was cast as Rue, the youngest tribute, who becomes an ally of Katniss's. Racists lit up Twitter, as is their wont: "Why does Rue have to be Black not gonna lie ruined the movie." And: "Awkward moment when Rue is some Black girl and not the little blonde innocent girl you picture." As Stenberg remembered it, being young helped her shrug off the invective, but the fact that she had to also gave her "an inkling" of what she would be up against as an actress of color. "People are stupid," she added. "It says in the book she's Black!" True: Collins at one point describes Rue as having "dark brown skin and eyes," and later "satiny brown skin." Not that it should have mattered.

The film shot for four mostly uneventful months in North Carolina. One ironic note: the production gussied up a deserted company town attached to a long-defunct mill to serve as the Seam, the nickname for Katniss's hometown in District 12; the site had been abandoned since the 1970s— meaning the location's present-day reality was arguably bleaker than the dystopian fantasy. The old company store served as Peeta's family bakery. (Curious? You can visit the Henry River Mill Village, an hour's drive northwest of Charlotte.)

Reviews were mixed when the film premiered in March 2012. Some critics objected to the toning down of violence, like David Thomson, writing in *The New Republic*:

> Whether filmmakers like it or not, this is a story about kids killing other
> kids with knives, bows and arrows, and anything else they can get their
> hands on. If you don't like that violence, and if you fear it will jeopar-
> dize the box office, then don't do the story. Instead the woeful director

Gary Ross has elected to present the combat as a mess of trembling handheld close-ups, rapid cuts, and an overall blurring, so that in effect we don't see the action. To my mind this is nearly un-American: From Ford and Hawks, through Sam Fuller and Anthony Mann, to Coppola and Scorsese, our cinema has reveled in what is called "action" and has made it something close to a philosophy. But in *The Hunger Games* you feel these scenes are like ink smudged in the rain.

I don't agree. I am more partial to the conflicted enthusiasm of *The National Review*'s John Podhoretz: "The thing is gripping as hell . . . I don't know that these books or the movie that springs from them are morally defensible, really—they glory in the violence that they view with horror—but my oh my they do get under your skin and into your head."

Simply put, the movies are well-made entertainments, suspenseful, and satisfying. But "simply put" is not my job here. One theme of this book, which I hope I've demonstrated, is that teen movies reflect their times every bit as much as westerns, science fiction, and horror films do. So what does it say about recent times that they produced this bizarre, convoluted, and brutal story that has resonated so profoundly and lucratively with young audiences—and older ones, too—but in another era might have made a few ripples as a provocation when dropped into the pond but otherwise sunk quickly to cult-movie status?

There are some obvious e-ticket answers anyone could recite without too much thought: 9/11, America's blundering Global War on Terror, the Great Recession, the degradations of online culture, climate change, the rise of right-wing populism and nationalism around the globe, and Trumpism here at home, the stain we can't seem to get out. The MAGA phenomenon postdates *The Hunger Games*, but both were incubating during the same period (and share cosmopolitan elites as their chief villains). Collins has said the initial inspiration struck one night in the mid-2000s when she was channel surfing back and forth between a reality show and the news, which might also be how certain voters got the idea that the star of *The Apprentice* would make a fine president. Collins's epiphany was even more fanciful. "I was very tired," she told one interviewer, "and I was flipping through images on reality TV where these young people were competing for millions of dollars or whatever, then I was seeing footage from the Iraq War, and those two things began to fuse together in a very unsettling way, and that is the moment where I got the idea for Katniss's story."

Like many parents of my generation, raising children in the 2000s and 2010s, I confess I was made deeply uneasy when my middle school–age children read the first novel and told me what it was about. Was this something I should let them read (assuming I still had any say in the matter)? Was it something I might want to read? The premise has a sick but undeniable hook, a come-on worthy of a classic exploitation film—so much so it's surprising the idea never occurred to anyone at American International Pictures.* But that's a reminder that teenagers getting slaughtered on screen is not a new form of entertainment, whether in AIP's drive-in horror movies or the slasher films that have seen waves of popularity since the original iteration of *Halloween* (1978). In *Carrie*, novelist Stephen King and director Brian de Palma surely killed off more high school students in the climactic prom massacre than have Collins and her adaptors, while the victims, killers, and survivors in *Boyz n the Hood* live in a virtual war zone nearly as confined and oppressive as Panem's miserable districts. And if you want to include the countless war films with youthful cannon fodder quaking in trenches, foxholes, jungles, and deserts, the carnage dates back at least as far as *All Quiet on the Western Front* (1930). In that context, *The Hunger Games* is merely a refinement, a conceptual tweak. Collins herself once said, when asked whether her books were too brutal and frightening for young people, "There are child soldiers all around the world right now who are nine, ten, carrying arms, forced to be at war. Can our children not even read a fictional story about it? I think they can."

---

*They might have come close. *Death Race 2000*, produced by Roger Corman in 1975 and starring David Carradine, could be seen as a distant, older relative of *The Hunger Games*. Corman made it not for AIP but for his own company, New World Pictures.

Another terrible fact of twenty-first-century life unfortunately relevant to this discussion: school shootings. They didn't begin with the 1999 tragedy at Columbine High School—the Naval Postgraduate School's Center for Homeland Defense and Security maintains a school shooting database going back to 1970—but the scale of that assault (thirteen dead, not including the two shooters, and twenty-one wounded) marked a divide in American life, a before and after akin to Pearl Harbor, the assassination of John F. Kennedy, and 9/11. The number of shootings have fluctuated in the years since, trending upward a bit in the second half of the 2010s, though it's not clear if that's a meaningful rise or a statistical blip, since the annual totals are relatively small, even if the impacts are huge. But the death tolls from specific attacks have continued to set horrifying records: the Columbine body count was surpassed by the 2012 shooting at Sandy Hook Elementary School, in Newtown, Connecticut, only to be surpassed again in 2018 at Marjory Stoneman Douglas High School in Parkland, Florida, and once more in 2022 at Robb Elementary School in Uvalde, Texas—a sickening, unspeakable tally, the terror magnified for children by years of increasingly realistic barricade-the-classroom drills, with fake shooters roaming the halls firing blanks. Why wouldn't Panem's fictional mayhem strike a chord with kids accustomed to literal trigger warnings?

That said, I think *The Hunger Games'* appeal is far more escapist than even minimally therapeutic; I mean, the movies aren't after-school specials. Teens (and adults) have long looked to Hollywood for vicarious, transgressive thrills, and twenty-first-century adolescent lives are circumscribed in multiple ways that might magnify such appeal. It's not just that kids are having less sex. They also drink less and don't smoke or vape as much, and, marijuana aside, their use of recreational drugs has dwindled (trends that all began in the 1990s).* Moreover, their interest in the adult-ish pursuits legally allowed them, traditional stepping-stones toward independence

---

*The story isn't the same for adults. According to a 2018 American Psychology Association report, binge drinking and marijuana use have increased steadily among adults since 1990. The opioid epidemic is also a mostly adult phenomenon.

such as part-time jobs, has also waned. According to Jean Twenge, a psychologist at San Diego State University who has written extensively about contemporary teenage life:

> Even driving, a symbol of adolescent freedom inscribed in popular culture from *Rebel Without a Cause* to *Ferris Bueller's Day Off*, has lost its appeal for today's teens. Nearly all boomer high school students had their driver's license by the spring of their senior year; more than one in four teens today still lack one at the end of high school . . . In conversation after conversation, teens described getting their license as something to be nagged into by their parents—a notion that would have been unthinkable to previous generations.

Well, yes, unthinkable at least to my sixteen-year-old self, back in 1974, intoxicated by the freedom granted by a car key. Society should, of course, celebrate the fact that less drinking, drug-taking, and driving means fewer kids crashing cars and killing or injuring themselves and otherwise ruining their lives. But even overanxious parents might feel pity for adolescent homebodies who, in Twenge's words, are "more comfortable in their bedrooms than in a car or at a party." To hear her tell it, aside from trudging to and from their lockdowned schools, teens barely even leave the house anymore. "The shift," she asserts, "is stunning: twelfth graders in 2015 were going out less often than *eighth graders* did as recently as 2009." (Her emphasis.) And even when teenagers do roam about, parents can reach and keep tabs on them in real time thanks to their cell phones–cum–tracking devices—not so different, a young person might feel, from the relentless scrutiny Katniss and Peeta are subjected to in the Hunger Games arena.

Unsurprisingly, study after study asserts that teenagers are more depressed than ever before. One example: the Centers for Disease Control's biannual Youth Risk Behavior Survey for 2021 found that 42 percent of all high school students reported "feeling so sad or hopeless that they could not engage in their regular activities for at least two weeks during the previous year," up from 28 percent a decade earlier. Over roughly the same period, the number of girls admitted to emergency rooms for "self-harm" tripled, and the suicide rate for people between the ages of ten and twenty-four (that's how the CDC breaks down the data) has increased steadily over the last two decades (as have the suicide rates for middle-aged and older adults).

Do we blame helicopter parenting for that? Crushing loads of homework? Not bothering to learn to drive? Social injustice? American carnage? Agoraphobia?

Covid and Zoom schooling surely didn't help. But the true culprits are literally at hand, according to multiple researchers, among them popular alarmists like Twenge and the psychologist Jonathan Haidt, author of the bestselling 2024 book *The Anxious Generation*, but also, in a 2023 report, Vivek H. Murthy, the US surgeon general under Joe Biden. All three have pointed the finger squarely at social media and smartphones, linked technologies that both reached critical masses of usership in the early 2010s, coinciding almost too perfectly with the abrupt decline in teen mental health; online porn and video games, each addictive and all-consuming in its own special way, also come in for blame. Haidt calls it "The Great Rewiring of Childhood":

> Gen Z became the first generation in history to go through puberty with a portal in their pockets that called them away from the people nearby and into an alternative universe that was exciting, addictive, unstable, and . . . unsuitable for children and adolescents. Succeeding socially in that universe required them to devote a large part of their consciousness—perpetually—to managing what became their online brand.

In a 2023 essay, the author and journalist Jessica Bennett (the first "gender editor" at *The New York Times*) offered an example of what this great rewiring looks like in the wild when she "shadowed" a group of thirteen-year-old girls "as they navigated middle school, puberty, and friendships amid constant access to a phone":

In many ways, their experience was familiar to anyone who's ever been a girl. But what stuck with me was how those devices seemed to ensure they could never get a mental health break from the insecurities of adolescence. From the moment they woke up until they fell asleep, whether or not the phone was locked away or they had access to social media, there was an underlying anxiousness about the things happening on it—friend drama, rumors, grade alerts, DMs—in ways no study could really capture.

"I just feel like I need it, you know?" a girl from Michigan, Addi, told me of her relationship with her phone. "Like, it helps me get through the day." In reality, of course, it often did the opposite: increased her anxiety, contributed to her self-consciousness, created drama with friends and families.

In two or three decades, will Haidt's and Bennett's warnings seem as hyperbolic as fears about comic books or smutty lyrics? Maybe . . . ? There are researchers who feel the phone/social media/depression link is overstated. But if I had to bet, I'd bet not. In October 2023, following the surgeon general's report, thirty-three states filed a suit in federal court against Meta, parent company of Facebook, Instagram, and WhatsApp, accusing it of ignoring "the sweeping damage" its platforms "have caused to the mental and physical health of our nation's youth." Eight other states and the District of Columbia filed a separate but aligned suit against Meta—which means that social media's allegedly deleterious effect on teens is the rare, maybe even sole, issue upon which more than four-fifths of state governments, both red and blue, can agree.

Surgeon General Murthy called for warning labels to be put on social media platforms spelling out the dangers for adolescents. My first thought: *That'll work*, followed by an eye roll emoji. But the impulse feels right. As Murthy wrote in a 2024 *New York Times* op-ed essay, "The moral test for any society is how well it protects its children."

On that score, I'd like to think we're doing better than Panem. But how do kids feel? Maybe for them—depressed, shadowed by horrific violence, living in fishbowls—*The Hunger Games* feels less like a metaphor than the day after tomorrow? "I think one reason this franchise was so successful is that this generation feels they are fighting for their survival all the time, and that survival is far from certain," Gary Ross observed in 2022, marking the first movie's tenth anniversary. "From climate change to authoritarianism, their generation feels a real sense of dread and jeopardy . . . I think, sadly, the themes in this movie are only more resonant now than when we made it."

No doubt. But for a less despairing analysis, I will turn to Madeline Joint, a millennial essayist, who in 2015 wrote a piece titled "Why Do Teenagers Love Dystopian Films?":

> Though the debate over whether this generation of teenagers have it easier than previous generations will rage for all eternity, the success of these stories reflects how young adults *feel* at the moment and how grateful they are for a little understanding. We are the generation that will suffer for the economic crash, increasing financial and social inequality and the inaction over climate change, yet we are powerless—we must simply wait until it is our turn and make the best we can of what we are given. These dystopian films all have two things in common: a respect for the legitimacy of young adult feelings, of their passions, power and love, and they each depict an unjust, cruel and unnavigable system torn down by the good in the younger generation . . . For the young adults flocking to see these films, they are not reveling in a dystopia, but a utopia. Crushed by the failings of the previous generation, they battle through the system that tries to control them and right their world's wrongs. What's depressing about that?

We'll see if millennials and Gen Z do any more to "right the world's wrongs" than have baby boomers and Gen X, who surely have big debits on their ledgers—and let's be fair, a few good things, too! But I'm old; I've earned my skepticism. As Joint reminds us, to be a teenager is not just to suffer torment but also to harbor hope that life can and will improve—that Dad will finally stand up and act like a real father, that escape from Modesto and South Central is possible, that romance can strike even in cableless Ridgemont.

That President Snow can choke on his own blood.

Katniss leads a successful revolt in *The Hunger Games* sequels, toppling a patriarchy *and* a matriarchy. But while those movies have interesting things to say about just-war theory, the uses and abuses of propaganda, and the inevitable excesses of revolutionary fervor, they land at a far remove from traditional teen movie concerns. More relevant here is the scene in the first movie during which Katniss and Peeta enjoy a quiet, confessional moment hiding from their prep teams on a rooftop in the Capitol. Call it the *Hunger Games* equivalent of the abandoned mansion sequence in *Rebel Without a Cause*.

"I just don't want them to change me . . . I don't know, turn me into something I'm not. I just don't want to be another piece in their game, you know?" Peeta says. "I just keep wishing I could think of a way to show them that they don't own me."

Here, "them" means the entire Panem power structure, and "something I'm not" means "a killer." But brutal context aside, isn't this an eternal cry? *They don't own me.* Peeta's lines could slip easily into dozens of teen movie screenplays. He's expressing the same defiance that Judd Nelson's Bender does in *The Breakfast Club*, when he tells Mr. Vernon to "Eat my shorts" and then, not backing down, racks up detention upon detention. It's the same defiance Pink vents at the end of *Dazed and Confused* when, as his school's starting quarterback, he refuses to sign the no-drugs pledge his hard-ass football coach insists is mandatory. "I may play ball next fall, but I'll never sign that," Pink promises, knowing his talent gives him the upper hand. "Now me and my loser friends are going to head out to buy Aerosmith tickets," he adds, by way of a kiss-off.

Katniss and Peeta, the last tributes standing, find their own perverse way to tell Panem's rulers to eat their shorts: at her suggestion, the two agree to a suicide pact rather than one killing the other in order to "win." It works, because Katniss and Peeta are leaning into their self-created roles of star-crossed lovers, which the Capitol audiences have embraced, and this act of rebellion flummoxes and frightens the powers that be enough that, in a first, the two are hastily declared co-victors before they can toast each other with the poisonous nightlock berries they've discovered. It's a nice piece of jiujitsu: beating the adults at their own game by giving them what they want.

Take that, world.

AFTERWORD

While researching and writing this book, I was frequently asked what grand conclusions I'd come to about teen movies. Alas, I've come to none. Themes and motifs, sure. I've followed threads and shed light as best I can. But I have no unified field theory of American adolescent cinema, and it's probably not a subject that warrants one. Art is messy, quicksilver, and full of contradictions. So are teenagers. So are teen movies.

They are also an ongoing story—a problem for a book like this. You cut off where you cut off, and then you cross your fingers and pray that whatever comes next doesn't hopelessly date what you've done. As of fall 2024, James Wolcott's 2003 observation that "girl power propels tween-teen culture" continues to hold true. The very funny *Superbad* notwithstanding, the best and/or most interesting teen movies of the past two decades, to my mind, have nearly all been female-centered and creatively driven: not just *Mean Girls* and the *Twilight* and *Hunger Games* series, but *Juno* (2007), *Easy A* (2010), *The Diary of a Teenage Girl* (2015), *Lady Bird* (2017), *The Hate U Give* (2018), *Booksmart* (2019), and *Bottoms* (2023)—the latter two further distinguished for centering queer characters. *Little Women* is often said to be the first YA novel, so you could add Greta Gerwig's 2019 adaptation to the list. Throw in Pixar's *Inside Out 2* (2024) as well. It's not that there aren't still films that celebrate and explore the adolescent male mindset; it's just that we don't call them teen movies anymore. We call them superhero movies.

That said, a shout-out to *The Perks of Being a Wallflower*, Stephen Chbosky's 2012 adaptation of his own novel, which stars Logan Lerman, Emma Watson, and Ezra Miller. Better than any film I know, it captures the exhilaration, almost romantic, of finally finding your people as a teenager, your tribe—a rush I remember as the high point of my own high school career. And a second shout-out to Paul Thomas Anderson for getting a mid-1970s California adolescence dead-on in *Licorice Pizza* (2021), despite being a member of his high school's class of 1989.

I've worried at times that this project might stray too deeply into nostalgia, but a little of that is unavoidable when you're dealing with eight decades' worth of movies. Despite whatever personal quirks and obsessions their creators imbued them with, these films inevitably serve as de facto yearbooks for their eras. *Yes! That's what we were like in high school! The hair! The slang! The cars! Not to mention, at times, the racism, the sexism, and the homophobia!*

One movie I haven't mentioned that confronts nostalgia head-on is *Peggy Sue Got Married*, Francis Ford Coppola's 1986 film (from a script by Jerry Leichtling and Arlene Sarner), which you might call a meta teen movie, or even an anti–teen movie. It opens with Kathleen Turner's middle-aged title character getting dressed for her twenty-fifth high school reunion. She's anxious about attending, dreading the inevitable questions about her pending divorce from her former sweetheart, Charlie, who she married right after graduation. At the reunion, he shows up unexpectedly—in the person of Nicolas Cage—and the evening overloads Peggy Sue's circuits to the point that she collapses.

When she comes to, it's 1960 and she's back in high school, waking up after fainting at a blood drive, only she remains middle-aged Peggy Sue, with all her life experience—the rest of the film being a fantasia on the theme of "If I knew then what I know now . . ." As she declares early on, "I want to have fun! I'm going to Liverpool to discover the Beatles!" As she murmurs later, "Mom, I forgot you were ever this young."

It's an odd movie that doesn't quite work, in part because Cage is too eccentric, skewing the central dilemma: Will Peggy Sue marry Charlie—*again*—even knowing the relationship will sour? You don't get why she's attracted to this jumpy, antic kid with an adenoidal Jerry Lewis voice in the first place. And Turner, who was thirty-two when the picture came out, is probably too young for her part. The film doesn't mean to pass her off as a teenager, but an actress who read as a fortysomething would have heightened the sense of dislocation that I think was the intent. (The device of adults playing teenagers while not hiding their ages works better in the middle school television series *Pen15*, which walks a thrilling tightrope between ironic distance and mortifying immediacy.)

But it's fun to see Turner in a majorette uniform, and the uneasy *feel* of the film has stuck with me ever since it came out, the way it yearns for the past yet renders that past discomfiting—its nostalgia somehow turned, like a corked wine. Maybe you can go home again, as we often do in our dreams, but it will be weird.

Contrary, however, to Ally Sheedy's famous *Breakfast Club* line, Peggy Sue's adult heart hasn't died; it's grown and even accrued some wisdom. Kudos to her therapist. Flung back to high school, she's distraught at moments—who wouldn't be, forced to take an algebra test for the first time in a quarter century?—anguished at others. For the most part, though, she's able to maintain a sympathetic but clear-eyed perspective on her own past, even as she relives it.

Has this book managed something similar? I hope so. That was the goal; the movies deserve it.

(And maybe there's my theory.)

ACKNOWLEDGMENTS

This book was a pleasure to research and write (mostly). Much of that pleasure is owed to:

Jennifer Joel, at CAA, and Jofie Ferrari-Adler, at Avid Reader, two of the smartest and most supportive people in publishing. I'm grateful to have them in my corner. Big thanks, too, to Sindhu Vegesena, at CAA, and Carolyn Kelly, at Avid Reader, and a shout-out to Sloan Harris.

Alison Forner, also at Avid Reader. She designed this book's knockout cover. And Clay Smith, who created the glorious endpapers.

The staffs at the New York Society Library and the New York Public Library of the Performing Arts, two of my favorite institutions. Both have collections I've relied on heavily and are also among the most pleasant places I know of to work.

Louise Hilton and the rest of the staff at the Motion Picture Academy of Arts and Science's Margaret Herrick Library.

Ned Comstock and Brett Service at USC, who guided me through the Warner Bros. Archives.

Alex Belth, Samantha Irwin, and Lucy Kaylin at Hearst Publications.

Everyone cited in my bibliography, excepting J. Edgar Hoover.

The late and much missed Cari Beauchamp, who offered valuable insights into early Hollywood and opened doors for me in the archival world.

Bob Cornfield, moviegoing buddy across four decades, who gave my manuscript an early read. His suggestions and occasional raised eyebrows made this book a lot better.

Kurt Andersen, Aimée Bell, Ash Carter, Graydon Carter, Jay Fielden, Michael Hainey, George Kalogerakis, David Kamp, Jim Kelly, and Susan Morrison—friends, colleagues, and the writer-editor-readers I've internalized.

Jack Barth, Tom Casciato, Trey Ellis, Steve Kessler, Jay Martel, Perry Vasquez, and Mike Wilkins. Early influences and best pals.

My siblings, Karen, Susan, and Todd Handy, and my late mother, Marlene.

My charming, talented, and beloved children, Zoë and Isaac Handy, and my charming, talented, and beloved wife, Helen Schulman, who is also my first and best reader, and my first and best everything else. You three complete me, to reference a Cameron Crowe movie not in this book.

Last, but not least, I need to salute the filmmakers, performers, and studio executives who created the movies I've had so much fun writing about—good, bad, heartfelt, venal, indelible. Thank you.

BIBLIOGRAPHY

Note: In quotes throughout the text I've standardized spelling and punctuation, particularly in regards to omitting the now mostly abandoned hyphen in "teen-ager."

BOOKS

Alexander, Paul. *Boulevard of Broken Dreams: The Life, Times, and Legend of James Dean*. Viking, 1994.

Arkoff, Sam, with Richard Trubo. *Flying Through Hollywood by the Seat of My Pants: From the Man Who Brought You* I Was a Teenage Werewolf *and* Muscle Beach Party. Birch Lane Press, 1992.

Armstrong, Jennifer Keishin. *So Fetch: The Making of* Mean Girls *(and Why We're Still So Obsessed with It)*. Dey Street Books, 2024.

Balio, Tino. *MGM*. Routledge, 2018.

The Beatles. *The Beatles Anthology*. Chronicle Books, 2000.

Biskind, Peter. *Easy Riders, Raging Bulls: How the Sex-Drugs-and-Rock 'n' Roll Generation Saved Hollywood*. Simon & Schuster, 1998.

Bogle, Donald. *Toms, Coons, Mulattoes, Mammies, and Bucks: An Interpretive History of Blacks in American Films*. (Fifth edition.) Bloomsbury Academic, 2016.

Brown, Kent R. *The Screenwriter as Collaborator: The Career of Stewart Stern*. Arno Press, 1980.

Champlin, Charles. *George Lucas: The Creative Impulse: Lucasfilm's First Twenty Years*. Harry N. Abrams, Inc., 1992.

Clarke, Gerald. *Get Happy: The Life of Judy Garland*. Random House, 2000.

Clarke, Jaime (editor). *Don't You Forget About Me: Contemporary Writers on the Films of John Hughes*. Simon Spotlight Entertainment, 2007.

Crowe, Cameron. *Fast Times at Ridgemont High: A True Story*. Simon & Schuster, 1981.

Crowther, Bosley. *Hollywood Rajah: The Life and Times of Louis B. Mayer*. Holt, 1960.

Dixon, Wheeler Winston. *Lost in the Fifties: Recovering Phantom Hollywood*. Southern Illinois University Press, 2005.

Driscoll, Catherine. *Teen Film: A Critical Introduction*. Berg, 2011.

Evans, Peter, and Ava Gardner. *Ava Gardner: The Secret Conversations*. Simon & Schuster, 2013.

Eyman, Scott. *Louis B. Mayer: Lion of Hollywood*. Simon & Schuster, 2005.

Fine, Benjamin. *1,000,000 Delinquents*. The World Publishing Company, 1955.

Frascella, Lawrence, and Al Weisel. *Live Fast, Die Young: The Wild Ride of Making* Rebel Without a Cause. Touchstone, 2005.

Funicello, Annette, with Patricia Romanowski. *A Dream Is a Wish Your Heart Makes: My Story*. Hyperion, 1994.

Gilbert, James. *A Cycle of Outrage: America's Reaction to the Juvenile Delinquent in the 1950s*. Oxford University Press, 1986.

Gora, Susannah. *You Couldn't Ignore Me If You Tried: The Brat Pack, John Hughes, and Their Impact on a Generation*. Crown Publishers, 2010.

Haidt, Jonathan. *The Anxious Generation: How the Great Rewiring of Childhood Is Causing an Epidemic of Mental Illness*. Penguin Press, 2024.

Hajdu, David. *The Ten-Cent Plague: The Great Comic-Book Scare and How It Changed America*. Farrar, Straus and Giroux, 2008.

Harris, Malcolm. *Kids These Days: Human Capital and the Making of Millennials*. Little, Brown and Company, 2017.

Hechinger, Grace, and Fred M. *Teen-Age Tyranny*. William Morrow and Company, 1963.

Higham, Charles. *Merchant of Dreams: Louis B. Mayer, M.G.M., and the Secret Hollywood*. Donald I. Fine, Inc., 1993.

Hiller, Jim (editor). *Cahiers du Cinéma: The 1950s: Neo-Realism, Hollywood, New Wave*. Harvard University Press, 1985.

Hine, Thomas. *The Rise and Fall of the American Teenager*. Avon Books, 1999.

Honeycutt, Kirk. *John Hughes: A Life in Film*. Race Point Publishing, 2015.

Howard, Ron, and Clint Howard. *The Boys: A Memoir of Hollywood and Family*. William Morrow, 2021.

Jones, Brian Jay. *George Lucas: A Life*. Little, Brown and Company, 2016.

Kazan, Elia. *Elia Kazan: A Life*. Alfred A. Knopf, 1988.

Kelly, Richard T. *Sean Penn: His Life and Times*, Canongate U.S., 2004.

Kett, Joseph F. *Rites of Passage: Adolescence in America, 1790 to the Present*. Basic Books, 1977.

Kline, Sally (editor). *George Lucas: Interviews*. University Press of Mississippi, 1999.

Kowinski, William Severini. *The Malling of America: An Inside Look at the Great Consumer Paradise.* William Morrow and Company, 1985.

Krassner, Paul. *Confessions of a Raving, Unconfined Nut: Misadventures in the Counterculture.* (Updated and expanded edition.) Soft Skull Press, 2012.

Lambert, Gavin. *Natalie Wood: A Life.* Knopf, 2004.

Lange, Alexandra. *Meet Me by the Fountain: An Inside History of the Mall.* Bloomsbury Publishing, 2022.

Lefourt, Peter, and Laura J. Shapiro (editors). *The First Time I Got Paid for It . . . : Writers' Tales from the Hollywood Trenches.* PublicAffairs, 2000.

Lertzman, Richard A., and William J. Birnes. *The Life and Times of Mickey Rooney.* Gallery Books, 2015.

Lewis, Jon. *The Road to Romance & Ruin: Teen Films and Youth Culture.* Routledge, 1992.

Lewisohn, Mark. *Tune In: The Beatles: All These Years, Vol. 1.* Crown Archetype, 2013.

Linson, Art. *A Pound of Flesh: Perilous Tales of How to Produce Movies in Hollywood.* Grove Press, 1993.

Maerz, Melissa. *Alright, Alright, Alright: The Oral History of Richard Linklater's Dazed and Confused.* Harper, 2020.

Marx, Arthur. *The Nine Lives of Mickey Rooney.* Stein and Day, 1986.

McCarthy, Andrew. *Brat: An '80s Story.* Grand Central Publishing, 2021.

McCarthy, Todd, and Charles Flynn. *Kings of the Bs: Working Within the Hollywood System: An Anthology of Film History and Criticism.* E.P. Dutton & Co., Inc., 1975.

McGee, Mark Thomas. *Faster and Furiouser: The Revised and Fattened Fable of American International Pictures.* McFarland & Company, Inc., 1995.

McGilligan, Patrick. *Nicholas Ray: The Glorious Failure of an American Director.* HarperCollins, 2011.

Michaud, Michael Gregg. *Sal Mineo: A Biography.* Crown Archetype, 2010.

Mintz, Steven. *Huck's Raft: A History of American Childhood.* The Belknap Press of Harvard University Press, 2004.

Orenstein, Peggy. *Girls & Sex: Navigating the Complicated New Landscape.* Harper, 2016.

Palladino, Grace. *Teenagers: An American History.* Basic Books, 1996.

Phillips, Mackenzie, with Hilary Liftin. *High on Arrival.* (Memoir.) Simon Spotlight Entertainment, 2009.

Poitier, Sidney. *This Life.* Alfred A. Knopf, 1980.

Pollack, Dale. *Skywalking: The Life and Films of George Lucas.* (Updated edition.) Da Capo Press, 1999.

Pye, Michael, and Linda Miles. *The Movie Brats*. Holt, Rinehart and Winston, 1979.

Rathgeb, Douglas L. *The Making of* Rebel Without a Cause. McFarland & Company, 2004.

Ray, Nicholas (edited by Susan Ray). *I Was Interrupted: Nicholas Ray on Making Movies*. University of California Press, 1993.

Rickles, Don, with David Ritz. *Rickles' Book*. (Memoir.) Simon & Schuster, 2007.

Rooney, Mickey. *Life Is Too Short*. (Memoir.) Villard Books, 1991.

Sales, Nancy Jo. *American Girls: Social Media and the Secret Lives of Teenagers*. Alfred A. Knopf, 2016.

Shary, Timothy. *Teen Movies: A Century of American Youth*. (Updated second edition.) Columbia University Press, 2023.

Shipman, David. *Judy Garland: The Secret Life of an American Legend*. Hyperion, 1993.

Short, Ann Elledge. *The Long-Term Impact of School Closings Due to Declining Enrollment on Elementary School Districts in Illinois*. (Dissertation.) Loyola University Chicago, 1983.

Spoto, Donald. *Rebel: The Life and Legend of James Dean*. HarperCollins, 1996.

Stein, Ellin. *That's Not Funny, That's Sick: The National Lampoon and the Comedy Insurgents Who Captured the Mainstream*. W. W. Norton & Company, 2013.

Watkins, S. Craig. *Representing: Hip Hop Culture and the Production of Black Cinema*. The University of Chicago Press, 1998.

Wertham, Frederick. *Seduction of the Innocent*. Rinehart & Company, 1954.

Wiseman, Rosalind. *Queen Bees & Wannabes: Helping Your Daughter Survive Cliques, Gossip, Boyfriends, and Other Realities of Adolescence*. Crown Publishers, 2002.

Wolfe, Tom. *Hooking Up*. Farrar, Straus and Giroux, 2000.

Wood, Lana. *Natalie: A Memoir by Her Sister*. G.P. Putnam's Sons, 1984.

ARTICLES

Albuhm, Sumner. "Are You Afraid of Your Teenager?" *Cosmopolitan*, November 1957.

Alexander, Bryan. "Q&A: Catherine Hardwicke, Director of *Twilight*." *Time*, November 19, 2009.

Ansen, David. "The Incredible Horror Mogul." (Profile of Sam Arkoff.) *Newsweek*, June 18, 1979.

Arentt, Jeffrey Jensen. "Getting Better All the Time: Trends in Risk Behavior

Among American Adolescents Since 1990." *Archives of Scientific Psychology*, August 20, 2018.

Ault, Susanne. "For Marketers, Teens Are Moving Target." *Billboard*, November 8, 2003.

Baker, Laura. "Screening Race: Responses to Theater Violence at *New Jack City* and *Boyz N the Hood*." *The Velvet Light Trap*, Fall 1999.

Barnosky, Jason. "The Violent Years: Responses to Juvenile Crime in the 1950s." *Polity: The Journal of the Northeastern Political Science Association*, July 2006.

Barth, Jack. "John Hughes: On Geeks Bearing Gifts." (Q&A.) *Film Comment*, May/June 1984.

Bates, Karen Grigsby. "They've Gotta Have Us." (The early-'90s wave of young Black filmmakers.) *The New York Times Magazine*, July 14, 1991.

Bennett, Jessica. "The Joy of Communal Girlhood, the Anguish of Teen Girls." *The New York Times*, December 31, 2023.

Bierly, Mandi. "Reminiscing with Jon Cryer about *Pretty in Pink*." *Entertainment Weekly*, August 24, 2006.

Binelli, Mark. "Drama Queen." (Profile of Lindsay Lohan.) *Rolling Stone*, August 19, 2004.

Biskind, Peter. "Rebel Without a Cause: Nicholas Ray in the Fifties." *Film Quarterly*, Autumn 1974.

Bitsch, Charles (translated by Liz Heron). "Interview with Nicholas Ray." *Cahiers du Cinéma* 89, November 1958.

Carr, David. "The Vampire at the Mall." (A stop on the *Twilight* promotional tour.) *The New York Times*, November 16, 2008.

Chambers, Veronica. "Poetry in Motion—The Director, John Singleton." *Vibe*, Fall 1992.

Christensen, Mark. "John Hughes: Making the Movies Young People Love." *Ampersand*, Summer 1986.

Clawson, Julie. "The Hunger Games: An Allegory of Christian Love." *The Huffington Post*, March 20, 2012.

Cohen, Rich. "The Glory Days of the American Mall." *The Wall Street Journal*, April 29, 2023.

Collier, Addore. "What's Behind the Black-on-Black Violence at Movie Theaters." *Ebony*, October 1991.

Crowe, Cameron. "The Actual, Honest-to-God Reunion of Crosby, Stills & Nash." *Rolling Stone*, June 2, 1977.

Crowe, Cameron. "The Durable Led Zeppelin: A Conversation with Jimmy Page and Robert Plant." *Rolling Stone*, March 13, 1975.

Crowther, Bosley. "A Ruin That Was Rooney: Andy Hardy Folds Up After Three

Days in Town, but Not Without a Word." (Mickey Rooney profile.) *The New York Times*, February 19, 1939.

Crowther, Bosley. "So Long, Andy: The Latest Hardy Family Picture Bids Adieu to That Bumptious Boy." (On Andy Hardy finally growing up.) *The New York Times*, February 21, 1943.

Day, Sara K. "Pure Passion: The Twilight Saga, 'Abstinence Porn,' and Adolescent Women's Fan Fiction." *Children's Literature Association Quarterly*, Spring 2014.

DeWitt, Jack. "Cars and Culture: The Cars of *American Graffiti*." *The American Poetry Review*, September/October 2010.

Dominus, Susan. "Suzanne Collins's War Stories for Kids." *The New York Times Magazine*, April 8, 2011.

Dresner, Lisa M. "Love's Labor's Lost?: Early 1980s Representations of Girls' Sexual Decision Making in *Fast Times at Ridgemont High* and *Little Darlings*." From *Virgin Territory: Representing Sexual Inexperience in Film*, edited by Tama Jeffers McDonald. Wayne State University Press, 2010.

Dyer, Peter John. "Youth and the Cinema: The Teenage Rave." *Sight and Sound*, Winter 1959.

Dyson, Michael Eric. "Between Apocalypse and Redemption: John Singleton's *Boyz N the Hood*." *Cultural Critique*, Spring 1992.

Eels, Josh. "America's Kick-Ass Sweetheart." (Jennifer Lawrence profile.) *Rolling Stone*, April 12, 2012.

Ellis, Trey. "The New Black Aesthetic." *Callaloo*, Winter 1989.

Farber, Stephen. "George Lucas: The Stinky Kid Hits the Big Time." *Film Quarterly*, Spring 1974.

Fattah, Hassan. "Hollywood, the Internet & Kids." *American Demographics*, May 2001.

Fey, Tina (as told to Jennifer Graham). "Mean Girls." (Fey's account of her own high school nastiness.) *Cosmo Girl*, April 2004.

Fingerhut, Lois; Deborah D. Ingram and Jacob J. Feldman. "Homicide Rates Among US Teenagers and Young Adults: Differences by Mechanism, Level of Urbanization, Race, and Sex, 1987 Through 1995." *JAMA: The Journal of the American Medical Association*, August 5, 1996.

Flanagan, Caitlin. "What Girls Want." (The *Twilight* novels and "the complexities of female adolescent desire.") *The Atlantic*, December 2008.

Freeman, Lucy. "Youth Delinquency Growing Rapidly Over the Country." *The New York Times*, May 20, 1952.

Garland, Judy. "Mickey and Me." (The star's account of her friendship with Mickey Rooney.) *Cosmopolitan*, March 1942.

Gibbs, Nancy. "Wilding in the Night." (Coverage of the "Central Park Jogger" case.) *Time*, May 8, 1989.

Gilbert, Eugene. "Why Today's Teen-Agers Seem So Different." *Harper's*, September 1959.

Gilbert, James. "Washington Diarist: Juvenilia." (Dismisses pop culture as a cause of teen criminality.) *The New Republic*, June 14, 1999.

Goldstein, Patrick. "His New 'Hood Is Hollywood." (John Singleton interview.) *Los Angeles Times*, July 7, 1991.

Goldstein, Patrick. "The Mission Beyond Hollywood." (John Singleton interview.) *Los Angeles Times*, May 31, 1992.

Goodman, Ezra. "Delirium Over Dead Star." (James Dean's posthumous popularity.) *Life*, September 24, 1956.

Grossman, Lev. "It's Twilight in America: The Vampire Saga." *Time*, November 23, 2009.

Heffernan, Virginia. "Anchor Woman." (Profile of Tina Fey.) *The New Yorker*, November 3, 2003.

Hill, Rebecca. "Capital or the Capitol?: The Hunger Games Fandom and Neoliberal Populism." *American Studies* 57, 2018.

Hintz, Cary and Elaine Ostry. "Interview with Lois Lowry, Author of *The Giver*." From *Utopian and Dystopian Writing for Children and Young Adults*, edited by Hintz and Ostry. Routledge, 2003.

Hoover, J. Edgar. "Youth . . . Running Wild." *Los Angeles Times*. June 27, 1943.

Hopper, Hedda. "Sinatra Waits Top Advice on Lawsuit." (Multiple items including prerelease praise for James Dean's performance in *Rebel Without a Cause*.) Syndicated column, September 7, 1955.

Horn, Stacey S. "Mean Girls or Cultural Stereotypes?" *Human Development*, 2004.

Howell, James C. "Youth Gangs: An Overview." A Juvenile Justice Bulletin (produced by the Office of Juvenile Justice and Delinquency), August 1998.

Hudson, Hannah Trierweiler. "Q&A with Hunger Games Author Suzanne Collins." www.scholastic.com, undated.

Hughes, John. "Vacation '58/Foreword '08." *Zoetrope All-Story*, Summer 2008.

Joint, Madeline. "Why Do Teenagers Love Dystopian Films?" *One Room with a View*, March 19, 2015.

Jordan, Don and Edward Connor. "Judge Hardy and Family: An American Story." *Films in Review*, January 1974.

Julian, Kate. "Why Are Young People Having So Little Sex?" *The Atlantic*, December 2018.

Kael, Pauline. "The Current Cinema: Un-People." (Review of *American Graffiti*.) *The New Yorker*, October 29, 1973.

Kamp, David. "John Hughes's Actors on John Hughes." Vanityfair.com, February 10, 2010.

Kamp, David. "Sweet Bard of Youth." (Posthumous profile of John Hughes.) *Vanity Fair*, March 2010.

Kanon, Joseph. "On the Strip." (Essay on *American Graffiti*.) *The Atlantic*, October 1973.

Kashner, Sam. "Dangerous Talents." (The making of *Rebel Without a Cause*.) *Vanity Fair*, March 2005.

Kashner, Sam. "George Lucas's Wild Ride: The Making of *American Graffiti*." Unpublished.

Kashner, Sam. "Hollywood in the Hood." (The making of *Boyz n the Hood*.) *Vanity Fair*, September 2016.

Kimble, Julian. "Once Upon a Time in LA: Revisiting the Ridiculous Fear of *Boyz n the Hood*." *The Ringer*, July 10, 2020.

Lamar, Jacob V. "A Bloody West Coast Story." (LA gangs.) *Time*, April 18, 1988.

Landau, Jon. "'American Graffiti': A Sixties Novella." *Rolling Stone*, September 13, 1973.

Levithan, David. "Suzanne Collins Talks About the Hunger Games, the Books and the Movies." (Q&A conducted by publisher at Scholastic Press.) *The New York Times*, October 18, 2018.

Macdonald, Dwight. "A Caste, a Culture, a Market." (Profile of Eugene Gilbert.) *The New Yorker*, November 22, 1958, and November 29, 1958.

Malooley, Jake. "So Hard to Say Goodbye: The Oral History of *Cooley High*." *Chicago* (website: chicagomag.com), January 2, 2023.

Mandel, Jerry and Harvey W. Feldman. "The Social History of Teenage Drug Use." From *Teen Drug Use*, edited by George M. Beschner and Alfred S. Friedman. Lexington Books, 1986.

Manter, Lisa and Lauren Francis. "Katniss's Oppositional Romance: Survival Queer and Sororal Desire in Suzanne Collins's The Hunger Games Trilogy." *Children's Literature Association Quarterly*, Fall 2017.

Matousek, Mark. "John Hughes." *Interview*, August 1985.

McNamara, Sylvie. "The Local Girls Who Inspired the Hollywood Classic *Mean Girls*." *Washingtonian*, May 13, 2024.

McNulty, Paul J. "Natural Born Killers?" (Essay urging tougher measures against teen crime.) *Policy Review*, Winter 1995.

Meadows, Susannah. "Meet the GAMMA Girls." (Report on *non*-mean girls.) *Newsweek*, June 3, 2002.

Miller, Cynthia J. and A. Bowdoin Van Riper. "Marketing, Monsters, and Music: Teensploitation Horror Films." *The Journal of American Culture*, June 2015.

Miller, Laura. "Fresh Hell." (Analyzing "the boom" in teen dystopian fiction.) *The New Yorker*, June 7, 2010.

Moak, Bob. "Heavy Run of Kid Films: Moppets Prove B.O. Naturals." *Variety*, September 20, 1939.

Morrison, Ewan. "YA Dystopias Teach Children to Submit to the Free Market, Not Fight Authority." *The Guardian*, September 1, 2014.

Murthy, Vivek H. "Surgeon General: Why I'm Calling for a Warning Label on Social Media Platforms." *The New York Times*, June 17, 2024.

Nordheimer, Jon. "Teen-Age Drivers Still Cruise, but Without That Old Fervor." *The New York Times*, April 7, 1974.

Ogersby, Bill. "Sleazy Riders: Exploitation, 'Otherness,' and Transgressions in the 1960s Biker Movie." *Journal of Popular Film & Television*, Fall 2003.

Ormond, Joan. "*Endless Summer* (1964): Consuming Waves and Surfing the Frontier." *Film & History*, 2005.

O'Rourke, P. J. "Don't You Forget About Me: The John Hughes I Knew." *The Daily Beast*, March 22, 2015.

Parker-Pope, Tara. "The Myth of Rampant Teenage Promiscuity." *The New York Times*, January 26, 2009.

Perez, Lexy. "*The Hunger Games* Turns 10: Director Gary Ross Reflects on Filming, Story's Resonant Themes." *The Hollywood Reporter*, March 21, 2022.

Ransom, James. "Beach Blanket Babies." (Behind the scenes at American International Pictures.) *Esquire*, July 1965.

Rau, Neil. "The Fight Was for Blood—and They Got It." (Report from the set of *Rebel Without a Cause*.) *Los Angeles Examiner*, May 22, 1955.

Ray, Nicholas. "Story into Script." (Making *Rebel Without a Cause*.) *Sight & Sound*, Autumn 1956.

Rensin, David. "John Singleton Talks Tough." *Playboy*, September 1993.

Ringwald, Molly. "Molly Ringwald Interviews Hit Filmmaker John Hughes." *Seventeen*, March 1986.

Ringwald, Molly. "What About *The Breakfast Club*? Revisiting the Movies of My Youth in the Age of #MeToo." *The New Yorker*, April 6, 2018.

Risker, Paul. "Can You Relate? Interview with Director Catherine Hardwicke." *PopMatters*, May 17, 2019.

Rohmer, Eric (translated by Liz Heron). "Ajax or the Cid?" (Review of *Rebel Without a Cause*.) *Cahiers du Cinéma* 59, May 1956.

Schmidt, Christopher. "Why Are Dystopian Films on the Rise Again?" *JSTOR Daily*, November 19, 2014.

Schwind, Jean. "Cool Coaching at Ridgemont High." *The Journal of Popular Culture*, 2008.

Scott, A.O. and Manhola Dargis. "A Radical Female Hero From Dystopia." (Analysis of Katniss Everdeen as a character.) *The New York Times*, April 4, 2012.

Scott, Sam. "Sam McDonald's Road." (Remembrance of Stanford University's first Black administrator, who began working there as a teenager.) *Stanford*, June 2023.

Seifert, Christine. "'Bite Me! (Or Don't).'" (Feminist reading of *Twilight* novels.) *Bitch Magazine*, January 2, 2009.

Sheff, David. "George Lucas." *Rolling Stone*, November 5, 1987.

Simpson, Jan. "Not Just One of the Boyz." (Profile of John Singleton.) *Time*, March 23, 1992.

Smith, Sean M. "Teen Days That Shook the World." (Oral history of *The Breakfast Club*.) *Premiere*, December 1999.

Spencer, Warren. "Your 100 Best Conservative Movies." *National Review*, March 11, 1996.

Springen, Karen. "Apocalypse Now." (YA dystopias on the bestseller lists.) *Publishers Weekly*, February 15, 2010.

Staehling, Richard. "The Truth About Teen Movies." *Rolling Stone*, December 27, 1969.

Steinberg, Shirley R. and Joe E. Kincheloe. "Privileged and Getting Away with It: The Cultural Studies of White, Middle-Class Youth." *Studies in the Literary Imagination*, Spring 1998.

Stern, Edith M. "Denver Students Learn Movie Making in the Classroom." *Popular Science*, April 1941.

Sturhahn, Larry. "The Filming of *American Graffiti*." *Filmmakers Newsletter*, March 1974.

Talbot, Margaret. "Girls Just Want to Be Mean." *The New York Times Magazine*, February 24, 2002.

Tavris, Carol. "Are Girls Really as Mean as Books Say They Are?" *The Chronicle of Higher Education*, July 5, 2002.

Touré. "What John Singleton Accomplished with *Boyz N the Hood*." *The New York Times*, April 30, 2019.

Twenge, Jean M. "Have Smart Phones Destroyed a Generation?" *The Atlantic*, September 2017.

Twenge, Jean M. and Heejung Park. "The Decline in Adult Activities Among U.S. Adolescents, 1976–2016." *Child Development*, March/April 2019.

Uncredited. "American Gangs: There Are No Children Here." *The Economist*, December 17, 1994.

Uncredited. "The Changes in Mickey Rooney." *Screen Guide*, January 1941.

Uncredited. "Film Men Strike Back at Kefauver." (Senate hearing on movies and juvenile delinquency.) *Los Angeles Times*, June 17, 1955.

Uncredited. "Interview with Stephenie Meyer." (Transcript of audience Q&A with Meyer, from a 2005 appearance at Arizona State University.) *Journal of Adolescent and Adult Literacy*, April 2006.

Uncredited. "*Look* Calls on Mickey Rooney." *Look*, May 7, 1940.

Uncredited. "Our Vicious Young Hoodlums: Is There Any Hope?" *Newsweek*, September 6, 1954.

Uncredited. "Subdebs: They Live in a Jolly World of Gangs, Games, Gadding, Movies, Malteds & Music." *Life*, January 27, 1941.

Uncredited. "Success Story." (Cover story on Mickey Rooney.) *Time*, March 18, 1940.

Uncredited. "Why Teen-Agers Go Wrong." *U.S. News & World Report*, September 17, 1954.

Uncredited. "Youth Delinquency Down." *The New York Times*, April 16, 1953.

Waxman, Sharon. "Cracks in Hollywood's Glass Slipper Genre." (Glut of movies aimed at teen girls.) *The New York Times*, April 26, 2004.

White, Armond. "Flipper Purify and Furious Styles." (Essay on *Jungle Fever*, *Boyz n the Hood*, and other early-'90s Black movies.) *Sight and Sound*, August 1, 1991.

Wolcott, James. "Teen Engines: Riding with the Kid Culture." *Vanity Fair*, July 2003.

Wolfe, Tom. "There Goes (Varoom! Varoom!) That Kandy Kolored (Thphhh-hhh!) Tangerine-Flake Streamline Baby (Rahghhh!) Around the Bend (Brum-mmmmmmmmmmmmmmmm . . . . . ." *Esquire*, November 1963.

Wood, Joe. "John Singleton and the Impossible Greenback Bind of the Assimilated Black Artist." *Esquire*, August 1993.

Zimmerman, Amy. "Catherine Hardwicke Broke Records with *Twilight* Then Hollywood Labeled Her 'Difficult.'" *The Daily Beast*, October 1, 2018.

OTHER

Camera Three. (CBS cultural affairs series.) Interview with Nicholas Ray, 1977. (https://www.youtube.com/watch?v=smSIk5yCjkQ).

The College Board. *Annual AP Program Participation 1956–2021*.

The Ezra Klein Show. (Podcast.) "Transcript: Ezra Klein Interviews Jean Twenge." *The New York Times*, May 19, 2023.

K–12 School Shooting Database. (k12ssdb.org).

The March of Time. "Youth in Crisis." (Newsreel.) 1943. (https://www.youtube.com/watch?v=RDs67J2JfkU).

NBC News, "Gangs, Cops & Drugs." (Special report.) 1989 (https://www.youtube.com/watch?v=tk9mR-zomkQ&t=6s).

Ramón, Dr. Ana-Christian, Michael Tran, and Dr. Darnell Hunt. *Hollywood Diversity Report 2023*. UCLA Entertainment and Media Initiative.

Rivas-Lara, Stephanie, Hiral Kotecha, Becky Pham, and Yalda T. Uhls. *Teens & Screens 2023*. Center for Scholars & Story Tellers, UCLA.

INDEX

Titles refer to films unless otherwise indicated.

ABOUT THE AUTHOR

BRUCE HANDY is a journalist, critic, humorist, and children's book author. His work has appeared in *The New Yorker, Vanity Fair, The New York Times, The Atlantic,* and more. He is the author of *Wild Things: The Joys of Reading Children's Literature as an Adult,* as well as five picture books, three of which were named *New York Times* best children's books. He began his career as a writer and editor at *Spy* magazine and also spent a season (1992–93) writing for *Saturday Night Live.*

Way fun times in English!
Maybe I'll finish "Emma" this summer.
(AS IF!!)
xoxo Cher ♡

This school bites.
—Bella

EAT MY SHORTS
EAT MY SHORTS
EAT MY SHORTS
—BENDER

Hope to see you on the beach this summer! I'll be the girl in the yellow polka-dot one-piece!
Dee Dee

PAR-TAY HAR-TAY, AMIGO!
WOODERSON
→ Class of 5 years Ago

SAFE TRAVELS THIS SUMMER.
—Jim Stark

What an adorable outfit! Did you get it at Talbots? Just kidding. Costco?
xo Regina